D1859629

TRIBES
OF
TRIPURA

TRIBES OF TRIPURA

Description, Ethnology and Bibliography

SIPRA SEN

GYAN

Published by

Gyan Publishing House
5, Ansari Road
Daryaganj, New Delhi-110002
Phone: 011-47034999, 9811692060
E-mail: books@gyanbooks.com

Distribution Network
gyanbooks.com
India, USA, Canada, UK, Australia, France

© Author

All rights reserved. No part of this work may be reproduced, stored, adapted, or transmitted in any form or by any means, electronic, mechanical, photocopying, micro-filming recording or otherwise, or translated in any language, without the prior written permission of the copyright owner and the publisher. The book is sold subject to the condition that it shall not, by way of trade or otherwise, be lent, resold, hired out, or otherwise circulated without the prior publisher's written consent in any form of binding or cover other than that in which it is published.

ISBN: 978-81-212-0448-4 (HB)

First Published, 1993

Printed at: Gyan Press, Delhi.

The views and opinions expressed in this book are author(s) own and the facts reported by them have been verified to the extent possible, and the publishers are not in any way liable for the same.

Tribes of Tripura, Description, Ethnology and Bibliography
Author: Sipra Sen

Dedicated
To the memory of my
Maternal Grandfather
Late Karuna Kr. Das Gupta, pleader
and,
Maternal uncles
Late Dr. Bhupesh Ch. Das Gupta and,
Late Dr. Nripesh Ch. Das Gupta, directors,
West Bengal Health Directorate, Calcutta,

CONTENTS

PART III

Key to Bibliography

All the references have been alphabetically arranged in a chronological order with reference to each author.

For books the author's name is followed by year, title of reference, place of publication and publisher's name with total number of pages.

For journals the author's name is followed by year, title of the article, name of the journal in which it was published, volume, number, month and page numbers.

In the case of newspapers, etc. the author's name or publisher's name which is followed by year, title of the article, name of the newspaper and date of publication, page number and column number.

Most of the references are in English but Bengali, Hindi, Tripuri, Lushai (Dulian), Manipuri publications have also been included in this Bibliography.

For books, journals, newspapers, etc. I have marked against few serial numbers as "n.p.". This means "not published". Similarly "n.d." indicates that "no date" (i.e. date of publication is not available in the book, journal, newspaper, etc). About question mark "?" it means regarding "doubtness" about author, date of publication, etc of the reference. "Sr" means Senior and "Jr" means Junior. Ed means "Editor", "Jt." means "joint" and "Jr" means "journal"

LIST OF ILLUSTRATIONS

List of Tables

PREFACE

The literature on Tripura and its tribes are scattered in several monographs, journals, edited books, reports, proceedings, etc. There is an urgent need to bring together all the references of main publications of this State and its people to provide a base for future research work. This book will facilitate macro and micro level researches on tribes of Tripura.

From this, one can get an idea about the region and people regarding geography, flora, fauna, climate, districts, religion, history, ethnology of tribes and almost all the references of published and unpublished research material which has been done so far on Tripura and its people. This bibliographical book will indicate the gaps of work in the field of research on the people of Tripura. It is hoped that, this will assist to fill the gap and select further research projects on Tripura and its tribes in various disciplines.

This bibliographical book covers all aspects of Social/Cultural/Biological Anthropology, Forestry, Geography, Sociology, Ethnology, Folklore, Archaeology, Social Psychology, History, Education, Political Science, Administration, Economics, Linguistics, Botany, Zoology, Geology, Soil Conservation and Tourism. Thus, it presents a multi-dimensional picture of the land, its people and their aspirations.

At the initial stage, the studies on Tripura and its people were undertaken in English mainly by the Britishers namely M.Barbe (1845), James Long (1851), Robert B.Smart (1866), T.H.Lewin (1969), W.W.Hunter (1876), Alexender Mackenzie (1884) and many others who published their reports, notes and accounts, articles, etc. on Tripura and its people in the shape of Hand Book, Census Report, District Gazetteers, Proceedings, Journals etc. Actually, from the Britishers we have got some earlier recorded documents on Tripura from the year 1845. It seems that, before 1845 there were no recorded English documents on Tripura and its people. In 19th century probably no Indian scholars published any document on Tripura and its people except Kailas Chandra Singha (1896).

Before Independence several ethnographic works had been attempted in the 20th century by a number of British scholars, especially B.C.Allen (1902), O.O.Lowis (1902), R.H.S.Hut-chinsen (1906), J.G.Cumming (1907), Peirre Bessaignet (1909), J.E.Webster (1910), C.M.Webb (1912), etc. In pre-Independence period few Indian scholars had published their books on Tripura and its people. These are:- Tripura Desher Katha(in Bengali) by Tripur Ch.Sen (1924), Tripurar Smriti and 1340 Tripurabder Census Bibarani (in Bengali) by S.C.Deb Barman (1927, 1933), The Rajmala by K.P. Sengupta (1932) and Tripura Buranji (in Assamese) Edited by S.K. Bhuyan (1938). All these are excellent literature and very much helpful. After Independence several works were written on Tripura and its people by J.B. Ganguly Gan Chaudhuri, S.B.K.Dev Varma, Malabika Das Gupta, Bhabananda Mukherjee, A.K.Mitra, Omesh Saigal, Mahadev Chakravarti, Banikanta Bhattacharyya, Nalini Ranjan Roychoudhury, Sudhanshu Bikash Saha, S.R.Bhattacharjee, S.N.Guha Thakurta, Sukhdev Singh Chib, S.N.Chatterjee, Bani Prasanna Misra, Tusher Kanti Niyegi, Tapan Kumar Som, Anil Bhattacharjee, Satyabrata Chakraborty, Swapan Sengupta, Ranjan Kr. Lahiri, S.T.George, G.K.Ghosh, Suchintya Bhattacharya and many others. There are many other Indian scholars who have published their written materials on Tripura. Very few insider-tribals of Tripura have carried out the work. Though they are now gradually publishing their works on Tripura but the major basic works have come out from the pen of Britishers and Bengalees.

The following monographs namely, The Hill Tracts of Chittagong and the Dwellers written by T.H.Lewin (1869), A Statistical Account of Bengal, volume VI by W.W.Hunter (1876),History of the Relations of the Government with the Hill Tribes of the North East Frontier of Bengal (1884) (i.e. The North East Frontier of India, reprinted by Mittal Publications, New Delhi) by Alexander Mackenzie (1989), Rajmala by Kailas Chandra Singha (1896), An Account of the Chittagong Hill Tracts by R.H.Sneyd Hutchinson (1906), Survey and Settlement report of Chakla Resonabad Estate in the Districts of Tipperah and Noakhali 1892-'99 by J.G.Cumming (1907), Eastern Bengal District Gazetteers: Tripura by J.E.Webster (1910) Tripura Desher Katha Edited by Tripur Ch.Sen (1924), Tripurar Smriti and 1340 Tripurabder Census Bibarani by Samarendra Chandra Deb Barman (1927 and 1933), Rajmala by K.P. Sengupta (1932) and Tripura Buranji

Edited by S.K.Bhuyan (1938) are quite informative. They have been used for their authenticity and vividness and may be considered as a first basic book on Tripura and its people. The following publications namely:- Tripura: The Land and its People Edited by Jagadis Gan Chaudhuri(1980), Tripura: Its History and Culture by Omesh Saigal (1978), A Political History of Tripura by Jagadis Gan Chaudhuri (1985), The Tribes of Tripura: A Dissertation by S.B.K.Dev Varman (1971), This Beautiful India: Tripura by Sukhdev Singh Chib (1988), An Anthology of Tripura Edited by Jagadis Gan Chaudhuri (1985), India-The Land and the People: Tripura by S.N.Guha Thakurta (1986),Techno-Economic Survey of Tripura by NCAER(1961), Tripura Through The Ages by Nalini Ranjan Roychoudhury (1983), Tripura Administration: The Era of Modernisation (1870-1972) by Banikanta Bhattacharyya (1986), Tribal Insurgency in Tripura: A Study in Exploration of Causes by S.R.Bhattacharjee (1989), Tribes of Tripura: A Historical Survey Edited by Sudhanshu Bikash Saha (1986), Tripura Prasanga Edited by Swapan Sengupta (1975), Tripura by DPRT (n.d.) and The Tribes of Tripura by S.B.K.Dev Varman (n.d.) are obviously dependable books about Tripura and its people.

This is a multi-disciplinary bibliography which covers the important writings on the tribes of Tripura in the pre-and post Independence period. A detailed study of this bibliography will reveal the important gaps in our knowledge about them. A large number of publications listed in this book are articles published in journals and presented at various Seminars and Conferences. It is observed that, Ethnographic Monographs are now gradually being published after Independence by new scholars. Some other types of monographic books are also published on Tripura about its History, Politics, Linguistics, Economics, Folklore, Insurgency, Refugee Problems, etc. it is also observed that there are a vast number of articles on ethnographical, political, historical and religious aspects by several new scholars who had published in several journals and also in edited books. Further, this bibliographical work indicates that a large number of studies have been done on the Tripuris, Reangs, Chakmas, etc. But not much work have been done on the Jamatias, Halams, Noatias, Mogs, Uchais and many other tribes and sub-tribes of this State.

The main purpose of compiling this bibliography is, however, to assist the scholars and researchers so that, the anthropologists, sociologists, ethnologists, archaeologists, historians, geographers, psychologists, linguists, politicians, economists, botanists, zoologists, geologists as well as librarians may get quick and ready references about the reference-queries without wastage of their precious time. Moreover, an individual researcher may select his own research theme from the bibliography.

In this book all the maps and sketches have been drawn by myself. Several old and new records, periodicals, books, newspapers, proceedings, dissertations, etc. were consulted from the year 1845 onwards. I have not found it necessary to annotate the references. Because, a serious scholar must read all the relevant materials himself and cryptic annotations are rarely of much use to him. I have here access to few unpublished research reports, papers on proceedings, Seminars, Symposia and even Dissertations, etc. along with selective published references. The preparation of bibliography is an ongoing process. I have to decide at some point of time to stop adding entries. As a result of this, there may be some omissions in publications which have been brought out after December, 1992. In spite of my best efforts few references are incomplete as these were collected from secondary sources and could not be verified. The choice before me was either to reject or to include them in this bibliographical book. I chose the latter because some information is better than nothing. Now, if this book can be of some help to make the tribes of Tripura better known and understood and in any way assist the scholars, it will be the great satisfaction for my hard and painstaking efforts.

I shall welcome and be grateful to the readers if they could kindly send their comments, suggestions, additional information, etc. directly to me to improve this document in the near future. And, as far as possible, I shall acknowledge them.

I must acknowledge that my best thanks are due to Shri. L.C.Das, Director of Research; Shri.U.C.Saha, Research Officer, Directorate of Statistics; Director, Information Cultural Affairs Tourism; Joint Director, Directorate of Statistics. I am very much grateful to them for their kind co-operation and help extended to me. I wish to express my sincerest gratitude to them. The photographs which I have used here have been kindly given by Shri. L.C.Das, Director of Research.

In the end, I must express my deep sense of gratitude to the National Library, Calcutta; Gauhati University Library, Guwahati, and Anthropological Survey of India Library, Shillong. I like to record my debt to my brother Dr. Salil Ranjan Sen who helped me to get the entire manuscript typed. Finally, I must express my most respectful regards to my mother Mrs. Malati Sen for her kind help and constant encouragement at every step to complete this work.

Rehabari,
Guwahati.

Sipra Sen

PART I

1

INTRODUCTION

LAND AND PEOPLE OF TRIPURA

Tripura is a fertile field to study Anthropology and Sociology for its colourful tribes like Tripuri, Riang, Chakma, Jamatia, Noatia, Mog, Halam, Uchai, Kuki, etc. Formerly, Tripura was an independent princely state. It was ruled by Tripuri *Maharajas* for about thirteen hundred years. This state is believed to have existed about 3000 years B.C. The rulers of Tripura had claimed that they are the descendents from *Chandra* (Moon).

It is said that, the *Nawab* of Bengal had helped Ratna Fa, during the medieval period, to occupy the throne of Tripura after the death of Dangar Fa (father of Ratna Fa) and presented the title *Manikya* to Ratna Fa. After that, the earlier title *Fa* was dropped and took *Manikya* title by Ratna Fa and the subsequent rulers of Tripura.

According to B.P. Misra (1976) the territory was known as "Hill Tippera" before 1920 and it was distinguished from the neighbouring "Tipperah" which constituted one of the districts of British India in the lower plains of East Bengal. But, since that year, on the representation of the *durbar*, the Government of British India agreed that the state should be known as "Tripura" instead of "Hill Tippera" (*Memoranda on the Indian States*, 1932, p. 218). According to Mahadev Chakravarti (1990) the State was formerly known as 'Swadhin Tripura' and later on as 'Hill Tippera' till 1920 when its name was changed to 'Tripura.'

Tripura merged with India on 15th October, 1949 by an *Agreement* which was signed in September, 1949, in Delhi. At this, Tripura became a *Part-C State* of India. Chief Commissioner (an Administrator) was appointed for Tripura by the Central Government on that day. He took over the administration from the Regent *Maharani Rajmata* Kamala Prabha Debi, mother of minor son Prince Kirit Bikram Manikya.

On 1st November, 1956, Tripura was converted as *Union Territory* and had a Lieutenant Governor. Thereafter, on 21st January, 1972, under the provisions of North Eastern Areas (Re-organisation) Act of 30th December, 1971, Tripura became a fullfledged "State". Tripura is popular for its beautiful temples, palaces, unique culture and tradition. At present, it is the only state of India where the *Bodo* people have retained their cultural tradition and habits (Chatterjee, S.K: 1951).

Tripura is covered by picturesque hills and dales covered with forest and luxurious vegetation. The handicrafts of Tripura are very much popular and attractive. According to 1981 Census only 11 per cent population of Tripura are urban dwellers and the rest rural dwellers.

GEOGRAPHY:- Tripura is situated approximately between $22^0 56'$ and $24^0 32'$ North Latitudes and between $91^0 10'$ and $92^0 21'$ East Longitudes. It is a small state but bigger than Sikkim with an area of 10,491 sq. kms. It covers 183.54 kms length and 112.70 kms width. The shape of the state is irregular and looks like a hanging (bend covered) sword. It also seems to be a bending head of an old lady facing towards South-West.

Tripura is an isolated land-locked state, sharing the international border of 832 kms long with Bangladesh's district of Sylhet on the north, Comilla on the west, Noakhali and Chittagong on the south and Chittagong Hill Tracts on the east. It maintains the geographical continuity with the main land India only on its north-east with Assam (Cachar district) and east with Mizoram (Aizawal district). Assam covers the border of Tripura about 51.52 kms and Mizoram about 61.18 kms. The *Tropic of Cancer* passes through West Tripura and North Tripura districts. Geopolitically Tripura is very much sensitive state as its longest part of the boundary is surrounded by the country Bangladesh.

NAME OF THE STATE:- Hunter (1876) remarks that the name "Tripura" was given in honour of the temple at Udaipur. This temple now ranks as the second *Tirtha* of Bengal; it was dedicated either to Tripurdhana, the Sun God or to Tripureswari, the mistress of the *"Three"* world (Heaven, Earth and Hell).

It is a believed that the name "Tripura" has been derived from *Tripurasundari*, the main deity of the land. Some believe that the name *Tripura* has been derived from two Tripuri words *viz. (Tui'* and *'pra'*. *'Tui'* means "water" and *'pra'* means "near").

According to R.M. Nath (1948) Tipperah people preferred to call themselves the children of water-goddess and were, therefore, known as the Tiphras or the Tippras; and later on they became known as the Tipperahs. Some other believe that the word "Tripura" has been sanskritised which originated from "Tipra", a native tribe of Tripura. Some people think that the name *Tripura* derived from *"Tri Puram"* meaning a "land of three cities" or, "three filled-up substance". Again some believe that a mythical king *Tripur* had named his kingdom "Tripura" after his own name.

MOUNTAIN :- About 60 per cent area of Tripura is hilly and the rest is flat land. Six main hill-ranges run almost parallel from north to south at a gradual increase in height. The average distance between the two ranges is about twelve miles. In between two successive hill ranges there lies a river-valley. The altitude of hills varies from 50 to 2000 feet above sea level. The hill slopes from east to west and south to north. For that, the eastern, south-eastern and north-eastern parts of the state are more hilly than the western part.

The main hill ranges are:- *Jampui* (highest points are *Betling Sib* (3,200 feet) and *Jampui* (1,860 feet); *Sakhan Tlang* (highest point is *Sakhan* (2,578 feet); *Longtarai* (highest point is *Phengpui* (1,581 feet); *Atharamura* (highest points are *Jarimura* (1,500 feet) and *Atharamura* (1,431 feet). The highest peak in the state is *Betling Siv* (3,200 feet). The hill consists of sandstone and shales of tertiary age.

RIVER:- The rivers of Tripura are neither broad nor deep enough for heavy navigation. There are twelve river basins, seven of which are important. The hills of Tripura form a watershed from which water runs towards north by the river *Khowai, Dhalai, Manu, Juri, Longai*: towards west by *Gumti, Hawra* and *Buriganga;* towards south-west by *Laogang* (Map-3). There are more rivers in Tripura. They are: *Deo, Muhari, Manugang, Surma, Raima,* etc. The most important and largest river is *Gumti* (133 kms length). People treat it as a sacred river as it is derived from *Tirthamukh,* where *Dambaru* falls is situated, which is considered a symbol of God *Siva.*

Most of the rivers are fed by rain water. During monsoon they are dangerous causing sometimes floods and during winter most of them dry up. Most of the rivers carry boat traffic, especially during the rainy season.

LAKE:- Truely speaking there is no lake in Tripura. *Rudrasagar,* an artificial lake, is situated at a distance of 53 kms south from Agartala. In the middle of this lake a beautiful palace *Nirmahal* is situated which was constructed during the time of Bir Bikram Kishore Manikya (1927-'47). *Dombur,* another beautiful artificial lake of Tripura is there. It is 30 miles from Amarpur.

CLIMATE:- Tropical climate is prevailing in Tripura. The climate is generally hot and humid. Maximum average temperature during May-August is 24^0C to 35^0C and minimum 10.5^0 C to 13^0C in December-January. Average rainfall is 301.9 cm (1983). Monsoon is from April to September. Pleasant weather is from October to February. In Summer strong wind blows sometimes thunderstorms.

FLORA:- The flora of Tripura is common to that of the neighbouring states of North East India and Bangladesh. Tripura is a paradise for medicinal plants. Three-fourth of the total area of the state is covered with forest. There are:- grass, cane, bamboo, wild herbs, cotton, timber, mango, lichi, guava, betel-nut, coconut, jackfruit, orange, lemon, pine apple, tobacco, etc. There are varieties of flower plants, such as:- rose, sun-flower, lotus, water-lily, *bokful, karabi, kadam, seuli,* etc. Medicinal plants are:- *amlaki, chailta, halencha, dumur, van-tulsi, arjun, basak, kalmegh, kantakari, ghrita kumari, lajjabati, sarpa gandha, thankuni, neem,* etc. In 1916 the first tea garden was set up in Kailashahar Division of Tripura.

AGRICULTURE:- People of Tripura generally practice the shifting (*jhum*) cultivation like South East Asia, part of Africa, Latin America and few parts of Germany. The physical composition of the soil is loose and porous. For that, it does not hold water. The mineral deficiencies effect on plants. The total cropped area of Tripura is 4,32,000 hectars (1982-'83)(P). The villagers select an area which is virgin or semi-virgin hilly forest land, cut down trees and burn the under growth. Thereafter, they clean the spot and plant crops for a few years and after that, they again select another site and repeat the same process. As shifting (*jhum*) cultivation process is not much gainful government is making efforts to bring more and more areas under permanent terrace-cultivation. According to which villagers have adopted permanent terrace cultivation in the plain areas of Tripura.

The *Gumti* valley is composed of alluvial soil and forms best cultivable land. The principal crops of Tripura are:- paddy, wheat, jute, tea, sugarcane, oilseeds, etc. All these are grown on 23 per cent of available agricultural land. Vegetables like gourd, potato, brinjal, radish, tomato, bean, etc. are grown much. Varieties of orange, pine apple fruits grow in plenty. The quality of these fruits are good.

FOREST:- The jungle products of Tripura is very rich. The common forest trees are:- oak, sal, timber, *garjan*, India-rubber, etc. Forest of Tripura could be divided into two types:- (a) evergreen and (b) moist deciduous forests. Trees in the hill-areas are gradually decreasing as people are using these for firewood, construction of houses and also for shifting (*jhum*) cultivation. In 1980-'82, the forest area of this state was 5,138 sq.km. which was 6,330 sq.km. in 1972-'75 (Table-I). Thus, the forest area has gone down in Tripura.

TABLE I : FOREST AREAS

State	*Forest area in Sq. Km.*		*Change of forest area in Sq. Km. (+) Increased (-) Decreased*
	1972-'75	1980-'82	
Assam	21,055	19,796	(-) 1,259
Manipur	15,090	13,572	(-) 1,518
Meghalaya	14,390	12,458	(-) 1,932
Nagaland	8,154	8,095	(-) 59
Tripura	6,330	5,138	(-) 1,192
Arunachal Pradesh	51,438	58,104	(+) 6,666
Mizoram	13,860	11,971	(-) 1,889

Source: *Himalaya: Man and Nature*, VIII (11), April 1985

FAUNA:- The fauna of Tripura resembles to that of the neighbouring states. The terrestrial fauna are richer than the aquatic fauna. These include varieties of insects, flies, mosquitoes, crabs, snakes, toads, frogs, elephants, tigers, deer, bears, monkeys, cats, pigs, dogs, goats, buffaloes, jackals, earthworms, leaches, butterflies, prawns, etc. Tripura is poor in piscean fauna. Common fishes available here are:- *Katla, koi, gorai, magur, mirigal, pabda, ghania, puthi, tengra, rohu, soul, singi*, etc. Tripura is partly dependent on Bangladesh for their supply of fresh and dry fish to Tripura.

The wild life of Tripura have mercifully fallen prey to the hunters. Thus, Tripura is losing her ecological balance and the climatic character is showing some change which has effects on nature. Tripura Government enacted game laws in 1955 to save and preserve wild life in Tripura. There is a sanctuary in Sepahijala (South Tripura). A - 45 minute drive from Agartala.

GEOLOGY:- Tripura seems to have risen from the sea-bed in late *Tertiary* period of about forty million years ago. The mineral resources are very meagre. The rocks are composed of *Lower Tertiary* to *Recent Age*. Sedimentary rocks are derived from the sediments. Rocks of Tripura can be divided on the basis of their lithological composition, depositional character and structural features.

The oldest rock of Tripura is known as *Surma* group. The youngest rock is *Dupi Tila* group. The oldest rocks are:- sandstone, siltstone, sandy-shale, mud-stone. The youngest rocks are:- sandy-clay, clayey sand-stone, white silica sand, ferruginous sandstone, unconsolidated silt and clay. The colour of the soil varies from reddish-brown to brown and also dark-brown to dark-grey.

The available minerals of Tripura are:- lignite, coal, limestone, ochre, etc. But the quality and quantity is too low of commercial value. Oil and gas minerals are available in South Tripura. Oil and Natural Gas Commission had discovered country's biggest gas zone in the state. Tripura is rich for its high quantity of hydrocarbon (natural gas) which is of high commercial value.

INDUSTRY:- There was no kind of industry till 1950. Progress has been made since 1951 onwards. Tripura is, however, much behind in large scale industry due to inadequate power, lack of river and rail transport. Twenty crore rupees World Bank aided forest based rubber plantation project would be undertaken soon in West and South Tripura in 5000 hectares of land. Tripura has already led the rubber revolution in North East region with 11,000 hectares under cultivation.

The Oil and Natural Gas Commission is now producing 250,000 cubic metres of natural gas per day in Tripura. On the recommendation of the Geological Survey of India, a glass factory has been set up at Arundhutinagar near Agartala with a capacity of 2 tonnes of glass-ware per day. According to ONGC,

Tripura has sufficient reserves of mineral oil. If so, it is hoped that a three million tonne capacity refinery may be set up in Tripura. As ONGC has discovered the country's biggest gas zone, we may expect rapid industrial development in the state.

Deposits of white sand with silica content helped to manufacture glass-ware in Tripura. Sand deposits of Agartala helps the demand of raw material for production of soda-ash for soap factory in Tripura. Rubber, tea, sugar, leather goods, fruit canning, handicrafts, loin-loom products are some of the industries of Tripura.

HANDLOOM AND HANDICRAFTS:- Loin looms and silk products of Tripura have achieved a good name. All these are practised by local people. *Dubris* (a piece of skirt), *riha* (breast garment), bedcover, screens, *asana* are beautiful and attractive. In villages, they have loom apparatus in every house like the Assamese, Manipuri, Naga and Mizo people. Generally they are using local cotton which grows in their *jhum* field.

Handicrafts made from bamboo, cane and palm leaves are beautiful. Hand bags, mat, basket, toys, trays, photo frames, *mora*, chair, etc. are their main products.

ENERGY AND POWER:- Availability of electricity in Tripura is inadequate. Before first Five Year Plan, the state was being served by a diesel station at Agartala which had five diesel sets with a total installed capacity of 476 kw and a firm capacity of 204 kw. At the end of the first plan period the installed capacity was 516 kw and firm capacity 350 kw. In 1957-'58 one more diesel set was added to Agartala Power House and raised the capacity to 500 kw. In 1959 and 1960 diesel power stations were introduced at four sub-divisional headquarters namely, Dharmanagar,. Kailashahar, Udaipur and Khowai. Except these, 11,000 volt lines were extended to Arundhutinagar, Ramnagar and Indranagar from Agartala. Afterwards, diesel sets have also been installed at Ambasa and Bogoti. The total installed capacity was 2,886 kws in the late 1960s.

In 1958-'59 investigation into the possibility of developing hydro-electric power projects over river *Gumti* was conducted. It was found that it is somehow economical to generate hydro-electricity on river *Gumti*. The water power potential of the *Gumti* was estimated to be 8,000 kw with a firm capacity of

4,000 kw. It was completed in 1976 with 10 mw within the *Gumti* valley of *Dambur* falls. About power supply, Tripura is still in a dark corner of India. Power is purchased by Tripura from Assam. Installed capacity and generation of electricity from *Gumti* Power Plant is 15 mw in 1981.

It is said that Tripura will have plenty of power soon when the North Eastern Council funded gas based 75 mw project and two units of 17 mw each would start functioning properly. The Council has funded 6.5 mw *Baramura* Gas Thermal Units in Tripura which has been successfully commissioned in March, 1990. The prospects of natural gas is launching a cash programme of rural electrification. Tripura State Electricity Department has consumed 120,000 cubic metres during 1989 per day. The state electricity department proposes to set up a 500 mw gas based thermal plant and also gas-based vanaspati plant of 15,000 tonnes. The Tripura State Electricity Board was the main customer of natural gas which is needing only 220,000 cubic metres of gas from ONGS (Tripura) daily.

PRE-HISTORIC ARCHAEOLOGY:- A large number of artifacts belonging to the stone age of Tripura ranging from the early stone age (Palaeolithic Period) to the new stone age (Neolithic Period) have been discovered in 1988 in Teliamura range in Tripura by Dr. N.R. Ramesh of Geological Survey of India. It is said that, the pre-historic people of Tripura has utilised fossil wood as their raw material of implements. Dr. Ramesh has located over half a dozen rich archaeological sites in Khowai and Haora valleys of West Tripura district. More than 700 stone implements have been collected from Teliamura, Jirania, Mohanpur, Bishalgarh and Agartala. The speciality of Tripura archaeology is that instead of stone, silicified fossil wood was used for 98 per cent of tools. This is because, fossil wood is locally available in the Tertiary Hill ranges which constitute the dominant geomorphological features in Tripura. The available tools are:- axes, cleavers, borers, knives, hammer stones, flakes, pebbles, ground and polished celts.

Basket-pattern design of potsheds have been found at Khas Kolyanpur, Seratali and Kolaghar in Khowai and Haora valleys of West Tripura district. Radio carbon dating of deposits ranging from 3450 ± 150 B.P. to 1190 ± 90 B.P.

CURRENCY OF TRIPURA:- In Tripura, during the reign of kings, they had their own currency. Bell metalled small sized regular-round figured coins were used by the people of Tripura. Goods were purchased with this coin. It is said that the art of icons on coins were first adopted by Ratna Manikya (the ruler of Tripura) which were symbolised with *'Chaturdasa Devata'* and *'Narasingha Abatar'*. Like these, different kings of Tripura had inserted different symbols on their coins and their names. All these coins are valuable from historical point of view which also indicates artistic talents of that period.

Coins from mid-part of the fifteenth century (from 1464 AD) upto Bir Bikram Manikya of 1931 have been discovered. A silver coin of early 16th century was discovered by Jahar Acharjee in early part of 1992 at Udaipur, former capital of Tripura. This coin pertains to the time of King Amar Manikya (1577-'85) of Tripura. All coins, so far found are round shaped. Most of the coins are made of silver, few are gold-made. No copper coin so far have been found. One side of the coin has the name of a king in Bengali scripts or so and on its other side depicts sometimes a picture of lion, *'trisul'* carried by a lion, *'chandra'* (moon), *'Siva-linga'*, *'Krishna'* standing on a lion, etc.

COMMUNICATION:- Lack of adequate and cheap transport has been an obstacle in the economic development of the state. Hilly surface, numerous streams and rivulets, etc. have created difficulties in the development and expansion of transport routes. Before independence, communication in Tripura was dependent on railways running close to its western, southern and northern borders which after independence fell within East Pakistan (now Bangladesh) territory. During First Five Year Plan period roads were built, some old timber bridges were replaced by concrete bridges and some new bridges were constructed. In Fourth and Fifth Five Year Plan periods some backward and hilly interior areas were linked by roads to Agartala. National Highway No. 44 runs through Silchar (Assam) to Agartala. It is known as Assam-Agartala road. It is 200 km long route and through this Tripura links with rest of the country. State highways run from Agartala to Sabrum, Belonia, Khowai, Kamalpur, Dharmanagar, Kailashahar. The construction of Assam-Agartala road was started in 1948 and completed in 1958. First it was only 9 feet width. Later on, it was widened to 12 feet and also built three concrete bridges to cross Khowai, Manu and Deo rivers. There are PWD roads, district roads, inter village bridle paths, etc. Innumerable motor services have been commissioned on regular traffic roads for carrying passengers and goods. But, the road remains closed very often during monsoon due to heavy landslides. South Tripura has not progressed much in economic development due to its road mileage.

The only railway MG line in the state links Dharmanagar with Patharkandi (Cachar district of Assam) when a 12 km track was laid in 1964. In 1986, this line was extended from Dharmanagar to Pancharthal. Again extended upto Kumarghat of North Tripura on 3rd January, 1990. There is a plan of Central Government (July, 1991) to bring the capital Agartala (West Tripura district) on the railway map of the country by extending 132 km of railway line. The 11 km long railway line from Kumarghat to Nalkata is under consideration since 1989 by NERAMAC which would be Asia's biggest frait. Tripura has the second largest tunnel in the country from Pancharthal to Kumarghat railway track. State Chief Minister Sri Samir Ranjan Barman flaged off the train on 12th July, 1992 from Kumarghat to Guwahati (Assam).

The air transport plays an important role in the state's economy. Indian airlines connects Agartala, the capital of Tripura, with other parts of the country. There is no other air-route, Tripura has less communication with the mainstream of Indian life due to geographic isolation and lack of proper communication system.

A TV transmission centre has been set up near Agartala town in October, 1991. Independent own TV centre has been opened in Agartala on 20th November 1992. There is a radio station at Agartala which provides the coverage of the whole area of the state. Postal services, telephone, telegraph services have been in operation since long.

Like Assam, Meghalaya and Manipur, *Inner Line* restriction is not there to visit Tripura. It is said that, Tripura is likely to introduce Inner Line permit regulation system in its tribal hilly areas to check "alien influx" and safe-guard the tribals and their socio-economic interests. The Government of India is trying to improve its Travel and Civil Aviation Department. So, it seems that, they are not at interested to introduce any Inner Line Permit.

LITERACY AND EDUCATION:- The king of Tripura Dharma Manikya (*c.*1431-1462) was a patron of Bengali and Sanskrit learning. The total literate persons of Tripura is 856,688 (Census 1981). The percentage of literacy has gone up from 20.24 per cent (1961) to 42.12 per cent (1981).

TABLE II : LITERACY OF TRIPURA (DECADAL VARIATION)

Year	*Total Population*	*Percentage of Literates*
1901	1,73,325	2.28 per cent
1911	2,29,613	4.03 per cent
1921	3,04,437	7.08 per cent
1931	3,82,450	2.84 per cent
1941	—	—
1951	6,45,707	15.52 per cent
1961	11,42,005	20.24 per cent
1971	15,56,342	30.98 per cent
1981	20,53,058	42.12 per cent
1991	27,44,827	

Source: *Census of India* 1901-1991

In 1976-'77 a Post Graduate Centre was opened at Agartala. In 1986-'87, there were 1,083 Nursery Schools, 1,927 Junior Basic Schools, 419 Middle or Senior Basic Schools, 280 High Schools, 100 Higher Secondary Schools, 9 Colleges, 1 P.G. Centre, 1 Government Law College, 1 Engineering and 1 Polytechnic College, 2 Music and Fine Arts College, one Nursing Training Centre, 2560 Adult (Social) Education Centre, one Physical Education Centre.

Tripura University was inaugurated on 2nd November, 1987 at old Post Graduate Centre Agartala. Before establishing of this University, all examinations of Tripura were held under Calcutta University. In tribal rural societies, there has been some drop-outs by the children in schools. If an Agricultural University could be started in Tripura that would bring fruitful results on agriculture, horticulture, forestry, etc. However, it is said, Agartala is to attain its full literacy by 1992-'93.

TABLE III : PERCENTAGE OF LITERATES (GENERAL AND TRIBAL)

Year	*Male*	*Female*	*Total*	*Tribal*		
				Male	*Female*	*Total*
1961	29.61	10.19	20.24	17.37	2.31	10.01
1971	40.20	30.98	30.98	23.60	6.04	15.03
1981	51.70	32.00	42.12	33.46	12.27	23.07

Source: *S.R. Bhattacharjee* (1989): 65

It is observed from table-II that the literacy rate has slowly improved during the princely-period. Table-III testifies that female literacy is low than male literacy. Literacy among the tribals is somehow increasing. According to 1981 Census urban-literacy of Tripura is 73.66 per cent and rural 38.23 per cent.

LANGUAGE:- According to Suniti Kumar Chatterji (1951)"Tripura State is now the only area where the Bodo people still retain a good deal of their medieval political and cultural *milieu*, although Hinduism has made rapid strides among them. But nearly 300,000 people in the State have still kept up their old Bodo language, the Tipra or Mrung" (1951 : 71). The important languages spoken in Tripura are:- Bengali, Kakbarak (Tripuri), Reang and Manipuri. Before merger of Tripura with India, the earlier rulers of the state, adopted Bengali language for their administration. Now about 80 per cent of population of the state is using Bengali language. The next important language is the dialect of the Tripuri which is known as *Kakbarak*. This dialect has no script of its own and is written in Bengali script. *Kakbarak* is one of the official languages of Tripura. Most of the tribal population of Tripura speaks *Kakbarak* language. It is also spoken by the people of Chittagong Hill Tracts of Bangladesh. This is a Bodo group of dialect which had originated in the Brahmaputra Valley. It belongs to the Tibeto Burman Group and Sino-Tibetan speech family.

LAND REFORMS:- There was no regular land revenue system in Tripura till 1880. Acts and Rules were introduced after 1880 for the following types of land tenure:-

(i) **Niskar**:- The tenure holder holds land without tax revenue.

TABLE IV

SINO-TIBETAN (OR TIBETO-CHINESE) LANGUAGE FAMILY

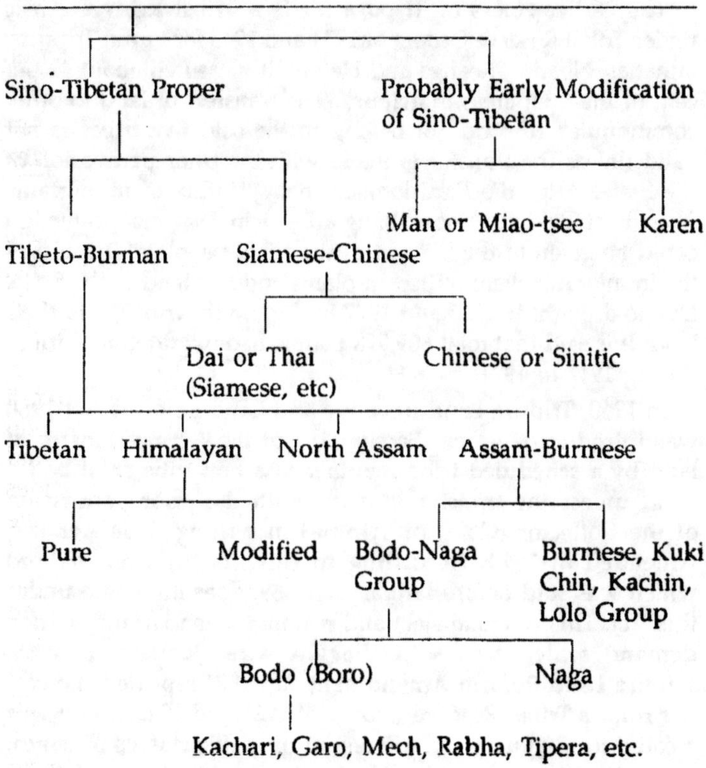

Source: *Suniti Kumar Chatterji* (1951) : 14, 15

(ii) **Dar Taluk**:- The intermediary right held under a 'Kayemi Taluk' or 'Taskishi Taluk' or under a revenue free tenure holder.

(iii) **Taskishi Taluk**:-The right of the *Talukdar* is transferable and heritable, but the rent can be revised after a contract period of 10 to 15 years.

(iv) **Kayemi Taluk**:- The right of the *Talukdar* is permanent, heritable and transferable and, the rent is fixed in an endless duration.

(v) **Jote**:- The right of a holder of *Jote (Raiyat)* is permanent, heritable and transferable, but the rent can be revised after a contracted period of 7 to 12 years.

(vi) **Korfa**:- The right of a holder who cultivates the land as under *Raiyat* or *Bargadar*.

The earlier rulers of Tripura made a Tribal Reserve Areas under Tribal Reserve Orders of 1931 and 1943 for Puran Tripuris, Jamatias, Noatias, Reangs and Halam. It measured,about 42 per cent of the total areas of Tripura. The transfers of land to other communities who do not belong to the said five tribes is not valid unless the transfer is made with the prior permission of the State. After the Partition, the heavy influx of immigrants from East Pakistan (now Bangladesh) in 1947 no protection could be given to the interest of the tribal people of Tripura as the immigrants were settled in plains and *tilla* land in the State. Due to drought in 1965 and 1972 in Tripura the tribals sold their land. It is said that total 609,998 people had migrated to Tripura during 1947 to 1971.

In 1960, Tripura Land Revenue and Land Reforms Act 1960 was introduced. As per Section 167 of the Act no transfer of land by a scheduled tribe member to a non-tribe shall be invalid unless the transfer is made with the prior permission of the Collector (Govt. of Tripura) in writing. This Act was Amended in 1974. According to this, the transfer of land which was sold before January 1, 1969, does not come under this Act. This Act is to eject and restore the land at the written demand which was sold illegally after January 1, 1969, Tripura Land Reform Amendment Act 1974 repealed the earlier ruler's Tribal Reserve Orders of 1931 and 1943 which was created to safeguard the interest of only five classes of tribes. Actually there are 19 classified tribes and majority of them are living outside of the Tribal Reserve. So it was meaningless to continue Tribal Reserve. Tripura Land Reforms Amendment Act 1975 provides that if any non-tribal desires to sell his land, then the tribals shall have the preferential right to purchase that.

Tripura Tribal Areas Autonomous District Council Bill 1979 has inspired creation of the Autonomous District Council in July, 1985 for the areas which is pre-dominantly inhabited by the tribals.

POPULATION:- There are Indo-Aryan (Bengalee) and Indo-Mongoloid (Tripuri, Reang, Jamatia, Noatia, Halam, Chakma, Mog, Kuki, Lushai, etc.) people. The total population of Tripura is 20,53,058 (1981 Census) of which 10,54,846 are male and 9,98,212 are female (Table V). The total Scheduled tribe population is 5,83,920 (28.44 per cent) and Scheduled caste is 3,10,384 (15.12 per cent), the urban population is 2,25,568 (11 per cent) and rural 18,27,490 (89 per cent), density of population per sq.km. is 196 persons in urban area.

TABLE V : POPULATION

District	*Male*	*Female*	*Total*	*Density per sq.km.*
Tripura West	4,99,605	4,76,647	9,76,252	322
Tripura North	2,79,832	2,61,410	5,41,248	140
Tripura South	2,75,403	2,60,155	5,35,558	150
Total	10,54,846	9,98,212	20,53,058	

Source: *Census of India (1981), Tripura*

Besides the above said tribes, there are the Khasi, Garo, Bhutiya, Lepcha, Oraon, Munda, Santhal, Bhil, Chaimal, Kunda or Kaur tribes in Tripura. There are also non-tribal population other than the Bengalee. They are :- Nepali, Behari, Assamese, etc. Rapid rise of population had taken place after the year 1941 due to influx of Bengalees from East Bengal (now Bangladesh) after a communal riot broke out on the issue of religion, in the district of Dacca (East Bengal). After independence, and the creation of East Pakistan (East Bengal, now Bangladesh) in 1947, Hindu refugees in large numbers came to Tripura from East Pakistan to settle here peacefully. Since then there has been constant flow of people from East Pakistan to Tripura. In 1986, a large number of the Chakma and Mog refugees migrated from Chittagong Hill Tracts of Bangladesh and took shelter in Tripura. Further, the establishment of tea-gardens during the second and third decades of this century led to immigration of the Santal, Oraon and Munda tribes. The Garos from Mymensing (Bangladesh) and Garo Hills (Meghalaya, India) immigrated to Tripura during early 1950s. The Khasis had also entered inside Tripura from Meghalaya (India) during the said period.

TABLE VI : POPULATION GROWTH

Year	Population	Decadal variation, in per cent
1901	1,73,325	25.98 per cent
1911	2,29,613	34.48 per cent
1921	3,04,437	32.59 per cent
1931	3,82,450	25.63 per cent
1941	5,13,010	34.14 per cent
1951	6,45,707	25.25 per cent
1961	11,42,005	78.71 per cent
1971	15,56,342	36.28 per cent
1981	20,53,558	
1991	27,44,827	

Source: *Census of India* (1901-1991)

TABLE VII : SCHEDULED TRIBE POPULATION

Year	Tribal Population	Decadal variation, in per cent
1901	91,679	52.89 per cent
1911	1,11,303	48.47 per cent
1921	1,71,610	56.37 per cent
1931	1,92,249	50.26 per cent
1941	2,56,991	50.09 per cent
1951	2,37,953	36.85 per cent
1961	3,60,070	31.53 per cent
1971	4,50,544	28.95 per cent
1981	5,83,920	28.44 per cent

In Tripura most of the people live in villages as agriculture is their main occupation. About 76 per cent of population are dependent on agriculture. However, the proportion of rural population is now gradually decreasing and urban population is remarkably increasing since 1981 onwards.

RELIGION:- The religious history of ancient Tripura was Vaisnavism, Saivaism, Saktism, Buddhism along with Animism. Hinduism is the earliest religion of Tripura (also Animism). It appears to have surfaced in the beginning of the 15th century. Most of the tribals of Tripura are following Animism along with Hinduism. There is a deep rooted impact of Saktism (Hindu cult) in their religion. Human sacrifices for the goddess Kali were very popular in earlier days among the Tipperas. This was abolished during the rule of *Raja* Dhana Manikya. The Lushai, Garo, Khasi, Mizos followed Christianity.

Among the Kukis, though the majority are Hindus, there are also Christians in large number. The Chakmas, Mogs follow Buddhism. The Tripuri, Reang, Jamatia, Noatia and Halam also follow Sakti cult. Kolois and Rupinis follow Vaishnavism.

TABLE VIII : RURAL / URBAN POPULATION

Year	*Rural Population*	*Urban Population*	*Percentage of R.P.*	*Percentage of U.P.*
1901	1,66,910	6,415	96.30	3.70
1911	2,22,782	9,831	97.02	2.98
1921	2,96,694	7,743	97.45	2.55
1931	3,72,870	9,580	97.50	2.50
1941	4,95,317	17,693	96.55	3.45
1951	5,96,434	42,595	93.14	6.86
1961	10,39,008	1,02,997	90.98	9.02
1971	13,93,982	1,62,360	89.57	10.43
1981	18,27,490	22,55,68	89.00	11.00

TABLE IX : MAIN TRIBES

District	*Headquarters*	*Main Tribes*
West Tripura	Agartala	Tripuri, Jamatia, Reang, Noatia, Kuki, Garo
North Tripura	Kailashahar	Tripuri, Reang, Chakma, Mizo
South Tripura	Udaipur	Tripuri, Jamatia, Reang, Uchai

TABLE X : RELIGION

Religion	*Population*	*Percentage of Total Population*
Hindu	18,34,218	89.34 per cent
Muslim	1,38,529	6.75 per cent
Buddhist	54,806	2.67 per cent
Christian	24,872	1.21 per cent
Sikh	285	0.01 per cent
Jain	297	0.02 per cent
Other Religion perssuanins	27	negligible
Religion not stated	24	negligible
Total	20,53,058	100.00

Source: *Census of India 1981, Tripura*

The following missionary organisations are active in Tripura. (1) Tripura Baptist Christian Union (TBCU), (2) Zorman Baptist Mission of Mizoram, (3) Roman Catholic Church, (4) United Pentecost Church of North East India and (5) Evangelical Church of India. The religious population of Tripura of five decades is as follows:-

TABLE XI : RELIGIOUS POPULATION OF FIVE DECADES

Religion	*1941*	*1951*	*1961*	*1971*	*1981*
Hindu	3,47,792	4,80,662	8,67,998	13,93,689	18,34,218
Muslim	1,23,570	1,36,940	2,30,002	1,03,962	1,38,529
Buddhist	7,724	15,403	33,716	42,285	54,806
Christian	328	5,262	10,039	15,713	24,872
Jain	—	—	195	375	297
Sikh	—	—	49	318	285
Other Religion perssuanin	—	—	—	—	27
Religion not stated	—	—	—	—	24

Source: *Census of India* 1941, 1951, 1961, 1971 and 1981.

SUPERSTITIONS AND BELIEF :- Most of the tribals of Tripura are superstitious. They believe in evil spirits. They worship *Tuima* or *Ganga* (the Ganges) when they are seriously ill. The priest of *Tuima* says the cause of ill-health in non-performance worship. *Burha-cha* god is worshipped to cure from illness.

They believe in re-birth and the law of *Karma* (self did). They are the believers of dreams, especially in the early-morning. If a dream is about buffalo, cattle, elephant, water, marriage ceremony, etc. it is believed that the cultivation would be profitable. Dreams of beggar, dead animal, fire, red cloth, somebody laughing, gathering of men, etc. is a bad symptom. A dream about building a new house means that the dreamer will die shortly.

It is further believed that eating a particular fish or animal when a woman is pregnant may effect her child's health which is in her womb.

FESTIVAL:- The Tripuris worship two brothers:- *Goraiya* (fair one) and *Kataiya* (dark one) on the last day of the Hindu Bengali year (*Chaitra Sankranti*). For this festival the Tripuris are to drink rice-beer for 2-3 days. A religious festival *Bara Puja* of the Halam tribe is celebrated once in four to five years. For this, large number of animals are sacrificed and people drink large quantity of rice-beer. Another festival, *navanna* (festival for new rice) also performed by them. *Durga Puja, Ganga Puja, Dewali* are their festivals. *Garia* and *Ker Pura* are their traditional festivals. *Dumbur* fair, *Ampinagar Mela (Saraswati Puja), Rathayatra Mela, Siva-ratri Mela, Baruni Mela, Kharchi Mela,* etc. are also celebrated by them in Tripura.

DANCE:- The *Garia* dance is very much popular among the Tripuris. They dance during *Garia* festival. The *Cherew* (bamboo-dance) is popular dance among the Lushai and the Mizo communities. Manipuri *Ras* dance is famous among the Manipuris. Balance-dance by the Reang and the Chakma are popular. The *Lebang Boomani* group dance are also popular. *Dailo Mairang Phawrmaw* is popular dance of the Reangs. Tagore's dance-dramas are popular in Tripura. The Reangs are accustomed to dance during their sorrow at the time of observing post-funeral rituals.

MUSIC:- Tripura has always been popular for music and cultural functions. The great singer of theater Sachin Deb Barman was from Tripura. Almost all the people of Tripura are fond of music. Before and after setting fire to the *jhum* fields and at the time of giving guard to the *jhum* field, they sing. They have festival songs, love songs, marriage songs, ritual songs. They usually sing with their indigenous musical instruments namely, *Sarinda, Chougpneng, Samu* (flute), etc. All these instruments are made of bamboo and strings. Some of them also use the modern instruments of the markets.

ADMINISTRATION (HISTORICAL AND POLITICAL):- In the ancient period Tripura had no distinct political status. Most of the western and southern parts of the state was politically attached to *'Samatata'* (called afterwards East Bengal, now Bangladesh) under various dynasties. It is somehow difficult to find out the actual date of establishment of the Tripura kingdom in its present form under the Tripura rulers.

The history of Tripura is almost a continuous one with glorious events. In the past many neighbouring countries such as Cachar, Sylhet, Jaintia, etc. were made to accept the superiority of Tripura. In 18th century the whole territory of Tripura fell indirectly under the *Nawab* of Dacca of Bengal. Most of its territory which is now part of Bangladesh was annexed by the Mughal Empire in 1733. Shamser Gazi (1748 to 1760 A.D.) became the virtual ruler of Tripura for twelve years. Following the assumption of British rule in Bengal in 1765, Muslim influence in Tripura was supplanted by the British. Thus the Mughals could not do any harm to the kingdom of Tripura. It was able to keep its independent status for more than 1,000 years. A British Political Agent was appointed for Tripura in 1871. In early part of 20th century Tripura was almost a feudatory colony to British-India.

Most of the scholars believe that the royal family of Tripura originally belonged to the Tipra (Tripuri) tribe. According to *Rajmala,* the *Rajas* of Tripura were the descendants of King Druhya, the third son of Yayati of *Lunar* dynasty of *Kshatriya* caste. According to Kaliprasanna Sen, Jujharu Fa was the founder of the Tripura era which was started from 590 AD (cf. *Shri Rajmala,* vol. I, 1926:208). Dharma or Dhankuru Fa, the fifth descendent of Jujharu Fa was a Buddhist and converted to Hinduism. It is said that the rulers of Tripura gave up their original title *Fa* and took the title *'Manikya'* which was perhaps at the influence of the Hindu society and culture of the neighbouring states. The earliest king who took first the title *Manikya* was *Raja* Ratna Fa who was the 139th *Raja* (cf. *Rajmala*) who ascended the throne in c1464 AD. It is believed that during his period coins were issued first time in Tripura. There is some controversy about the period during which Ratna Fa (Manikya) ruled in Tripura and also the question whether he was the first ruler to use the title *Manikya.* But it is somehow observed that from *Raja* Ratna Fa, the names of all the descendant kings ended with the word *Manikya* and their queens either *Sundari* or *Devi.*

From the last part of the Mughal Period, the zamindari of *Chakla Roshnabad* was given to the *Rajas* of Tripura on conditional basis that the Mughals should get an annual tribute from the rulers of Tripura. This arrangement was also made by the East India Company (British-India Government) with the *Raja* Krishna Manikya for *Chakla Roshnabad* in lieu of annual rent of Rs. 1,00,001/- for its annexation by the British in February, 1761. The British resident Mr. Leak took the zamindari of *Chakla Roshnabad* in 1782 for direct management for ten years.

Finally, *Chakla Roshnabad* was returned to the ruler of Tripura *Raja* Rajdhar Manikya in 1792 and formed a district *Roshnabad Tripura* and a British Collector was appointed under the king for its administration. After Independence of India, the zamindari of *Chakla Roshnabad* went to East Pakistan (now Bangladesh). Thus, Tripura lost unwillingly the territorry of its fertile plain land of *Chakla Roshnabad* and also, its main rail heads of west, south and northern parts of the state.

The modern era of Tripura was perhaps started from the reign of Birchandra Manikya (1862-'96). He succeeded his brother *Raja* Ishan Chandra Manikya. During his time both slavery and the custom of self-immolation by the Hindu widow were abolished in the state in 1877 and 1889 respectively. On 4th December 1829, William Bentink declared self-immolation illegal in India. *Raja* Birchandra followed some administrative set-up after the British-India fashion.

In 1863 the Jamatias under their leader Parikshit revolted against Tripura Government. It was due to the cruelty of the Tripura Government officials to them. It was restrained with the help of the Kukis by the Government at Kailasahar.

The Kukis raided Tripura several times. They gave much trouble to the Government of Tripura. Lord Mayo, the then Governor General of British India, had appointed Mr. A.W.B. Power as a *Political Agent* for the first time in Tripura in 1871 to reside at Agartala to protect the state from the Lushai Kuki raids. At the advice of the Political Agent, judiciary reform of Hill Tripura was introduced by the King. In 1872, he established *Khas Appeal Adalat* (Royal Court of Appeal) for final judgement of the civil and criminal cases. It was constituted with two judges. He kept with him the supreme power of justice. In 1877, Birchandra received his personal title of *Maharaja*. He divided the state into seven administrative divisions. These are:- Agartala, Udaipur, Sonamura, Belonia, Khowai, Dharmanagar and Kailashahar. In 1878, *Pahari Adalat* (Hill Court) and the post of Political Agent was abolished and a District Magistrate was nominated. In 1890, it was decided that the king should select and appoint a Minister with full powers of administration. The king was the proprietor of the soil of Tripura. The subjects of Tripura held their land either directly as a collector or under taluk grants, which was either temporary or permanent. In the hills, a family-tax was realised from *jhum* cultivators and rents were paid for the land in the plains. He opened departments of Excise, Stamps and Registrations. A military force was there under Superintendent of Police. The king was a great patron of literature, art and music. He encouraged poet Rabindra Nath Tagore. He established Birchandra Public Library. After his death in 1896 his son Radhakishore Manikya (1896-1909) ruled Tripura. He formed some departments such as education, health, agriculture, public works, etc. He founded a college at Agartala in 1901, established a technical school, Victoria Memorial Hospital, temple of Lord Jagannath, a museum, etc. Tripura State Gazette was first published during his reign in *Bengali*. He was a lover of Bengali language and literature. Bengali was the official state language of Tripura. His son Birendra Kishore Manikya (1909-1923) succeeded the throne after his death. He established several schools and dispensaries in various parts of the state. He founded model school for agricultural and sericultural education and training. He introduced tea-gardens in waste lands. He granted to Burma Oil Company in 1916 a license for exploring mineral oil in the state. *Amatya Sabha* (Advisory Council) was reconstituted by him.

Maharaja Bir Bikram Kishore Manikya (1923-1947) was the last ruling King of Tripura. At the age of 14 he had succeeded the throne of his father on August 14, 1923. As he was a minor (at that time), the administration was to run under a council of administrators. He became the ruler in 1927. He beautified Agartala town, the only Municipality area. He constructed new roads which connected Agartala with its sub-divisions and improved the road-communications in the interior areas. He set up State Electricity Scheme in 1936. He held *Durbars* (meetings) with the tribal-chiefs. He encouraged *jhum* cultivators to do permanent plough cultivation. He established *Rajsabha* (Privy Council), improved *Khas Adalat* (High Court), appointed *Mantri Parishad* (Council of Ministers), established *Vyavasthapak Sabha* (Legislative Assembly), *Gramya Mandalis* (Village Unions), introduced financial administration and audit and separated the State budget from the budget of the Ruler. But, due to Second World War he could not take much action on all these matters. *Maharaja* gave free shelter to the refugees who came to Tripura after the communal riots in 1941 at Dacca and in 1946 at Noakhali of East Bengal (now Bangladesh). He died on 17th May, 1947, at the age of thirty-nine. Before his death he settled the question of Tripura's merger with India by agreeing to it affirmatively.

There was a Reang revolt in 1942-'43 during the reign of *Maharaja* Bir Bikram. This was partly due to socio-religious and partly anti-feudal. Ratanmoni was the leader of that revolt. Their movement was suppressed by the royal forces.

After the death of *Maharaja* Bir Bikram his minor son King Kirit Bikram became the *Maharaja*. As he was a minor one, a Council of Regency under the presidentship of his mother *Maharani* Kanchanprava Devi was to run the administration through Vice-President, Member, Chief Minister and *Dewan*. Before and mostly after the death of Bir Bikram Kishore Manikya there were communal riots in Noakhali, Dacca, Mymensingh and other places of East Bengal (East Pakistan, now Bangladesh). For that, Hindu refugees had migrated to Tripura for their safety. But this led a violent communal politics among the tribal and Muslims in Tripura. They formed a secret organisation called *Sengkrak* and made trouble to the refugees. The tribals tried to drive out the Bengalees and in the mean time the Muslims were keen to annex Tripura with East Pakistan. One of the local Muslim leaders Gedu Mia (Abdul Barik Khan Chaudhuri), the brain behind the *Anjuman Islamia* had conspired with some of the palace-people that he was to be appointed as Chief Minister by replacing *Maharajkumar*. After that, Muslim League National Guards in East Pakistan made a propaganda that Tripura state belongs to East Pakistan. They distributed pamphlets to the public which indicated that, Muslims were to conquer Tripura and annex it to East Pakistan. The pamphlets were widely circulated in East Pakistan and preparation was made to invade Tripura. It happened soon after the Independence of India. Regent Maharani was also alerted at this dangerous situation of Tripura. She was anxious about the difficult condition of the state as it was about to be isolated from the main land of India by the Award of the *Boundary Commission*. For that, she saw Sardar Ballabbhai Patel, Home Minister of India, in July 1947. During conspiracy *Maharani* Kanchanprabha Devi and her minor son Kirit Bikram Manikya fled to take shelter in Shillong (capital of Assam, now Meghalaya). On 21st August 1947 Sardar Ballabbhai Patel instructed Sir Akbar Hydari, Governor of Assam, to take proper action for the protection of Tripura. The conspiracy thereafter failed at the quick action taken by the Indian Government and keen interest of the *Maharani*.

The Council of Regency of Tripura was dissolved and *Maharani* Kanchanprava Devi became the only Regent on 12th January, 1948. A new Chief Minister designated as the *Dewan* of Tripura State was appointed who with the help of one Adviser and two to three Secretaries had to look after the administration. An Agreement, about the merger of Tripura with India, was signed on 9th September 1949 in New Delhi by *Maharani* as Regent and on behalf of her minor son Kirit Bikram Kishore Deb Barman Manikya. It was agreed to transfer the administration of Tripura to India on October 15, 1949 and *Maharaja* of Tripura could retain all his private properties, personal rights, privileges, immunities and dignities which he received before 15th August 1947 as a ruler of Tripura. According to this agreement the age-old rule of a dynasty came to an end on 15th October 1949. It is strange as nothing was mentioned about the share of *Chakla Roshnabad* zamindari in that agreement. It was, however, included in East Pakistan (now Bangladesh) as stated earlier.

Since October 15, 1949, Sri Ranjit Kumar Ray, the then *Dewan* of Tripura, was appointed by the Government of India as the Chief Commissioner of Tripura. He was the head of the state in place of the Regent *Maharani*. The new Constitution of India had converted Tripura on 26th January 1950 as a Part-C State. For a period of 8 years (1949-1956) Tripura was a Part-C State. Tripura was administered by a Chief Commissioner, as stated earlier, under the direct control of the Union Government. After the first general election in 1952, an Advisory Council was formed with three advisers, two of whom were top leaders of Congress Party in Tripura and one, a retired civil servant. They were Sri Sacindralal Singha, Sri Sukhamay Sengupta and Sri Jitendra Devbarman. They were appointed by an order of the President of India on April 14, 1953. Their duty was only to advise the Chief Commissioner on nineteen subject matters which were divided among them.

The Government of India had appointed the State Reorganisation Commission (1954-'56). They recommended for merger of Tripura and Manipur with Assam. But, it was strongly objected in Tripura by the CPI(M) for the rights of Tripura tribes. After that, at the recommendation of the States' Re-organisation Commission, the Government of India converted Tripura as a Union Territory on November 1, 1956. A 32 member Territorial Assembly (Council) was formed in 1957 with some power. Out of 32 members, 30 were elected representatives of the States' electorate while the rest two were nominated by the President of India. 27 members out of 30 elected in Territorial Assembly constituencies in the first ever general election held in 1952. Pro-Congress stand of the former *Maharaja* had tilled the balance in favour of the Congress during second general election in 1957. This Territorial Assembly began to function from August 15, 1957. It had the power to deal with total nine State-matters and one concurrent subject-matter of the Concurrent List under its jurisdiction. It could pass bye-laws on those subjects which had to effect soon after the approval of the Parliament. The designation of Chief Commissioner was upgraded as Administrator. The Territorial Assembly had a Chairman (elected by the Assembly members) who acted as a political chief and a Chief Executive Officer (appointed by the Administrator i.e. Chief Commissioner), who acted as a head of the bureaucracy of three departments *viz.* Education, Engineering and Health Services. These were headed by three Principal Officers respectively.

Around 1961, some tribes of Tripura under Eastern India Tribal Union (EITU) demanded the 5th Schedule of the Constitution to apply to Tripura. Later on, the tribes of Tripura had also demanded the extension of the Sixth Schedule of the Constitution and formation of autonomous districts for Tripura tribes. There was a large victory of Congress in the Assembly election of 1962. In 1963, Constitution was amended to provide Tripura with its first Legislative Assembly and a Council of Ministers. With the enforcement of Union Territories Act, 1963, which came into force from 1 July, 1963, a Legislative Assembly was set up in Tripura (Misra, 1976). This had 30 elected members and 3 nominated members, nominated by the President of India. Previously, a bill could be passed by the Territorial Assembly only after the approval of the Parliament before it was submitted to the President of India for giving his assent. But the new Legislative Assembly had power to pass laws on all the State and concurrent subjects. A bill could be passed by the Legislative Assembly which goes directly to the President of India for his assent. The Legislative Assembly had a Speaker and a Deputy Speaker and power to conduct its proceedings and business. The Council of Ministers with the Chief Minister as the head to aid and advise the Administrator who refers the bills to the Legislative Assembly and to the President for decision. In case of urgency he himself has to take action on behalf of the President. The member of Ministers was raised from three to five. The Chief Minister is appointed by the President as well as other Ministers on the advise of the Chief Minister. These were Chief Minister Sri S.L. Singha, Minister Sri S. Sengupta and three Deputy Ministers Sri M.L. Bhowmik, Dr. B. Das and Sri Raj Prasad Choudhuri. Tripura was at that time one District Territory with a District Magistrate and a Collector. The territory was divided into ten revenue sub-divisions.

Perhaps at the influence of the CPI(M) and the difference between tribes and non-tribes led to the formation of Tripura Upajati Juba Samity (TUJS) on June 10, 1967. Their demands were to recognise Kok-Barak language, to adopt Roman script, to regain the lands possessed by the non-tribes from tribes and to create an autonomous District Council for Tripura tribes under the Sixth Schedule of the Constitution of India.

The North Eastern Areas (Re-organisation) Act No. 81 of 1971 was passed in the Parliament and assented by the President of India on December 30, 1971. According to this Act, Tripura attained the Statehood on January 21, 1972. As per this Act, the North Eastern Council (NEC) was formed to co-ordinate the development and security in the area of North-East-India. The office of the NEC was established at Shillong (Meghalaya) in 1972. At the Statehood of Tripura, the Legislative Assembly became sixty seated according to the Constitution. The status of Administrator was upgraded to that of Lieutenant-Governor in 1971 and Joint Secretary upgraded to Chief Secretary.

First general election of the State Assembly was held in March, 1972. In this, Congress won 42 seats out of 60. The Congress Ministry was formed by Sri Sukhamoy Sengupta. He resigned on March 29, 1977 soon after the defeat of the Congress in 1977 election where CPI(M) won 53 seats out of 60. On April 1, 1977, Sri Prafulla Kumar Dass, Janata-CPI(M) formed the coalition government. But he was replaced after a short period by Sri Radhika Ranjan Gupta. After 95 days he also left his Janata-CPI(M) coalition Ministry and Sri Nripen Chakraborty led by CPI(M) government came into office in August, 1977, as Chief Minister and continued till the Congress(I)-TUJS alliance was voted to power in the State Assembly election in February, 1988. Scheduled tribes of Tripura have twenty reserved seats (in Feb. '93) instead of seventeen in the sixty member State Legislature for Tripura, the 75th Constitution amended Article 332 for the election in February, 1993. At this, three along more with 17 earlier tribal reserved constituencies become effective.

MOVEMENTS IN TRIPURA :- a) *Jamatia Revolt*:- In the year 1863, the Jamatias under their leader Parikshit revolted. This happened as they protested against coolie-labour to Sri Okhirai Hazari, a tax collector of *Raja* Bir Chandra Manikya. Before that, till *Raja* Ishan Chandra Manikya (1849-'61), the Jamatias were exempted from doing forced coolie-labour work to pay tax collector. For that, they agreed and refused to do coolie work even to pay tax and they prepared themselves for revolt. The revolt was suppressed by the *Raja* with the help of the Darlong Kukis of Kailasahar. It was stated (Bengal Judicial Proceedings, October, 1864, No. 47) that, about 200 Tipperahas (Jamatias) had been killed, many villages burnt down and the inhabitants wandered in the plains of Tipperah. Parikshit, the leader, was captured and brought to the *Raja* by the Darlong Kukis. It is stated that, the king released him after converting him to *Vaishnavism* faith.

b) *Reang Movement*:- Under the leadership of Ratanmani (Noatia) a movement was started in 1942-'43 by the Reangs. It was partly socio-religious and partly anti-feudal movement. This happened due to anger with their village headmen, *Choudhuries.* They were not satisfied with the unequal taxation system of the *Raja*. The Tripuris had to pay minimum taxes while the Reangs and Noetias had to pay the maximum. It is said that they not only paid highest house taxes but also on bamboo and cane. As their *Choudhuries* did protest to the king about this inequality they approached a religious person Ratanmani, who followed Ramayana-Mahabharata and his dogma was *'Om Prana*

Rama'. In the mean time, an ambitious *Choudhuri* of Bagafa, Sri Khagendra Reang wanted to become *Rai* (Chief) of the Reang community of Tripura. There was a rule among the Reang that one can not be a *Rai* till the death of the existing *Rai*. As *Maharaja* Bir Bikram Manikya favoured him, he illegally dismissed Sri Debi Sing Reang, a *Rai* of Amarpur and appointed, Khagendra Reang as *Rai* by promoting him from *Choudhuri*. At this, the Reangs were not happy, especially when Khagendra Reang's supporters had to harass the supporters of Debi Sing Reang. Moreover, when there was a food crisis during the Second World War they observed the hoarding tendencies of some *Choudhuries* to profit from the distress situation as-well-as they observed that the king had purchased all available paddy to feed some limited persons of war-army and to people of Agartala town. Ultimately, famine started in Amarpur, Udaipur, Belonia and Sabroom. In this great trouble, Ratanmani's disciples started to distribute food in their own villages.

During war, *Maharaja* wanted to recruit some youths from Reang community through the *Choudhuries*. But, the *Choudhuries* could not recruit any single Reang youth and reported to the king that the disciples of Ratanmani disallowed them to recruit the Reang youth and they had prepared for a revolt against the king. Actually the Reangs were not against the king but against the *Choudhuries* and later on they had looted the houses of *Choudhuries*. A royal force was sent to suppress the Reang revolt. They controlled them, burnt the Reang villages and arrested many famine victims and brought them to Agartala. At the instance of king, they were forcefully asked to leave their religion *Saivism* and adopt *Vaishnavism*. Ratanmani and some of his followers fled to Chittagong Hill Tracts due to fear. The British police, however, arrested them. According to a request dated November 29, 1943, by the king they handed Ratamani to Agartala Central Jail authorities. Soon after his arrival in Agartala Ratanmani died. His death was un-natural. But, the people of *Maharaja* declared that the death was due to cholera. Till today Ratanmani is respected as a religious *guru* by many of his disciples.

c) *Tripura Massacre*:- There was communal tension in 1979-'80 in North East India including Tripura. The expulsion of foreigners' movement which started first in Assam and then spread to

Tripura and other States of North East India. The Tripura Upajati Juba Samiti (TUJS) made publicity about the tribal backwardness. According to them, this was due to large scale immigrant of Bengalees from East Pakistan (now Bangladesh) made the tribals as "minority" and "second class citizen." in their own land Tripura. Some tribal extremists formed Tripura National Volunteers (TNV) in July 1979 with the aim to establish an independent Tribal State of Tripura through their armed struggle. In 1978-'79 Sri Vijay Rankhal and his co-extremist tribals organised Tripura *Sena* in all the Sub-Divisions of Tripura. They got inspiration at the instance of Laldenga of Mizoram and Phizo of Nagaland. They tried to maintain their links with Mizo National Front (MNF) of Mizoram. Rankhal became the Commander-in-Chief of Tripura *Sena*. In 1979 he attacked Amarpur Police Station and looted it. He was expelled from TUJS on August 5, 1979, for anti-party activities.

On March 15, 1980, the agitators raised a slogan "oust the aliens". It meant that all those (Bengalees) who entered Tripura after 1949 should quit the State Tripura. On March 15, 1980, the agitators of TUJS adopted a resolution in their 12th general meeting held at Taidu (South Tripura) to drive out the "foreigners" who came to Tripura after October 15, 1949. TUJS attended a meeting of all hill leaders of the North-East India at Dibrugarh (Assam) on March 28, 1980. Taidu (South Tripura) meeting adopted two types of action viz. demonstration and deputation in front of all block offices simultaneously on May 21, 1980 and (ii) boycott of all markets in the State by the tribal people during first week of June, 1980. Everyday the situation was deteriorating. The bazar boycott programme was the effect of communal tension between tribals and non-tribals. Scattered violent movements were reported from June 2, 1980. Tripura Chief Minister, Sri Nripen Chakraborty, appealed on June 4, 1980 to withdraw 'Foreigner-Movement'. The massacre which was the worst one occured in Tripura on June 7, 1980. In Mandai Bazar, at a distance of about 25 kilometres from Agartala, a large number of Bengalees were killed. According to Jagadis Gan-Choudhuri (1985 : 64) "the flame of fire spread very rapidly from village to village burning thousands of houses and huts, cattle and crops. Numerous villages were laid waste. Lakhs of people were rendered homeless. Properties, both movable and immovable, of several crores were destroyed, damaged, burned, looted and captured. Hundreds were murdered." It appears from several violent clashes, in diffenent parts of Tripura that there was no administration in the State since June 7 to 9, 1980. The Central Reserve Police Force (CRPF) was late in arriving there. The situation was, however, controlled when the Army reached there. Bijoy Hrangkhawl was the brain behind the *"Foreigner Movement"*. Binanda Jamatia and other underground extremists formed "Army of Tripura Peoples' Liberation Organisation" (ATPLO) in December, 1980. The members of ATPLO were trained by the Mizo National Front (MNF) in Chittagong Hill Tracts. Sri Jamatia made an agreement with CPI(M) and surrendered to the Left Front Government with his followers on July 23, 1983. He was murdered on February 17, 1985. On May 4, 1988, TNV leader Bijoy Hrangkhawl wrote a letter to the Governor of Tripura for a peaceful solution of tribal problems through negotiation within the framework of the Constitution of India. As a result, a tripartite Agreement was signed by the Union Government, Government of Tripura and the militants of TNV. This ended the eight year old insurgency. For this, there was an understanding between Government and TNV to amend the Representation of People's Act, 1950 so as to provide 20 reserved Scheduled Tribe's seats in Tripura State Legislative Assembly, restoration of alienated land to the tribals and, a re-drawing of the boundaries of the Autonomous District Council in Tripura. The TNV extremists assured to come overground and surrender with their arms, ammunition and equipment within one month of the signing of the Agreement and Government will rehabilitate all the TNV militants who will surrender and take all measures for socio-economic development of the tribals of Tripura. The formal 'surrender' was observed at Ganganagar (North Tripura) Peace Camp on August 13, 1988 in presence of Chief Minister and the Governor of Tripura. Tripura Peace Accord was signed by the TNV, the Centre and the State government on August 12, 1988. But, this Peace-Accord with TNV seems to run into rough weather as some clashes are still going on in Tripura.

DISTRICT COUNCIL:- The tribal areas of 7,132,54 sq.km. are under the Autonomous District Council which came into being on January 18, 1982, in terms of *"Tripura Tribal Area*

Autonomous District Council Act, 1979." The 6th Schedule for the Tripura Autonomous District Council was passed by the Parliament (*49th Constitutional Amendment*) Act, 1984. The Autonomous District Council was constituted through democratic election in July, 1985, under the *Schedule VI* of the Constitution. It safeguards the tribal interest, quick development of tribal areas. It helps to solve the problems on socio-economic and cultural aspects of the tribes. It has power on certain matters *viz.* a) Executive (i.e. private disputes in between two persons and public disputes for a whole tribal village); b) Administrative (i.e. market, water supply, footpath, finance, etc.) and, c) judicial (i.e. murder, theft, divorce, etc.). Tripura Tribal Areas Autonomous District Council had passed a resolution in September, 1991 unanimously urging the Tripura Government to enforce the *Inner Line Permit* system for regulating movement of outsiders in the States' Autonomous Hill Region to protect the tribal population within the autonomous tribal region.

There was a movement in 1991-'92 by All Mizo Convention (AMC) of Tripura for its long-standing demand to set up a Mizo Regional Council for the people of Jampui Hills bordering Mizoram. They wanted this to get protection from exploitation and allow them to have their own autonomous administration.

VILLAGE COUNCIL :- The formation of Village Council of the tribes of Tripura is simple. Village Chief or *Gaon Bura* is a head man who ruled on certain matters of the villagers. *Gaon Bura* enjoyed certain customary powers and privileges. The Provinces Panchayati-Raj Act of 1947 had been extended to Tripura in 1959. Single tier Village Council at the village level was formed. according to this Act. The designation of the selected office-bearers of the Village Council varies from tribes to tribes. The Council has two parts *viz.* administrative known as *Gaon Panchayat* and judicial called *Naya Panchayat*. The term of office of the members of a *Gaon Panchayat* and its *Pradhan* is 5 years and *Upa-Pradhan* is one year. A *Naya-Panchayat* is formed by taking some elected members of *Gaon-Panchayat*. The head of this *Panchayat* is called *Sar-Panch*.

The function of the Village Council are on administrative, economic, judicial, defensive and socio-religious. For administration, the Council looks after construction and maintenance of paths and bridges, site selection for new village allotment of house sites to individual families, sanitation and water-supply, etc. For economic activities, the Council includes site selection for shifting cultivation, allotment of *jhum* fields to each family, organisation of co-operative labour for *jhum* cultivation, organisation of fishing, hunting, gathering, etc. For judicial, the Council settles inter-village disputes, cases of elopment, adultery, theft, quarrel, etc. For defensive, the Council is to look after safety and security of the village. For socio-religious function, the Council observes the festivals, looking after the poor, disposal of dead, regulation of marriages, preservation of social customs, etc.

The Village Council used to get its income by imposing fees and taxes on sale of animals, fairs, festivals, slaughter-houses, trade, profession, supply of water, etc. Every Village Council has to prepare its estimates of income and expenditure twice in a year and lay it before the *Gaon Sabha* (Village Assembly). A Village-Assembly usually starts in the evening at the *Kachari Ghar* of the Village Chief to settle disputes and for other matter.

CHIEFTAINSHIP- Besides Village Councils of each tribe, there are the suprima traditional council headed by the respective tribal village chief or *Raja*. In between village council and supreme traditional council, there is a zonal office among few tribes. The Reang has this. They made three zones on the basis of three famous rivers of Tripura *viz.* the Muhuri river, the Gumti river and the Khowai river. Three zonal chiefs are there for the said three areas. They called them *Hukai Chaudhuri*. The village administration is conducted by the *Chaudhuri* (Chief of the village), *Karbari* (Secretary), minister to the Chief and *Daoa* (Manager).

LOCAL GOVERNMENT- There are two categories of statutory institutions of local government *viz.* the Municipality and the *Panchayat*. The Municipal administration was introduced by *Raja* Bir Chandra Manikya in 1871 in Agartala town. The number of wards were set up in 1937. In March 1978, the number of wards had increased. The function of the Municipality involves water supply, sanitation, scavenging drainage, roads, public health, etc. They get their income by imposing taxes on property, trade, business, water-supply, house-tax, fees from markets, revenues from vehicle, etc. At present, there are total ten towns under Municipality in Tripura. These are : Agartala, Dharmanagar, Radhakishorpur, Kailashahar, Belonia, Khowai, Amarpur, Sonamura, Kamalpur, Subroom. Each Municipality has one elected Chairman and one elected Vice-Chairman.

GAMES AND SPORTS- They like all types of modern and indigenous games and sports. Young boys and girls are fond of modern sports and they are participating in different competitions of Inter-State and national sports and games. Some of them know wrestling, judo, karate, etc. The Education Directorate is giving them training for Scouts and Guides, physical education and sports.

Most of them are fond of fish and meat. For that, they are trapping their games.

WEAPONS- Most of the tribes of Tripura are brave and good fighters. Their main weapons are *dao* (dagger), bow, arrow, knife; etc. Some of them know "guerilla" warfare and also the art of trench fighting.

HEALTH- People of Tripura suffer much from malaria, pox, gastro enterities, cholera, diarrhoea, dysentery, typhoid, etc. Epidemic diseases happened several times in a year. Progress of health services are made at Agartala and other parts of the State. Before the starting of the first Five Year Plan (1951-56) there was only one "Victoria Memorial Hospital" at Agartala which had started in 1903. There were several dispensaries throughout the territory of Tripura. The condition of the health services have been improved after independence. Hospitals, Primary Health Centres and dispensaries have been established throughout the State. Large number of patients are treated in different hospitals of Tripura. Less number of people now believe in magic and sacrifice to cure diseases through indigenous medical care. It is reported that the rate of cancer in the north-east, especially in Tripura, is higher due to tobacco leaf chewing and lack of sense of hygiene, for eating pesticide and uncleaned vegetables.

LIQUOR, DRUGS, ETC- Most of the tribes are fond of liquor. Indigenous rice-beer is popular among them. This home-made liquor plays an important item in their life and culture. It is an essential item for religious ceremonies, festivals and social functions. *Ganja*, *Charas*, Opium, etc. are now-a-days popular among the younger generation. Some of them have the habit of chewing dry tobacco leaf. Most of them chew betel nuts with lime and betel leaves.

FOOD AND DRINK- Rice is their main food which is taken with meat, fish, boiled vegetables and pulses along with chillies. They like eating both fresh and dried fish. The Mizos eat several kinds of animals and birds.

Besides their indigenous liquor, they drink tea and milk. Some of the Mizos prefer to drink tea without milk.

PHYSICAL FEATURES OF THE TRIBES- According to E.T. Dalton (1872) the physiognomy of some of the tribes of Tripura is like that of the Manipuris. But the greater part of them, according to him, bears more resemblance to the Khasis, having strongly marked Mongolian features with flat face and thick lips. They are not shorter in stature than the Bengalees and far more muscular and strongly made.

The tribes of Tripura are generally medium to above medium stature, mesocephalic to brachycephalic head, broad high cheek bones, flat platyrrhine to leptorrhine nose, brownish yellow skin colour. They are strong and sturdy. The women are generally medium to short statured people.

DRESS AND ORNAMENTS- Modern educated young men and women have almost rejected the dress and ornaments of their ancestors. Their traditional dresses are simple like *'pachras'*, *'riyas'*, *'chaddar'* etc. Some time the women use *'Saris'*. In olden days, the men used short *dhotis*. But now mill-made *dhoties* from market are used. The young boys use pant and shirt with *genji*.

In early days, the women folk used necklace of coins and beads, silver bangles different types of ear ornaments, bracelets, etc. The Reang women are fond of ornaments. But due to change of economic condition, influence of modernity, education, etc. they are not using their out dated ornaments. At present women are using simple earings, necklace, glass bangles.

MARRIAGE:- They are patrilineal, patrilocal and patriarchal people. Each tribe has its own rule for selection of mates. Their marriages are three types. These are : negotiation, service and rarely elopment. Marriage is considered "legal" soon after the formal marriage ceremony. They follow endogamy but they are exogamous in respect of clans. Marriage between members of same clan is generally discouraged but it is not prohibited to the Mizos.

In earlier days boys and girls rarely mixed freely with one another. Mizo boys and girls free mix. Each tribe has its own rules for selection of mates. For the Tripuri, Reang and Halam marriage, the would-be groom is required to stay and work in his would-be father-in-law's house for certain period. This procedure applies also in case of negotiated marriage.

There is a dowry system among the Jamatias. They take dowry from the groom's house. Child marriages are not there. Among the Chakmas few child-marriages are found now-a-days. Among the Reangs and the Noatias widow re-marriage is allowed, but not within a year of the death of her husband. Similarly, a widower cannot re-marry within a year of the death of his wife. Monogamy is normally practised by them. Polygamy and polyandry are not allowed. A Kuki man can marry a second wife during the-life time of his first wife. But their women can not re-marry during the life-time of her husband. They do not allow divorce unless both wife and husband desire a separation.

DIVORCE- Divorce is allowed by mutual consent. The bond of matrimony among them is very strong. Still some of them desire to divorce. They need not to go for this to court. They can separate by mutual consent or if the husband does not like his wife he can send her back to her parent's house for good. If divorce is wanted by a wife she has to refund the bride-price of her husband. If it is sought by a husband for the reason other than barrenness, adultery, sickness or incurable diseases, he has to pay some fine to the village-elders and to his wife.

POSITION OF WOMEN- Tribal women of this region hold a high position. They are maintaining same status with their men. They co-operate with their men in house-hold work and play an important role in agricultural activities.

The married women have almost no right in the property of her father. All the movable and immovable property of her dead father has to be inherited generally by her brothers.

CUSTOMARY LAW OF INHERITANCE- It is stated earlier that father's property is generally inherited by the sons.

In some Mizo tribes and sub-tribes either the youngest or eldest son is to inherit all the property of his dead father and he is compelled to look after his widowed mother by staying in the house of his father. Sometimes their property is inherited equally by all the sons. Among the Reangs, the youngest son stays in the house of his parents and looks after them. When the parents die, the youngest son automatically becomes the owner of all the property which is left by his father. In case a father has daughters and no son his property is to be shared equally by all his daughters. If a couple has no issue, after the death, their property is to be inherited by the husband's brother or father or nearest relatives of father's side.

BIRTH RULE- They consider more children for better living. They generally welcome a male child. The mother after the birth of a child can not come out for 7 days and consider the room unpurified where the child was born. There are some ceremonies and sacrifices related with the birth of a child and it varies from tribe to tribe.

NAME GIVING CEREMONY- The most important ceremony in connection of birth of a child is the name giving ceremony which they perform two or nine days after the birth. It varies from tribe to tribe. Among some tribes they give name to a new born baby immediately after the birth. The maternal uncle of a new born child is to occupy an important place on birth ceremony.

DISPOSAL OF DEAD- The dead body is cremated by the Tripuris, Reangs, Jamatias, Halams, Moghs, Chakmas. The Kuki-Mizos, Garo, Khasi bury their dead in a common burial ground. If anyone dies unnaturally in water, the Mizo has to pay great honour to bury his dead body. When any one dies, the news of the death is sent through the relatives and friends to others. Mizos come to pay their homage to the dead person in the shape of money and other gifts.

The Tripuris, Jamatias, Halams, Mogs bury, if it is a child below 18 months. The dying person is attended by elderly persons of the locality. The dead body is burnt near a river or stream. If a man dies of an unnatural death, he is considered to be a sinner. Generally the process of disposal of dead by the Tripuris, Reangs, Jamatias, Halams, etc. is almost like the Hindu custom.

2

BRIEF DESCRIPTION OF THE DISTRICTS

The present state of Tripura consists a part of pre-independence Hill Tipperah. Till August 31, 1970, Tripura was a single district territory with 10 sub-divisions and 45 tehsils. On September 1, 1970, the Government of Tripura had divided the territory into three districts *viz.* West Tripura, North Tripura and South Tripura without creating any change in the boundary of the sub-divisions. The number of tehsils was increased from 45 to 177 without changing the territorial jurisdiction of the ten sub-divisions.

Originally Tripura was a princely state. It was merged with India on October 15, 1949 and became its Part-C State on January 26, 1950. formally declared as a Union Territory on Novermber 1, 1957 and elevated to the status of a State on January 21, 1972.

WEST TRIPURA DISTRICT- This district is situated in the middle part of Tripura. It is bounded on the south with South Tripura District, north with North Tripura District and Bangladesh, west with Bangladesh and east with Bangladesh.

This district is mainly the home of the Tripuris. The other tribes that inhabit here are Jamatia, Reang, Noatia, Kuki, Garo, etc. Agartala town is the capital of Tripura and headquarters of West Tripura District. Agartala is a plain town. *Maharaja* Krishna Kishore Manikya (1830-1850) had shifted his capital site to present Agartala from old Agartala. The area of the West Tripura District is 2995.36 sq. km. The total population is 9,76,252. The density of population per square kilometre is 322 and percentage of literacy is 46.21 per cent (Census of India 1981).

The available mineral deposits of this district is limestone, glass sand, plastic clay, natural gas and oil. No big industries have so far been set up here. Handlooms and handicraft industries have been set up. Tailoring, furniture workshop, knitting industry, printing press, blacksmith, etc. have set up. Due to almost isolation, inadequate transport facilities, marketing difficulties, less availability of raw material and electricity-power no heavy industry could be set up here.

Parts of Baramura and Atharamura are hill ranges. There are Khowai, Haora and parts of Gumti as major river valleys. A dam has been constructed on Khowai river to control floods and to irrigate the agricultural fields. In West Tripura district average annual rainfall is approximately 250 cm. The reserved forest area of this district is 1,434,88 sq. km.

West Tripura is a beautiful and developed district. Agartala town is connected with most of the town and big villages of the state. National Highway No. 44 runs through Agartala. This district has three Sub-Divisions. They are:- Sadar Sub-Division, Khowai Sub-Division and Sonamura Sub-Division, There are total nine Community Development Blocks (C.D. Block) in West Tripura district. These are :- Bishalgarh, Jirania, Mohanpur, Teliamura, Khowai, Melaghar, Agartala Town, Khowai Town and Sonamura Town development block.

In West Tripura district a total 128 High Schools, 51 Higher Secondary, 5 Colleges, 2 Music of Art College, one Government Law College, one Engineering College, one Polytechnic College, one Nursing Training College and one University were till 1987. Tripura University started functuning since 2nd November, 1987 at old Post Graduate Centre at Agartala. Previously, old P.G. Centre (MA/M.Sc) was under Calcutta University till 1986-87.

Important places of this district are :- Agartala, *Puran* (old) Agartala, *Chouddha Devatar Mandir, Sipahijala,* etc.

Agartala- This is the capital town of Tripura. It is connected by the satelite station for STD telephone facility. A TV transmission centre was set up here in October, 1991. Independent own TV centre opened in Agartala on 20th November, 1992. A radio station is situated here. Indian Airline's air-services are available here in between Calcutta-Guwahati-Agartala, Silchar-Agartala, Guwahati-Silchar-Agartala-Guwahati and vice versa. Vayudoot services are available in between Agartala-Kamalpur, Agartala-Kailashar, Calcutta-Guwahati-Agartala. Daily road transport services are there from Silchar-Agartala, Agartala-Belonia-Sabroom. The National

Highway No. 44 from Agartala towards Assam is almost zigzag way. After passing three hillocks of Tripura (towards Agartala) the road has several turns, especially at *Athara Mura*. Naturally many passengers generally get sick during their travel here. The Government is trying to make the road straight by cutting the hillocks to make travel comfortable and easy.

Agartala town is always busy with political, cultural and commercial activities. Picturesque view of Agartala looks extremely beautiful. *Maharaja' Ujjayanta Palace* is situated at the heart of the town. Three main roads touch this palace. Houses, shops, etc. are situated on road sides. The architecture of the houses is remarkable. Most of the houses are white coloured. All the houses have front side veranda. From a distance, it looks like a single veranda runs continuously the whole of the roadside. The construction of the *Ujjayanta Palace* was started by *Maharaja* Radha Kishore Manikya in 1899 and completed in 1901 at a cost of over rupees ten lakhs. The palace is a two-storied mansion. The Throne Room, Durbar Hall. Library, Reception Hall, etc. all furnished with art, curio, etc. Recently it was taken over by the State Government and transformed into State Legislative Assembly. *Maharaja's* old Palace was built in 1862 which was damaged due to severe earthquake in 1898 and was unfit for habitation. *Kunjaban Palace* is situated within a mile of the *Ujjayanta Palace*. It is constructed on a hillock known as *Kunjaban* which stands to the north of Agartala town. This has green beauty of gardens and a small zoo.

Maharaja Bir Bikram College Campus has a number of lakes; Government Museum has old archaeological findings of Tripura. Budhha temple, *Uma Maheswar* temple, Handloom and Handicrafts Corporation, *Jagannath* temple of late 19th century, etc., are situated in Agartala.

Puran (old) Agartala:- *Puran* Agartala was the capital of Tripura since the time of *Maharaja* Krishna Manikya (1760-'83) who had shifted the earlier capital site from Udaipur to old Agartala on the bank of the river *Haora* to avoid hostility with Samsher Gazi (1748-1760) who attacked Udaipur in 1748. *Maharaja* Krishna Kishore Manikya (1830-1849) had shifted the capital from old Agartala to the present Agartala site, a few miles far from old Agartala.

Temple Chaudda Devatar Mandir- It is situated in *Puran* (old) Agartala. Every year in the month of July pilgrims visit this place during *Kharchi Puja*. Fourteen good-heads have been indentified here. They are : *Siva, Durga, Vishnu, Lakshmi, Saraswati, Kartik, Ganesh, Brahma, Samudra, Ganga, Agni, Kamadeva, Himadri,* and *Prithivi*. Besides the temple, the ruins of old Palace of *Maharaja* is still there.

Sipahijala:- The place is situated 30 kms from Agartala town. It is said that *Maharaja* Bir Bikram Manikya gave this watery land as a gift to one of his loyal *sipahi* (soldier). For that, it is named as *Sipahijala*. There is a beautiful lake and a mini zoological garden surrounded all around by dense forests.

NORTH TRIPURA DISTRICT- This district is bounded in the north with Bangladesh, west with West Tripura district, south with Bangladesh and east with Assam and Mizoram. This district is mainly the home of the Tripuri, Reang and Chakma. Other tribes also reside here, Kailashahar is the headquarters' of this district. The area of this district is 3881.24 sq. kms. The total population is 5,41,248. The density of population per sq. km. is 140 and percentage of literacy is 41.96 per cent (Census of India 1981).

The available minerals are small scale of limestone, lignite, clay deposits (suitable for ordinary pottery and roofing tiles). No big industry is set up here. Tripura Government has now taken all possible steps to develop this district.

Longtarai, Shakhanunokoti and *Jampui* hill ranges are there. River valleys are *Dhalai, Manu, Deo* and *Juri*. A dam was constructed on river *Manu* to control floods and to irrigate agricultural fields. Average annual rainfall is approximately 231 cm. Available reserved forest land is 2,364,39 sq. km.

National Highway No. 44 passed through the district from Assam. M.G. Railway line links *Dharmanagar* with Assam. It has been extended upto *Kumarghat*. There are three sub-divisions of this district. These are: Dharmanagar Sub-division, Kailashahar Sub-division and Kamalpur Sub-division. There are total eight Community Development Blocks. They are: Panisagar, Kanchanpur, Dharmanagar, Kumarghat, Chawmanu, Salema, Kailashahar town, Kamalpur town.

In North Tripura district there was a total of 72 High Schools, 23 Higher Secondary, 2 Colleges, one Regional Physical Institution and one Nursing Training College till 1986-'87. Important places of this district are:- *Jampui* Hills, *Pancharthal, Unakoti Tirtha* etc.

Jampui Hills- Its highest peak is *Belting Sib.* This hill has beautiful landscape. Sylhet (Bangladesh) is situated in the north and the Langten Range of Chittagong (Bangladesh) lies in the south, Jampui Range is situated in between Mizoram and Tipura as a boundary in the east. Best quality of oranges are grown here. The people of this hill are mostly Mizos. They are Christians. *Fuldang Sai, Chhabwal, Tlang Sang, Bangla Bari, Behliang Chhip, Vanghmun, Tlakshi, Hmunpal, Hormung Chuang Bhai Sum,* etc., are the Mizo villages of this hill. Kanchanpur and Dasda Bazar are two important markets of this area.

Pancharthal- Here a big sized brass image of Lord Buddha, in sitting position, is an attraction of the visitors. Here an important local market is situated which sells *jhum* products and oranges of *Jampui* hills. *Pancharthal* has M.G. Railway line from *Dharmanagar* to *Pancharthal.* It is situated on the Assam-Agartala road, at a distance of about 128 km far from Agartala town.

Unakoti Tirtha- *Unakoti* means one less than a crore. It is situated at a distance of about five miles from *Kailasahar.* It is a holy shrine in the hilly part. Numerous rock-cut images are scattered in its rocky walls. Among the rock cut images the *Shiva* head and the gigantic figure of *Ganesa* are famous. Ten feet high *Siva's* head deserves special interest. According to archaeologist these images may be dated back to 11th to 12th centuries. Every year during *Asokastami* a great fair is held here.

SOUTH TRIPURA DISTRICT- This district is bounded with Bangladesh in its south, east and west. West Tripura district is bounded in its north and north-west. Udaipur is head quarters' of this district. Tripuri, Jamatia, Reang are the main tribe of this district. Other tribes also reside here. The area of this district is 3615.25 sq. kms. The total population is 5,35,558. The density of population per sq. km. is 150 and percentage of literacy is 34.83 per cent (Census of India 1981).

Available mineral deposits are small scale of lignite, small pockets of plastic clay and huge quality of natural gas. *Debtamura, Baramura, Kalajhari, Atharamura, Takka Tulsi* are hill ranges of this district. *Gumti, Muhari and Manu Nala* are the river valleys of South Tripura district. Hydro-Electric Project is situated at *Gumti* installed with approximately 10 mw. power products. Average annual rainfall of this district is approximately 307 cm.

Total 2,161,30 sq. km. area is under reserved forests and 5,960.57 sq. km. protected forests.

State highway runs from Agartala to Subroom town, the extreme southern place. There are four Sub-divisions of South Tripura district. These are: Udaipur Sub-division, Amarpur Sub-division, Belonia Sub-division and Subroom Sub-division. There are total nine Community Development Blocks. These are: Matabari, Radhakishorepur town (Udaipur), Amarpur, Dumburnagar, Amarpur town, Rajnagar, Bagafa, Belonia town, Satchand, and Sabroom town.

In South Tripura district total 80 High Schools, 26 Higher Secondary Schools, 2 Colleges and one Nursing Training College till 1986-'87. Important places of this district are :- Tripurasundari Temple, Udaipur Trithamukh, Nir Mahal, Bhubaneswari Temple, etc.

Tripurasundari Temple (Udaipur):- It is considered as one of the oldest *Pithasthan*. The temple consists of a square type structure of the typical Bengali hut-type and situated on a hillock at Udaipur. It was built by *Maharaja* Dhanya Manikya about 450 years back. A large number of people are visiting this temple during *Diwali* festival every year.

It is said that the temple was first built by *Maharaja* Dhanya Manikya in 1501. Thereafter it was repaired by *Maharaja* Rama Manikya in 1681 and again it was repaired by *Maharaja* Radhakishore Manikya (1896-1909) in the beginning of the 20th century.

There are two identical images inside the temple *Matabari*. One is called *Chhotima* which is now worn out and it is about 2 feet in height and the other one is called *Tripura Sundari* which is about 5 feet in height. The goddess *Tripurasundari* is a guardian deity of the royal family.

Udaipur- There are several temples in Udaipur. *Jagannath* temple is situated on the south-west bank of the *Jagannath Dighi* (tank) in Udaipur town. *Bhubaneswari* temple, *Gunavati* temple, etc., are situated in Udaipur. *Govinda Manikya's palace, Bhubaneswari* temple are situated on the right bank of the river *Gumti*. *Maharani Gunavati* temple, wife of *Maharaja* Govinda Manikya situated on the eastern part of the town of Udaipur.

Tirthamukh:- It is about 117 km. far from Agartala and about 8 km from Sonamura town. A hydro-electric power generating station has been set up here. During *Uttarayan Sankranti* (middle of the month January) both tribals and non-tribals pilgrims take a holy dip in *Tirthamukh* water.

Nirmahal:- It is situated at a distance of about 53 km from Agartala. It is surrounded on all sides by an artificial deep lake called *Rudra Sagar. Maharaja* Bir Bikramkishore Manikya (1927-'47) built this *Nirmahal* (palace in water) at the centre of the said lake. *Nirmahal* has electricity and a small beautiful garden.

Pilak Pathar:- Many old stone images are there. A number of terracotta temple plaques are found in *Pilak Pathar*.

Dumbur Lake:- Dumbur lake is the water reservoir of the *Gumti* Hydel Project, which covers an area of 40 sq. km. A ride by a motor boat is allowed here.

Deotamura:- It is a peak situated in between Udaipur and Amarpur Sub-Divisions. This is an interesting site due to its panel of images found which are covered on the hills facing towards the river Gumti.

Bhubaneswari Temple:- It is situated on the right bank of the *Gumti* river at Udaipur. It was built by *Maharaja* Govinda Manikya (1660-1675).

TABLE XIII : DISTRICTS, SUB-DIVISIONS, BLOCKS AND TOWNS

District and Headquarters (Total villages)	*Sub-Divisions*	*Blocks*	*Towns*
WEST TRIPURA	Sadar	Bishalgarh	Agartala
Hqs. Agartala		Jirania	
(Total 281 villages)		Mohanpur	
	Khowai	Teliamura Khowai	Khowai
	Sonamura	Melagarh	Sonamura
NORTH TRIPURA	Dharmanagar	Panisagar	Dharmanagar
Hqs. Kailashahar		Kanchanpur	
(Total 280 villages)	Kailashahar	Kumarghat	Kailashahar
		Chamanu	
	Kamalpur	Salema	Kamalpur
SOUTH TRIPURA	Udaipur	Matabari	Radhakishorepur (Udaipur)
(Total 303 villages)	Amarpur	Amarpur	Amarpur
		Dumburnagar	
	Belonia	Rajnagar	Belonia
		Bagafa	
	Sabroom	Satchand	Sabroom

Source : Census of India 1981 : Tripura.

3

BRIEF DESCRIPTION OF THE TRIBES

Tripura is the ancient home of the Bodos. Various tribes had migrated in ancient time to this land and they resided in different parts of the hilly regions. During the reign of the earlier Tripura *Rajas*, the tribes maintained their freedom of adiminstration through their Chief or *Sardars*.

The Mags immigrated to Tripura long back from Burma through *Arakan* and *Chittagong Hill Tracts* and spread upto *Chittagong Noakhali*, southern part of *Comilla* (Bangladesh); Mizoram and Tripura. The archaeological ruins, which still existed in the southern part of Tripura, made it sure that a Buddhist Kingdom was there in Tripura in remote past. The Mags and the Chakmas are two Buddhist dominant communities of South Tripura. *Rangamati* (the present Udaipur in South Tripura) was the capital of the Buddhist Kingdom. It was situated on the southern bank of the *Gumati* river.

The Tripuris immigarted from China through the north east corner of Tripura. They got obstructions from the *Bachal* tribe (a branch of the greater Kuki tribe) and the Mags. But the Tripuris overpowered them and spread not only in Tripura but also to Chittagong, Noakhali, Comilla and Sylhet (Bangladesh). The Tripuris made their appearance in Tripura politics in about eighth century. In 1941 and 1943 *Maharaja* Bir Bikarm reserved an area of land of 1950 sq. miles for Tripuri, Noatia, Jamatia, Riang and Halam communities for permanent plough cultivation in the fertile valleys.

TABLE XIII : DATA OF THE RESERVATION

Sub-Division	*Locality*	*Area in sq. miles*
Amarpur	Raima Valley	527 sq. miles
Khowai	Kalyanpur	412 sq. miles
Kailashahar	Manu Valley	308 sq. miles
Belonia	Bagafa Laugang and Khalashi	198 sq. miles
Sadar	Takarjala and Jampaijala	195 sq. miles
Sabroom	Jalefa	160 sq. miles
Udaipur	Maharani and Pitra	150 sq. miles
		Total 1950 sq. miles

Source : Jagadis Gan Chaudhuri (1885) : 48

There are total 19 classified Scheduled tribes along with other immigrant people of Tripura.

TABLE XIV : TRIBAL POPULATION OF TRIPURA

Sl.No.	*Tribes*	*Population*			
		1951	1961	1971	1981
1.	Tripuri	1,50,971	1,89,799	2,50,382	3,31,191
2.	Reang	8,471	56,597	64,722	83,476
3.	Jamatia	2,764	24,359	34,192	44,554
4.	Chakma	7,277	22,386	28,622	35,097
5.	Halam	1,644	16,298	19,076	29,040
6.	Noatia	1,916	16,010	10,297	7,073
7.	Mag	3,789	10,524	13273	18,291
8.	Kuki	2,721	5,532	7,775	5,432
9.	Garo	7,362	5,484	5,559	7,311
10.	Munda	51	4,409	5,347	7,911
11.	Lushai	1,947	2,988	3,672	3,778
12.	Oraon	—	2,875	3,428	5,306
13.	Santal	736	1,562	2,222	2,709
14.	Uchai	—	766	1,061	1,295
15.	Khasia	151	349	491	458
16.	Bhil	41	69	169	791
17.	Lepcha	5	7	177	103
18.	Bhutia	19	7	3	19
19.	Chaimal	—	50	—	11

The main tribes of Tripura are Tripuri Reang, Chakma, Jamatia, Mag, Halam, Noatia and Uchai There are other tribes also namely: Kuki, Lushai, Garo, Khasi, Munda, Oran, Santal, Bhil, Lepcha, Bhutia, Chaimal, etc. The Chaimal had immigrated to Tripura after the year 1951 and most of them left the state after 1961. The Munda, Oraon, Santal, Bhil, Lepcha and Bhutia had migrated to Tripura for employment in tea garden and rubber plantation, etc. from North Bengal and Bihar after the year 1951. The Garos had immigrated from Meghalaya (India) and Mymensing (Bangladesh) and the Khasis from Meghalaya and Assam. The Kuki-Lushai had migrated to Tripura from Mizoram.

The tribes of Tripura are racially Mongoloid origin and they belong to Tibeto-Burman linguistic group.

TRIPURI- Numerically the Tripuris constituted the largest tribe of Tripura. Since the time of *Maharaja* Kalyan Manikya, the members of the royal family were given the title *"Thakur"*. They were also known as *Bara Ghariya*. The Tripuris were formerly the rulers of Tripura. They are commonly known as *"Kshatriya"*. They settled in and around Agartala and are quite advanced in education. Plain Tripuris are not like the Tripuris who are living on the hill slopes of Tripura. The upper rank of the Tripuri tribe is constituted by the *Maharajas*, the princes and the *Thakurs*. According to Omesh Saigal (1978 : 93) there are 12 classes of *Thakurs*, who enjoy the higher status among the *Tripuri Kshatriyas*.

The Tripuris mainly resided in West Tripura but now scattered all over the state. Their mother tongue is *Klokbarak*, a Tibeto-Burman language. They are divided into two groups namely *Puran Tripuri* and *Deshi Tripuri*. The *Puran Tripuris* are said to be the original inhabitants of the state. They resided in Sadar Agartala town and Khowai sub-divisions. The title of the *Puram Tripuris* are *Deb Barman*. The Puran Tripuris, belongs to the Indo-Chinese stock of Tibeto-Burman and Bodo group. They traced their descent from *Kshatriya* warriors. Their mode of living, social customs, culture, etc. are almost similar to that of the Aryan Hindu Bengalees.

The Tripuris are sub-divided into 12 *Haddas* (groups) according to their types of work which they were entitled to perform in the *Darbar* of the earlier *Maharajas*. These are: Bachhal, Siuk, Koatia, Daityasing, Hujuria, Ciltia, Apiya, Chhatratuiya, Deorai or galim, Subenarayan, Sera and Julai. At the end of *Maharaja's* rule all these *Huddas* disappeared except galim to perform *Ker and Kharchi pujas*. The Julais are again sub-divided into eleven sub-groups depending on their type of work in a house hold. Such as: Das Paiya, Manarai, Totarai, Mamiplaksa, Maichhaplaksa, Golchhari, Chelargrai, Machharai, Adrai, Jitrai and Suikasa.

Generally, the *Puran Tripuris* or Tripuris live in a 'Tong' or pile house on hill tops and hill slopes in a group. They construct their houses five to six feet high from the ground in order to escape from the attack of wild animals. In the plains and in the foot hills Puran Tripuri's houses are made similar to that of the Bengalees. They live in a small group of 5 to 30 families in their selected place known as *'Parah'* or *'Punzi'* which usually bear the name of their *Sardars* or Headman. The ground, just below the hut, is fenced off and used to keep domestic animals like hens, cattle, pigs, etc. The hut of the Headman or the *Sardar* of the *Parah* hamlet is situated among them in the middle part.

The Tripuris, in the past used to live on *Jhum* cultivation. Now many of them have adopted plough cultivation. *Gharchuk-ti,* a kind of house tax, is levied to the shifting cultivators. Previously their Headman was to allot the *Jhum* area for each house owner. Their main crops are : paddy, maize, cotton, cucumber, pumpkin, gourd, jungle potato, etc. Agriculture is their main source of livelihood. The crop cultivated in three types of land, namely a) Upland, b) Intermediate land and, c) Low land.

Sometimes the Tripuris go out for hunting expedition. Fishing is also done by them.

Among them two types of marriages are there *viz. Hiknamani* and *Kaijagmaṇi*. The first one is by mutual consent between the boy and the girl. For this there is no elaborate rituals for their marriage. A feast is given to the friends and relatives. The second type of marriage is performed through negotiation between the parents of the boy and the girl. In earlier days, the prospective bridegroom had to stay for one year in the house of the bride before his marriage and to extend his assistance in agricultural activities of the bride's house. Now it is simplified by paying bride-price in cash. Widow remarriage and divorce are allowed. Generally, the Tripuris live in a nuclear family. They practise monogamy. Few rich Tripuris occasionally practised polygyny. Cross-cousin marriage and levirate are not allowed.

Village panchayat is there in each village. It is headed by a *Choudhury*. The elder male member of each family can participate in the panchayat. The *Choudhury* is elected by the panchayat members.

Women make their garments from hand woven fabrics. They use loin-loom for this. Their garments are: *Dubra*, skirt, *Pachhra Rias* and *Saris*. The females wrapped round their body upto their ankle with a skirt. They use blouse and *Rias* to cover their breasts. The men wear pant, shirt and small *dhotis*. Women like silver made ornaments. They keep their hair long. They wear less ornaments.

The Tripuris profess to be Hindus. But they were previously *animist*. They still worship *Chaturdas Debata, Ganga Balagnni* (the presiding deity of jungles), *Kharchi Ker*, etc. They have two types of priests *viz.* Brahmin Pandit and *Ojhas*. Hindu ways of religious rites are performed by Brahmin Pandit and the tribal way of religious rites by the *Ojhas*. The tribal priest is also known as *Achais*. The high ranked Tripuris perform their religious rites with the help of their priest known as *Chantai*.

The Tripuri dialect belongs to Bodo group of Assamese- Burmese branch of Tibeto-Burman family of languages. Tripuri language has no alphabets of its own. It is written in Bengali alphabets. Most of the Tripuris can speak and understand Bengali language.

Their dead are cremated. After the completion of cremation, the crematory is cleaned. A *tulsi* (basil) plant is planted by cleaning a part of the front portion of the deceased's hut. An earthen lamp lights near the *tulsi* plant. At the site rice and meat is cooked for seven days.

DESHI TRIPURI- The *Desi Tripuris* are said to have originated as a result of admixture between the Bengali Hindus and the Tripuris. They are very much akin to the Hindu Bengalees. Many of them follow the *Sakti* cult. They mainly reside in the plain areas of Agartala. They don't know *jhum* cultivation. As they live in plains they are efficient in plough cultivation. .Their occupations are: agriculture, animal husbandry and trade. Their huts are similar to those of the Bengalis. Like the married Bengali women, vermilion and *sakha* (conch bangle) are their symbols of a married person. Among them, dowry system is there. They pay their dowry either in cash or land. Among them, there are four types of marriages *viz.* negotiation, love marriage, elopment and marriage by service. They can marry Bengali caste groups. Divorce is allowed. Re-marriage of widow, widower, divorcee is permitted. Like the Bengalees, they arrange marriage-feast (on the day of marriage) in the house of the bride and thereafter in the groom's house when the bride comes after her marrriage to her husband's place.

Cultivation is their main occupation. Some of them tie their marriage life with the Bengali *Namasudra Kayastha*, etc. Many educated Tripuris are now working in Government offices, schools, colleges and university.

Their dead are cremated. On the thirteenth day after death they purify by performing *Sradha* ceremony.

REANGS- Reang is also spelt as Riang. They are said to have inhabited originally at *Mayanithlang* of Lushai Hills (Mizoram). Later on, some of them migrated to Tripura and Chittagong Hill Tracts under their Chiefs. They resided in Udaipur, Amarpur, Sonamura, Belonia, Kailasahar, Kamalpur and Khowai sub-divisions of Tripura. It is said that the Reangs migrated from *Shan* kingdom of Burma during the reign of Ratna Manikya-I in 14th Century. There were two Reang commanders in the army of *Raja* Dhanya Manikya (1463-1515).

The Reang tribe is divided into two groups. Namely : *Meska* or *Mechka* and *Mailsoi* or *Malchhui*. The first group again divided into 7 sub-groups. Namely :- Cheki, Meska, Tuimaiya fak, Musa or Muchha, Raichak or Raikachak, Takh Mayakcha and Waring or Wairem. The second group divided into 7 following sub-groups:- Molsai, Apet, Nakhyam or Nagkham, Chmrong, Darbong, Sagrai and Reang or Ria Kachak. All these sub-groups *(dafa)* have their own Chiefs. Their Chiefs are divided into two groups :- one is under the leadership of the *Rai* and the other under the *Kachak*.

They belong to the Mongoloid racial group. They have their own dialect known as *'Polong-O'*. It also known as Reang language. This is according to Grierson belong to the Tirbeto-Chinese family of Tibeto-Burman sub-family of Assam Bunmese branch of Bodo group. They are an endogamous tribe and have had very little contact with the Bengalis. Hinduism among them is slowly introduced.

The Reangs are mainly agriculturists. They generally practice *jhum* cultivation like the *Puram Tripuris* and the *Kukis*. They select a fertile site on the slope of a hill which is known as *Haping Halap* for *jhuming* and a cross-fence with bamboo is to make on the ground and also a cross like bamboo pole is to fix on the ground. This means a warning to trespassers. Thereafter, they worship *Bura-chha* the deity or *jhum* for rich growth of argicultural products. The sowing is done after the first rain of the season and the crop is harvested in winter. They learnt plough cultivation from the *Mags* about a century ago. Their main crops are:- cotton, paddy, maize, cereals, mustard, chilli, gourd, potato, pumkin, etc. Both male and female are harvesting. Women generally collect edible jungle roots and creepers throughout the year. They have to pay house tax for their shifting *(jhum)* cultivation. Now-a-days some of them have adopted settled cultivation. They hunt for getting meat to eat.

Generally they live on the top of the hills and sometimes on narrow strips of valley between hillocks *(tilla)*. They choose their area of habitation which is situated in such a place so as to protect themselves and their property from enemy, easy availability of water and so on. They live in a group of families of 3 to 10. Each settlement is known as *Parah* (village) or hamlet which is named after the name of an influential leader *(Sardar)*. Typical Reang hut is built on a high bamboo platform *(machang)* is called as *'Tong'* which is erected on pillars of 4-6 feet in height. The walls are made of split bamboos. Usually two sloped hempen gabled roofs are there. Thatched roofs are also there with *san* grasses.

Their traditional dress is very simple. Men wear a loin cloth (hand woven) and a piece of cloth as a wrapper for upper part of their body. Women wear a long piece of cloth called *rignai* or *pachhra*. They wrap it around their waist. It hangs down upto their knees. They use breast garment which is known as *'Riah'*. This is artistic in design. Due to spread of education among them their traditional dress is gradually changing. Men prefer now to wear mill-made shirt, pant, *dhoti* and head gear. Women are now using *saris* and blouses as their fashion. The Reang women stand first among other tribes of Tripura for their ornaments of silver coined necklaces *(Rangbatang)* beads, etc. They take pride in their personal decoration with ornaments. Men do not wear ornaments.

Among the Reang, addiction to alcohol is very much. They prepare their drinks from rice, dance and music are the main part of their life and culture. They do not marry outside their tribal community. Their marriages are two types *viz. Halakchaai* and *Halakchham*. The first one is by mutual consent between the boy and the girl. The second one is by negotiation between the parents of the boy and the girl. Parallel cousin marriage is most common among them though it is declining. Cross cousin marriage is rare. Their marriage system is somehow like the Tripuris. The bride-groom is required to stay for years in the house of his future father-in law before his wedding where he has to work physically including in the agricultural field of his father-in-law. Child marriage is not allowed. Monogamy is practised by them. Divorce is permitted by mutual consent. Marriage is arranged through *Andra* (match-maker) who is sent for negotiation to prospective bride's house. Then the bride's party is invited to finalise the proposal. They are served pork, rice and drink. After finalisation the bride-groom feeds the bride's party with pork, fowl, drink, etc. as per their demand. The final day of marriage is fixed by the *Ojhai*.

They have many god and goddesses. They follow both *animism* and Hinduism. Some Christian Reangs are also there. The Hindu deities *Shiva Vishnu Krishna Kali*, etc. are worshipped by many Reangs. Their important deities are : *Matai Katar* (Supreme deities like *Shiva* and *Durga), Tuima* (deity of river), *Sangrama* (deity of the hills) *Burachha* (Jungle God), *Khulongma* (goddess of cotton), *Mailong-Ma (Laksmi), Buduirao* (god of evil sprits) and *Lampra* or *Ksh amdhi* (presiding deity of the seas and the sky). Their important religious festivals are : *Ker, Ganga Puja, Garia, Matangi puja*, etc. These they perform with a huge gathering and each family has to contribute money which they call *Khain*. Such religious festivals are also held-up with meetings of their tribal Chiefs. In that meeting religious, social and political matters are discussed. Their surplus collection of *Khain* is to utilise for welfare of their society.

They cremate their dead. Before cremation they first bathe the dead body and then dress the male with new *Dhuti* or *Kamcha* and a *rituku* is tied round the head as a headgear. In case of women, a new *riah* and *rignai* (a short hand woven *sari*). Then cooked meat and rice in an earthen pot is placed at the feet of the dead body. A dance ritual is performed throughout the night. Rice beer is served among the mourners, except the family of the deceased who neither drink nor join in the dance. The next morning they keep the dead body on a pyre and burn it. They keep a little portion of burnt bone ash or bone for a year. Among the Christains and the *Vaishnava* Reangs the custom is burial. After a year, the Hinduised Reangs throw the bone-ash or bone of the deceased in water preferably in a river and perform a *sraddha* ceremony. At that time they feed some of their people. The widows are prohibited from wearing any oranments for one year after the death of their husbands.

JAMATIAS:- Previously they were mainly inhabited in Sonamura and Udaipur Sub-Divisions. Now they have scattered all over the state. *'Jamat'* in Urdu means an assembly of persons. The name *'Jamatia'* is supposed to be derived from *Jamat*. Some believe that in ancient times the Jamatias were recruited in the army of the kings of Tripura which was called *'Jamat'* and subsequently they came to know as *'Jamatia'*. Others believe that as they are in the habit of living jointly or in groups led to such nomenclature. Perhaps they are an admixture of many tribes of Tripura.

They do not live in *Tongs* built on *machans* on the hillocks. Their houses are like their Bengali neighbours. Ethnologically they are akin to the Tripuris and their physical character are like that of the Tripuris. Their dialect is Tripuri.

In the past, the kings of Tripura had given them a special position among the tribes of Tripura by exempting them from *ghar chukti* tax for their shifting cultivation and given settlement of vast region of fertile land mainly in Udaipur Division. For this, the Jamatias, though they once belonged to the Tripuri tribe, managed to develop a political system of their own and economically and socially they are more advanced than other tribes except Tripuris.

By 1931 almost all of them had given up *jhuming* and adopted plough cultivation (1931 Census Report). They fall under the category of cultivator and agriculture is their main source of livelihood. The Jamatias are peace loving people.

They live in big *paras* (villages or hamlets). They construct their huts plastering the walls with mud and making the floor with earth after the fashion of their Bengali neighbours. They have big courtyards and grow fruit-trees in the rear of their compound.

Simple disputes among the Jamatias are settled by the *Mulluk* (native land) *Sardars*. According to gravity of the dispute sometimes he consults with two or more *Mulluk Sardars* to give judgement. These two *Mulluk Sardars* are the Headmen of the

Reang community who are elected persons. They are :- Kripa Moi Sardar of the Bagma area and the other is Chander Mohan of the Baisha bari-Mahrani area. They are to decide the critical cases. Murder cases are reported to the Police.

Tripura is divided into 16 Jamatia *Mahals*, each under the charge of 2 *Panchais*. The *Panchais* are elected persons, elected by all the village headmen *(Choudhury)*. They have no fixed tenure to serve. They can continue as long as they enjoy the confidence of the people, after which they are replaced. Their posts are not hereditary.

The Jamatias adopted Hinduism. It is said that during the reign of *Maharaja* Bir Bikram there was a tax collector Okhiral Hazari who was cruel and tyrannical. The Jamatias rose in revolt against him. The King of Tripura sent his army to control the revolt with the help of the Darlong Kukis. They succeeded in putting down the revolt and brought with them over 200 Jamatias with their leader Parikshit to Agartala. King Bir Bikram, however, spared the life of their leader and released him. He returned to his area and asked all the Jamatias to follow Hindu *(Vaishnava)* customs. In 1931 Census Report it is mentioned that apart from 803 Jamatias, who adopted to the *Vaishnava* faith, all others belonged to the *Shakti* cult. Many of them go every year for pilgrimage to Kashi (Banaras) and Brindaban. They worship *Shiva, Durga*, etc. In addition to the Hindu rituals, they also perform their old indigenous *pujas*. They perform these *pujas* by collecting subscription. They worship on the banks of *Gumti, Burima Khowai* rivers. They also perform the *pujas* of the Goddess *Tripura Sundari*. Their rituals are to perform by the *Ojhai*. Their *Dharia* is one who beats the drum in their *pujas*. The *Matai bainai* is the bearer of the idols. The owner of the house where big *pujas* held are known as *Kherpang*. This is also called by the person who offer the *pujas*.

Their custom of marriage is similar to those of the Tripuris but service by marriage or *Jamaikhata* is not compulsory. Monogamy is practiced by them. Few rich persons have more than one wife. Divorce is permitted. Adultery is a great offence. Widow re-marriage is allowed. The system of bride price is absent. But both the parties have to offer *Langi* (a sweet variety of liquor brewed from *mami* rice). Invitation to marriage ceremony is done by the Jamatia community by sending around to the huts of their relatives and friends with cloves and betel-nuts in a large plate of plaintain leaves.

Previously they wore handwoven cloth. Women used a piece of big cloth which they put round their waist upto ankles and another small cloth to cover their breasts. Now they wear mill-made cloth and ready made dresses.

They cremate their dead. Keep their personal *asuj* (impurity) for 13 days from the day of death and keeps *asti* (a little portion of burnt bone-ash or bone) to immerse later-on in a river and if possible, in the Ganges river.

NOATIA:- Noatia means new. They are largely found at Udaipur, Sabroom, Khowai, Kamalpur, Dharmanagar and Belonia Sub-Divisions. Their culture, customs and manners, dress, etc, are very much similar to that of the Tripuris and the Jamatias. It is believed that, the Noatia is a mixed tribe consisting of people from the Tripuris and the Jamatias. They migrated from the then East Pakistan (Bangladesh). The Noatias are divided into eleven classes *viz.* Keoya, Murasing, Asiang, Garyan, Khalicha, Tengbai, Leitong, Deildak, Anaokia, Khakta and Totaram. Out of these only six classes are living in Tripura.

They are short in stature and fair in complexion. They like to live in groups. Previously they practised *jhum* cultivation and live in bamboo made platform *'Tong Ghar'*. Now the Noatias practice plough cultivation. Their females weave their cloth *Dubra* and *Risa (Sari* and breast-tying a small piece of cloth) from loin looms. *Dubra* they put to cover their waist upto knee which has various colourful designs. The males make in their leisure time bamboo baskets.

Noatia girls generally marry after 14 years of her age and the boys after 18. Marriage with close relatives and between blood relations is strictly prohibited. Monogamy is in their marriage rule but few rich Noatias have more than one wife which is approved by their society. Divorce is permitted.

Adultery is a great offence. Widow re-marriage is allowed. Marriage is arranged through a match-maker *(Ghatak)* who is sent first to the house of a selected bride for negotiation. *Jamai Khata* (marriage by service) system of marriage is there. In this system, before marriage, the groom is to stay at least for two years to his proposed bride's house to do work physically. If the bride-side is satisfied with his work the marriage takes place, otherwise, he goes back. There is no bride price system. At the time of marriage, drinking of rice beer, community feasts are there and these continue for two days.

Their Chief is known as *'Dalpati'*. All cases usually are settled by him except murder cases which they report to the Poliçe. They speak in Tripuri language. They also worship *Shiva (Matai Katar), Garia Debta, Laxmi Puja* like the Tripuris and the Jamatias. They sacrifice pig, goat, fowl, duck, etc. for their *pujas*, The *'Sakti'* cult is pre-dominant among them though *'Vaisnavism'* is also there.

They cremate their dead according to Hindu custom. They observe thirteen days *asuj* (impurity) from the day of death. The asthi (a little part of bone-ash or bone) they immerse later on in the river preferably in the river Ganges. The *shradha* ceremony is performed after one year of death in the pattern of Tripuri customs.

HALAM:- The Halams are scattered all over the Sub-Divisions mainly in the Central and Northern areas of the State. They belong to the Kuki Groups. They came in contact with the King Tripura. It is said that the *Maharaja* had given them the title *Halam* which means in Tripuri *Ha* = earth, *lam* = road. They are also known as *Mila Kukis*. The Kukis call them *Rang-long*. The Halam had collected taxes from the rest of the Kukis of Tripura and they had good relations with the *Maharajas*.

As per their myths the Halams are said to have migrated from *Khurpuitabhum*, a place in the hills just to the north of Manipur. In Kuki language *Khur* means 'source', *pui* is *'river'*, *ta* stands for 'from'. Thus, it seems that their orginal home was perhaps near the source of a big river which may be the *Surma* river.

They are divided into 17 *dafas* (clans) *viz*. Kaloi, Kulu or Khulong. Korbong, Kaipang, Kaireng, Chadai, Deb, Sakachef, Thangchep, Nabeen, Bongshel, Morchhum, Murdhakang or Murasing, Rangkhol, Rukpini or Rupini, Langai and Langlung. It is said that the Murasing though included in the above list seems to be the Noatia. The above *dafa* either bears the name of the leaders of Halam community or according to their professions.

The Halam dialect is akin to the Kuki-Chin group of Tibeto-Burman family. Most of the Halam can speak the *Mrung* or *Tripuri* language fluently. Though they are the branch of the Kukis but due to the influence of socio-economic contact with the Tripuri neighbours, their customs, habits, religion, etc. are nearer to the Tripuris.

Their religion is a mixed form of Hinduism and animism. Few of them follow Christianity. They believe in evil spirits. They are *Sakti* worshippers but some of them follow *Vaisnavism*. Their language is akin to the Tripuris. They worship many god and goddesses namely *Shiva, Durga, Kali, Sundralopa, Dhaleswari*, etc. *Bara Puja* is an important festival which is held once after 4 to 5 years. They worship near the *Surma* river. They raise money for this *puja* from their community. Goat, duck, fowl, pig, etc. are killed to offer in that *puja*. Liquor is consumed at the occasion. The *puja* ends with discussion-meeting where the elders give lectures on religious, cultural, social matters, etc.

Monogamy is in their marriage rule. Ploygamy and child marriages are also practised by few of them. The boy has to pay a bride price in cash to his parent-in-law for marriage which may go above one hundred rupees. The period of voluntary service by the bridegroom is called *Damad Utha*. Proposal for marriage is finalised by the groom side. The bride side can't say anything. The marriage parties are offered drink at the marriage function. Divorce is allowed. If it is sought by the husband he has to pay a fine and offer drinks. If by the wife, a child if born, is claimed by the ex-husband.

The political structure of the Halams consists of the *Kanskow*, the *Ghalim*, the *Gabor* and the *Rai*. Ordinary cases of criminal and civil matters are decided by the *Rai* in his court who is head of the case settler. The *Rai* is appointed for a five year term. After him the next man in the rank gets promotion and becomes *Rai*. Similary, others also occupy one after another vacant promotion-posts. They have volunteers who assist the court of the *Rai*.

Previously their village was situated almost in a circular shape and all the houses were faced to the centre where a common youth dormitory (*Vaisginn)* was situated. Male youths sleep at night in this dormitory. The youth leader (*Thangval U)* was in-charge to look after the youth of that house. The youth looked after their village. Their dwelling huts are similar to that of the Tripuris.

They practice *jhum* cultivation and have not adoped settled or plough cultivation. Women are fond of ornaments. Beads, conchs, etc., are their ornaments. They have beautiful ear rings. *Dubra* or a single piece of handwoven cloth is wrapped by the females. It covers their of upper and lower part of the body and hangs down upto their knees.

The dead are cremated,

MAG:- It spelt also as Mog and Mugh. As per G.K. Ghosh (1992) The Mogs are also called Jhumiah Tribe. They mainly reside in Sabroom and Belonia Sub- Divisions. It is said that they migrated to Chitagong from Arakan in 17th century. Later they entered the low hills along the borders of Tripura. It is further said that, the Arakanese are known as the Mag who prefers to be called by the name *Marma* which was the ancient name of the Burmans (Burmese).

Their dialect is akin to Arakanese which is similar with Burmese. They have their own scripts. According to Grierson Mag language belongs to Assam Burmese group of the Tibeto-Chinese family. Now many of them are bilingual. Their huts are constructed on mud plinths. Kitchen and the granaries are built separately. Generally their houses are facing towards east. Bachelor's dormitories are there; *Sabosagong* dormitory is meant for the boys and *Aseragong* for the girls. But there is no compulsion to live in the dormitory by the girls at night.

Their main food is rice. They prefer meat and dried fish along with vegetables. Edible roots are also eaten. Home brewed rice-beer is consumed by them. But, they do not drink much liquor. They practice *jhum* cultivation. Many of them have adopted plough cultivation.

They have two endogamous divisions. Their clan *Palemsa* is sub-divided into two exogamous sub-classes *viz. Bara Palemsa* and *Chota Palemsa*. A girl of *Bara Palemsa* can marry only to the boy of *Chota Palemsa*. A girl of *Chota Palemsa* is sometimes allowed to marry a boy who belongs to the clan of the other moiety. Some of the clans belonging to the second moiety. as follows :- Farengsa, Regeiasa, Rekhoisa, Karaonurasa, Lugdungsa, Khemsa.

The Mags generally live in nuclear families. Extended families are sometimes found among them. The eldest son gets half of the property of his dead father. The remaining half is divided equally among other sons. All the daughters inherit the ornaments of their mother. But, the eldest daughter gets the lion's share.

Three types of marriages are there. These are :- *Khobo miyanijare* (love marriage), *Khobomiboprijare* (Negotiated marriage) and *Khamatoore* (Marriage by service). They allow women freedom which is their characteristic feature of the Mag society. Widow re-marriage and divorce are allowed. But the cases of divorce and separation are not many. Though these are allowed in their society but, they dislike it. Child marriage is not practiced. Their marriage ceremonies are simple. For marriage there is no compulsion to give feasts to their community.

The Mags have concept of heaven and hell which are known as *Nerefun* and *Sagrafun*. Most of them are Buddhists. Very few of them are either Hindus or Christians. Their supreme God is *Phora* (Buddha). The other deities worshipped by them are *Sani(Chini), Kali* and *Ganga*. They also worship *Buradevta (Chichi)*. A *Kheyang* (temple of Lord Buddha) is there in each Mag Village. It is a single roomed hut thatched with a four sloped roof designed in the form of 'pagoda'. Inside the temple there is an image of Lord Buddha in Yoga-form is made of mud. The temple is looked after by the villagers by raising subscription. There is a priest for this temple who is known as *Shamphura*.

Their important festivals are :-

Boat festival:- It happens in full-moon night in the month of September-October (*Aswin*, Bengali month).

Water festival:- This is akin to Holi festival. It takes place on the first day of March-April (*Chaitra*, Bengali month).

Buha Chakra:- This comes after the full moon day in the month of December-January (Magh, Bengali month).

Phungyi burning ceremony:- When a *Phungyi dies (a priest of high rank), they are to preserve the dead body in a Keyang* (coffin) for one year. At the end of the period on a fixed day, the dead body is to be cremated. The ceremony is observed on this occassion.

They have Village Councils in every-four villages which are grouped together. The head of their Council is known as *Bemarang* or *Choudhury* or *Tahsildar*. He is an elected person by the Council members on consideration of his wealth, property and personality. He is assisted by an assistant known as *Karbari* and a messenger known as *Peada*. The *Choudhury* is to preside over the council meetings. The council is to decide all the disputes except murder cases which they have to report to the police.

They cremate the dead body. Before cremation they observe funeral rites by offering food and water to the dead.

CHAKMA- The Chakmas mostly reside in the Sub-Divisions of Kailasahar, Amarpur, Sabroom, Udaipur and Belonia. Most of them are Arakanese immigrants. They inhabit till to-day in Central part of Chittagong Hill Tracts (Bangladesh) which is adjoining to the hills of Arakan or Arakan Yoma in Burma.

They speak a corrupt form of Bengali language which is an admixture of Assamese and Burmese groups of languages. Previously their dialect was written in Burmese script. According to Arakanese folklore there was a battle with the Chakmas against the local kings of Arakan as early as in 16th century. As per their own historical tradition, their earlier inhabitation was in the southern part of Chittagong Hill Tracts which extended along the *Matamuri* river. On 8th August 1880, by a Gazette notification it was described about the Chakma Chief's circle of Chittagong Hill Tracts. The Chakma Chief was allowed to collect revenue from the people under his jurisdiction. His headquarters was at Rangmati (Bangladesh).

According to Risley, the name Chakma has been derived from *Tsamka Tsak Thek*, a Lohitic tribe of the Chittagong Hill Tracts. According to Dr. Leeffer, the *sak* in the border areas of Arakan and Chittagong descended the Chakma and linguistically spoke *Sak* dialect. They are akin to the *Kader* of Upper Burma or to the *loi* of Manipuri. Further it seemed to Dr. Leeffer that the *Saks* have adopted Bengali language and became Chakma. According to Dev Varman (1986) their original home was in Burma.

The Chakmas of Tripura are divided into 35 sects (gozas) which are sub-divided into *gustis*. These are :- *Milima, Tanja, Burua, Koda, Wuangsa, Buma, Kurchya, Kadua*, etc. They can not marry within their same *gusti* though they can marry in the same *goza*. Divorce is permissible. Widow re-marriage is allowed within their community. Child marriage is not practised. Marriages are performed by negotiation. Payment of bride price is there.

They have Village Council consisting of elders. Their chiefs called *Sardars or Dewans*. He plays an important role in managing the economic affairs of the Chakma community. Their social discipline is very strict. Minor offences, communal disputes, petty thefts, etc. are settled by their *Sardar,* Below the rank of *Sardar (Dewan)* there is *Karbaris* whose duty is social work. There are *Talkudars* whose role is to look into religious matters. There is *Khijayat* also.

Most of them are Buddhist. There are four types of workers in the temple of Lord Buddha in a Chakma village. They are :- *Bhikkus, Raulees, Ojhas* and *Gankulies*. The *Bhikkus* are monks. The *Raulees* are to perform the customary rites from cradle to grave. The *Ojhas* appease the evil spirits. The *Gankulies* sing sentimental narrative religious songs from village to village. Old religious manuscripts even of hundred years old are sometimes available with the Chakma chiefs who read all these holy books.

Jhum cultivation is their main source of livelihood Now, few of them practice settled cultivation. At present, many of them have joined service and trade. Educationally, the Chamas are progressing day by day. Their food habits are some what like that of the Kukis but they are not addicted to drink like the Kukis.

Their dress has some similarities with the dress of the *Burmese* and the *Shan* people. The Chama women weave their clothes in their leisure time. Generally they use their own hand-woven clothes. A piece of cloth is tied by them around their body covering the upper and lower part of the body. Now many of them wear *saree* blouse. Men wear mill-made *Dhoti,* gengi and shirt. Women use ornaments which somehow look like the Bengali women.

The Chakmas cremate their dead. The family members of the deceased dive money in honour of the dead person. Sometimes they keep the dead-body in a wooden box for several days till the family members could arrive there from differnt places for funeral rites.

KUKI- They inhabit mainly in Dharmanagar, Kailashahar and Amarpur Sub-Divisions. They also live in Mizoram, Manipur and a few in Assam. According to their legends the Kukis originally belong to a place called *Sinlung* on the bank of the river *Mekong* in south-western part of China. Due to some natural calamities, famine and nomadic habit they migrated to *Shan* country. Again they migrated towards Chin Hills, Irrawadi Valley and Chindwin of Burma. In search of more fertile land for cultivation, they gradually migrated to Mizo Hills, Manipur, Tripura and Assam.

The Kukis of Tripura are also known as *Hre-em.* Some believe that they are the *Halam* people of Tripura. The Kukis are not a single group of people. The term *Kuki* is a generic word which covers a number of tribes, sub-tribes and clans of common character.

They are divided into twenty-six classes. These are as follows:- *Paitu, Chothang , Khareng, Baibek, Amrai, Chamlen, Batle, Riyete, Balta, Rangchon, Rangchiya, Chhailoi, Jangte, Pailai, Beltu, Paite, Phun, Phuntei, Lextai, Hraltei, Sowalai, Powaktu, Dhum, Burdoia, Chhaljen, and Rangte.* Their clans are not fully exogamous. Marriage within the same clan is discouraged but not prohibited. There is no restriction of inter-marriage among different tribes of Kuki groups. Their marriage is generally of two types:- negotiation and love-marriage. Adultery is alomst nil. Divorce is allowed. Widow re-marriage is permissible. Younger brother is to marry the widow of his elder brother (Levirate) but, the elder brother can not mary the widow of his younger brother. Polygamy is found among some rich people but he can not marry a fourth-one if the other three wives are alive.

Their traditional occupation is *jhum* cultivation and hunting. Their economic condition is almost good. Cane and bamboo products are manufactured by them for their domestic use. Women are expert weaver. Few men are good carpenters and blacksmiths.

They prefer to live on hill tops. The Kuki villages have a cluster of houses and are closely constructed with one another. Their houses are built on wooden or bamboo platform. Timber is used for very big houses. Their rooms are quite spacious. Their domestic animals are kept below their *machanes* or houses. In the middle of the room there is an earthen hearth. Their room has two doors, one at the front and other at the rear. Generally their rooms do not have any window. Now-a-days they have constructed their houses having several rooms. doors, windows and ventilation. Long ago, the Kukis had no habit to repair their houses. When their huts were unfit for habitation they had built new huts in the new site nearby their old huts.

They have their hereditary Village Chief who has some power. Their traditional religion is *animism.* At present, most of the Kukis are Christians. Some of them follow their traditional religion. Physically the Kukis are strong and stout. They are short and medium in stature. Height of men is generally 5 to $5\frac{1}{2}$ feet and women are $4\frac{1}{2}$ to 5 feet. Their legs are muscular and complexion is dark.

Traditionally the Kukis both men and women wear a cloth wrapped round their waist and hang it upto ankles. To cover their upper part they use shirt. Generally they cary a netted bag with steel pipe, tobacco, etc. Pipes are smoked by both men and women. They are expert archers. They are fond of meat. *Zu* (rice beer) is their favourite drink. They believe in life after death and re-birth. They bury their dead.

UCHAI- They are inhabited mainly in South Tripura district and some of them in North Tripura. In South Tripura they live in Amarpur and Belonia sub-divisions and in Dharmanagar Sub-division of North Tripura. They are the immigrants from Arakan (Burma, now Myanmar) to Chittagong (Bangladesh) and thereafter to Tripura. They are also known as Oichai. They are a small ethnic group in Tripura.

They speak *Kokbarak* language which belongs to the Bodo group of Tibeto-Burman group of language. They use Bengali scripts. They can speak a corrrupted form of Bengali language. They have Village Council of elders. They have their Chiefs known as *Choudhury*. He plays an important role in managing the affairs of the Uchai community.

They do not allow marriage among relatives nor inter-community marriage. There are four types of marriages among them. These are:- negotiation, mutual consent, elopment and marriage by service. The traditional system of marriage among the Uchai is marriage by service. The period of service is three to four years. Sometimes the bridegroom lives permanently, after his service period, in the house of his father-in-law. Bride price is found among them. They are monogamous. Child marriage is not there. Adultery is a great offence. Widow and widower re-marriage is allowed. Divorce is permissible. They have twelve clans *(panji)*. Nuclear family is common. Extended family is also found in good number.

They practice *jhum* cultivation. Now few of them have adopted plough cultivation. Their cultivable *jhum* fields are rain fed. The Uchai are mainly Christians. Some of them are Hindus and few are Buddhists. The Hindus are divided into *Sanatan* and *Vaishnav* sub-groups. Hindu Sanatan, Vaishnav and Buddhist groups worship their own deities including *Ganga, Bura Devta, Lakshmi, Choudda Devta, Ker,* etc.

Their stature is medium to short and strongly built. Their skin colour is light yellow to dark brown. The Uchai women weave their own clothes. The traditional dress of a male is *Kasha* and *Khutaitak borak,* Kasha seems to be a cotton muffler which they wear to cover their private parts and Khutaitak borak is a hand made indigenous shirt. But, most of the Uchai males are now using mill-made small *dhoti,* shirt and genji, etc. Younger generation now wear pants, shirts, shoes, slippers, etc. The women use their traditional dresses *Risha* or *Rhia* and *Rignai.* Risha or Rhia is a small piece of breast-cloth which is multi-coloured and looks like a cotton muffler. Rignai is a multi-coloured hand made cloth which they wrap around their waist and it hangs down to cover their knees and sometimes it extends from waist to feet. Modern young girls wear *saree,* blouse, slipper, etc. Women wear necklaces, ear rings bracelets, etc. Men in their leisure time prepare excellent varieties of baskets, etc. They are skillful in making their baskets with cane and bamboo.

The Uchai eat meat, fish and all types of vegetables. Rice is their main food. The Hindus and Buddhists do not eat beef. Uchai women are hard workers. They help their men folk in agriculture, animal husbandry, etc. Generally they prefer to use their indigenous medicines.

They bury their dead except the Hindus and the Buddhist. They observe death rituals. The eldest son gets his father's property. But he shares the property equally among his younger brothers.

LUSHAI (MIZO)- They are inhabited mainly in *Jampui* Hill areas under Dharmanagar Sub-Division of North Tripura District. It seems that, the Hmar and Paite tribes have been mixed up with the Lushais of Tripura. It is said that their original home was Mizoram. They come to Tripura due to the availability of plenty of *jhum* fields. It is said that the Kacharis had used the word *Lushai* a derogatory term which means the head hunters. The terms the Mizos and the Lushais are used synonymously. The word Mizo has been recently adopted which means "Hillman" in *Zoumi* language. The word Lushai is presumed to have derived from "Luchhai".

The Lushais are Christian. They are educationally and economically much advanced tribe. Their houses are built about 2 feet above the ground and have wooden roofs and walls. The floor is either made of wooden planks or bamboos. Though they are Christians still they observe *animistic* rituals and worship *animistic* objects.

They belong to the Chin-Kuki group. The Malay and the Burmese elements are present more or less in the Lushai dress and culture. The Lushais came to Mizoram from Chin Hills of Burma. Some of them migrated to Tripura in search of *jhum* field.

In their village they live in thatched and bamboo made huts on hill tops. Lushai women weave their clothes. Women wear full-sleeve blouses and hand woven *puanchai* which they tie round their waist which hangs upto their ankle to cover their lower part. Some of them are now using all kinds of modern dresses like skirts, frocks, mini, middi, etc. Men prefer to wear western dresses. They wear trousers and shirts. Valuable ornaments of women are amber necklaces and cornelian beads.

They have their hereditary Chief *(Rengpui)* who takes advice from the *Upas* (Councillors). Traditional occupation of the Lushai is *jhum* cultivation and hunting. A patch of jungle in the hill slopes cleared by burning down trees, herbs and shrubs. The burnt ashes serves as the only manure in the hill slopes of their agricultural fields. With the help of *'Trakkal'* (chopper) they dig little holes and sowed the seeds of paddy, cotton, sesame, cucumber, maize, etc. They are now also cultivating orange and red-pepper.

The boys and girls are mixing freely. The boys get married between 18 to 25 years of their age and girls 16 to 22 years. There is a bride price which is payed to the groom. Divorce is allowed with the consent of the community. Widow or widower can remarry. Child marriage is not there. Polygamous type of marriage is not prevalent.

The Lushai male, female and children are smokers. Lushai or *Dulian* is their dialect. Their main food is rice with boiled vegetables with sufficient quantity of chillies. Tea is popular drink among them. Beef and pork are considered delicious food. The Lushai men are expert archers.

Younger sons inherit all the moveable and immoveable properties of their father. They have their traditional bamboo dance *(cheraw)* by women. They bury their dead according to Christian convention.

DARLONG:- It is said that the Darlongs came from eastern Burma more than three centuries ago. They came to Tripura *via* the Mizo Hills where there is a range called *Darlong Hang*. They first came to Unakuti (Tripura) and thereafter to Srimangal (Tripura). Some of them proceeded to Brahman Baria (Bangladesh).

The Darlongs occupied Teliamura to Unakuti. They have their Chief *(Lal)*. Their Chief is hereditary. A Village Council *(Napa)* is elected by the villagers. This is to function in criminal and civil matters of the Darlong villages. The Darlongs love music and song. They practice jhum cultivation.

They bury their dead.

RUPINI:- According to the Rupinis they have come from the *Lengdi* mountain beyond Aizawl (Mizoram) where there is a big legendary lake. Their origin is perhaps same as the Lushais (Mizo) and the Kukis. They mainly inhabit near the foothills on both sides of the *Baramura* Range in Sadar and Khowai Sub-Divisions.

They have become Hindus on the influence of their neighbours. They are devotees of Vishnu. The older generation avoid meat, fish and wine. Long before, it is said, they kept fowls and domesticated animals. The new educated generation is not strict in eating meat, fish, etc., as they dislike vegetables. Now most of the Rupinis are strict *Vaishnavists* and most of their customs and social rules conform to its forms. At the same time, the Rupinis are following *animism* and believe in the existence of God in all elements of nature. They offer *Puja* to a deity of stone which they believe is benevolent to them.

There is a myth about the name *Rupini*. It is said that once a white elephant was found in a forest. People went to see and trap it. But they could not. Suddenly a lightskin fair and beautiful youth appeared there who captured the white elephant and disappeared. Every body was surprised at this. They could not get time to ask the name of that youth. For that, they called that youth *Rupini* (fair one). From that day, they came to be known as "Rupinis".

They are economically sound. Some of them are land-holders. Some Rupinis practice *jhum* cultivation and they are now cultivating in plain land. They prefer to live on hillocks. Their houses are generally 3 metres in width and 8 meters long. There is no partition inside their room. They cook in a corner of their room. They generally make a small machan type of projection about 2 metres from the ground in the room. This is made of bamboo. They keep here dried vegetables, utensils, clothes, etc. The roof of their hut is of dried bamboo leaves or chan grass. The floor and wall are made of mud plaster.

Their every village has a *Visnu* temple. Only priest is allowed to enter the temple, others sit outside the temple. The construction of the temple is almost same to those made by the Manipuri Vaisnavs in Khowai and Sadar Sub-Division of Tripura. 'Rai Kanchan', a supreme authority of the Rupini Society, meets once in a year on the Maghi Purnima day (December-January) with the Rupini people to review the social structure, degeneration of social culture, social value and issue an instruction to regenerate the age old social spirit. Some of them were forced to opt for Christianity leaving their traditional 'Vaisnavism'. But most of them again came back to Vaisnav society after paying token-penalty and performing 'prayaschitta'.

The Rupinis are classified into four sub-clans namely-Puran Rasti, Nutan Rasti, Thaithak and Paithak. Their social hierachy is as follows higher to lower:- Rai, Karim, Kabor, Chapiakha, Kanskow, Yaksong and Singja.

They can not marry without the consent of their parents. They follow the rule of endogamy for their marriage custom. But, now marriages outside their clan has increased among the educated Rupinis. Child marriage is not there. Divorce is allowed. Widow and widower re-marriage is permissible.

The Rupini tribe, belonging to the Indo-Mongolian racial family. They did not have any literate member till 1947. The language of the Rupinis was somehow like the Kuki-Chin characteristics. Now, their grammar and vocabularies are akin to Tripuri language.

Their musical instruments are sarangi, violin, flute, *dholak* (drum) etc. Thy are fond of singing and dancing. Their Council allots punishment and penalties according to the gravity of the infringement. Generally it aims at resolving disputes amicably.

The dead body is burnt and buried if it is child below 18 months of age.

GARO:- They are inhabited in the Sub-Division of Sadar and Udaipur. They mainly reside in Garo Hills of Meghalaya. They migrated from Garo Hills of Meghalaya and plains of Mymensingh of Bangladesh to Tripura due to the availabitlity of plenty of jhum land. According to Playfair (1909) their original home was Tibet. But it is said that they were driven out by the Tibetan from Bhutan. However, it is certain that they came from northern mountains beyond Assam and finally settled in Garo Hills and plains of Mymensingh. Their name Garo is said to have derived from one of their original leader "Garo".

The Garos of Tripura are mainly agriculturists and those who have their own land now practice settled cultivation like the Bengali neighbours. The landless Garos practice shifting cultivation in the remote areas. Their other occupations are service, business etc. The Garo dialects belong to the Assam-Burmese family. They can speak Bengali language fluently. They belong to the Tibeto-Chinese family of Tibeto-Burman sub-family of Bodo group.

They are mainly divided into three exogamous clans called *Kathohis viz.* the *Momins Maraks* and *Sangma* as well as the sub-division known as the *Machong*. Marriage among the Garos is strictly exogamous and the husband and wife must belong to different clans. They are matrilineal in descent. Their clans descended from a common ancestress - mother. Cross-cousin marriage is popular and very common. There is no bride-price or bride-groom price. Divorce is allowed. But, among the Christians, all these rules are not common. Mariage within the same 'Machong' or motherhood is very rare. The *Mahari* basically includes all the males and females who are *'Machong'*.

Their dwelling houses are made of painted bamboo splits with two thatched hampen roofs. Their houses are raised on piles. Generaly they live in their colonial pattern. Their houses are exceedingly long with doors at each end but no windows. Majority of them in Tripura are now Hindus as compared to Christian and Muslim Garos. Hindu Garos offer light (pradip) near Hindu images and holy plant 'Tulshi' (Basel).

Their main food is rice. The Hinduised Garos do not eat beef. They like dry fish. They drink liquor which is produced from rice. In Tripura, the Garos are well known for their 'Pachua' a kind of beer brewed from 'Binni rice'. It tastes very sweet and is sipped through bamboo pipettes from a small earthen pitcher *(langi)*.

Their cremation ground is situated in their village which is called *Maungruram*. The burial gound is known as *Gopram*. The Hindus cremate their dead while the Christians and Muslims bury their dead. The Hindu Garos generaly sacrifice *(Rang)* a buffalo at the time of funeral done by the Mahari.

SANTALS, MUNDAS AND ORAONS:- They are inhabited in the forest areas of Khowai, Kamalpur and Sadar Sub-Divisions. They had migrated to Tripura for employment from North Bengal and Bihar after the year 1951. Actually they had come to Sylhet (Bangladesh) few generations ago. Some of them came to Tripura from the tea gardens of Sylhet.

They have their *Sardars*. They have also Councils of Sardars known as *Mandal*. They believe in Supreme being. They worship *Dharmes* and *Singbonga* who saves, according to them, the family from the evil eye and ill matters. They can marry with the consent of their parents. They have *Raibar* to negotiate for marriages. They have bride price in the form of money. Divorce is permissible with the consent of their Sardar.

They prefer their indegenous medicine. They have their medicine-man called the *Baidh*. They have also *Deonrahs* (witch doctors), *Bhagats* (devotees), etc.

KHASI- The Khasis had immigrated from Meghalaya and Assam. Some of them migrated from Mymensingh and Sylhet (Bangladesh).

The Khasis of Tripura are mainly agriculturists. Some of them are engaged in bee-keeping, labourers are employed on road construction, etc. The origin of the Khasis is uncertain. Some are of the opinion that the Khasis are first Mongolians who migrated to India. Another view is that they came from the North and spread upto Sylhet (Bangladesh).

They are matrilineal in descent. They belong to the Aust family of Mon Khmer branch like the Nicobarese. The Khasis are divided into four groups namely:- the Bhoi, the Lyngngam, the Wars and the Khynriam. Marriage within the clan is strictly prohibited.

Khasi houses and courtyards are highly neat and clean. The main structure of the house rests upon stone pillars or wooden pillars. The youngest daughter known as *Ka Khadduh* inherits the property.

They cremate their dead except the Christians who bury their dead.

PART II

FULL BIBLIOGRAPHY OF TRIPURA AND THE TRIBES

A

1. **Abbi, B.L. (Ed)** : 1984 : *North East Region : Problems and prospects of development*. Chandigarh, Centre for Research in Rural and Industrial Development.

2. **Abraham, A.S.** : 1988 : The CPM after Tripura : Fears of declining influence. *Times of India*, Feb. 26.

3. **Acharjee, J.** : 1980 (?) : Two rare coins of hitherto unknown Tripura King Isvaramanikya. *Memoirs No. 7, NSI* (Varanasi), 118p.

4. ——— : 1985 : Some important and rare coins of Tripura, Jour. of NSI (Varanasi), XLVII : 49.

5. ——— : 1985 : Unique early coin of the Manikya Dynasty of Tripura. *Proceedings of North East Indian History Association*, vol. 6 : 56-8.

6. ——— : 1986 : Coins of Tripura : A Historical Survey, *(In) Tribes of Tripura (Ed.)* by Sudhanshu Bikash Saha. Agartala, Rupali Book Store : 165-172.

7. ——— : 1989 : A rare coin of Tripura. *(In) Fifty Years of Indological Study (Ed.) by K.D. Bajpai, New Delhi.*

8. **Acharjee, N.** : 1985 : *Kok-Borok Sauraunoma Kaulaya*. Khowai (Tripura), Published by the author, 57p.

9. **Acharyya, N.N.** : 1983 : *Historical Documents of Assam and Neighbouring States : Original Record in English*. New Delhi, Omsons Publications : 222-32.

10. ——— : 1985 : *Cursory glance on the early Historical Perspectives of Tripura. Proceedings of NEIHA No. 6 (Ed)* by J.B. Bhattacharjee. Shillong, NEHU (History Deptt.) : 91-8.

11. ———. 1985 : *North East As Viewed by Foreigners*. Gauhati, Omsons Publications : 58.

12. **Acharja, S.** : 1982 : *Bastaver darpane yuba samitir mukh (in Bengali)*. Agartala, Pub. by the author.

13. **Acharya, S.K.** : 1988 : Ethnic Processes in North Eastern India. *Economic and Political Weekly* (Bombay), XXIII (21), May 21 : 1068-77.

14. **Adhikari, C.S.** : 1982 : *The problem of indebtedness among the tribals in Sadar Sub-Division of Tripura.* Agartala, Directorate of Research, 49p.

15. ——— : 1985 : Immigrant tribes in Tripura : A few observations. *Proceedings of NEIHA, No.6* : 469- 77.

16. ——— : 1988 : *Four Immigrant Tribes of Tripura.* Agartala, Directorate of Research, 30p.

17. **Adhikari, Pradip Kumar** : 1990 : Asant boni huie hai Chatgaon ki pahariya *(in Hindi). Purbanchal Prahari* (Guwahati), Feb. 20 : 1(col. 2-5).

18. ——— : 1991 : Chakma soronarthi : Swadesh bapasi ki asha jagi *(in Hindi). Saptasetu* (Guwahati), January 10 : II (I-II).

19. **Agarwal, A.K.** : 1983 : Land ownership system in the Hill Areas of the N.E. Region and its effect on development of agriculture. *Social Research,* 3(1), Jan.-March : 32-39.

20. ——— (Ed.) : 1987 : *Economic problems and planning in North East India.* New Delhi, Sterling Publishers : 17-9, 28-34, 55- 8, 261-63, 294-315, 394-413, 543-60, 475-99.

21. **Agarwal, V.C.** *and* Bhattacharya, T.A. : 1977 : Report on collection of mammals from Tripura. *Record : Zoological Survey of India,* 73 : 135-57.

22. **Agnihotri, M.** : 1970 : Mizo Folk Tales : Zawlpala and Tualvungi. *Folklore,* 11 : 51-5.

23. **Agriculture Deptt.** : 1974 : *Report on World Agricultural Census (1970-'71) in Tripura.* Agartala, Govt. of Tripura, Agriculture Deptt.

24. **Agricultural Finance** : 1983 : *A Study on Shifting Cultivation in Tripura.* Agartala, Agricultural Finance Corporation.

25. **Agro Economic** : 1962 : *Kathaliacherra : A Jhumia settlement colony in Tripura.* Jorhat, Agro Economic Research Centre for N.E.I. *(Mimeo.).*

26. **Agro Economic** : 1969 : *An Assessment of Colonisation Scheme of Shifting Cultivators in Tripura*. Jorhat, AERC (*Mimeo.*).

27. ——— : n.d. : *Impact of colony scheme on Jhumias (1961-1967)*. Jorhat, AERC (*Mimeo.*).

28. ——— : 1969 : *Rural life in Assam Hills*. Jorhat, AERC.

29. ——— : 1971 : *Resurvey of the village Kathaliacherra (Belonia Tripura)*. Jorhat, AERC (*Mimeo.*).

30. **Ahluwalia, Shashi** : 1986 : *Social and Economic Development in North East India*. Delhi, Gyan Publishing House.

31. **Ahmad, Mahiuddin** : 1970 : *Agartala Sarajantra Mamlaye Abhijeger Purna Bibaran (in Bengali)*. Agartala, January.

32. **Aitchison, C.U.** (*Comp.*) : 1892 : *A collection of treaties, engagements and sanads, vol I, II*. Calcutta, Supdt. Govt. Ptg. (*Reprinted* by Mittal Publications, Delhi in 1981, vol. xii).

33. **Akbar, M.J.** : 1980 : Mandai massacre. *Sunday*, June 15 : 14-9.

34. **Ali, Liaquat** : 1990 : Fresh influx worries Tripura. *Shillong Times*, June 18 : 3(4-6).

35. **Ali, Rahman** : 1967-'72 : *Art and architecture of the Kalabuvis of Tripura*. Ph.D. Thesis, Poona University (*Unpublished*).

36. **Allen, B.C.** : 1902 : Tipperah, (*In*) *Census of India 1901, vol. IV, Assam, pt. I, Report*. Shillong, Govt. Press : 144.

37. **Allen, B.C.** *et al* : 1979 : *Gazetteer of Bengal and North East of India*. Delhi, Mittal Publications : 605-12 (*Reprinted*).

38. **Amnesty International** : ? : *Bangladesh : Unlawful killings and torture in the Chittagong Hill Tracts*. London, Amnesty International.

39. **Amrita Bazar Patrika** : 1904 : Tripura Notes. *Amrita Bazar Patrika*, Sept. 1.

40. ——— : 1979 : Panchayat System : A Success in Tripura. *Am. Baz. Pat.*, Sept. 10.

41. **Amrita Bazar Patrika** : 1979 : Tripura soon to be a major silk producing state. *Am. Baz. Pat.*, Oct. 30.

42. ——— : 1979 : Insurgency in Tripura. *Am.Baz.Pat.*, Nov. 1.

43. ——— : 1981 : 400 tribals enter Tripura. *Am.Baz.Pat.*, June 29.

44. ——— : 1981 : Tripura Government preparing for Poll. *Am.Baz.Pat.*, July 29.

45. ——— : 1981 : Tribal Influx : Tripura's concern. *Am.Baz.Pat.*, Sept. 25.

46. ——— : 1981 : Editorial : Tripura's new problem. *Am.Baz.Pat.*, Oct. 3.

47. ——— : 1981 : Tribals raid 3 houses. *Am.Baz.Pat.*, Oct. 14.

48. ——— : 1981 : What ails the ancient house of Bodos? *Am.Baz.Pat.*, Oct. 18.

49. ——— : 1982 : 2 tribals shot dead. *Am.Baz.Pat.*, Jan. 21.

50. ——— : 1982 : Tripura Scheduled Tribes Population declining. *Am.Baz.Pat.*, Oct. 12.

51. ——— : 1983 : Tripura tribal ultras want to lay down arms. *Am.Baz.Pat.*, March 8.

52. ——— : 1983 : Demand to save Chakmas from victimisation. *Am.Baz.Pat.*, Oct. 5.

53. ——— : 1985 : Tripura Tribal Council comes under Central control. *Am.Baz.Pat.*, May 25 : 3.

54. ——— : 1985 : Tripura concerned over rise in crimes. *Am.Baz.Pat.*, July 9 : 7.

55. ——— : 1985 : Panchayat controversy in Tripura. *Am.Baz.Pat.*, Sept. 30 : 7(1-4).

56. ——— : 1985 : Big scope for horticulture in Tripura. *Am.Baz.Pat.*, Dec. 14 : 7(2-4).

57. ——— : 1985 : Tripura can expand rubber potential. *Am.Baz.Pat.*, Dec. 17 : 5(1-2).

58. ——— : 1986 : TUJS's grand show of strength. *Am.Baz.Pat.*, Jan. 4: 7(2-5).

59. ——— : 1986 : Tripura Jhum land. *Am.Baz.Pat.*, Jan. 21.

60. **Amrita Bazar Patrika** : 1986 : Drilling for gas in Tripura. *Am.Baz.Pat.*, Jan. 28 : 7(5-7).

61. ——— : 1986 : Woes of bonded labour in Tripura. *Am.Baz.Pat.*, Jan. 29 : 7(6-7).

62. ——— : 1986 : Tripura's murder 'A case of retaliation'. *Am.Baz.Pat.*, March 7 :7(5).

63. ——— : 1986 : Labour unrest bogs rationing in Tripura. *Am.Baz.Pat.*, March 16 : 3(7-8).

64. ——— : 1986 : TNV-MNF truck : Delhi in touch with Tripura. *Am. Baz. Pat.*, April 9: 1(2-3).

65. ———: 1986 : Furore in Tripura over move to withdraw riot cases. *Am. Baz. Pat.*, April 9 : 7(2-3).

66. ——— : 1986 : Editorial : TNV escalates violence. *Am. Baz. Pat.*, April 10 : 6(1-2)

67. ——— : 1986 : Operation 'energy agents' by TNV. *Am. Baz. Pat.*, April 11 : 7(2-4).

68. ———: 1986 : Plight of Reang tribals in Assam. *Am. Baz. Pat.*, April 24 : 7(1-4).

69. ———: 1986 : Troops prevent migration : BDR massacres 150 Tripuris *Am. Baz. Pat.*, May 24 : 1(4-5).

70. ——— : 1986 : Tripura plans to take over sick tea gardens. *Am. Baz. Pat.*, June 5: 5(2-3).

71. ———: 1986 : PREPAK sets up secret hideouts. Am. Baz. Pat., June 15 : 6(3).

72. ———: 1986 : Desertion plagues TNV. *Am. Baz. Pat*, June 19:7 (1-4).

73. ——— : 1986 : 5,000 refugees enter Tripura in 3 days. *Am. Baz. Pat.*, June 21 : 7(2-4).

74. ——— : 1986 : "Tribal influx on". *Am. Baz. Pat.*, June 29: 1(4).

75. ———: 1986 : Mizo accord may put TNV off gear. *Am. Baz. Pat.*, July 7: 7(1-5).

76. ——— : 1986 : TUJS objects to Laldenga's remark. *Am. Baz. Pat.*, July 12: 7(6-7).

77. ———: 1986 : A battle of surival for Chakmas. *Am. Baz. Pat.*, July 18 : 7(4-7).

78. **Amrita Bazar Patrika** : 1986 : TNV rebels gun down CPM backer. *Am. Baz. Pat.*, July 23 : 7 (7-8).

79. ———: 1986 :Tribal influx continues. *Am. Baz. Pat.*, July 25: 10(4).

80. ——— : 1986 : Rajya Sabha questions : Intelligence set up in N-E region geared up to curb terrorism. *Am. Baz. Pat.*, Aug. 8: 12(1-3).

81. ——— : 1986 : Roaring Trade in banned drugs alleged *Am. Baz. Pat.*, Aug. 7: 7(2-4).

82. ——— : 1986 : Protecting N-E Eco-system. *Am. Baz. Pat.*, Aug. 26 : 7(4-5).

83. ——— : 1986 : Tripura Congress (I) in doldrums. *Am. Baz. Pat.*, Aug. 27 : 7(2-4).

84. ——— : 1986 : Editorial : Tripura's heavy burden. *Am. Baz. Pat.*, Aug. 29 : 6(1-2).

85. ——— : 1986 : TNV ultras gun 14 down: Bandh today. *Am. Baz. Pat.*, Aug. 31 : 1(5-7).

86. ——— : 1986 :Tripura to get more forces. *Am. Baz. Pat.*, Sept 3:1(4).

87. ——— : 1986 : TNV guerillas gun down six policemen. *Am. Baz. Pat.*, Sept. 14: 1(1-3).

88. ——— : 1986 : Editorial : Terror in Tripura. *Am. Baz. Pat.*, Sept. 17: 6(1-2).

89. ——— : 1986 : TNV guerillas butcher nine non-tribals. *Am.Baz.Pat.*, Nov. 15 : 1(1-2).

90. ——— : 1986 : Tripura gaon panchayat by elections on Jan. 4. *Am.Baz.Pat.*, Dec. 6 : 7(4-5).

91. ——— : 1986 : Chakma refugees seek safety guarantee. *Am.Baz.Pat.*, Dec. 19 : 7(3-5).

92. ——— : 1986 : TNV attacks shatter morale of BRO workers. *Am.Baz.Pat.*, Dec. 24 : 7(5-6).

93. ——— : 1986 : TNV rebels massacre 10 non-tribals. *Am.Baz.Pat.*, Dec. 24 : 1(5-7).

94. ——— : 1986 : Bandh cripples life in Tripura : Killings worry Centre. *Am.Baz.Pat.*, Dec. 25 : 1(7-8), 12(4-5).

95. **Amrita Bazar Patrika** : 1986 : Curfew in Amarpur : 5 more killed in Tripura. *Am.Baz.Pat.*, Dec. 26 : 1(1-2), 12(3).

96. ——— : 1986 : Editorial : TNV strikes again. *Am.Baz.Pat.*, Dec. 26 : 6(1-2).

97. ——— : 1986 : Third TNV strike in 72 hours : All 8 members of a family killed. *Am.Baz.Pat.*, Dec. 27 : 1(1-3).

98. ——— : 1986 : More forces for Tripura urged. *Am.Baz.Pat.*, Dec. 29 : 1(1).

99. ——— : 1986 : Steps to tackle TNV to be decided in Delhi. *Am.Baz.Pat.*, Dec. 30 : 1(6-7).

100. ——— : 1986 : "Disturbed areas act won't help": Nripen. *Am.Baz.Pat.*, Dec. 31 : 1(7-8).

101. ——— : 1986 : Bangla to take back Chakma refugees. *Am.Baz.Pat.*, Dec. 31 : 1(7-8).

102. ——— : 1987 : Editorial : Need for Joint strategy. *Am.Baz.Pat.*, Jan. 1 : 6(1-2).

103. ——— : 1987 : Chakma influx from Bangladesh continues. *Am.Baz.Pat.*, Jan. 8 : 1(7-8), 12(1).

104. ——— : 1987 : Editorial : Progress in Tripura. *Am.Baz.Pat.*, Jan. 9 : 6(1-2).

105. ——— : 1987 : Security forces gearing up to combat TNV violence. *Am.Baz.Pat.*, Jan. 10 : 5(5-7).

106. ——— : 1987 : 'Indians go back'. *Am.Baz.Pat.*, Jan. 13 : 1(2-3).

107. ——— : 1987 : Editorial : Smouldering North East. *Am.Baz.Pat.*, Jan. 14 : 6 (1-2).

108. ——— : 1987 : 38 killed in Tripura in 2 days. *Am.Baz.Pat.*, Jan. 15 : 3(6).

109. ——— : 1987 : TNV to be outlawed. *Am.Baz.Pat.*, Jan. 15 : 1(4-5).

110. ——— : 1987 : 'Extra vigil' call on TNV. *Am.Baz.Pat.*, Jan. 19 : 1(2-5).

111. ——— : 1987 : Bangladesh to take back Chakma DPs. *Am.Baz.Pat.*, Jan. 25 : 12(3-4).

112. **Amrita Bazar Patrika** : 1987 : Amnesty wants : India not to repatriate tribal refugees. *Am.Baz.Pat.*, Jan. 21 : 7(2-5).

113. ——— : 1987 : Massive anti-extremist drive in Tripura. *Am.Baz.Pat.*, Jan. 24 : 7(2-5).

114. ——— : 1987 : TNV kills five of a non-tribal family. *Am.Baz.Pat.*, Jan. 28 : 1(1).

115. ——— : 1987 : Editorial : Joint steps in Tripura. *Am.Baz.Pat.*, Jan. 30 : 6(1-2).

116. ——— : 1987 : Blood-bath in Tripura hamlets. *Am.Baz.Pat.*, Feb. 1 : 3(2-3).

117. ——— : 1987 : Fresh influx of Chakmas. *Am.Baz.Pat.*, Feb. 1 : 3(1-2).

118. ——— : 1987 : Six TNV collaborators arrested. *Am.Baz.Pat.*, Feb. 1 : 3(4).

119. ——— : 1987 : India's protest against Chakma influx. *Am.Baz.Pat.*, Feb. 3 : 1(2-5).

120. ——— : 1987 : Editorial : Not by arms alone. *Am.Baz.Pat.*, Feb. 3 : 6(1-2).

121. ——— : 1987 : TNV declared 'unlawful association'. *Am.Baz.Pat.*, Feb. 5 : 1(1).

122. ——— : 1987 : TNV goading tribals to join ranks. *Am.Baz.Put.*, Feb. 7 : 7(1).

123. ——— : 1987 : 'Quit Tripura Order' by TNV. *Am.Baz.Pat.*, Feb. 7 : 12(6).

124. ——— : 1987 : Chakma influx continues. *Am.Baz.Pat.*, Feb. 11 : 12(2-4).

125. ——— : 1987 : Tripura alerted 'Raising Day' on eve on TNV. *Am.Baz.Pat.*, Feb. 13 : 3(1-3).

126. ——— : 1987 : TUJS wants army to tackle TNV activities. *Am.Baz.Pat.*, Feb. 14 : 3(3), 9(2-3).

127. ——— : 1987 : Chakma influx worries Tripura. *Am.Baz.Pat.*, Feb. 15 : 7(7-8).

128. ——— : 1987 : Two projects for Tripura tribal sectors. *Am.Baz.Pat.*, Feb. 17 : 3(1-2).

129. ——— : 1987 : Tripura on the verge of rubber revolution. *Am.Baz.Pat.*, Feb. 20 : 3(2-3).

130. **Amrita Bazar Patrika** : 1987 : Dhaka impeding return of Chakmas. *Am.Baz.Pat.*, March 6 : 7(5-8).

131. ——— : 1987 : Rehabilitation projects for Jhumia tribals. *Am.Baz.Pat.*, March 7 : 3(5).

132. ——— : 1987 : Fresh TNV assault feared. *Am.Baz.Pat.*, March 9 : 3(4-5).

133. ——— : 1987 : Power shortage in Tripura. *Am.Baz.Pat.*, March 10 : 3(3).

134. ——— : 1987 : Editorial : Another Chakma massacre. *Am.Baz.Pat.*, March 11 : 6(1-2).

135. ——— : 1987 : Development efforts to counter insurgency. *Am.Baz.Pat.*, March 11 : 7(1-4).

136. ——— : 1987 : Tripura CM claims Bangladesh helping TNV. *Am.Baz.Pat.*, March 11 : 3(2).

137. ——— : 1987 : Some Tripura areas declared disturbed. *Am.Baz.Pat.*, March 12 : 1(2).

138. ——— : 1987 : Conspiracy against tribal leader Tripura. *Am.Baz.Pat.*, March 14 : 3(2).

139. ——— : 1987 : TUJS wants powers to be rested with tribal council. *Am.Baz.Pat.*, March 18 : 3(4).

140. ——— : 1987 : 48000 Chakmas in Tripura. *Am.Baz.Pat.*, March 21 : 3(1).

141. ——— : 1987 : 'Amra Bangali' activists arrested in Tripura. *Am.Baz.Pat.*, April 3 : 3(4-5).

142. ——— : 1987 : Editorial : The return of Chakmas. *Am.Baz.Pat.*, April 6 : 6(1-2).

143. ——— : 1987 : Chakmas fleeing to India to escape death. *Am.Baz.Pat.*, April 13 : 8(4-5).

144. ——— : 1987 : Food crisis in Tripura tribal areas. *Am.Baz.Pat.*, April 15 : 3(6).

145. ——— : 1987 : Tourism given industry status in Tripura. *Am.Baz.Pat.*, April 17 : 3(1).

146. ——— : 1987 : N-E parties to settle inter-state border issues. *Am.Baz.Pat.*, April 25 : 3(1-2).

147. ——— : 1987 : Horticultural Corporation in Tripura soon. *Am.Baz.Pat.*, April 25 : 3(3).

148. **Amrita Bazar Patrika** : 1987 : Editorial : Accord on Chakmas. *Am.Baz.Pat.*, April 29 : 6(1-2).

149. ——— : 1987 : TNV rebel surrenders to CM. *Am.Baz.Pat.*, May 3 : 3(4-5).

150. ——— : 1987 : Power crisis grips Tripura. *Am.Baz.Pat.*, May 1 : 5(3-4).

151. ——— : 1987 : TNV rebels kidnap CPI(M) MLA. *Am.Baz.Pat.*, May 14 : 1(7-8).

152. ——— : 1987 : 'Bangladesh to take back all Chakmas'. *Am.Baz.Pat.*, May 15 : 5(1-2).

153. ——— : 1987 : Tripura schemes for welfare of tribals. *Am.Baz.Pat.*, June 6 : 3(4-5).

154. ——— : 1987 : Tripura denies allegations on Chakmas. *Am.Baz.Pat.*, June 8 : 8(8).

155. ——— : 1987 : 3 N-E states to be on rail map by 1990. *Am.Baz.Pat.*, June 17 : 3(1-3).

156. ——— : 1987 : Editorial : Tripura tribals attacked. *Am.Baz.Pat.*, July 14 : 6(1-2).

157. ——— : 1987 : Gas struck near Agartala. *Am.Baz.Pat.*, July 27 : 3(7-8).

158. ——— : 1987 : Gas struck in Tripura basin again. *Am.Baz.Pat.*, July 27 : 7(1).

159. ——— : 1987 : Chakmas want tripartite agreement. *Am.Baz.Pat.*, July 27 : 7(2-5).

160. ——— : 1987 : Tripura's efforts to attract tourists. *Am.Baz.Pat.*, July 28 : 7(7-8).

161. ——— : 1987 : NEC to promote balanced regional development. *Am.Baz.Pat.*, Aug. 2 : 10(2-3).

162. ——— : 1987 : 1,000 children go blind in Tripura every year. *Am.Baz.Pat.*, Aug. 4 : 5(1-2).

163. ——— : 1987 : Tripura illiterates to be 4'26 lakhs by 1990. *Am.Baz.Pat.*, Aug. 4 : 5(5).

164. ——— : 1987 : Centre urged to check infiltration into Tripura. *Am.Baz.Pat.*, Aug. 6 : 5(5-6).

165. ——— : 1987 : Tripura to grow medical plant. *Am.Baz.Pat.*, Aug. 7 : 5(8).

166. **Amrita Bazar Patrika** : 1987 : Tri-lingual dictionary for Tripura, Manipur tribes. *Am.Baz.Pat.*, Aug. 7 : 5(6-7).

167. ——— : 1987 : Power position may improve in Tripura. *Am.Baz.Pat.*, Aug 8 : 5(2-3).

168. ——— : 1987 : Political tension mounts in Tripura. *Am.Baz.Pat.*, Aug. 26 : 7(5-6).

169. ——— : 1987 : Tripura Government's help to Chakmas. *Am.Baz.Pat.*, Sept. 13 : 7(4-5).

170. ——— : 1987 : Concern at condition of Tripura monuments. *Am.Baz.Pat.*, Sept. 14 : 7(2-3).

171. ——— : 1987 : Bangladesh yet to settle Chakma issue. *Am.Baz.Pat.*, Sept. 14 : 5(1-2).

172. ——— : 1987 : Editorial : Chakmas again. *Am.Baz.Pat.*, Sept. 16 : 6(1-2).

173. ——— : 1987 : 'Marriage by service' among Riangs. *Am.Baz.Pat.*, Sept. 19 : 5(1-2).

174. ——— : 1987 : Bangladesh forms committee to look into Chakma problem. *Am.Baz.Pat.*, Sept. 27 : 10(3).

175. ——— : 1987 : Editorial : TNV's desparate game. *Am.Baz.Pat.*, Oct. 16 : 6(1-2).

176. ——— : 1987 : TNV raids despite 'strong vigilance'. *Am.Baz.Pat.*, Oct. 18 : 1(2-5).

177. ——— : 1987 : Mental diseases increases in North Eastern Region. *Am.Baz.Pat.*, Nov. 2 : 7(6).

178. ——— : 1987 : Editorial : Peace keeping in Tripura. *Am.Baz.Pat.*, Nov. 11 : 6(1-2).

179. ——— : 1987 : Tripura tea industry faces crisis. *Am.Baz.Pat.*, Nov. 16 : 10(3-5).

180. ——— : 1987 : Efforts to bring Tripura on country's tourist map. *Am.Baz.Pat.*, Dec. 9 : 4(6-8).

181. ——— : 1987 : TAI wants Central panel for Tripura. *Am.Baz.Pat.*, Dec. 14 : 10(3-4).

182. ——— : 1987 : Editorial : The task now in Tripura. *Am.Baz.Pat.*, Dec. 30 : 6(1-2).

183. ——— : 1988 : Multi-cornered contests for most Tripura seats. *Am.Baz.Pat.*, Jan. 18 : 9(1-3).

184. **Amrita Bazar Patrika** : 1988 : Women to play decisive role in Tripura polls. *Am.Baz.Pat.*, Jan. 19 : 8(5-8).

185. ——— : 1988 : Army moving into disturbed areas in Tripura. *Am.Baz.Pat.*, Jan. 23 : 12(2-3).

186. ——— : 1988 : Urban electorate hold trump card in Tripura. *Am.Baz.Pat.*, Jan. 25 : 8(4-5).

187. ——— : 1988 : TNV : Union Minister meets army, State Officials. *Am.Baz.Pat.*, Jan. 25 : 8(4-5).

188. ——— : 1988 : Editorial : Precaution in Tripura. *Am.Baz.Pat.*, Jan. 29 : 6(1-2).

189. ——— : 1988 : Chakmas : The anguished cry. *Am.Baz.Pat.*, Jan. 30 (Saturday Weekend Reading) : I(1-8).

190. ——— : 1988 : Entire Tripura declared disturbed: Army Alerted. *Am.Baz.Pat.*, Jan. 30 : 1(1-3).

191. ——— : 1988 : 'State has sabotaged Accord' — says P.M. *Am.Baz.Pat.*, Jan. 30 : 1(4-6).

192. ——— : 1988 : Will Chakma presence affect Tripura polls? *Am.Baz.Pat.*, Jan. 30 : 7(1-3).

193. ——— : 1988 : 'Tripura Government fails to curb insurgency' : P.M. *Am.Baz.Pat.*, Jan. 30 : 12(2-4).

194. ——— : 1988 : TNV kills 30 even as army patrols streets. *Am.Baz.Pat.*, Jan. 31 : 1(1-3).

195. ——— : 1988 : Troops enter towns : 13 more killed; CRPF, TNV exchange fire. *Am.Baz.Pat.*, Feb. 2 : 1(2-4).

196. ——— : 1988 : Left Front rule ends in Tripura : Congress - TUJS alliance wins majority. *Am.Baz.Pat.*, Feb. 5 : 1(1-3), 12(6-8).

197. ——— : 1988 : Tripura Government to probe left front 'scandals'. *Am.Baz.Pat.*, Feb. 8 : 1(7-8).

198. ——— : 1988 : Selection of Ministers raises problems in Tripura. *Am.Baz.Pat.*, Feb. 8 : 7(1-4).

199. ——— : 1988 : Order on arms surrender. *Am.Baz.Pat.*, Feb. 9 : 1(1).

200. ——— : 1988 : Tripura Minister says : We're ready to have recounting in all constituencies. *Am.Baz.Pat.*, Feb. 9 : 1(2-4).

201. **Amrita Bazar Patrika** : 1988 : Left front's Tripura Day today. *Am.Baz.Pat.*, Feb. 10 : 1(6), 12(4).

202. ——— : 1988 : Tripura : Panja denies Central interference. *Am.Baz.Pat.*, Feb. 10 : 12(2-6).

203. ——— : 1988 : CPI(M)-TNV nexus? *Am.Baz.Pat.*, Feb. 11 : 7(5-8).

204. ——— : 1988 : Centre to probe CPI(M) - TNV link. *Am.Baz.Pat.*, Feb. 17 : 1(7-8).

205. ——— : 1988 : 'TUJS not a regional party'—Majumdar. *Am.Baz.Pat.*, Feb. 19 : 12(3-4).

206. ——— : 1988 : 'Tripura Election : Behind the scenes (The MLA Maharani)'—R.C. *Am.Baz.Pat.*, Weekend Reading, Saturday, Feb. 20 : 4(1-8).

207. ——— : 1988 : 8 TNV extremists held. *Am.Baz.Pat.*, Feb. 23 : 8(6-7).

208. ——— : 1988 : Editorial : Meeting the TNV menace. *Am.Baz.Pat.*, March 3 : 6(1-2).

209. ——— : 1988 : Panel to probe Tripura tribal council affairs. *Am.Baz.Pat.*, March 25 : 8(5).

210. ——— : 1988 : Meghalaya to supply power to Tripura. *Am.Baz.Pat.*, March 25 : 8(8).

211. ——— : 1988 : Per capita income less in hills. *Am.Baz.Pat.*, March 29 : 7(5).

212. ——— : 1988 : Editorial : The TNV surrender. *Am.Baz.Pat.*, Sept. 13 : 6(1-2).

213. ——— : 1988 : TNV gets a temporary political mileage. *Am.Baz.Pat.*, Sept. 17 : 7(4-5).

214. ——— : 1988 : TUJS will not accept Hrangkwal. *Am.Baz.Pat.*, Sept. 22 : 7(4).

215. ——— : 1988 : Congress-CPI(M) clash in Tripura: 14 dead. *Am.Baz.Pat.*, Oct. 14 : 1(2-3).

216. ——— : 1988 : Tripura orders judicial probe : LF to agitate. *Am.Baz.Pat.*, Oct. 15 : 1(2-3).

217. ——— : 1988 : Editorial : Tripura clashes. *Am.Baz.Pat.*, Oct. 16 : 6(1-2).

218. ——— : Editorial : Disunity in Tripura. *Am. Baz. Pat.*, Oct. 26: 6(1-2)

219. **Amrita Bazar Patrika** : 1988 : Editorial : Change in Tripura CPI(M). *Am.Baz.Pat.*, Nov. 3 : 6(1-2).

220. ——— : 1988 : Editorial : Chakmas of Bangladesh. *Am.Baz.Pat.*, Nov. 6 : 6(1-2).

221. ——— : 1988 : Tripura Ministry in trouble over Laskar tribe. *Am.Baz.Pat.*, Nov. 14 : 7(3).

222. ——— : 1988 : Cashewnut project in Tripura. *Am.Baz.Pat.*, Nov. 11 : 7(4).

223. ——— : 1988 : Tripura government to improve lot of listed class. *Am.Baz.Pat.*, Dec. 7 : 8(3-4).

224. ——— : 1988 : Tribal bodies seek protection of rights. *Am.Baz.Pat.*, Dec. 7 : 8(3-4).

225. ——— : 1988 : Autonomy for Jhampui Hill areas under consideration. *Am.Baz.Pat.*, Dec. 8 : 7(2).

226. ——— : 1988 : Tripura Upajati's protests on 'Khas' land allotment. *Am.Baz.Pat.*, Dec. 10 : 9(4).

227. ——— : 1988 : TNV to demand village councils. *Am.Baz.Pat.*, Dec. 10 : 9(6-8).

228. ——— : 1988 : Editorial : New factor in Tripura. *Am.Baz.Pat.*, Dec. 14 : 6(1-2).

229. ——— : 1988 : Serious financial crisis in Tripura. *Am.Baz.Pat.*, Dec. 31 : 12(3).

230. ——— : 1989 : TNV heading for a showdown with State Govt. *Am.Baz.Pat.*, Jan. 14 : 7(1-3).

231. ——— : 1989 : TNV not merging with TUJS. *Am.Baz.Pat.*, Jan. 16 : 7(4).

232. ——— : 1989 : Reang bridegrooms have to work for father-in-law to get married. *Am.Baz.Pat.*, Jan. 16 : 7(5-6).

233. ——— : 1989 : Chakmas reject Ershad's move for District Councils. *Am.Baz.Pat.*, Jan. 16 : 12(4-5).

234. ——— : 1989 : Tripura holiday resort reintroduces toy train. *Am.Baz.Pat.*, Jan. 24 : 7(4).

235. ——— : 1989 : 'Jungle rule in Tripura'—Nripen. *Am.Baz.Pat.*, Feb. 3 : 7(5-6).

236. ——— : 1989 : Tripura Govt. advised to raise more revenue. *Am.Baz.Pat.*, Feb. 4 : 7(4).

237. **Amrita Bazar Patrika** : 1989 : Jampui Mizos .ay launch agitation soon. *Am.Baz.Pat.*, Feb. 16 : 7(5-7).

238. ——— : 1989 : Non-implementation of accord : TNV leaders criticise Tripura government. *Am.Baz.Pat.*, March 3 : 8(5-6).

239. ——— : 1989 : Tripura to be industrially advanced by 2000 AD. *Am.Baz.Pat.*, March 9 : 9(7-8).

240. ——— : 1989 : Heroin worth Rs. 1-cr. seized in Tripura. *Am.Baz.Pat.*, March 15 : 7(3).

241. ——— : 1989 : TUJS supports ABSU demands. *Am.Baz.Pat.*, March 15 : 7(5).

242. ——— : 1989 : Tripura Mizos threaten stir. *Am.Baz.Pat.*, March 29 : 7(6).

243. ——— : 1989 : Buddhist monk to contest from Tripura East. *Am.Baz.Pat.*, Nov. 17 : 7(5).

244. ——— : 1989 : Tripura assured of enough gas supply. *Am.Baz.Pat.*, Dec. 12 : 7(1-2).

245. ——— : 1989 : Farmer's wages in Tripura raised. *Am.Baz.Pat.*, Dec. 24 : 7(1-2).

246. ——— : 1989 : TNV leaders to meet P.M. *Am.Baz.Pat.*, Dec. 27 : 7(6).

247. ——— : 1990 : TUJS demands pushing back 'foreigner'. *Am.Baz.Pat.*, Jan. 9 : 7(3-5).

248. ——— : 1990 : ISKCON plans to set up complex near Agartala. *Am.Baz.Pat.*, Jan. 12 : 8(1-3).

249. ——— : 1990 : Two spectacle monkey escape from Tripura zoo. *Am.Baz.Pat.*, Jan. 15 : 7(1).

250. ——— : 1990 : Demand to repatriate refugees with 'honour'. *Am.Baz.Pat.*, Jan. 22 : 7(1-2).

251. ——— : 1990 : Tripura panel to redemarcate boundary. *Am.Baz.Pat.*, Jan. 30 : 7(5).

252. ——— : 1990 : 19th Century copper coins found. *Am.Baz.Pat.*, Feb. 5 : 9(5).

253. ——— : 1990 : Congress in Tripura : A ship without radar. *Am.Baz.Pat.*, Feb. 8 : 5(6-8).

254. ——— 1990 : Planning panel praises Tripura's performance. *Am.Baz.Pat.*, Feb. 12 : 7(1-4).

255. **Amrita Bazar Patrika** : 1990 : Rs. 10 cr. sought to implement TNV Accord. *Am.Baz.Pat.*, Feb. 16 : 3(3-4).

256. ——— : 1990 : Identity cards in Tripura to check Bangla influx. *Am.Baz.Pat.*, Feb. 17 : 8(7-8).

257. ——— : 1990 : ONGC to invest Rs. 73 crore in Tripura. *Am.Baz.Pat.*, Feb. 21 : 10(7-8).

258. ——— : 1990 : Passport camp in district town. *Am.Baz.Pat.*, March 4 : 7(6).

259. ——— : 1990 : Tripura Cong. student front to launch stir. *Am.Baz.Pat.*, March 5 : 7(5).

260. ——— : 1990 : Hrankhawl, sayed talk TNV Accord. *Am.Baz.Pat.*, March 6 : 7(1).

261. ——— : 1990 : Thermal plant switched on in Tripura. *Am.Baz.Pat.*, March 8 : 7(5-6).

262. ——— : 1990 : Inner Line permit for Tripura area demanded. *Am.Baz.Pat.*, March 11 : 7(1-2).

263. ——— : 1990 : Gas leak. *Am.Baz.Pat.*, March 11 : 7(5).

264. ——— : 1990 : TUJS conference. *Am.Baz.Pat.*, March 11 : 7(8).

265. ——— : 1990 : TUJS demands 2 more berths in Tripura Ministry. *Am.Baz.Pat.*, March 13 : 7(5).

266. ——— : 1990 : Tripura to set up tribal research institute. *Am.Baz.Pat.*, March 14 : 7(5).

267. ——— : 1990 : Viral disease hits bee-keeping in N-E. *Am.Baz.Pat.*, March 20 : 5(3-4).

268. ——— : 1990 : TUJS, CPI(M) demand more job quota for tribals. *Am.Baz.Pat.*, March 20 : 5(1).

269. ——— : 1990 : Tripura L F plea to seal border. *Am.Baz.Pat.*, March 23 : 7(4).

270. ——— : 1990 : Press Council condemns attack on Tripura daily. *Am.Baz.Pat.*, April 4 : 7(1-4).

271. ——— : 1990 : Tripura ADC polls on July 8. *Am.Baz.Pat.*, April 21 : 7(1-3).

272. ——— : 1990 : Tripura ADC polls likely on July 15. *Am.Baz.Pat.*, April 27 : 7(2-4).

273. ——— : 1990 : TNV. *Am.Baz.Pat.*, April 29 : 7(1).

274. **Amrita Bazar Patrika** : 1990 : TUJS wants TNV alliance to join during polls. *Am.Baz.Pat.,* April 30 : 7(7-8).

275. ——— : 1990 : New industrial policy for Tripura. *Am.Baz.Pat.,* May 3 : 10(3-6).

276. ——— : 1990 : Arms looted from Tripura police camp. *Am.Baz.Pat.,* May 6 : 1(4).

277. ——— : 1990 : Tripura Cong., urged to renew talks with TNV. *Am.Baz.Pat.,* May 6 : 7(2-5).

278. ——— : 1990 : Tripura wants Central forces. *Am.Baz.Pat.,* May 7 : 7(1).

279. ——— : 1990 : Agartala airport being modernised. *Am.Baz.Pat.,* May 9 : 7(1).

280. ——— : 1990 : Tripura tea industry faces problems. *Am.Baz.Pat.,* May 24 : 10(6).

281. ——— : 1990 : Tripura's agitation threat on gas supply. *Am.Baz.Pat.,* May 25 : 7(6-8).

282. ——— : 1990 : Tripura C.M. for poll pact with TNV. *Am.Baz.Pat.,* May 27 : 7(5-6).

283. ——— : 1990 : TNV's participation in ADC poll to split vote bank. *Am.Baz.Pat.,* June 1 : 7(6-8).

284. ——— : 1990 : Chakma refugees offer terms. *Am.Baz.Pat.,* June 5 : 11(2-4).

285. ——— : 1990 : Conversion on the rise in Tripura. *Am.Baz.Pat.,* June 8 : 7(5).

286. ——— : 1990 : Rival parties prepare for Tripura's ADC polls. *Am.Baz.Pat.,* June 16 : 5(1-2).

287. ——— : 1990 : Drive to make Agartala a literate city by Nov.'90. *Am.Baz.Pat.,* June 26 : 5(1).

288. ——— : 1990 : N-E states plan to boost tourism. *Am.Baz.Pat.,* June 26 : 5(2-4).

289. ——— : 1990 : Minister denies allegation : TUJS bags last ADC seat. *Am.Baz.Pat.,* July 13 : 11(2-3).

290. ——— : 1990 : Chakma DP's prolonged stay troubles Tripura. *Am.Baz.Pat.,* July 13 : 5(1-3).

291. ——— : 1990 : TUJS largest party in ADC polls. *Am.Baz.Pat.,* July 13 : 5(1-2).

292. **Amrita Bazar Patrika** : 1990 : Attempt to forment communal riots in Tripura. *Am.Baz.Pat.,* July 14 : 5(6).

293. ——— : 1990 : Editorial : Poll violence in Tripura. *Am.Baz.Pat.,* July 14 : 6(1-2).

294. ——— : 1990 : Editorial : The Chakma question. *Am.Baz.Pat.,* July 16 : 6(1-2).

295. ——— : 1990 : Tripura ADC members have MLA status. *Am.Baz.Pat.,* July 17 : 7(1-4).

296. ——— : 1990 : ADC Chief. *Am.Baz.Pat.,* July '19: 5(7).

297. ——— : 1990 : Tripura C.M. smells plot in peace panel. *Am.Baz.Pat.,* July 26 : 7(4-5).

298. ——— : 1990 : Tripura poll violence : 'Govt not told of NF probe team's visit'. *Am.Baz.Pat.,* July 27 : 7(4-5).

299. ——— : 1990 : Tripura wants buffer stock of food supplies. *Am.Baz.Pat.,* July 27 : 3(6).

300. ——— : 1990 : Tense week ahead in Tripura. *Am.Baz.Pat.,* July 30 : 5(6-7).

301. ——— : 1990 : 44 km railway line laid in 26 years. *Am.Baz.Pat.,* July 30 : 5(1-4).

302. ——— : 1990 : Tripura areas still disputed. *Am.Baz.Pat.,* July 31 : 5(6-7).

303. ——— : 1990 : NF team's conclusion : Tripura ADC election totally rigged. *Am.Baz.Pat.,* Aug. 1 : 3(1-2).

304. ——— : 1990 : Rajiv's statement boosts Tripura Govt. *Am.Baz.Pat.,* Aug. 6 : 5(6-8).

305. ——— : 1990 : Editorial : Case in Tripura. *Am.Baz.Pat.,* Aug. 7 : 6(1-2).

306. ——— : 1990 : Furore in LS over Tripura violence. *Am.Baz.Pat.,* Aug. 9 : 1(7-8).

307. ——— : 1990 : Tripura, Centre heading for confrontation. *Am.Baz.Pat.,* Aug. 13 : 7(2-4).

308. ——— : 1990 : Financial crisis : Tripura seeks Central help. *Am.Baz.Pat.,* Aug. 25 : 7(5-7).

309. ——— : 1990 : Plea to disperse Chakmas from Arunachal. *Am.Baz.Pat.,* Aug. 27 : 3(3).

310. **Amrita Bazar Patrika** : 1990 : TUJS to severe links with TNV. *Am.Baz.Pat.*, Aug. 27 : 5(5-6).

311. ——— : 1990 : Charge and counter-charge on Tripura gas utilization. *Am.Baz.Pat.*, Aug. 27 : 7(5-8).

312. ——— : 1990 : 'Adventurist' forms extremist group. *Am.Baz.Pat.*, Aug. 28 : 5(1-2).

313. ——— : 1990 : Volatile political situation in Tripura. *Am.Baz.Pat.*, Aug. 29 : 5(6- 8).

314. ——— : 1990 : Tripura to have plenty of power soon. *Am.Baz.Pat.*, Sept. 3 : 7(1-4).

315. ——— : 1990 : RKM English medium school of Agartala. *Am.Baz.Pat.*, Sept. 3 : 5(1-2).

316. ——— : 1990 : Controversy over vegetable diet. *Am.Baz.Pat.*, Sept. 4 : 9(2-4).

317. ——— : 1990 : TUJS threat to opt out of coalition. *Am.Baz.Pat.*, Sept. 5 : 11(1).

318. ——— : 1990 : TUJS threatens to withdraw Ministers. *Am.Baz.Pat.*, Sept. 6 : 3(3).

319. ——— : 1990 : Tripura CPI(M) supporters on the run. *Am.Baz.Pat.*, Sept. 7 : 7(8).

320. ——— : 1990 : Tripura Congress (I) squabbles. *Am.Baz.Pat.*, Sept. 7 : 7(2-4).

321. ——— : 1990 : 2 Congress men killed in Tripura. *Am.Baz.Pat.*, Sept. 9 : 7(8).

322. ——— : 1990 : Concern over 'eviction' of Chakma DPs. *Am.Baz.Pat.*, Sept. 10 : 7(4).

323. ——— : 1990 : NEC seeking ways to solve power problem. *Am.Baz.Pat.*, Sept. 10 : 7(2-3).

324. ——— : 1990 : R.K. Mission's project opens new chapter in Tripura. *Am.Baz.Pat.*, Sept. 11 : 5(7-8).

325. ——— : 1990 : President's Rule in Tripura under study. *Am.Baz.Pat.*, Sept. 11 : 5(7-8).

326. ——— : 1990 : Tripura incentives for gas-based units. *Am.Baz.Pat.*, Sept. 12 : 10(2-4).

327. ——— : 1990 : Tripura CM rebuts CPI(M) allegations. *Am.Baz.Pat.*, Sept. 16 : 7(2-5).

328. **Amrita Bazar Patrika** : 1990 : Tripura CM scoffs at demand for President's rule. *Am.Baz.Pat.*, Sept. 17 : 7(7-8).

329. ——— : 1990 : Subscription collection menace in Tripura. *Am.Baz.Pat.*, Sept. 19 : 7(6).

330. ——— : 1990 : Cong.-TUJS attack on left activists unabated. *Am.Baz.Pat.*, Sept. 20 : 5(1-3).

331. ——— : 1990 : Tripura's plan proposal for Rs. 1600 cr. *Am.Baz.Pat.*, Sept. 22 : 5(2-3).

332. ——— : 1990 : 20 p.c. bonus for Tripura tea garden workers. *Am.Baz.Pat.*, Sept. 22 : 7(5).

333. ——— : 1990 : Rly Board's decision disheartens North Eastern States. *Am.Baz.Pat.*, Sept. 24 ; 5(1-3).

334. ——— : 1990 : Cong (I)-TUJS meeting. *Am.Baz.Pat.*, Sept. 24 : 7(4).

335. ——— : 1990 : Tripura CM's plea for perspective plan for N.E. *Am.Baz.Pat.*, Oct. 13 : 5(2-3).

336. ——— : 1990 : Call to link Agartala by rail via Assam. *Am.Baz.Pat.*, Oct. 14 : 9(1-3).

337. ——— : 1990 : Agartala-Calcutta rail link demanded. *Am.Baz.Pat.*, Oct. 15 : 5(7-8).

338. ——— : 1990 : Shortage of coal supply hits tea output in Tripura. *Am.Baz.Pat.*, Oct. 22 : 10(7-8).

339. ——— : 1990 : Tripura CM warns against fundamentalism. *Am.Baz.Pat.*, Oct. 24 : 7(1).

340. ——— : 1990 : Centre blamed for Tripura's backwardness. *Am.Baz.Pat.*, Oct 30 : 7(5-8).

341. ——— : 1990 : Tripura fears large-sclae influx. *Am.Baz.Pat.*, Oct. 31 : 7(5-6).

342. ——— : 1990 : Tripura's demand may now be settled. *Am.Baz.Pat.*, Nov. 13 : 5(1-4).

343. ——— : 1990 : Tripura Govt. announces new industrial policy. *Am.Baz.Pat.*, Nov. 30 : 5(4-5).

344. ——— : 1990 : Tripura archieve to help scholars. *Am.Baz.Pat.*, Dec. 3 : 7(2-3).

345. **Amrita Bazar Patrika** : 1990 : Plan to supply natural gas to N.E. States under study. *Am.Baz.Pat.*, Dec. 5 : 5(6-8).

346. ——— : 1990 : Cupid worship growing in Chakma camps. *Am.Baz.Pat.*, Dec. 11 : 5(2-4).

347. ——— : 1990 : Gas supply at subsidized rate for Tripura. *Am.Baz.Pat.*, Dec. 12 : 5(4).

348. ——— : 1990 : 'RV to talk with Shekhar on Tripura'. *Am.Baz.Pat.*, Dec. 13 : 5(8).

349. ——— : 1990 : Tripura to raise forest protection force. *Am.Baz.Pat.*, Dec. 14 : 5(2-3).

350. ——— : 1990 : Centre urged to take over Tripura Varsity. *Am.Baz.Pat.*, Dec. 14 : 5(1).

351. ——— : 1990 : ATTF menace on the rise in Tripura. *Am.Baz.Pat.*, Dec. 16 : 7(2-4).

352. ——— : 1990 : Rate of smuggling rises on Tripura border. *Am.Baz.Pat.*, Dec. 18 : 7(6-8).

353. ——— : 1990 : Mass influx in Tripura claimed. *Am.Baz.Pat.*, Dec. 19 : 11(1-2).

354. ——— : 1990 : Rs. 225 cr. Tripura annual Plan outlay. *Am.Baz.Pat.*, Dec. 30 : 5(5-6).

355. ——— : 1991 : Tripura Ministry rift worries Cong. *Am.Baz.Pat.*, Jan. 1 : 11(1-2).

356. ——— : 1991 : TUJS under pressure from rank and file. *Am.Baz.Pat.*, Jan. 3 : 5(7-8).

357. ——— : 1991 : N-E States prepare for mid-term polls. *Am.Baz.Pat.*, Jan. 9 : 7(2-5).

358. ——— : 1991 : 'Movement needed for railway line extension up to Agartala'. *Am.Baz.Pat.*, Jan. 14 : 5(1-5).

359. ——— : 1991 : Plan panel approach to Tripura 'Unfortunate'. *Am.Baz.Pat.*, Jan. 31 : 5(4).

360. **Ananda Bazar Patrika** : 1988 : Tripura. *An.Baz.Pat.*, Aug. 13.

361. ——— : 1988 : Editorial. *An.Baz.Pat.*, Aug. 15.

362. **Anand, Madhusudan** : 1987 : Tripura-1 : Ativadi andolan ki jar aur jamin. *Nava Bharat Times*, Jan. 15 : 4(5-8).

363. **Annual Reports** : 1985 : *Annual Reports and Accounts of the Public Sector undertakings in Tripura for the period 1981-'82 to 1984-'85*. Agartala. Information and Public Relations.

364. **Anonymous** : 1872 : Tipra and Chittagong Kukis. *Indian Antiquary*, vol I; : 225-26.

365. ——— : 1891 : Baiti-Chunari. *(In) District Census Report, 1891. Burdwan Division, Birhbum District*. p.34.

366. ——— : 1929 : Murungs. *Assam Review* (Gauhati), March.

367. ——— : 1957 : Traditional arts and crafts : Tripura, Manipur and Assam. *Bulletin of the Institute of Traditional Cultures* (Madras) : 200-205.

368. ——— : 1957 : Lullabies of India (Karnataka, Punjab, Tripura, Hindi). *Kurukshetra*, Vol. 6, No. 2, November : 204.

369. ——— : 1962 : *Survey of the living conditions of tea plantation labourer in Tripura*. Calcutta, Central Tea Board, p.43.

370. **Archaeological Survey** : 1924 : *India, Central Publication Branch : Annual Report, 1921-22*. Calcutta, Manager of Publications : 85-7.

371. ——— : 1931 : *India, Central Publication Branch: : Annual Report, 1927-28*. Calcutta, Manager of Publications : 184-85 (Report on Dharmanagar Hevajna).

372. **Archives** : ? : *Tripura Secretariat Archives*. Agartala. Tripura Secretariat.

373. **Arora, C.K.** : 1980 : Tripura : Bureaucracy in control. *Economic and Political Weekly*, XVII(31) : 1386.

374. **Asom Jagriti** : 1980 : Indian citizens versus foreign nationals : Memorandum to the Prime Minister of India. *Asom Jagriti*, January 25, p.10.

375. **Assam Tribune** : 1975 : Tribal problems of Tripura placed before P.M. *A.T.*, Feb. 3 : 5.

376. ——— : 1979 : Tripura village burnt down by Mizo Insurgents. A.T., March 22.

377. ——— : 1980 : Tribals have suffered more in Tripura. *A.T.*, July 10.

378. **Assam Tribune** : 1980 : Tribals in Tripura go on mass fasting. *A.T.*, Oct. 26.

379. ——— : 1982 : Tribal extremists in Tripura active. *A.T.*, Sept. 21.

380. ——— : 1980 : Tribals have suffered more in Tripura. *A.T.*, July 10.

381. ——— : 1981 : Plea to give arms to village resistance parties in Tripura. *A.T.*, June 25 : 1.

382. ——— : 1985 : I-A to start copter service in Tripura. *A.T.*, July 28 : 1.

383. ——— : 1986 : Police Stations in South Tripura alerted. *A.T.*, March 7 : 1(7).

384. ——— : 1986 : TNV leader Debbarma believed killed. *A.T.*, April 2 : 3(3).

385. ——— : 1986 : Embankment work on Muhuri River continues. *A.T.*, April 15 : 1(1-2).

386. ——— : 1986 : Disturbed areas belt on Indo-Burma border. *A.T.*, April 15 : 6(5).

387. ——— : 1986 : More tribal evacuees enter Tripura. *A.T.*, May 6 : 1(2-4).

388. ——— : 1986 : TUJS stir in support of Bangla tribals. *A.T.*, May 13 : 1(2-3) and 8(5).

389. ——— : 1986 : Refugee influx into Tripura continues. *A.T.*, May 26 : 1(3-5).

390. ——— : 1986 : Editorial : Chakma Exoders. *A.T.*, May 27 : 4(1-2).

391. ——— : 1986 : 11872 Bangla refugees in Tripura. *A.T.*, June 16 : 1(5-7).

392. ——— : 1986 : More refugees enter Tripura. *A.T.*, July 5 : 1(4-6).

393. ——— : 1986 : TUJS against demand for greater Mizoram. *A.T.*, July 13 : 4(1-2).

394. ——— : 1986 : Fresh Chakma Influx in Tripura. *A.T.* July 19 : 1(4), 8(5).

395. ——— : 1986 : Activities of NEHHDC. *A.T.*, July, 29 : 5(5).

396. **Assam Tribune** : 1986 : Tribal Influx Continues in Tripura. *A.T.*, July 30 : 6(6).

397. ——— : 1986 : Tourism schemes in N.E. region. *A.T.*, Aug. 2 : 1(3-5).

398. ——— : 1986 : Ten killed by Shanti Bahini. *A.T., Aug. 21 : 1(6-8).*

399. ——— : 1986 : Tripura Govt. to fight against divisive forces. *A.T.*, Sept. 2 : 4(1-2).

400. ——— : 1986 : Editorial : Terrorism in Tripura. *A.T.*, Sept. 4 : 4(1-2).

401. ——— : 1986 : Chakma Rajguru calls for International intervention. *A.T.*, Nov. 5 : 3(3).

402. ——— : 1986 : Tripura Panchayat Poll on Dec. 28. *A.T.*, Nov. 13 : 6(5).

403. ——— : 1986 : TNV Extremists step-up activities : 8 killed. *A.T.*, Nov. 14 : 1(5-6).

404. ——— : 1986 : 12 hour West Tripura Bandh observed. *A.T.*, Nov. 14 : 5(3).

405. ——— : 1986 : Guerrillas kill 17 people in Tripura. *A.T.*, Nov. 15 : 1(2-3) 8(4).

406. ——— : 1986 : Editorial : TNV Problem. *A.T.*, Nov. 26: 4(1-2).

407. ——— : 1986 : Two killed in TNV attack. *A.T.*, Nov. 30: 1(8).

408. ——— : 1986 : 13 killed by TNV Extremists. *A.T.*, Dec. 6 : 1(7-8).

409. ——— : 1986 : Tripura's Mizos want Regional Council. *A.T.*, Dec. 9 : 4 (7-8).

410. ——— : 1986 : Chakma refugees fear atrocities. *A.T.*, Dec. 18 : 4(7-8).

411. ——— : 1986 : TNV Guerrillas kill 10 in Tripura. *A.T.*, Dec. 24 : 1(1-3).

412. ——— : 1986 : TNV Rebels kill 4 non-tribals. *A.T.*, Dec. 26 : 1(6-7).

413. ——— : 1986 : 8 more killed by TNV Extremists. *A.T.*, Dec. 27 : 1(2-4).

414. Assam Tribune : 1986 : Editorial : Killings in Tripura. *A.T.*, Dec. 28 : 4(1-2).

415. ——— : 1986 : Concern over Law and Order Situation in Tripura. *A.T.*, Dec. 29 : 1(4-5).

416. ——— : 1987 : North Tripura Police Outposts alerted. *A.T.*, Jan. 3 : 3(5).

417. ——— : 1987 : 400 more Chakmas enter Tripura. *A.T.*, Jan. 7 : 1(1).

418. ——— : 1987 : India and Bangla to end TNV insurgency. *A.T.*, Jan. 9 : 1(1-3).

419. ——— : 1987 : More refugees enter Tripura. *A.T.*, Jan. 13 : 1(2-4).

420. ——— : 1987 : Repatriation of Tribal Refugees deferred. *A.T.*, Jan. 17 : 4(7-8).

421. ——— : 1987 : 7 killed by Shanti Bahini. *A.T.*, Jan. 20: 1(7-8).

422. ——— : 1987 : TNV being banned. *A.T.*, Jan. 23 : 1(4-6).

423. ——— : 1987 : Notification to ban TNV under consideration. *A.T.*, Jan. 24 : 1(5).

424. ——— : 1987 : Chakmas fleeing due to BDR violence. *A.T.*, Jan. 25 : 6(3-6).

425. ——— : 1987 : India urged to postpone returning of refugees. *A.T.*, Feb. 1 : 1(7-8).

426. ——— : 1987 : Plastic clay found in Tripura. *A.T.*, Feb. 3 : 5(1).

427. ——— : 1987 : TNV declared unlawful Association. *A.T.*, Feb. 5 : 1(5-7).

428. ——— : 1987 : Banning of TNV a 'stern' warning to insurgents. *A.T.*, Feb. 7 : 7(2-3).

429. ——— : 1987 : 'Quit Tripura Order' to Indians. *A.T.*, Feb. 7 : 1(1-3).

430. ——— : 1987 : Concern at killings of Chakmas. *A.T.*, April 13 : 1(3-5).

431. ——— : 1987 : Call to observe 'TNV-Day' on Feb. 14. *A.T.*, Feb. 13 : 1(6-8).

432. ——— : 1987 : 625 tribal refugees cross over to Tripura. *A.T.*, March 4 : 4(7-8).

433. **Assam Tribune** : 1987 : 100 Chakmas massacred. *A.T.*, March 9 : 1(1).

434. ——— : 1987 : Indo-Bangla Talks on Chakmas soon. *A.T.*, April 18 : 4(7-8).

435. ——— : 1987 : Early repatriation of Chakmas agreed. *A.T.*, April 27 : 1(1-3).

436. ——— : 1987 : Insurgency : Political Solution Urged. *A.T.*, May 26 : 1 (2-4).

437. ——— : 1987 : Scope for plastic based industry. *A.T.*, June 7 : 3(3).

438. ——— : 1987 : Separate Scientific Cell for N.E. Tribal Population. *A.T.*, June 18 : 4(7-8).

439. ——— : 1987 : 3 N-E States will be on rail map by 1990. *A.T.*, June 18 : 4(1-2).

440. ——— : 1987 : Solution of Chakma problem soon. *A.T.*, *June 29 : 1(5-7).*

441. ——— : 1987 : Socio-Religious customs of the Rupini. *A.T.*, Aug. 15 : 7(3-6).

442. ——— : 1987 : Editorial : Rebels in North East. *A.T.*, Aug. 21 : 4(1-2).

443. ——— : 1987 : Terrorist activity in North East. *A.T.*, Sept. 1 : 6(3-4).

444. ——— : 1987 : Editorial : Inner Line Regulations. *A.T.*, Sept. 21 : 4(1-2).

445. ——— : 1987 : Modern Tea factory in Tripura. *A.T.*, Sept. 22 : 7(5-6).

446. ——— : 1987 : Hill Tribal Liberation Organisation formed. *A.T.*, Sept. 28 : 1(1-2).

447. ——— : 1987 : Editorial : TNV strikes again. *A.T.*, Oct. 18 : 4(1-2).

448. ——— : 1987 : Concern over plight of Chakma refugees. *A.T.*, Dec. 5 : 4(7-8).

449. ——— : 1987 : TNV Serves Tax Notice on Tripura Minister. *A.T.*, Dec. 25 : 1(2-5).

450. ——— : 1987 : Editorial : Tripura Scene. *A.T.*, Dec. 28: 4(1-2).

451. **Assam Tribune** : 1988 : Tribal Guerrillas 'Out to disrupt' Tripura poll. *A.T.*, Jan. 4 : 4(1-2).

452. ——— : 1988 : Plan to deal with TNV extremists. *A.T.*, Jan. 6 : 1(1-3).

453. ——— : 1988 : Buta criticises Tripura Govt's comment. *A.T.*, Jan. 7 : 5(5-6).

454. ——— : 1988 : Reserved seats to play decisive role in Tripura. *A.T.*, Jan. 8 : 1(1-2).

455. ——— : 1988 : Poll campaign gains momentum in Tripura. *A.T.*, Jan. 9 : 7(3).

456. ——— : 1988 : Chittagong insurgency gaining momentum. *A.T., Jan. 11 : 1(1-4).*

457. ——— : 1988 : Security tightened in Tripura. *A.T.*, Jan. 14 : 6(1-2).

458. ——— : 1988 : Army deployed against TNV. *A.T.*, Jan. 17 : 1(1-3).

459. ——— : 1988 : Tight Security for Tripura Poll. *A.T.*, Jan. 21 : 1(3-5).

460. ——— : 1988 : Army to take over Tripura disturbed areas. *A.T.*, Jan. 28 : 1(4-7).

461. ——— : 1988 : P.M. lashes out at Tripura Govt. *A.T.*, Jan. 29 : 1(1-2).

462. ——— : 1988 : In Tripura : Deployment of armed forces ordéred. *A.T.*, Jan. 30 : 1(3), 8(4).

463. ——— : 1988 : 30 non-tribals killed in Tripura. *A.T.*, Jan. 31 : 1(2-4).

464. ——— : 1988 : 13 More killed by TNV rebels. *A.T.*, Feb. 2 : 1(1-3), 6(7).

465. ——— : 1988 : Record turn out of voters in Tripura. *A.T.*, Feb. 3 : 1(5-7).

466. ——— : 1988 : Ruling parties suffer set backs in Meghalaya, Tripura. *A.T.*, Feb. 4 : 1(5-8).

467. ——— : 1988 : Editorial : TNV depredations. *A.T.*, Feb. 4 : 4(1-2).

468. ——— : 1988 : Left front rule ends in Tripura. *A.T.*, Feb. 5 : 1(5-8).

469. **Assam Tribune** : 1988 : Counter offensives against TNV. *A.T.*, Feb. 11 : 1(5-6).

470. ——— : 1988 : Tripura Police Armoury sealed. *A.T.*, Feb. 11 : 1(5-7).

471. ——— : 1988 : Left Front was not defeated. *A.T.*, Feb. 12 : 3(6).

472. ——— : 1988 : Jamatia rules out dialogue with TNV. *A.T.*, Feb. 18 : 4(1-2).

473. ——— : 1988 : New Railway Lines in N-E Region. *A.T.*, Feb. 24 : 4(7-8).

474. ——— : 1988 : 14 Rifles received from TNV Gun Factory. *A.T.*, March 3 : 1(4-5).

475. ——— : 1988 : Tripura C.M's appeal to people. *A.T.*, March 8 : 5(3).

476. ——— : 1988 : Tripura Govt. terms for talks with TNV. *A.T.*, March 23 : 6(3-4).

477. ——— : 1988 : Centre urged to save Tripura's Tea Gardens. *A.T.*, March 30 : 6(6).

478. ——— : 1988 : Tripura Govt's Concern over Chakma Refugees. *A.T.*, April 19 : 5(2).

479. ——— : 1988 : Chakma refugees complete 2 years. *A.T.*, May 1 : 5(5-6).

480. ——— : 1988 : Dioscorea successfully introduced in Tripura. *A.T.*, May 3 : 3(3-4).

481. ——— : 1988 : Ershad's warning to Chakma tribals. *A.T.*, May 11 : 7(5-6).

482. ——— : 1988 : ZRV Enrolment drive launched. *A.T.*, June 15 : 7(1-2).

483. ——— : 1988 : Fresh Chakma influx into Tripura. *A.T.*, June 27 : 5(5).

484. ——— : 1988 : ONGC's exploration plan in Tripura. *A.T.*, July 9 : 6(5-6).

485. ——— : 1988 : Agartala to have railway link. *A.T.*, Aug. 8 : 7(1-2).

486. ——— : 1988 : Editorial : Accord of Peace. *A.T.*, Aug. 17 : 4(1-2).

487. **Assam Tribune** : 1988 : TNV to maintain separate identity. *A.T.*, Aug. 19 : 1(2-4) and 8(7).

488. ——— : 1988 : Evidence of Tripura in Stone Age. *A.T.*, Sept. 11 : 5(1-2).

489. ——— : 1988 : Editorial : Home coming in Tripura. *A.T.*, Sept. 15 : 4(1-2).

490. ——— : 1988 : P.M.'s 'Secret Pact' with TNV alleged. *A.T.*, Sept. 25 : 1(3-5).

491. ——— : 1988 : Centre wanted TNV to create tension. *A.T.*, Sept. 27 : 3(6-7).

492. ——— : 1988 : Tripura security act comes into effect. *A.T.*, Sept. 30 : 1(5-7).

493. ——— : 1988 : Hrangkhwal for economic revolution of Tribals. *A.T.*, Oct. 1 : 9(6-7).

494. ——— : 1988 : Tripura wants rail line to Agartala. *A.T.*, Oct. 1 : 11(3-4).

495. ——— : 1988 : 132 KV transmission line completed. *A.T.*, Oct. 16 : 6(4).

496. ——— : 1988 : Chakma refugees face uncertain future. *A.T.*, Nov. 8 : 7(1-4).

497. ——— : 1988 : Tripura to have second largest tunnel. *A.T.*, Nov. 26 : 7(6).

498. ——— : 1988 : Indo-Bangla talks on return of Chakmas. *A.T.*, Dec. 2 : 5(1-2).

499. ——— : 1988 : Tripura Govt. to set up methanol plant soon. *A.T.*, Dec. 8 : 6(4).

500. ——— : 1988 : TNV emerges as political party. *A.T.*, Dec. 12 : 6(2-3).

501. ——— : 1989 : Surrendered TNLF members are dacoits. *A.T.*, Feb. 7 : 6(5-6).

502. ——— : 1989 : Stalemate in ADC in Tripura. *A.T.*, Feb. 27 : 7(3-5).

503. ——— : 1989 : Tripura accord runs into rough weather. *A.T.*, March 7 : 3(1-2).

504. ——— : 1989 : TNV unhappy over delay in accord implementation. *A.T.*, March 9 : 6(7-8).

505. **Assam Tribune** : 1989 : Editorial : Danger to North East. *A.T.*, March 10 : 4(1-2).

506. ——— : 1989 : Helicopter service Centre considering Tripura Govts' proposal. *A.T.*, March 24 : 3(6).

507. ——— : 1989 : Tripura Mizos threaten Stir for regional Council. *A.T.*, March 27 : 1(8).

508. ——— : 1989 : What led to tribal unrest in Tripura. *A.T.*, April 4 : 3(4-5).

509. ——— : 1989 : Tripura lies in active seismic zone. *A.T.*, April 17 : 1(8).

510. ——— : 1989 : Polluted drinking water affects health in Tripura. *A.T.*, April 18 : 3(1-3).

511. ——— : 1989 : Concern at destruction of forest wealth. *A.T.*, April 18 : 3(6-7).

512. ——— : 1989 : Tripura CPI(M) supports Bodo autonomy. *A.T.*, April 19 : 1(4).

513. ——— : 1989 : Delay in land allotment hits rubber project. *A.T.*, April 24 : 6(4-6).

514. ——— : 1989 : More Chakma refugees entering Tripura. *A.T.*, May 17 : 5(3-6).

515. ——— : 1989 : Modalities for return of tribal refugees. *A.T.*, May 18 : 1(2-5).

516. ——— : 1989 : Trans-Border crimes on increase. *A.T.*, May 31 : 5(4-6).

517. ——— : 1989 : Chakma refugees demand Political settlement. *A.T.*, 3(3-4).

518. ——— : 1989 : Chakma influx to Gohpur Area. *A.T.*, June 5 : 5(3-4).

519. ——— : 1989 : Tripura farmers affected by drought. *A.T.*, June 6 : 6(1-3).

520. ——— : 1989 : Chakma leaders refuse to visit Chittagong. *A.T.*, June 8 : 3(3-4).

521. ——— : 1989 : 100 yr. old Tripura temple may not be raised. *A.T.*, June 15 : 6(1).

522. ——— : 1989 : Self sufficiency in rubber in three years possible. *A.T.*, June 18 : 7(1-3).

523. **Assam Tribune** : 1989 : Rubber cultivation picking up in N-E. *A.T.*, June 24 : 5(5-6).

524. ——— : 1989 : ONGC starts drilling in Tripura. *A.T.*, June 25 : 3(3-5).

525. ——— : 1989 : Buta Singh to visit Tripura. Chakma refugee's camps. *A.T.*, June 30 : 7(3-4).

526. ——— : 1989 : Memorandum to P.M. : TNV alleges 'Irregularities'. *A.T.*, July 13 : 3(3-5).

527. ——— : 1989 : Chakma issue : Centre urged to hold talks with Bangladesh. *A.T.*, July 13 : 5(4-5).

528. ——— : 1989 : Tripura CM criticises ADC's functioning. *A.T.*, July 21 : 5(1-3)

529. ——— : 1989 : Tripura Hopes self sufficiency in power. *A.T.*, July 24 : 3(3-5).

530. ——— : 1989 : NH 44 to be converted into double line. *A.T.*, Sept. 7 :1(1).

531. ——— : 1989 : Project dantak entrusted with widening of NH 44. *A.T.*, Sept. 10 : 3(4-5).

532. ——— : 1989 : Mizos in Tripura call for poll boycott. *A.T.*, Nov. 2 : 5(3).

533. ——— : 1989 : TNV dissatisfied with accord implementation. *A.T.*, Dec. 24 : 7(3).

534. ——— : 1989 : No hope of early repatriation of Chakmas. *A.T.*, Dec. 25 : 1(1-2), '(4).

535. ——— : 1990 : Fernandez to inaugurate 2 MG lines on January 3, 4. *A.T.*, January 2 : 1(2), 8(6).

536. ——— : 1990 : Centre urged to settle problem of Chakma refugees. *A.T.*, Jan. 13 : 7(5).

537. ——— : 1990 : Assam financial corporation (Joint SFC's : Assam, Meghalaya, Manipur and Tripura). *A.T.*, Jan. 20 : 5(1-8), 6(1-3).

538. ——— : 1990 : Tripura : CPM opposes demand for territory. *A.T.*, Feb. 6 : 2(7-8).

539. ——— : 1990 : Tribal refugees seek PM's intervention. *A.T.*, Feb. 7 : 5(2).

540. ——— : 1990 : Govt. proposes to issue Identity Cards to citizens: In Tripura. *A.T.*, Feb. 17 : 5(6-8).

541. **Assam Tribune** : 1990 : ONGC to invest Rs. 743-Cr. in Tripura. *A.T.*, Feb. 20 : 5(3).

542. ——— : 1990 : 437 TNV members rehabilitated. *A.T.*, March 3 : 5(1).

543. ——— : 1990 : Gas Turbine comes up in Tripura. *A.T.*, March 8 : 5(4).

544. ——— : 1990 : TUJS demands corruption-free Govt. *A.T.*, March 13 : 1(1-4).

545. ——— : 1990 : Deficit Budgets for Mizoram, Tripura, *A.T.*, March 20 : 1(1-4), 8(6-7).

546. ——— : 1990 : Seminar on Agrarian situation in North East. *A.T.*, March, 24 : 7(3). [*"Agrarian Structure and Land Relations in NE Region"*, organised by the National Institute of Rural Development, N.E. Regional Centre, Guwahati, 22nd March to 24th March, 1990].

547. ——— : 1990 : Concern over issue of citizenship certificates. *A.T.*, March 31 : 5(3-4).

548. ——— : 1990 : Cong(I) TUJS seat adjustment talk with TNV fail *A.T.*, May 5 : 1(1).

549. ——— : 1990 : Two killed in police firing in Tripura. *A.T.*, May 5 : 1(3).

550. ——— : 1990 : Armed men loot rifles from Tripura Police. *A.T.*, May 6 : 1(5-6).

551. ——— : 1990 : Advisory panels for development of Chakma language. *A.T.*, May 15 : 6(3).

552. ——— : 1990 : Tripura tribal students to launch movement. *A.T.*, May 21 : 3(3).

553. ——— : 1990 : Tripura Govt. to boost State tea industry. *A.T.*, June 5 : 5(3-4).

554. ——— : 1990 : Stalemate over use of gas in Tripura. *A.T.*, June 5 : 5(3-6).

555. ——— : 1990 : Rs. 13 Cr. Plan to widen Agartala airport. *A.T.*, July, 4 : 5(3-4).

556. ——— : 1990 : Alternative railway plan for Tripura. *A.T.*, July 27 : 3(5-7).

557. ——— : 1990 : In Tripura : Political Scenario may be tense this week. *A.T.*, July 31 : 2(7-8).

558. **Assam Tribune** : 1990 : Body formed to sort out TUJS-Cong(I) differences. *A.T.*, Aug. 4 : 5(7-8).

559. ——— : 1990 : Concern over influx of foreigners to Tripura. *A.T.*, Aug. 8 : 5(3-4).

560. ——— : 1990 : Tripura requests Centre to keep Para-Military forces. *A.T.*, Aug. 18 : 5(6-8).

561. ——— : 1990 : Tripura on threshold of Industrial take-off. *A.T.*, Aug. 22 : 3(1-3).

562. ——— : 1990 : Tripura's chasma bandars' migrating to Assam. *A.T.*, Aug. 28 : 5(4).

563. ——— : 1990 : ONGC "Too keen" to set up new project in Tripura. *A.T.*, Sept. 1 : 3(3-5).

564. ——— : 1990 : TUJS threatens to withdraw Ministers. *A.T.*, Sept. 6 : 3(3).

565. ——— : 1990 : No: threat to Cong (I)-TUJS relationship : Tripura CM. *A.T.*, Sept. 7 : 5(4-5).

566. ——— : 1990 : Ban on foreign tourists yet to be lifted. *A.T.*, Sept. 25 : 3(1-3).

567. ——— : 1990 : Volatile Political situation in Tripura. *A.T.*, Sept. 26 : 3(3-5).

568. ——— : 1990 : Tripura plans to revamp TTDC (i.e. Tripura Tea Development Corporation). *A.T.*, Oct. 6 : 5(4).

569. ——— : 1990 : Introduction of Inner-Line Regulation in N-E States urged *A.T.*, Oct. 12 : 3(1-4).

570. ——— : 1990 : Tripura News Letter : Cong(I)-TUJS relationship deteriorating. *A.T.*, Oct. 26 : 5(1-4).

571. ——— : 1990 : More employment to combat insurgency in N-E. *A.T.*, Nov. 3 : 3(5-6).

572. ——— : 1990 : Coins of Sultans of Bengal discovered. *A.T.*, Nov. 26 : 5(4).

573. ——— : 1990 : Tripura Govt. to issue I-Cards. *A.T.*, Nov. 30 : 6(5).

574. ——— : 1990 : Orange farming picking up in Tripura. *A.T.*, Dec. 3 : 5(4-6).

575. ——— : 1990 : Red alert along Assam-Tripura border. *A.T.*, Dec. 5 : 1(1).

576. **Assam Tribune** : 1990 : Rubber cultivation in North East picks up. *A.T.*, Dec. 10 : 5(4-5).

577. ——— : 1990 : Chakma camps' cupids. *A.T.*, Dec. 11 : 5(1-2).

578. ——— : 1990 : Spl. Forest protection force for Tripura. *A.T.*, Dec. 14 : 5(5).

579. ——— : 1990 : Tripura seeks Central Assistance. *A.T.*, Dec. 15 : 3(6-8).

580. ——— : 1990 : Smuggling in Indo-Bangla border increasing. *A.T.*, Dec. 16 : 5(5-6).

581. ——— : 1990 : Minimum wage for Tripura workers. *A.T.*, Dec. 16 : 3(3-4).

582. ——— : 1990 : International gang of smugglers active in Tripura. *A.T.*, Dec. 18 : 5(2-4).

583. ——— : 1990 : 'The Abode of Eternal Peace'. *A.T.*, Dec. 19 : 6(7-8).

584. ——— : 1990 : BSF asked to ignore influx—Tripura CPI(M). *A.T.*, Dec. 19 : 6(1-3).

585. ——— : 1990 : TNV's threat to launch movement. *A.T.*, Dec. 20 : 3(1-2).

586. ——— : 1990 : Unchecked infiltration 'A Major Issue in Tripura'. *A.T.*, Dec. 21 : 5(4-5).

587. ——— : 1990 : 30,000 Bangla Nationals pushed back from Tripura. *A.T.*, Dec. 23 : 1(2-3).

588. ——— : 1990 : Chakma refugees' want to return home. *A.T.*, Dec. 23 : 5(4).

589. ——— : 1990 : Tripura Tea : A Cindevella in Indian Tea Market. *A.T.*, Dec. 26 : 3 (3-5).

590. ——— : 1990 : Tripura to seek more forces to deal with ATTF. *A.T.*, Dec. 30 : 3(6-8).

591. ——— : 1991 : Schools in Tripura in doldrums. *A.T.*, Jan. 1 : 5(6-7).

592. ——— : 1991 : Steps to develop tourism in NE. *A.T.*, Jan. 2 : 1(1), 8(7).

593. ——— : 1991 : Ah! Jampui Hills, Thou Turning Barren. *A.T.*, Jan. 3 : 6(1-2).

594. Assam Tribune : 1991 : Rs. 11 Cr. agreed for airport expansion. *A.T.*, Jan. 6 : 6(6).

595. ——— : 1991 : Demand to identify foreigners in Tripura. *A.T.*, Jan. 7 : 5(3-4).

596. ——— : 1991 : Plea to extend Rly line upto Agartala. *A.T.*, Jan. 8 : 3(5-6).

597. ——— : 1991 : Tripura for 'free trade' with Bangladesh. *A.T.*, Jan. 8 : 5(4).

598. ——— : 1991 : Tripura CM orders action against ATTF. *A.T.*, Jan. 9 : 2(8).

599. ——— : 1991 : Insurgency in N-E increasing. *A.T.*, Jan. 17 : 1(1-3), 8(7-8).

600. ——— : 1991 : Plea to Tripura Governor. *A.T.*, Jan. 28: 5(4).

601. ——— : 1991 : Tripura Governor flays at 9th Finance Commission. *A.T.*, Jan. 30 : 3(3-5).

602. ——— : 1991 : Inner Line Permit in Tripura ADC urged. *A.T.*, Feb. 2 : 3(4-5).

603. ——— : 1991 : Chakmas asked to return home. *A.T.*, Feb. 18 : 1(5).

604. ——— : 1991 : TUJS demands early Panchayat Poll. *A.T.*, Feb. 27 : 5(1)

605. ——— : 1991 : Delhi in awkward situation over Chakma issue. *A.T.*, March 2 : 3(1-4).

606. ——— : 1991 : Cong(I) to forge alliance with TUJS. *A.T.*, March 15 : 5(4-5).

607. ——— : 1991 : 'No simultaneous poll in Tripura'. *A.T.*, March 23 : 3(6-8).

608. ——— : 1991 : Tripura to come under industrial map. *A.T.*, March 29 : 5(2-3).

609. ——— : 1991 : Tripura Govt. considering report on OBC. *A.T.*, April 2 : 3(6-8).

610. ——— : 1991 : TUJS to snap ties with Cong(I). *A.T.*, April 3 : 5(1-3).

611. ——— : 1991 : Good prospects for Coffee in N-E States. *A.T.*, April 7 : 2(1-2).

612. **Assam Tribune** : 1991 : Over 15,58 Lakh voters in Tripura. *A.T.*, April 9 : 2(6-8).

613. ——— : 1991 : RSP to support CPI(M) in Tripura. *A.T.*, April 10 : 3(8).

614. ——— : 1991 : Boost to tourism in NE likely. *A.T.*, April 10 : 3(4).

615. ——— : 1991 : CPI(M) to confront Cong(I) in Tripura. *A.T.*, April 10 : 3(3).

616. ——— : 1991 : Cong(I) in Tripura facing serious infighting. *A.T.*, April 11 : 5(6-8).

617. ——— : 1991 : Plea to stream line transport network in N-E Region. *A.T.*, April 11 : 3(3-5).

618. ——— : 1991 : Call for Poll boycott in Tripura. *A.T.*, April 14 : 5(7-8).

619. ——— : 1991 : Cong(I) TUJS to fight Tripura East (ST) seat. *A.T.*, April 15 : 2(4-5).

620. ——— : 1991 : Enterprises employ over 2 Lakh people in Tripura. *A.T.*, April 15 : 5(1-2).

621. ——— : 1991 : EC urged to hold parliamentary poll on May 20. *A.T.*, April 15 : 5(6).

622. ——— : 1991 : TNV to put candidate for East Tripura seat. *A.T.*, April 18 : 3(1-2).

623. ——— : 1991 : Tripura may witness fight between Cong(I), CPI(M). *A.T.*, April 19 : 5(1-2).

624. ——— : 1991 : Demographic Balance in N-E States "Unprecedented". *A.T.*, April 22 : 3(3-5).

625. ——— : 1991 : TUJS concern over ATTF activities. *A.T.*, April 25 : 3(1).

626. ——— : 1991 : TUJS member shot dead. *A.T.*, April 26: 1(8).

627. ——— : 1991 : Tripura fears violence during poll. *A.T.*, April 27 : 3(1-4).

628. ——— : 1991 : BJP likely to make dent in Tripura. *A.T.*, April 27 : 6(7-8).

629. ——— : 1991 :Tripura Government against Disturbed Areas Act. *A.T.*, May 1 : 3(3).

630. **Assam Tribune** : 1991 : Tripura Maharani in electoral battle. *A.T.*, May 4 : 5(6-7).

631. ——— : 1991 : 12 Tripura Cong-I workers hurt. *A.T.*, May 7 : 8(4).

632. ——— : 1991 : Tripura poised for "rapid growth". *A.T.*, May 7 : 3(4-5).

633. ——— : 1991 : Forest protection force to be set up in Tripura. *A.T.*, May 8 : 3(4).

634. ——— : 1991 : Rs. 20 Cr. aid for Tripura urged. *A.T.*, May 8 : 3(6).

635. ——— : 1991 : Tripura to come under Industrial Map. *A.T.*, May 29 : 5(2-3).

636. ——— : 1991 : Tripura opposition worried over ATTF's treat. *A.T.*, June 11 : 3(1-3).

637. ——— : 1991 : Tripura goes to poll tomorrow. *A.T.*, June 11 : 3 (4-5).

638. ——— : 1991 : Cong-I Hopeful of getting 'walkover' in Tripura. *A.T.*, June 11 : 3(5-8).

639. ——— : 1991 : Centre to send more forces to Tripura. *A.T.*, July 5 : 5(2).

640. ——— : 1991 : Steel plant in Tripura likely. *A.T.*, July 23 : 3(6).

641. ——— : 1991 : Tripura thermal project shelved. *A.T.*, Aug. 7 : 3(4-6).

642. ——— : 1991 : Dissidence in Tripura Congress takes new turn. *A.T.*, Aug. 7 : 5(3-4).

643. ——— : 1991 : Tripura worried over rise in influx. *A.T.*, Aug. 9 : 3(3-5).

644. ——— : 1991 : ULFA's plan to help ATTF (i.e. All Tripura Tribal Front). *A.T.*, Aug. 11 : 1(1-2), 2(8).

645. **Asthana, A.N.** *et al (Eds.)* : 1981 : *Proceedings of workshop on Agricultural Research in North Eastern Hill Region.* Shillong, ICAR Research Complex for NEHR (1980) [The other editors are S.P. Ghosh, PSRC Murti, R.N. Verma].

B

646. **Bagchi, D.P.** : 1979 : Role of farming and forestry. *Economic Times*, Jan. 5 : 5(1).

647. **Baidya, Ashish Kumar** : 1985 : Pilak civilization of Tripura. *Proceedings of NEIHA* (Agartala), No. 6 : 48-50.

648. **Balfour, Edward** : 1976 : *Encyclopaedia Asiatica.* New Delhi, Cosmo Publications *(Reprinted).*

649. **Bali, Surya Kanta** : 1987 : Kayen lorti hai purbachal ki Sat bahanen! *Nava Bharat Times*, Nov. 7 : 4(3-6).

650. ——— : 1988 : Tripura ke bahane bichardhara par bahas. *N.B.T.* Feb. 13 : 4(3-6).

651. **Bandopadhyaya, Amiya Kumar** : ? : *Desheya Rajyae Praja-Andolane Tripura.* : 236-44.

652. **Bandapadhyay, Asit Kumar** : ? : *Bangla Sahitter Itibrittya* (3rd Part) 2nd Chapter, (XIIth Section) : 1226-1229 *(Rajmala).*

653. **Bandopadhyay, Bibhuti Bhusan** : ? : *Abhijatrik* : 96-107 (Tripura).

654. **Bandopadhya, Brajendra Nath** : ? : *Sangbad Patro Sekaler Katha* : 241, 273-74, 270-71.

655. **Bandopadhyaya, Jagadis** : 1975 : Shikhya Prasange Tripura *(In) Tripura Prasanga (Ed)* by Swapan Sengupta *(in Bengali)* Agartala, Directorate of Public Relations and Tourism : 148-68.

656. **Bandopadhyay, P.K.** : 1980 : Book Review : Tripura, the land and its people Edited by Jagadish Gan Chowdhury, Published by Leeladevi Publications. Delhi, Pp.186, Price Rs. 60/- *Jr. NEICSSR*, IV(II), Oct. : 26-7.

657. **Bandopadhyay, Rakhal Das** : ? : *Banglar Itihas (Ist Part)* : 8, 39, 90, 96, 108.

658. **Bandopadhyay, Rakhal Das** : ? : *Banglar Itihas (2nd Part)* : 52, 53, 57, 112, 150, 180, 225, 217.

659. **Bandopadhaya, Suprasanna** : 1982 : *Tripurar Itihas* (Sachitra). Calcutta, Firms KLM Pvt. Ltd *(in Bengali).*

660. ——— : 1954 : *Itihas ashrita Bangla Kabita* : 11, 19, 20, 22, 23, 24, 25, 89, 90, 92, 94, 95, 99, 100, 101, 102, 104, 105, 106, 107, 111, 112, 113, 114, 116, 117, 118.

661. ——— : 1965 : A Tripuri folktale. *Folklore,* VI(8), August : 337-40.

662. ——— : 1967 : Bride in exchange of a fly : A Tripuri folktale. *Folklore,* 8 : 63-4, 58.

663. ——— *(Ed.)* : 1971 : *Tripura State Gazette Sankalan.* Agartala, Directorate of Education, Govt. of Tripura.

664. ——— : 1975 : Bangla Godyer Krama Vikase Tripurar Abadan, *(In) Tripura Prasanga, (Ed)* by Swapan Sengupta. Agartala, Directorate of Pub. Rel. and Tourism: 1-4 *(in Bengali).*

665. **Banerji, Adris** : 1968 : *Temples of Tripura.* Varanasi, Prithivi Prakashan, 22 p.

666. **Banerjee, Anil Chandra** : 1946 : *Eastern Frontier of British India, 1784-1826.* Calcutta, M. Mukherjee & Co. : 34-42.

667. **Banerjee, Asis** *and* **Das Gupta, Malabika** : 1984 : Shifting the location jhumia villages in Tripura : An empirical study. *Man in India.* 64(4), Dec. : 362-68.

668. ——— : 1984 : Jhuming as a way of life of the Jhumias : An Analysis of data from Tripura. *Jr. NEICSSR,* 8(1), April : 17-25.

669. **Banerjee, Asis, Das Gupta, Malabika** *and* **Roy Omkar Prasad** : 1986 : The Importance of forests in the Economic Life of the Jhumias of Tripura, *(In) Forestry Development in North East India, (Eds).* by Malabika Das Gupta et al. Guwahati, Omsons Publications : 23-30.

670. **Banerjee, Haripada** : 1360 TE : *Tripura-Raj-Kuhini.* Agartala *(Unpublished).*

671. **Banerjee, N.K.** : 1972 : An appraisal of shifting cultivation in India, *(In) Agro Economic Problems of Tribal*

India by M.L. Patel. Delhi, Bhopal Progress Pubs. : 105-16.

672. **Banerjee, R.D.** : 1917 : *Annual Report, 1913-14*. New Delhi, Archaeological Survey of India. Manager of Publications: 249-53. (Notes on Indian numismatics, dealing with Tripura coins).

673. **Banerjee, Sivadas** : 1981 : Poll prospects in Tripura-II. *Times of India*, July 27.

674. ——— : 1981 : Tripura presents no clear picture. *T.O.I.*, July 28.

675. **Banerjee, Uttam** : 1988 : Letters to the Editor : How TNV helped Congress (I). *Statesman*, Feb. 14 : 8(6).

676. **Bangiya Sahitya Parishad** : ? : *Bharatkosh* (3rd Part) : 759-60 (Tripura).

677. **Bangiya Sahitya Parishad** : ? : *Bharakosh* (1st Part). Agartala, 212 p.

678. **Bank of India** : 1972 : *Industrial potential Surveys of Arunachal Pradesh, Assam, Manipur, Nagaland and Tripura*. Bombay, Industrial Development, Bank of India.

679. **Bapat, N.V.** : 1967 : The social worker in border area. *Vanyajati*, 15 : 3, 127-30.

680. **Barbe, M.** : 1845 : Some account of the Hill tribes in the interior of the District of Chittagong, in a letter to the Secretary of the Asiatic Society. *Jr. Asiatic Society of Bengal*, 14, pt. I : 380-91.

681. **Bardoloi, Gopal** : 1986 : *Economy of North-East India : A Statewise analysis*-Guwahati, LBS Publications.

682. **Bareh, Hamlet** : 1967 : Patterns of Economic enterprises in the Hill areas of North East India, *(In) A Common Perspective for North East India, (Eds)* by Rathin Mitra *and* B. Das Gupta. Calcutta, Pannalal Das Gupta : 223-31.

683. **Baresh, Meyer** : 1967 : The concept of a 'Tribe' in East Pakistan: The case of the Chakma of the Chittagong Hill Tracts. *(In) Abstract, American Anthropological Association, 66th Annual Meeting*.

684. **Barkataki, S.** *(Ed.)*: 1969 : Tripura *(In) Tribes of Assam, (Ed)* by S. Barkataki. New Delhi, National Book Trust (India) : 156-59.

685. **Barkataki, S.N.** : 1982 : *Tribal Folk Tales of Assam (Hills).* Gauhati, Publication Board, Assam (1970, *reprinted* in 1982) : 244 (Lushai).

686. **Barman, Satya Bhusan** : 1979 : *Interim report.* Agartala, Govt. of Tripura.

687. **Barooah, S.R.** : 1990 : Letters to the Editor : Railways in NE Region. *Assam Tribune,* Feb. 17 : 4 (3-4) (Tripura).

688. **Barthakur, D.N.** : 1985 : Development of Human Resources for Agriculture and allied sectors in the N.E.H. Region, *(In) Planning in North East India, (Ed)* by K. Alam. New Delhi, Omsons Publications : 33-46 (Tripura).

689. **Barthakur, D.N., Awasthi, R.P.** *and* **Ghosh, S.P.** : 1976 : Alternative system of farming for increasing productivity in *jhum* lands. Proceedings of a Seminar on *"Socio Economic Problems of the Shifting Cultivation in the North East India" NEICSSR, Shillong (Mimeo.)*

690. **Barthakur, J.K.** : 1967 : A Note on the agricultural background of the Assam Hills. *(In) a Common Perspective for North East India, (Eds)* by R. Mitra *and* B. Das Gupta. Calcutta, Pannalal Das Gupta : 194-99.

691. **Barthakur, M.** : 1985 : Formation of Planning and development strategies for N.E. India : The land of seven sisters, *(In) Planning in North East India, (Ed.)* by K. Alam. New Delhi, Omsons Pubs : 260-67.

692. **Barthakur, P.B.** : 1987 : Trouks in Tripura. *Shillong Times,* Feb. 7 : 2 (3-5), 5(1).

693. ——— : 1987 : Insurgency galore in N.E. *Shillong Times,* Nov. 28 : 2(3-6).

694. ——— : 1990 : North East is a volcano. *Shillong Times,* July 30 : 2(3-6), 3(1-3).

695. **Barua, B.P.** : 1973 : *British relation with Hill Tippera and Chittagong Hill Tribes*. Ph.D. Thesis, Calcutta University (*Unpublished*).

696. **Baruah, J.N.** : 1991 : Scientific innovations in North-East. *Assam Tribune*, April 24 : 4(3-6), 6(7-8).

697. **Barua, P.C.** (*Ed.*) : 1990 : *Development planning of North-East India : Agricultural, Economic, Environmental, Financial, Industrial, Manpower and Rural*. New Delhi, Mittal Publications.

698. **Basak, Hariganga** : 1956 : Tripura Rajya Praja Andolaner itikatha (History of the Praja Movement in Tripura). *Samaj*, 3(31), Independence No., Aug. 15.

699. **Baska, R.G.** : 1920 : Tippera copper-plate of Lokanatha. *Epigraphia Indica, XV (19), 301-15.*

700. ——— : 1967 : *History of North Eastern India*. Calcutta, Sambodhi Publication, 432 p.

701. **Basu, Amitabha, Majumder, Partha P., Ghosh, Aloke K.** *and* **Biswas, Suhas K.** : 1980 : Human Biological variations in Asia, with special reference to India, *(In) La Diversite Biologique humaine : Human Biological Diversity, (Eds)* by A. Basu *et al.* Paris, Masson : 197-273.

702. **Basu, A.** : 1978 : *Report on shifting cultivation on Mizoram and Tripura*. Report submitted to Anthropological Survey of India, Shillong *(Unpublished)*.

703. **Basu, Arati** : 1981 : *Shifting cultivation in Tripura*. Seminar of Anthropological Survey of India, Calcutta, 18p *(Mimeo)*.

704. **Basu, Ashish** : 1968 : Tripura and its village industry. *Khadi Gramodyog*, 14(4), Jan. : 354-56.

705. **Basu, Girindra Shekhar** : ? : *Puran Prabesh* (Tripura) : 235.

706. **Basu, Mirendra Nath** : 1957 : The dance among the Koms of Manipur. *Indian Folklore*, 2(2), Oct-Dec. : 9-10.

707. **Basu, Nagendra Nath** : ? : *Viswakosh* (8th part) : 195-215 (Parbatta Tripura).

708. ——— : ? : *Viswakosha* (22nd Part) : 529 p.

709. **Basu, Provash Chandra** : 1931 : The Social and Religious Ceremonies of the Chakmas. *Jr. and Proceedings of the Asiatic Society of Bengal, N.S.,* vol. 27(2) : 213-223.

710. **Basu, Salil Kumar** : 1959 : Finger dermatoglyphic study of the Riangs of Tripura. *Jr. Asiatic Society,* 1(2) : 161-68.

711. ——— : 1960 : A Note on the Simian crease of the Riangs of Tripura. *Science and Culture* (Calcutta), 26, July.

712. **Basumatari, K.K.** : 1984 : Letters to the Editor : "Army presence in Tripura : Other side of the shield." *Shillong Times,* Oct. 20 : 2(3-5).

713. **Bechert, Heinz** : 1968 : Contemporary Buddhism in Bengal and Tripura. *Educational Miscellany,* 4(3-4), Dec. 1967-March 1968: 37-50.

714. **Beg, Hamdi** : 1987 : Bringing Tripura gas to Calcutta. *Amrita Bazar Patrika,* Aug. 24 : 6(7-8).

715. **Bengal Census** : 1896 : *Report on the Census of the District of Tripura.* Calcutta, 33 p.

716. **Bengal District Gazetteer** : 1914 : *Tippera District (Statistics, 1900-1901 to 1910-1911).* Calcutta, The Bengal.

717. **Beshart, Heinz** : 1975 : Samasamayik Boudha Dharma : Bangla O Tripuraye *(In) Tripura Prasanga (Ed.)* by Swapan Sengupta. Agartala, Direc. of Pub. Rel. and Tourism : 51-6. *(in Bengali).*

718. **Bessaignet, Peirre** : 1909 : Chakma Circle. *(In) Gazetteer : Chittagong Hill Tracts.* Dacca, Govt. Press, 15 p.

719. **Besseignet, P.** : 1958 : *Tribesmen of the Chittagong Hill Tracts.* Dacca, Asiatic Society of Pakistan, 109 p. (Tripura).

720. **Bez Baruah, R.N.** : 1982 : Anti Jhumming measures in the North East. *Himalaya : Man and Nature,* 5(6), Nov. : 13-4.

721. **Bhadra, Gautam** : 1975 : The Kuki (?) uprising (1917-1919) : Its cause and nature. *Man in India,* 55(1) : 10-56.

722. **Bhadra, R.K.** : 1975 : Indian Tribes and their modernisation. *North Eastern Research Bulletin,* VI, Summer : 41-50.

723. **Bhagabati, A.C.** : 1981 : Some aspects of emergent tribal identity in North East India. *Bulletin Deptt. of Anthropology, Dibrugarh University* , vol. 7-8, 1978-'79 : 78-95.

724. **Bhardwaj, Gopal** : 1977 : Socio-Political Movements Among the Tribes of India. *(In) Tribal Heritage of India, vol. I : Ethnicity, Identity and Interaction, (Ed)* by S.C. Dube. New Delhi, Vikas Pubg. House : 152-54.

725. **Bhat, S.** : 1975 : *The Challenge of the North East.* Bombay, Popular Prakashan : 54-6, 57-61.

726. **Bhattacharjee, Amit** : 1990 : Bengali script for Kokbarak language demanded. *Amrita Bazar Patrika,* Dec. 11 : 7(2-5).

727. **Bhattacharyya, Angsu Narayan** : 1988 : Letters to the Editor : How TNV helped Congress(I). *Statesman* (Calcutta), Feb. 14 : 8(4-5).

728. **Bhattacharjee, Anil** : 1974 : Tribal youths demand fair deal : Movements in Tripura. *Am.Baz.Pat.,* Nov. 18.

729. ——— : 1986 : Huge backlog of court cases in Tripura. *Am.Baz.Pat.,* Feb. 5 : 7(2-7).

730. ——— : 1986 : Extremists active in South Tripura District. *Am.Baz.Pat.,* March 7 : 7(2-4).

731. ——— : 1986 : Tribal Infiltration continued. *Am.Baz.Pat.,* June 3 : 7(1-4).

732. ——— : 1986 : Harrowing tales of tribal migrants. *Am.Baz.Pat.,* July 21 : 7(2-6) (Chakma Refugee of Tripura).

733. **Bhattacharjee, Anil** : 1986 : Gory massacres by TNV desperados. *Am.Baz.Pat.,* Sept. 20 : 7(1-5).

734. ——— : 1986 : TNV men to surrender soon. *Times of India,* Oct, 15 : 7(1-3).

735. ——— : 1986 : Bangladesh 'supporting' TNV. *Times of India,* Dec. 1 : 4(1-3).

736. **Bhattacharjee, Anil** : 1986 : TNV guerrillas gun down 13. *Am.Baz.Pat.*, Dec. 6 : 1(7-8), 10(4-5).

737. ——— : 1986 : Fear psychosis in Tripura. *Am.Baz.Pat.*, Dec. 19 : 7(2-5)

738. ——— : 1987 : What made Tripura CM change stand on TNV. *Am.Baz.Pat.*, March 4 : 7(1-4).

739. ——— : 1987 : BRO's tough job in N-E. *Am.Baz.Pat.*, April 24 : 7(1-3) (Border Road Organisation).

740. ——— : 1987 : Chakma Influx. *Am.Baz.Pat.*, April 26 : 7(1-6).

741. ——— : 1987 : Tripura Engineering College in bad shape. *Am.Baz.Pat.*, May 3 : 7(1-2).

742. ——— : 1987 : Chaos in Tripura Congress. *Am.Baz.Pat.*, May 15 : 7(1-3).

743. ——— : 1987 : Staggering loss in Tripura Jute Mill. *Am.Baz.Pat.*, May 23 : 3(1-2).

744. ——— : 1987 : Acute food shortage in Tripura. *Am.Baz.Pat.*, May 27 : 7(4-6).

745. ——— : 1987 : CPM wooing Tripura tribals. *Am.Baz.Pat.*, June 21 : 7(1-6).

746. ——— : 1987 : Tripura gearing up for election. *Am.Baz.Pat.*, July 7 : 7(6-8).

747. ——— : 1987 : Tripura fights malaria. *Am. Baz. Pat.*, Aug. 14:7 (3-5).

748. ——— : 1987 : Lottery scandal shakes Tripura Assembly. *Am.Baz.Pat.*, Aug. 30 : 5(5-7).

749. ——— : 1987 : National party gains popularity over regionalism in N-E India. *Am.Baz.Pat.*, Dec. 9 : 7(4-5).

750. ——— : 1988 : BSF accused of polling with TNV. *Am.Baz.Pat.*, Jan. 29 : 7(1-5).

751. ——— : 1988 : Tripura CPI(M) questions validity of commission. *Am.Baz.Pat.*, March 30 : 7(1-4).

752. ——— : 1988 : 'Reign of terror' in Tripura. *Am.Baz.Pat.*, Sept. 8 : 7(1-3).

753. ——— : 1988 : Hrangkhawl in a tight spot. *Am.Baz.Pat.*, Oct. 10 : 7(5-6).

754. **Bhattacharjee, Anil** : 1988 : Tripura killings a glaring case of police apathy. *Am.Baz.Pat.*, Oct. 17 : 7(1-3).

755. ——— : 1988 : Border problems plague Tripura. *Am.Baz.Pat.*, Dec. 2 : 7(2-4).

756. ——— : 1988 : Chakma terms impending solution of CHT problem. *Am.Baz.Pat.*, Dec. 4 : 7(2-3).

757. ——— : 1988 : "Congress(I) violating peace accord" Hrangkhawl. *Am.Baz.Pat.*, Dec. 23 : 7(1-3).

758. ——— : 1988 : Large-scale smuggling, inflitration along Tripura border. *Am.Baz.Pat.*, Dec. 28 : 7(1-3).

759. ——— : 1989 : Discord in Tripura coalition. *Am.Baz.Pat.*, Jan. 9 : 7(1-3).

760. ——— : 1989 : Tripura facing big budget deficit. *Am.Baz.Pat.*, Jan. 19 : 7(5-6).

761. ——— : 1989 : Hrangkhawl trying to stage a comeback. *Am.Baz.Pat.*, Jan. 24 : 7(5-6).

762. ——— : 1989 : Congress ignoring tribals' interest : Alleges TUJS. *Am.Baz.Pat.*, Feb. 16 : 7(1-3).

763. ——— : 1989 : Mizo tribals in Tripura demand separate council. *Am.Baz.Pat.*, Feb. 22 : 7(4-5).

764. ——— : 1989 : Railway line being extended in Tripura. *Am.Baz.Pat.*, March 2 : 7(6).

765. ——— : 1989 : Majority of tribals in ADC areas going down. *Am.Baz.Pat.*, March 5 : 7(1).

766. ———: 1989 : Tripura Government, autonomous council trade changes. *Am.Baz.Pat.*, March 9 : 7(2-4).

767. ——— : 1989 : Tripura fears it won't get aid from Centre. *Am.Baz.Pat.*, Dec. 9 : 7(5-7).

768. ——— : 1989 : Plan expenditure in Tripura to be curtailed. *Am.Baz.Pat.*, Dec. 18 : 10(7-8).

769. ——— : 1989 : Tripura initiates process to send back tribal refugees. *Am.Baz.Pat.*, Dec. 20 : 7(1-4).

770. ——— : 1989 : Tripura tense over clashes between CPI(M), Cong(I). *Am.Baz.Pat.*, Dec. 30 : 7(1-3).

771. ——— : 1990 : All parties demand end to infiltration in Tripura. *Am.Baz.Pat.*, Feb. 11 : 7(1-4).

772. **Bhattacharjee, Anil** : 1990 : Tripura urges centre to fix gas price. *Am.Baz.Pat.*, Feb. 17 : 9(3-6).

773. ——— : 1990 : Campus beat : Education in Tripura in a State of crisis. *Am.Baz.Pat.*, Feb. 20 : 9(1-5).

774. ——— : 1990 : Tripura politics turning complex. *Am.Baz.Pat.*, March 7 : 8(4-7).

775. ——— : 1990 : Gas leak from Tripura drill site continues. *Am.Baz.Pat.*, March 16 : 7(4).

776. ——— : 1990 : Tripura minister's move against CM falls flat. *Am.Baz.Pat.*, April 3 : 7(1-3).

777. ——— : 1990 : Solar energy project success in Tripura. *Am.Baz.Pat.*, April 12 : 7(3).

778. ——— : 1990 : Tripura official denies report on Chakma. *Am.Baz.Pat.*, April 24 : 6(1-2).

779. ——— : 1990 : ADC election now at centre of Tripura politics. *Am.Baz.Pat.*, May 5 : 11(2-4).

780. ——— : 1990 : School burning a regular feature in Tripura. *Am.Baz.Pat.*, May 11 : 8(7-8).

781. ——— : 1990 : Tripura Mizos demand regional council. *Am.Baz.Pat.*, May 16 : 7(2).

782. ——— : 1990 : Tripura ADC poll on July 8 will be crucial. *Am.Baz.Pat.*, June 12 : 8(6-8).

783. ——— : 1990 : Tripura telecom services in disarray. *Am.Baz.Pat.*, July 1 : 5(3).

784. ——— : 1990 : ADC polls boost morale of Cong-TUJS alliance. *Am.Baz.Pat.*, July 19 : 5(6-8).

785. ——— : 1990 : Tripura Govt's threat to launch stir. *Am.Baz.Pat.*, Aug. 8 : 5(2-4).

786. ——— : 1990 : Tripura farmers in distress. *Am.Baz.Pat.*, Sept. 8 : 5(4).

787. ——— : 1990 : Centre obstructing Tripura's development. *Am.Baz.Pat.*, Sept. 9 : 7(2-3).

788. ——— : 1990 : Tripura CPI(M) a divided lot. *Am.Baz.Pat.*, Sept. 11 : 7(1).

789. ——— : 1990 : Differences widen in Tripura CPI(M). *Am.Baz.Pat.*, Sept. 22 : 5(1-4).

790. **Bhattacharjee, Anil** : 1990 : Essentials cost 30 p.c. more in Tripura. *Am.Baz.Pat.*, Sept. 22 : 5(6-7).

791. ——— : 1990 : Govt. leadership change, now the talk of Tripura. *Am.Baz.Pat.*, Oct. 6 : 7(1-3).

792. ——— : 1990 : Tripura to have second battalion of State Rifles. *Am.Baz.Pat.*, Oct. 6 : 7(2-3).

793. ——— : 1990 : Discontent in ADC over Cong-TUJS roll brewing. *Am.Baz.Pat.*, Oct. 13 : 7(6-8).

794. ——— : 1990 : Tripura spends much on security for politicians. *Am.Baz.Pat.*, Oct. 21 : 7(1-2).

795. ——— : 1990 : Cong-TUJS talks on memorandum inconclusive. *Am.Baz.Pat.*, Oct. 31 : 7(6- 8).

796. ——— : 1990 : Drive against infiltration in Tripura. *Am.Baz.Pat.*, Oct. 31 : 5(5-6).

797. ——— : 1990 : Chakma cause. *Am.Baz.Pat.*, Dec. 5 : 7(2-4).

798. ——— : 1990 : Refugees in Tripura hail Ershad ouster. *Am.Baz.Pat.*, Dec. 12 : 5(1-4).

799. **Bhattacharya, Anil Chandra** : 1975 : Tripuray Bangla Natyacharcha, *(In) Tripura Prasanga (Ed)* by Swapan Sengupta. Agartala, Directorate of Pub. Rel. and Tourism : 29-45 *(in Bengali).*

800. **Bhattacharjee, Apurbachandra** : C 1930 : *Progressive Tripura.* Calcutta, the author, 114 p (*Reprinted* in 1985 by Inter India Pubs., New Delhi, 114 p.).

801. **Bhattacharyya, Asit Ranjan** : 1981 : *Panchayati Raj in Tripura with special reference to Panisagar Community Development Area.* Ph.D. Thesis, G.U. *(unpublished).*

802. **Bhattacharyya, A.K.** : 1971 : *Census of India 1971, Tripura series 30, paper No. 1, Provisional Population Totals.* Agartala, Directorate of Census, 19 p.

803. ——— : 1973 : *Census of India 1971, Tripura : A Portrait of Population.* Agartala, Directorate of Census Operation, 260 p.

804. ———: 1973 : *Census of India 1971, Tripura, part II-A, General Population Table.* Agartala, Dir. of Cen. Ope. Tripura.

805. **Bhattacharyya, A.K.** : 1973 : *Census of India 1971, Tripura, part II-C(i) Social and Cultural Tables.* Agartala, Dir. of Cen. Ope. Tripura, 165p.

806. ——— : 1973 : *Census of India 1971, series 20, Tripura part X-A&B : District Census Handbook (West Tripura District).* Agartala, Dir. of Cen. Ope. Tripura.

807. ——— : 1973 : *Census of India 1971, series 20, Tripura, part X-A&B: District Census Handbook (South Tripura District).* Agartala, Dir. of Cen. Ope. Tripura.

808. ——— : 1973 : *Census of India 1971, series 20, Tripura, part X-A&B: District Census Handbook (North Tripura District).* Agartala, Dir. of Census Ope. Tripura.

809. ——— *(Ed.)* : 1973 : *India, Census 1971, Tripura, pt. III : Establishments Reports and Tables.* Delhi, Controller of Pubs, 485p.

810. ——— : 1976 : *India, Census 1971- Tripura II-(i) C-Social and Cultural Tables and Part V-A- Special Tables on Scheduled Castes and Scheduled Tribes.* Delhi, Manager of Pubs., 139p.

811. ——— : 1977 : *Census of India 1971, India, Pt. I-A: General Report, Tripura.* Delhi, Controller of Pubs., 182p.

812. **Bhattacharyya, B.** : 1978 : Political Development in Tripura. *(In) North East India : A Sociological Study, (Ed.)* by S.M. Dubey, Delhi, Concept Pub. Company : 245-59.

813. **Bhattacharjee, Banga Chandra** : 1897 : *Letter from Babu Banga Chandra Bhattacharjee,* Officer-in-Charge, Political Department, Agartala, to the Political Agent of the Hill Tipperah, No. 140-111-88, dated Agartala, the 1st Dec. 1897.

814. ——— : 1897 : (?) : *Arya Jatir Utpatti O Deergha Prayan* : 187 (i.e. Jahhur Uttarbartigan dwara Tripura Rajyer Bhitti Sthapan).

815. **Bhattacharjee, Bani Kanta** : 1980 : Patterns of Administrative Organisation, *(In) Tripura : The Land and its People, (Ed.)* by Jagadis Gan Choudhuri, Delhi, Leeladevi Publications : 44-54.

816. **Bhattacharjee, Bani Kanta** : 1984 : Tripura : Progress and Problems since Independence. *Himalaya : Man and Nature*, VIII(4), Sept : 15-6.

817. ——— : 1985 : Tripura : Maharaja and his subjects. *Proceedings of NEIHA*, (Agartala), No. 6 : 265-70.

818. ——— : 1986 : *Tripura Administration : The era of modernisation (1870-1972)*. Delhi, Mittal Publications, 328p.

819. **Bhattacharyya, Buddhadev** : ? : *Himalayer Tin Sangee*. Calcutta, Asia Pub. House : 1-96 (Tripura).

820. **Bhattacharjee, C.R.** : 1986 : Tripura looks up to prospect of gas based power. *Economy and Business Review of Am.Baz.Pat. Suppliment* : 7(1-3).

821. **Bhattacharjee, Dinesh Chandra** : 1938 : Swadhin Tripura Rajmala. *Prabasi* (Calcutta), Falgoon, 1345B.S.

822. **Bhattacharyya, Gayatri** : 1981 : *Impact of refugee rehabilitation on Tripura's economy*. Ph.D. Thesis, Calcutta University *(Unpublished)*.

823. ——— : 1985 : Refugee Rehabiltiaiton, *(In) An Anthology of Tripura (Ed.)* by Jagadis Gan Choudhuri. New Delhi, Inter-India Pubs : 45-50.

824. ——— : 1988 : *Refugee Rehabilitation and its Impact on Tripura's Economy*. Delhi, Omson Publications, 175p.

825. **Bhattacharyya, H.** : 1989 : *Communism in Tripura up to 1965. Unpublished* Ph.D. Thesis, University of London.

826. ——— : 1989 : The Emergence of Tripuri Nationalism. *Economic and Political Weekly*.

827. **Bhattacharyya, Harihar** : 1990 : Communism, Nationalism and Tribal Question in Tripura. *Eco. and Pol. Weekly*, XXV(39), Sept. 29.

828. ——— : 1990 : *Communism, Nationalism and Tribal Question in Tripura*. Proceedings of Seminar, Deptt. of Pol. Sc., University of Burdwan, West Bengal, January 6, 1990.

829. **Bhattacharjee, Ila** : 1986 : Uprisings of Tribal Women in Tripura, *(In) Tribes of Tripura, (Ed.)* by Sudhanshu Bikash Saha. Agartala, Rupali Book Store : 128-32.

830. **Bhattacharjee, J.B.** : 1977 : *Cachar under the British Rule in North East India.* New Delhi, Radiant Publishers (also about Tripura).

831. **Bhattacharjee, J.B.** : 1982 : Tripura state formation in Medieval Tripura. *Proceedings of NEIHA* (Imphal), No. 3 : 57-72.

832. ——— *(Ed.)* : 1982 : *Social Tension in North East India.* Calcutta, Research India Publications.

833. ——— *(Ed.) : 1985 : Proceedings of the North East India History Association,* Session VI. Agartala, NEIHA, 542p.

834. ——— : 1988 : Physical divisions and cultural zones in North East India : A brief outline *(In) National Seminar on "The Archaeology of North East India",* Oct. 26-28, 1988 *(Ed.)* by Jai Prakash Singh. Shillong, Deptt. of History, NEHU *(Mimeo.).*

835. **Bhattacharya, Jogendra Nath** : 1896 : Kahar. Calcutta, *Hindu Castes and Sects* : 310-11(Sch. Caste of Tripura).

836. **Bhattacharya, K.K.** : 1970 : *Tripura : A select and annotated bibliography on Tripura.* Agartala, Tripura Library Association, 33p.

837. **Bhattacharyya, Nossiter** : 1988 : *Communism in a Micro State : Marxist State Government.* 164p.

838. **Bhattacharyya, N.N.** : 1989 : Viability of the States of North East India. *Jr. NEICSSR,* 13(1), April : 1-4.

839. **Bhattacharyya, Nossiter** *and* **Bhattacharyya, H.** : 1989 : The Emergence of Tripuri Nationalism, 1948-'50 *(In) South Asia Research* (London), 9(1), May.

840. **Bhattacharyya, Padmanath** : ? : *Kamrup shashanabali* (5th part). Gauhati, Deptt. of Historical and Antiquarian Studies, Assam, 7-8.

841. **Bhattacharya, Prabhas** : 1985 : Economic Base Analysis Income Leakage and Regionalism Growth, *(In) An Anthology of Tripura, (Ed.)* by Jagadis Gan

Chaudhuri, New Delhi, Inter India Publications : 57-64.

842. **Bhattacharya, Pramod Chandra** : 1962 : Pahar Vaiyamar Annanna Janajati, Tippra *(In) Asamar Janajati (Ed.)* by Pramod Chandra Bhattacharya. Jorhat, Asom Sahitya Sabha : 333-34.

843. **Bhattacharya, Priyabrata** : 1980 : Art and Archaeology *(In) Tripura : The Land and its People, (Ed.)* by Jagadis Gan Chaudhuri. Delhi, Leeladevi Publications : 55-70.

844. **Bhattacharya, Priyabrata** : 1985 : Religious History of the Tipras on the background of Kharchipuja. *Proceedings of NEIHA* (Agartala), No. 6 : 99-106.

845. ——— : 1986 : Historical Evaluation of the Rock-Cut sculptures of Unakoti. *Proceedings of NEIHA* (Pasighat), No. 7 : 77- 86.

846. **Bhattacharjee, Pradip Nath** : 1980 : *Lokabritter aloke Koloi sampraday* [The Koloi : In the light of People's History]. Agartala, Directorate of Research, 127p (English verison by Ram Gopal Singh, 1983).

847. **Bhattacharyee, P.N.** : 1983 : *The Jamatias of Tripura*. Agartala, Govt. of Tripura, Dir. of Research, 101p.

848. **Bhattacharjee, R.P.** : 1991 : Anachronism of the conventional idea of shifting cultivation : A review of Tripura's situation *(In) Shifting Cultivation in North East India, (Ed.)* by D.N. Majumdar. New Delhi, Omsons Publications : 312-17.

849. **Bhattacharjee, P.R.** : n.p. : *Singificance of income leakage in the export base model of regional growth : A case study of Tripura. (Unpublished* Ph.D. Thesis).

850. ——— : 1984 : Cropping pattern in the plains and valleys of Tripura. Proceedings of a Seminar on *"Land, Land Relation and land Reforms in the Plains and Valleys of N.E.I."*, April 17-18, NEICSSR. (This *Edited* by Atul Goswami).

851. ——— : 1984 : Manpower Planning and Industrialisation of Tripura. *Jr. NEICSSR*, 8(2), Oct. : 1-5.

852. **Bhattacharjee, P.R.** : 1985 : Tea-plantation labour in Tripura : Trend in employment, productivity and wages. Proceedings of a Seminar on *"Tea Garden Labourers in North East India : A Multi Dimensional Study"*, 25th to 27th Feb. '85, Shillong, NEICSSR in collaboration with Sacred Heart Theological College, Shillong, 9p *(Mimeo)*.

853. ——— : 1986 : Cropping pattern in the Plains and Valleys of Tripura *(In) Land Reforms and Peasant Movement: A Study of North East India (Ed)* by Atul Goswami. New Delhi, Omsons Pubs. : 145-55.

854. ——— : 1987 : New Horizon of tribal antonomy and tribal development in Tripura. *Jr. NEICSSR*, XI(1), April : 33-42.

855. **Bhattacharjee, P.R.** : 1989 : In quest of growth boosters in the rural economy of Tripura. Proceedings of a Seminar on *"Perspective, Issues and Experiences of Rural Development in North East India"* held on 26-27 May '89 by NEICSSR, Shillong, 10p.

856. ——— : 1990 : Development and social movement in Tripura : A normative analysis. Proceedings of a Seminar on *"Social Movements in societies of Tripura since Independence"* organised by Tripura University, Agartala on 10th Feb. 1990 *(Mimeo)*.

857. ——— : 1990 : Self-sufficiency in food grains *vs* optimal resource use : An exercise in choice of Agricultural strategy in Tripura. Proceedings of a Seminar on *"Constraints of Agricultural Development in North East India"*, 2-3 July, 1990, NEICSSR, Shillong, 10p. *(Mimeo)*.

858. ——— : 1990 : Tea-plantation labour in Tripura, *(In) Tea Garden labourers of North East India : A Multidimentional Study on the adivasis of the Tea Gardens of North East India, (Eds)* by S. Karotemprel and B. Dutta Roy. Shillong, Vendrame Institute.

859. ——— : 1991 : In quest of growth : Boosters in the rural economy of Tripura, *(In) Rural Development in North East India: Perspectives, Issues and Experiences*,

(Ed) by R.K. Samanta, New Delhi, Uppal Pub. House : 301-11.

860. **Bhattacharjee, R.** : 1972 : Adult education in Tripura. *Indian Journal of Adult Education*, 33 : 12, 19.

861. **Bhattacharya, Suchintya** : 1978 : Life Pattern of the Reangs : A study of a tribal community of Tripura. *Jr. NEICSSR*, II(I), April : 10-2.

862. ——— : 1980 : *The Kaipengs*. Agartala, Directorate of Research, 89p.

863. ——— : 1985 : Historical Survey of Tribal Uprisings in Tripura. *Proceedings of NEIHA* (Agartala), No. 6 : 450-53.

864. ——— : 1992 : *Genesis of Tribal Extremism in Tripura*. Delhi, Gyan Pub. House, 208p.

865. **Bhattacharya, S.C.** : 1958 : Tripurar Rupkatha, Part I and II. Agartala, District Publicity Office, Tripura, 21p.

866. **Bhattacharya, S.C.** : 1967 : *Tripura on the March*. Agartala, Public Relations Office, Govt. of Tripura : 6-8, 11, 16-7, 31-3, 41-2.

867. **Bhattacharjee, S.R.** : 1989 : *Tribal Insurgency in Tripura : A Study in exploration of causes*. New Delhi, Inter-India Publications, 211p.

868. **Bhattacharya, S.S.** : 1976 : *Report on the Socio Linguistic Survey of Tripura*. Calcutta, Anthropological Survey of India, *(unpublished)*.

869. ——— : 1976 : Historical development of tribal movement in Tripura with special reference to language and script. (Paper presented in the Seminar on *"Contemporary Tribal Movement in India"*). Calcutta, Anthropological Survey of India.

870. ——— : 1979 : Socio-linguistic profile of Tripura. *Jr. of the Indian Anthropological Society* (Calcutta), 14(3), Nov. : 189-98.

871. **Bhattacharya, T.** *and* **Chakraborty, D.** : 1986 : Wild Mammalian Resources of Tripura, *(In) Forestry Development in North East India, (Eds.)* by M. Das

Gupta *et al.* Guwahati, Omsons Publications : 207-16.

872. **Bhattasali, N.K.** : 1923 : Notes on the coinnage of Tipperah. *Jr. of the Asiatic Society of Bengal*, 23.

873. ——— : 1929 : *Iconography of Buddhist and Brohnmical sculptures in the Dacca Museum*. Dacca, Dacca Museum Committee, 274p.

874. **Bhikkhu, Pragya Jyoti** : 1989 : Letters to the Editor : Facilities for Chakma. *Shillong Times*, Aug. 21 : 2(3-4).

875. **Bhikshu, Srimat Dharma Rakshit** : ? : *Mainamatir Itihas*. Agartala.

876. **Bhowmik, D.C., Sipra Sen** *and* **Mukherjee, S.K.** *(Comps.)* : 1979: *Silver Jubilee Celebration, North East India, Shillong, 1953-1978 : Anthropological Literature of North East India (Researches conducted by Anth. Surv. of India)*. Shillong, Anth. Surv. of India *(Mimeo.)*.

877. **Bhowmick, Kanailal** : 1982 : *The development of social education in Tripura and Cachar*. Ph.D. Thesis, Gauhati University *(Unpublished)*.

878. **Bhowmick, Kanailal** : 1986 : Traditional Tribal System of Social Education in Tripura, *(In) Tribes of Tripura, (Ed.)* by Sudhanshu Bikash Saha. Agartala, Rupali Book Store : 159-64.

879. **Bhaumik, Kirit** : 1981 : Basic District Stalls of Tripura Tribal Council. *Times of India*, Aug. 24.

880. **Bhowmik, Sharit K.** : 1988 : Strangling worker's initiatives : Fate of workers' co-operatives in Tripura. *Economic and Political Weekly*, 23(49), Dec. 3 : 2566-67.

881. **Bhuyan, J.C.** : 1971 : Census of India 1971, Tripura. Proceedings of a Seminar on "Social, Economic and Cultural Aspects of Tripura." Agartala.

882. **Bhuyan, S.K.** *(Ed.)* : 1938 : *Tripura Buranji*. Gauhati, Deptt. of Historical and Antiquarian Studies, Assam, 103p *(Reprinted* in 1962).

883. **Bidyabhushan, Amulyacharan** : ? : *Srehatter Itibritya.* Dacca.

884. **Bidyavinode, Chandrodaya** : 1905 : An open Letter. *Arun* (Brahmanbaria, Tripura), Vol, I(22), 1st Chaitra, 1312B.S.

885. **Bikram-Kisor, Maharaj Kumar Sahadev** *and* **Gan-Choudhuri, J.**: 1986 : Princely Tripura's constitution act, 1941. *Proceedings of NEIHA,* (Pasighat), No. 7 : 192-200.

886. **Biswas, Asha** : 1970 : Features : Bamboo craft. *Hindustan Times,* Oct. 23.

887. **Biswas, K.** : 1958 : Vegetable resources of Tripura. *Amrita Bazar Patrika, Puja Annual* : 168-70.

888. **Blochmon, M.A.** : 1873 : *Contributions to the Geography and History of Bengal ; Mahammedan Period, 12-3-1538 AD.* Calcutta, Calcutta Madrasha : 24-31.

889. **Bora, A.K.** : 1986 : Problems and prospects of better utilisation of land in the Hills of North East India, *(In) Land Use Pattern in North East India, (Ed.)* by B.B. Dutta. Ludhiana, Gogan Publishers : 41-54.

890. **Borah, Aswhini Kr.** : 1989 : Input of modern technology for rural development in N.E. India : A Case Study. Proceedings of a Seminar on *"Perspective, Issues and Experiences of Rural Development in North East India"* held on 26-27 May by NEICSSR, Shillong : 7p (Mimeo).

891. **Bora, Munindra** : 1987 : Shifting cultivation in North East India. *Souvenir, North East India Geographical Society,* Dec. : 18-21.

892. **Borgohain, B.K.** *and* **Roy Chaudhury, P.C.** : 1975 : *Folk Tales of Nagaland, Manipur, Tripura, and Mizoram.* New Delhi, Sterling Publications : 105-20.

893. **Borthakur, D.N.** *et al.* : 1978 : Shifting cultivation in the North Eastern Region. *(In) Resources Development and Environment in the Himalayan Region.* Delhi, Deptt. of Science & Technology, Govt. of India : 330-42.

894. **Bose, Manjula** *(Ed.)* : 1981 : *Land Reforms in Eastern India.* Calcutta, Jadavpur University.

895. **Bose, M.L.** : 1979 : *Historical and constitutional documents of North Eastern India (1824-1973).* Delhi, Concept Publishing Company.

896. **Bose, N.K.** : 1969 : Book Review : Temples of Tripura by Adris Banerji, Pp.22+Frontispiece+half tone plates+2 line drawings, 1968, Prithivi Prakashan, Varanasi 5, Rs. 10/- only. *Man in India,* 49(1), Jan.-March : 116.

897. **Bose, Saradindu** : 1984 : Shifting cultivation in India. *Jr. Indian Anthropological Society,* 19(1), March : 55-65.

898. ——— : 1989 : Shifting cultivation in India *(In) Man and Environment, (Eds)* by Surajit Sinha, Arabinda Basu and Amitabha Basu. Calcutta, Indian Anthropological Society : 55-65.

899. **Bose, Saradindu, Ghatak, S.** *and* **Bera, R.K.** : 1982 : Shifting cultivation in India, *(In) Economies of the Tribes and their transformation, (Ed)* by K.S. Singh. New Delhi, Concept Publishing Company : 216-25.

900. **Bose, Saradindu, Saha, Vaskar** *and* **Thangam, E.S.** *(Eds)* : 1982: *Population Data regarding forestry communities practising shifting cultivation.* New Delhi, Inspector General of Forests : 32-4.

901. **Bose, S.K.** : 1961 : Land use survey in a Juang village. *Man in India,* 41(3), July-Sept.

902. ——— : 1988 : Coinage of Tripura, *(In) National Seminar on The Archaeology of North East India,* Oct, 26-28, 1988 *(Ed)* by Jai Prakash Singh. Shillong, Deptt. of History, North Eastern Hill University : 1-36 *(Mimeo.)*

903. **Bose, Satyaranjan** : 1957 : Desatmobodh O Maharaja Radhakishore Manikya. *Samaj* (Agartala), Aug. 24 : 4.

904. **Boucheseiche, M.** : 1800 : *Account of the Religion, Manners, Laws and Customs of the Cucis, or the inhabitants of the Tipra Mountains (in French).* [Translated from the English of James Rennell, F.R.S.]

905. **Bowles, Chester** : 1954 : *Ambassador's Report.* London, Victor Gallancz Ltd, 415p.

906. **Butler, John** : 1978 : *Travels and adventures in the province of Assam.* Delhi, Vivek Publications (*Reprinted,* 1st Pub. in 1855): 79-101.

C

907. **Call** : 1973 : Tribal problem in Tripura. *Call,* 25(4) : 15-20.

908. **C., A.K.** : 1987 Tripura. *Now,* May 12, 3(32) : 22.

909. **Campbell, A.** : 1874 : The Looshais. *Jr. of Anthropological Institute,* (London), vol. 3 : 57-65.

910. **Carey, B.S.** *and* **Tuck, H.N.** : 1896 : *The Chin Hills, vol. I and II.* Rangoon (Burma), The Supdt. of Govt. Printing, 236p (*Reprinted* in 1983 by Cultural Publishing House, Delhi).

911. **Census** : 1896 : *Census of India 1891, Bengal, vol. II : Report on the Census of the District of Tripura.* Calcutta, Govt. Press, 33p.

912. ——— : 1953 : *Census of India 1951, vol. XII, pt. I-A : Assam, Manipur and Tripura (Report).* Shillong, Assam Govt. Press : 145-64.

913. ——— : 1953 : *Census of India 1951 : Assam, Manipur and Tripura (Paper I-B, vol. XII_.* shillong, Assam Govt. Press.

914. ——— : 1961 : *Census of India 1961, vol.I, pt.II-C(ii) Language Tables.* Delhi, Manager of Publications.

915. ——— : 1963 : *Census of India 1961, vol. XXVI Tripura General Report.* Delhi, Manager of Publications.

916. ——— : 1963 : *Census of India 1961, vol. XXVI Tripura, General Population Tables and General Economic Tables.* Delhi, Manager of Publications.

917. ——— : 1963 : *Census of India 1961, vol. XXII Tripura, Cultural and Migration Tables.* Delhi, Manager of Publications.

918. ——— : 1965 : *Census of India 1961, vol. XXVI Tripura : Report on Housing and Establishments.* Delhi, Manager of Publications.

919. ——— : 1965 : *Census of India 1961, vol. XXVI : Tripura, Fair and Festivals.* Delhi, Manager of Publications.

920. **Census** : 1965 : *Census of India 1961, vol. XXVI : Tripura, village Monograph, Kamalghat.* Delhi, Manager of Publication.

921. ——— : 1965 : *Census of India 1961, vol. XXVI Tripura, Village Survey Monograph : Rudijala.* Delhi, Manager of Publication.

922. ——— : 1965 : *Census of India 1961, vol. XXVI : Tripura, village Survey Monograph, Dwarika Talukdar para.* Delhi, Manager of Publication.

923. ——— : 1965 : *Census of India 1961, vol. XXVI Tripura, village Survey Monograph, Sekerkot.* Delhi, Manager of Publication.

924. ——— : 1967 : *Census of India 1961, vol. 15, Pt. I-(i) General Report, Tripura.* Delhi, Manager of Publication, 166p.

925. ——— : 1967 : *Census of India 1961, Tripura, vol. 26. pt. III-Household Economic Tables and part V-A- Special Tables for Scheduled Castes and Scheduled Tribes.* Delhi, Manager of Publications, 404p.

926. ——— : 1967 : *Census of India 1961, Tripura, vol. 25, pt. II-C : Cultural and Migration Tables.* Delhi, Manager of Publications, 306p.

927. ——— : 1973 : *Census of India 1971 : Tripura, part II-C(i), Seminar Papers on Social, Economic and Cultural aspects of Tripura.* Delhi, Controller of Publications, 165p.

928. ——— : 1975 : *Census of India 1971 : Tripura, Housing Report and Tables.* Delhi, Controller of Publications, 109p.

929. ——— : 1975 : *Census of India 1971 ; Tripura : A Potrait of Population.* Delhi, Controller of Publications, 200p.

930. ——— : 1975 : *Census of India 1971 : Tripura : Establishment Report and Tables.* Delhi, Controller of Publications, 485p.

931. ——— : 1976 : *Census of India 1971 : Tripura, Social and Cultural Tables and Special Tables on Scheduled Castes and*

Scheduled Tribes. Delhi, Controller of Publications, 139p.

932. **Census** : **1977** : *Census of India 1971 : Tripura, General Report*. Delhi, Controller of Publications, 182p.

933. ——— : 1979 : *Census of India 1971 : Tripura, Social and Cultural Tables and Fertility Tables*. Delhi, Controller of Publications, 151p.

934. ——— : 1981 : *Census of India 1981, series 21, pt. IX, Tripura*. Agartala, Directorate of Census Operations.

935. ——— : 1981 : *Census of India 1981, series 21, Tripura, Pt. IX, Special Tables on Scheduled Caste and Scheduled Tribes*. Agartala, Directorate of Census Operations.

936. ——— : 1981 : *Census of India 1981, series 21, Tripura, part II-B, Primary Census Abstract*. Agartala, Directorate of Census Operation, 77p.

937. ——— : 1981 : *Census of India 1981, Tripura : Final Population Report*. Agartala, Directorate of Census Operations.

938. **Central Gazetteers Unit** : ? : *The Gazetteer of India, Indian Union, vol. I : Country and People*. Delhi, Publications Divisions (Tripura).

939. **Central Institute** : 1973 : *India, Central Institute of Indian Language (Distribution of Languages in India in States and Union Territories)*. Mysore, Central Institute of Indian Languages, 264p.

940. **Central Road Research** : 1978 : *Report on development of Damcherra-Monpai Phuldangshi Road (Tripura State) using soil stabilisation techniques*. New Delhi, Central Road Research Institute, 25p.

941. **Chakma, Pradipmoy** *et al* : n.m. : *Chakma Adi Ballya Shikhya (in Bengali)*. Dayon (Tirap of Arunachal Pradesh), Pub. by Srimat Jyotipal Mahasthavir (Printed by Lakshmi Narayan Press, Digboi, Assam).

942. **Chakma, Punnyadhan** : *c*. 1980 : *Chakma Itihas : Oyetejjha O Sanskriti Grantha*. Dayon (Tirap, Arunachal Pradesh), Pub. by Srimat Jotipal Mahasthavir.

943. **Chakma, Sirsendu** : 1989 : Letters to the Editor : Chakma refugees. *Assam Tribune,* May 29 : 4(4).

944. **Chakma, Sneha Kumar** : 1974 : Tribal problem in Tripura. *Call,* 25(7), March : 12-20, 22.

945. **Chakrabarti, Anirban** : 1988 : 'Congress won Tripura polls by manipulation' : Basu. *Amrita Bazar Patrika,* Feb. 5 : 1(4- 6).

946. **Chakraborty, Bhabesh** : 1974 : Tribes of Tripura : A short ethnographic account. *Bulletin of the Cultural Research Institute* (Calcutta), 10(3-4) : 130-37.

947. **Chakraborty, B.C.** : 1964 : *British Relations with the Hill Tribes of Assam since 1858.* Calcutta, Firma K.L. Mukhopadhyay.

948. **Chakravarty, D.N.** : 1972 : Tripura in transition. *Yojana,* March 5 : 197-99.

949. ——— : 1986 : Planning in North Eastern Region. *Assam Tribune,* January 26, *Republic Day Supplement* ; 7(6-8) *and* 10(1-4).

950. **Chakraborty, Jiban** : 1983 : *Tripura tirish theke ashi (in Bengali)* [i.e. Tripura from 1930 to 1980]. Agartala, Barnamala Prakashan.

951. **Chakraborty, Jogesh** : 1986 : The Tribals of Tripura and the R.S.P. *(In) Tribes of Tripura (Ed)* by Sudhanshu Bikash Saha. Agartala, Rupali Book Store : 89-92.

952. **Chakraborty, K.P.** : 1970 : Agricultural development in Tripura. *Tripura Review,* 1(1) : 32-6.

953. **Chakravarti, Mahadev** : 1984 : Ziratia problem of Tripura *(In) Proceedings of North East Indian History Association,* No. 5 (Aizawl) : 179-94.

954. ——— : 1985 : Continuity and Change : A case study in Tripura. Proceedings of a Seminar on *"Sequences in Development in North East India (A Study of Tradition, Continuity and Change)"* held on 9-10 December 1985, organised by NIECSSR, Shillong *(Mimeo.).*

955. ——— : 1985 : Communist activities in Tripura, 1939-42. *Proceedings of NEIHA,* No. 6 (Agartala) : 363-70.

956. **Chakravarti, Mahadev** : 1986 : *The Tribal Autonomous District Council, and Tribal Problem : A Perspective.* Agartala, Govt. of Tripura : 17-8.

957. ——— : 1986 : Tea and tea plantation workers of Tripura in the Past and Present. *Proceedings of NEIHA,* No.7 (Pasighat) : 435-44.

958. ——— : 1986 : Tribal chief and his people : A Case Study *(In) Tribes of Tripura (Ed.)* by Sudhanshu Bikash Saha. Agartala, Rupali Book Store : 81-7.

959. ——— : 1986 : Forestry in Tripura : Its Past and Present *(In) Forestry Development in North East India, (Eds)* by M.Das Gupta *et al*. Guwahati, Omsons Publications : 31-41.

960. ——— : 1988 : Boundary disputes between the princely State of Tripura and the British Government : A case study. *Jour. NEICSSR,* 12(2), October : 36-44.

961. ——— : 1988 : Land in Tripura : The Tenurial system and transfer. *Proceedings of NEIHA,* No. 9 (Guwahati) : 469-76.

962. ——— : 1988 : The TUJS : From protest to power. Proceedings of a Seminar on *"Regional Political Parties in North East India"*, 9-10 December, 1988, NEICSSR, Shillong : 1-13 *(Mimeo.)*

963. ——— : 1989 : Structure of Socio-Economic under development and exploitation of tribals of Tripura. Proceedings of a Seminar on *"Structures of Socio- Economic under Development and Exploitation in North East India" , 27-28 Feb. 1989, organised by Sacred Heart College, Shillong (Mimeo.)*

964. ——— : [illegible] New Zealand Baptist Mission in Tripura since 1909. *Proceedings of NEIHA,* Xth Annual Session, No. 10 (Shillong), Shillong, History Deptt., NEHU : 229-240.

965. ——— : 1989 : Rural development and people's participation : Tripura a case study. Proceedings of a Seminar on *"Perspective, Issues and Experiences of Rural Development in North East India"* held on 26-27 May 1989 by NEICSSR, Shillong : 1-11 *(Mimeo).*

966. **Chakravarti, Mahadev** : 1989 : Continuity and Change : A Case Study in Tripura, *(In) Sequences of Development in North East India, (Ed)* by J.B. Bhattacharjee. New Delhi, Omsons Publications : 215-222.

967. ——— : 1990 : Growth of Christianity in Tripura and some tribal movements since Independence. Proceedings of a Seminar on *"Social Movements in Societies of Tripura since Independence"* organised by Tripura University, Agartala on 10th Feb. 1990 *(Mimeo).*

968. ——— : 1991 : Peoples participation in rural development, *(In) Rural Development in North East India : Perspectives, Issues and Experiences, (Ed)* by R.K. Samanta. New Delhi, Uppal Publishing House : 69-93.

969. ——— : 1991 : *The Administrative Reports of Tripura State, 4 vols.* Delhi, Gyan Publishing House, 1000p.

970. **Chakravarti, M., Das Gupta, M.** *and* **Sarkar, B.** : n.p. : *The Lushais of Tripura in the past and present.* Agartala, Govt. of Tripura *(Unpublished).*

971. **Chakravartti, M.R.** *and* **Basu, Salil Kumar** *: 1960 : A Note on the Simian crease of the Riangs of Tripura. Science and Culture* (Calcutta), 5 : 28-34.

972. **Chakraborty, N.** : 1969 : Folk tale of the Chakma tribe. *Vanyajati,* XVII (2), April : 62-3.

973. **Chakrabarti, Nalini Kanta** : 1974 : *Government and Administration of Tripura. Unpublished* Ph.D. Thesis, Calcutta University.

974. **Chakravartty, Nikhil** : 1988 : Using the army for petty politicking. *Amrita Bazar Patrika,* Feb. 3 : 6(3-6).

975. ——— : 1988 : Tripura : A Bitter Point of Dispute. *Amrita Bazar Patrika,* Feb. 10 : 6(3-6).

976. **Chakraborti, Nripen** : 1974 : Tribal question : Urgent problem before the democratic movement. *People's Democracy* (Agartala), July 14 : 6-8.

977. ——— : 1979 : Battle for democracy in rural Tripura. *Economic Times,* Jan. 5 : 4(1).

978. **Chakraborti, Nripen** : 1986 : Village Road : Whether towards Development or Exploitation? *(In) Tribes of Tripura, (Ed.)* by Sudhanshu Bikash Saha. Agartala, Rupali book Store : 13-8.

979. ——— : 1988 : Letters to the Editor : Who's to blame in Tripura ? *Statesman*, Oct. 25 : 6(4-5).

980. **Chakraborty, N.K.** : 1984 : Plant resources of Tripura Forests. Proceedings of a Seminar on *"Planning for Forestry Development in the N.E. Region"*. Shillong.

981. ——— : 1986 : Plant Resources of Tripura Forests, *(In) Forestry Development in North East India, (Eds)* by M. Das Gupta *et al.* Guwahati, Omsons Publications : 217-24.

982. **Chakrabarti, Nalini Kanta** : 1985 : Plant Resources *(In) An Anthology of Tripura (Ed)* by Jagadis Gan Choudhuri. New Delhi, Inter India Publications : 11-20.

983. **Chakravarty, Padmini** : 1979 : Social structure of the tribals of Tripura as reflected through their dances. *Folklore*, 20(2): 30-9.

984. **Chakraborty, Santimay** : 1980 : *Tripurani Kareng Kathama.* Agartala, Directorate of Research, 142p.

985. ——— : 1980 : *Tripurar Rupkatha.* Agartala, Directorate of Research, 138p.

986. **Chakrabarty, Saroj** : 1984 : *The Upheaval Years in North-East India (A documentary in depth study of Assam holocausts), 1960- 1983.* Calcutta, Pub. by Saroj Chakrabarty and R. Chakrabarty : 100-02, 116-19.

987. **Chakraborty, Satyabrata** : 1987 : Repatriation of Tribal refugees put off. *Statesman*, Jan. 16 : 1(2-7).

988. ——— : 1987 : TNV trying to drive out Bengalis. *Statesman*, Oct. 20 : 9(2-5).

989. ——— : 1987 : Round the region : Growing 'Tribalism' a threat to Tripura Marxists. *Statesman*, Nov. 24 : 7(2-3).

990. ——— : 1988 : Loan-Mela and TNV dominate campaign. *Statesman*, Jan. 19 : 1(5-8) and 9(4).

991. **Chakraborty, Satyabrata** : 1988 : Front has the edge in Tripura. *Statesman,* Jan. 31 : 9(2-4).

992. ——— : 1988 : Floating votes turned the tables. *Statesman,* Feb. 5 : 9(2-3).

993. ——— : 1988 : Tripura Left Front to launch agitation. *Statesman,* March 29 : 14(2-3).

994. ——— : 1988 : Tripura Tribal bands cross over to Chittagong. *Statesman,* April 7 : 4(2-3).

995. ——— : 1988 : TUJS dead against talks with TNV. *Statesman,* April 15 : 4(3-5).

996. ——— : 1988 : And now, peace in Tripura : But will it last? *Statesman,* Aug. 27 *(Saturday's Supplement)* : 1(1-8).

997. ——— : 1988 : Implementation of TNV Accord hardly possible. *Statesman,* Aug. 28 : 11(3-4).

998. ——— : 1988 : TNV Surrender. *Statesman,* Sept. 10 : 1(6-7).

999. ——— : 1988 : Fresh controversy in Tripura over Loan Mela. *Statesman,* Nov. 10 : 4(1-3).

1000. ——— : 1988 : Tripura Front plans much. *Statesman,* Dec. 29 : 4(3-5).

1001. ——— : 1989 : Tripura's problem of infiltration turning acute. *Statesman,* Feb. 16 : 4(7-8).

1002. ——— : 1989 : Growing intolerance towards Chakmas. *Statesman,* June 12 : 1(1-5).

1003. ——— : 1989 : Resurgence of Tripura tribal insurgency. *Statesman,* July 6 : 7(1-4).

1004. ——— : 1990 : Poll violence feared in tribal Tripura. *Statesman,* July 8 : 1(1-5).

1005. ——— : 1990 : Battle lines being drawn between Tripura tribals. *Statesman,* Oct. 17 : 16(3-5).

1006. ——— : 1990 : Chakma camps invite international scrutiny. *Statesman,* Nov. 24 : 7(2-6).

1007. ——— : 1991 : Cong(I) optimistic over poll prospects in North East. *Statesman,* May 3 : 7(2-4).

1008. ——— : 1991 : No cake walk for Congress-I in Tripura. *Statesman,* May 3 : 13(1).

1009. **Chakraborty, Satyabrata** : 1991 : CPI-M opts out in Tripura. *Statesman,* June 9 : 7(2-4).

1010. ——— : 1991 : Tripura CM's nephew killed : CPI(M) urged to rethink poll decision. *Statesman,* June 10 : 1(2-6).

1011. **Chakrabarti, S.B.** : 1989 : Antyodaya : The Revised Strategy for rural development, some perspective. Proceedings of a Seminar on *"Perspective, Issues and Experiences of Rural Development in North East India"* held on 26-27 May 1989 by NEICSSR, Shillong : 1-11 *(Mimeo).*

1012. ——— : 1991 : Antyodaya : The Revised Strategy for Rural Development, some perspective. *(In) Rural Development in North East India : Perspectives, Issues and Experiences, (Ed)* by R.K. Samanta. New Delhi, Uppal Publishing House.

1013. **Chakraborti, S.K.** : 1971 : Reflection on Tipra Numerals. *Pines* (Shillong), 1(1), March : 74-77.

1014. **Chakraborty, Shyamal Kumar** : 1979 : Tripura is on refugee : Tribals and Bengalis are on a collision path. *Sunday,* June 17 : 43.

1015. **Chakraborty, S.R.** : 1972 : Editorial : Working of co-operative societies in Tripura, 1970-1971. *Indian Review of Public and Co-operative Economy,* April-May 2 : 2.

1016. ——— : 1981 : *Provisional Population Total.* Agartala, Direc. of Census.

1017. ——— : 1981 : *Provisional Population Total, part-I of 1981 Supplement,* Agartala, Direc. of Census.

1018. ——— : 1981 : *Census of India, Tripura, Pt. I of 1981* Agartala, Direc. of Census.

1019. **Chakraborty, S.R.** : 1982 : *Final Population figures, paper 2 of 1982.* Agartala, Direc. of Census.

1020. **Chakraborty, Sujit** : 1990 : The changing face of Tripura. *Assam Tribune,* Dec. 16*(Sunday Reading Supplement)* : 1(1-8).

1021. **Chakravarty, Sumit** : 1988 : Tripura Accord : Landmark for North-East. *Shillong Times*, Sept 2 : 2(3-6), 3(3-4).

1022. ——— : 1988 : New hope for Tripura tribals. *Amrita Bazar Patrika*, Sept. 8 : 6(7-8).

1023. **Chakraborty, Swadesh** : 1988 : Tripura victory a boost for Assam Cong(I). *Statesman*, Feb. 11 : 4(2-4).

1024. **Chakravarti, Tapati** : 1989 : The Riang women of Tripura : Their participation in Economic Activities and Social Status. Proceedings of a Seminar on *"Perspective, Issues and Experiences of Rural Development in North East India"* held on 26-27 May 1989 by NEICSSR, Shillong : 1-7 *(Mimeo)*.

1025. ——— : 1991 : The Riang women of rural Tripura: Their participation in economic activities and social status *(In) Rural Development in North East India (Ed)* by R.K. Samanta, New Delhi, Uppal Publishing House : 205-15.

1026. **Chakravorty, Ujjayant** : 1987 : India : Home of World's wettest desert. *Himalaya : Man & Nature*, XI(1), June : 11-2.

1027. **Chaliha, Bhaba Prasad** : 1987 : North East India : A Cultural Panorama. *Assam Tribune*, Dec. 6 : 4(3-6) and 6(4-5).

1028. **Chanda, Arup** : 1988 : Drug trafficking on the rise in North East. *Statesman*, Oct. 25 : 4(1-5).

1029. ——— : 1989 : Nagaland Election Scene-II : Tripura game may be repeated. *Statesman*, Jan. 11 : 14(1-4).

1030. **Chander, K.** : 1971 : Mizo Hills : Indians' Eastern Frontier. *Mirror*, 10 : 34-6.

1031. ——— : 1978 : Lushais of Mizoram. *Social Welfare*, 25 : 20-2.

1032. **Chaptwala, C.D.** : 1967 : Rural industries in Tripura : Problems and Prospects. *Panchayati Raj*, 8(7), Oct. : 7-8.

1033. **Chari, Pushpa** : 1987 : Interview of C.Z. Ghafoor "Poor Communication affects BSF performance" on Chakma. *Shillong Times*, Dec. 20 : 2(1-6).

1034. **Chari, R.B.** : 1973 : *Census of India 1971, series I, pt. I of 1975 : Scheduled Castes and Scheduled Tribes*. Delhi, Manager of Publications.

1035. **Charls, Stewart** : 1904 : *History of Bengal*. Calcutta.

1036. **Chatterjee, Gobinda Narayan** : 1967 : Research design-setting : Tripura and its people. *Educational Miscellany*, 3(3-4) : 64-8. (Dec. '66-March '67).

1037. **Chatterji, G.N.** : 1968 : Differences in identification of teachers and non-teachers. *Indian Educational Review*, 3 : 1, 20-45.

1038. ——— : 1972 : A Brief Note on the Linguistic Problems in Tripura Territory, *(In) Conference of Heads of Tribal Research Bureaus/Institutes, etc. in India* by Central Institute of Indian Languages. Manasagangotri (Mysore), Central Institute of Language : 45-6.

1039. **Chatterjee, Gobinda Narayan** *and* **Gangopadhyaya, Himangshunath** *(Eds.)* : 1961 : *Rabindranath -O-Tripura*. Calcutta, Pub. by editors in 1368 B.S.

1040. **Chatterjee, H.L.** : 1955 : The Story of Assamese Envoys in Tripura. *Prachi*, 7.

1041. ——— : 1961 : Tripurar Itihas Prasanga. *Rabi*, I *(new) : 35 (Pub. in 1368 B.S. in Bengali* from Agartala).

1042. **Chattopadhaya, Kamaladevi** : 1978 : *Tribalism in India*. New Delhi, Vikas Publishing House.

1043. **Chatterjee, Neera** : 1965 : Tripura and its tribal population. *Educational Miscellany* (Agartala), 2(1-2) : 61-9.

1044. ——— : 1966 : Research design for the assessment of intelligence of Tribal and Non-Tribal Boys of Tripura. *Educational Miscellany*, 2(3-4).

1045. ——— : 1967 : Comparison of performance of tribal and non-tribal boys of Tripura on five performance tests. *Educational Miscellany*, 3(3-4) : 8-14.

1046. **Chatterjee, N.** : 1972 : Tripura and its tribal population. *North Eastern Affairs* (Shillong), 1(2).

1047. **Chatterjee, S.** : 1988 : Rural water supply in Tripura. *Himalaya : Man and Nature,* XII(4), Sept. : 5-7.

1048. **Chatterjee, Shankar** : 1990 : Duck breeding farm in Tripura : Problems and Prospects. *Himalaya : Man and Nature* (Delhi), XIII (7-8), Dec. '89-Jan.'90 : 10-11.

1049. **Chatterjee, Suhas** : 1972 : *Tripura Kok-Borok Bhasar Likhita Rupe Uttaram (in Bengali).* Cálcutta, 52p.

1050. **Chatterjee, Suhas** : 1985 : Role of the Raja of Tripura and the English in capturing the Mizo Chief Lalchukla. *Proceedings of NEIHA,* vol. 6 (Agartala) : 197-200.

1051. ——— : 1985 : *Mizoram under the British Rule.* Delhi, Mittal Publications : 13- 35 (Tripura).

1052. **Chattopadhyay, Srish Chandra** : ? : *Debayatan O Bharat-Sabhayata.* : 73, 78, 128.

1053. **Chatterjee, Suniti Kumar** : 1951 : Kirata-Jana-Krti : The Indo-Mongoloids. *Royal Asiatic Society of Bengal, Letters* (Calcutta), XVI(2), 1950 : 71-5.

1054. ——— : 1967 : Letter of Prof. Suniti Kumar Chatterji containing his views on the status of the Chakma language and the need to preserve it (23rd June, 1967), *(In) The Chakmas* by S.P. Talukdar. Delhi, Gyan Publishing House (1988) : 219-21.

1055. **Chatterjee, S.N.** : 1984 : *Tripura : A Profile.* New Delhi, Inter-India Publications, 67p.

1056. ——— : 1990 : Shifting cultivation in Tripura : Some strategies for development. Proceedings of a Seminar on *"Constraints of Agricultural Development in North East India"*, 2-3 July, 1990, NEICSSR, Shillong, 5p *(Mimeo).*

1057. **Chaube, S.K.** : 1969 : Early British Policy on the North East India. *Assam Tribune,* May 5.

1058. **Chaube, Shibanikinkar** : 1973 : *Hill Politics in North East India.* Bombay, Orient Longman : 189-200.

1059. **Chaube, Shibanikinkar** : 1982 : Nation Building and Politics in the North East Indian Hills, *(In) Tribal Movements in India, vol.I, (Ed)* by K.S. Singh. New Delhi, Manohar Publications : 27-37.

1060. ——— : 1984 : *Electoral Politics in North East India*. New Delhi, Orient Longman Ltd.

1061. ——— : 1985 : *Electoral Politics in North East India*. Madras, University Press : 172-90.

1062. ——— : 1990 : Tribal societies and the problem of nation building *(In) Nationality, Ethnicity and Cultural Identity in North East India, (Ed)* by B. Pakem. New Delhi, Omson Publications.

1063. **Chaudhwari, D.K.** : 1977 : *Chakmas of Tripura and Bangladesh : A Study in Social Change and Folklore Patterns*. ICSSR Project 1976-'77. Agartala, Fakirchand College, Diamond Harbour Pargana : 76-7.

1064. **Chaudhuri, Dipak Kumar** : 1984 : Problem of Sati : Conflict between the British and the Maharaja of Tripura. *Proceedings of NEIHA*, vol. 5 (Aizwal) : 116-26.

1065. ——— : 1985 : British Policy and the Indian Princes : A Case Study of the reactions of the Maharajas of Tripura. *Proceedings of NEIHA*, vol. 6 (Agartala) : 271-84.

1066. ——— : 1986 : Tripura in 1886 : A Socio Economic Profile. *Proceedings of NEIHA*, vol. 7 (Pasighat) : 400-406.

1067. **Chaudhuri, D.K.** : 1988 : The Mission civilisatrice : The appointment of Political Agent in Tripura *(In) Indian Archives*. New Delhi, Ministry of Education, Archives Deptt.

1068. **Chaudhuri, K.C.** : 1987 : Letters to the Editor : Chakmas wait for justice. *Statesman*, Aug. 8 : 8(4-5).

1069. **Chib, Sukhdev Singh** : 1984 : *Caste, Tribes and Culture of India, vol. 8 : North Eastern India*. New Delhi, Ess Ess Publications, 384p.

1070. ——— : 1988 : *This Beautiful India : Tripura*. New Delhi, Ess Ess publications, 124 p.

1071. **Chinikok** : 1988 : Tripura. *The Chinikok* (Agartala), issue 71st, dated Sept. 25, 1988.

1072. **Chitharangadan, V.K.** : 1986 : Role of the Rubber Plantation Industry in the Economic Development of the North Eastern Region, *(In) Forestry Development in North East India, (Ed)* by M. Das Gupta *et al.* Guwahati, Omsons Publications : 67-71.

1073. **Chonkar, Raj** : 1987 : Solar Power in Tripura. *Amrita Bazar Patrika,* Aug. 23 : 7(1).

1074. ——— : 1987 : Repatriation plan a lie : Say Chakmas. *Amrita Bazar Patrika,* Dec. 29 : 7(5-6).

1075. ——— : 1988 : Saga of Chakma children adopted in France. *Amrita Bazar Patrika,* Jan, 18 : 7(5-6).

1076. ——— : 1988 : Poojary to go ahead with Loan -Mela. Amrita *Bazar Patrika,* Jan. 25 : 1(2- 5).

1077. ——— : 1988 : Shanti Bahini may be used to crush TNV. *Amrita Bazar Patrika,* Feb. 11 : 12(3-4).

1078. **Chonkar, Raj** : 1988 : Clashes feared in Tripura. *Amrita Bazar Patrika,* Jan. 28 : 7(5).

1079. ——— : 1988 : North District results to be deciding factor in Tripura : Hills and Plains. *Amrita Bazar Patrika,* Jan. 30 : 7(1-3).

1080. ——— : 1988 : Chakmas : The Anguished Cry. *Amrita Bazar Patrika,* Jan. 30 : 7(1-8).

1081. ——— : 1988 : Tripura, Meghalaya go to the polls today amid light security. *Amrita Bazar Patrika,* Feb. 2 : 1(6-8), 12(4-5).

1082. ——— : 1988 : The forgotten Chakmas. *Amrita Bazar Patrika,* Feb. 11 : 6(7-8).

1083. —— : 1988 : Changes in 'Tipperah'. *Statesman, Miscellany Supplement,* Oct. 9 : 13(4-5). [This is the Review of *"Tripura Administration : The Era of Modernisation"* by Banikanta Bhattacharyya, Mittal Publications, Rs. 180/-].

1084. **Choudhury, A.C.** : 1317 B.S. : *Shrihatter Itibritta.* Sylhet (Bangladesh), Pub. by author, 96p.

1085. **Choudhuri, Bikash** : 1975 Tripurar Unnayaner Samashya, *(In) Tripura Prasanga, (Ed)* by Swapan

Sengupta. Agartala, Directorate of Public Relations & Tourism : 195- 204.

1086. **Choudhuri, Buddhadeb** *(Ed)* : 1982 : *Tribal Development in India : Problem and Prospects.* Delhi, Inter-India Publications : 49, 72, 217, 218, 358-356.

1087. **Choudhuri, B.** *and* **Chanda, S.** *(Eds.)* : 1984 : *Glimpses of Tripura.* Agartala, Tripura Darpan Publications.

1088. **Choudhury, Dibyendu** : 1957 : Palmar main lines configuration among the Riang of Tripura. *Bulletin of the Deptt. of Anthropology* (Anth. Survey of India), 6(1).

1089. **Choudhury, Dulal** : 1975 : Chakmader Adibas Bhumi, *(In) Tripura Prasanga (Ed)* by Swapan Sengupta. Agartala, Directorate of Public Relations & Tourism : 46-50.

1090. ——— : 1975 : Marriage rituals of the Chakmas of Chittagong Hill Tracts, Bangladesh. *Bulletin of the Cultural Research Institute* **(Calcutta), 11 : 1-2, 91-94.**

1091. ——— : 1980 : *Chakma Prabad (in Bengali).* Agartala, Bipani Publications.

1092. **Choudhuri, J.** ; 1973 -'74 : Village Administration and Justice in Old Tripura. *Quarterly Review of Historical Studies, 13(3) : 157-68.*

1093. **Choudhury, Jayanta Nath** : 1969 : *Abrita Itihas : Unakoti, (in Bengali).* Agartala, Govt. of Tripura.

1094. ——— : 1976 : (?) : *Abrita-Itihas Unkoti (in Beng* Calcutta, Saraswat Library, 206 Bidhan Saran (Ranchi, Smti, Sulata Sarkar), 77p + 20 plates.

1095. **Choudhury, Pratap** : 1986 : Law and Legal System in Tripura in Nineteenth Century. *Proceedings of NEIHA*, vol. 7 (Pasighat): 183-91.

1096. ——— : 1988 : Savism in Tripura. *Proceedings of NEIHA*, vol. 9 (Guwahati) : 232-37.

1097. ——— : 1988 : Reigonal Political Parties in Tripura : A Genesis. Proceedings of a Seminar on *"Regional Political Parties in North East India"*, held on 9-10

December, 1988 by NEICSSR, Shillong : 1-7 *(Mimeo).*

1098. **Choudhury, P.C.** : 1959 : *The History of Civilization of the People of Assam to the Twelfth Century A.D.* Gauhati, Deptt. of Historical and Antiquarian Studies, Assam. (*Reprinted* in 1987 by Spectrum Publications, Guwahati).

1099. **Choudhury, Rabi** : 1968 : Sinkrak of Tripura. *Swarajya,* Aug. 3 : 29.

1100. **Choudhury, Rabijit** : 1988 : TNV supports TUJS-Congress(I) alliance. *Shillong Times,* Jan. 25 : 1(1-2).

1101. ——— : 1988 : Why TUJS is silent on foreigners' issue. *Shillong Times.* Feb. 12 : 3(1-5), 4(3).

1102. ——— : 1988 : Pressure for autonomy of Jampui Hills, *Shillong Times.* Nov. 24 : 1(3-5).

1103. ——— : 1989 : Mizos in Tripura Press for Autonomous Council. *Shillong Times,* March 10 : 3(1-4).

1104. ——— *(Ed.)* : 1990 : *News of North East : A Monthly compilation of Clippings.* Guwahati, Dighalipukhuri East, Tayebulla Compound (June, 1990). Pub. N.E.R.C., D.D.A.U.

1105. **Choudhury, Rabindra Kumar** : 1983 : Unemployment problem in the North Eastern region with Special reference to Assam. *Social Research* (Shillong), 3(3-4), July-Dec. : 1-12.

1106. **Choudhury, Rabindra Kumar** : 1989 : Rural poverty in North East India : Its absolute and relative magnitude. Proceedings of a Seminar on "*Perspective, Issues and Experiences of Rural Development in North East India*" held on 26-27 May 1098 by NEICSSR, Shillong : 1-12 *(Mimeo).*

1107. **Chowdhury, Sudhangsu** : 1952 : Traditional arts and crafts of Tripura, Manipur and Assam. *Art in Industry,* III(3).

1108. **Choudhury, V.** *and* **Roy, P.** : 1980 : A Unique coin of Virabhadra, Manikya : Hitherto unknown to the chronology of 'Tripura', *(In) Coinage of Bengal and its neighbourhood,* N.S.I., Varanasi : 32-35.

1109. **Choudhurani, Sarat Kumar** : ? : 1) *Late Tripur Raj Radha Kishor Manikya* and, 2) *Story of Tripura (in Bengali)*. Agartala.

1110. **Choudhuri, Shashi Bhusan** : 1975 : Sipahee Vidroha O Tripura, *(In) Tripura Prasanga, (Ed)* by Swapan Sengupta. Agartala, Directorate of Public Relations & Tourism : 28-35.

1111. **Chowdhuri, A.T.** : 1924 : *Tripura Katha*. Agartala, Pub. by author.

1112. **Chowdhuri, Mohan** : 1979 : Tripurar Praja Andolan : Kichu Tathya-Er-Prekshapate. *Dainik Sangbad* (Agartala), Dec. 13, 15.

1113. **Chowdhury, Vasanta** *and* **Ray, Parimal** : 1975 : Representation of the Chaturdasa devatas on a coin of Ratnamanikya deva of Tripura. *JNSI*, vol. XXXVII, pt. I-II : 121-13.

1114. ——— : 1978 : Tripura coins : Their social significance. *Bulletin of the Cultural Research Institute*, 13(1-2) : 42-45.

1115. **Chowla, N.L.** : 1980 : Tripura Holocaust. *Hindustan Times*, June 18.

1116. **Chowmuhani, Bijoy Kumar** : 1988 : TRPC aims at. *Himalaya : Man and Nature*. XII(1-2), June-July : Last cover page.

1117. **Chunda, Devi** : 1990 : Buddhist Goddess. *Assam Tribune*. Oct. 22 : 6(4).

1118. **Citizen Weekend Review** : 1969 : Protest in Manipur : Trouble in Tripura. *Citizen Weekend Review*, Sept. 27 : 27-8.

1119. **Commissioner** : 1842 : Letter from the Commissioner of 16th Division and Sudder Board to the Collector of Chittagong by Henry Ricketts on 26th Aug. 1842 *(In) The Chakma*, by S.P. Talukdar, Delhi, Gyan Publishing House (1988) : 141-42.

1120. **Communist Party** : 1988 : *"TNV agreement and some questions"*. Agartala, CPI(M)'s Tripura State Committee.

1121. **Controller of Publications** : 1982 : *Report on development of North Eastern Region.* New Delhi, National Committee on the Development of Backward Areas, Planning Commission, Govt. of India, 67p.

1122. **Copland, Ian** : 1982 : *The British Raj and the Indian Princes, Chapter-IV : Mission Civilisation 1870-1890.* Pune.

1123. **Cumming, J.G.** : 1907 : *Survey and settlement report of chokla Resonabad Estate in the Districts of Tipperah and Noakhali, 1892-99.* Shillong, Eastern Bengal and Assam Secretariat Press : 4, 119 (xxxii), 17.

1124. ——— : 1913 : *Letter from the J.G.Cumming, LCS, Officiating Chief Secretary to the Govt. of Bengal, Political Deptt. to the Commissioner of the Chittagong Division, No. 1391-P.D. dated Darjeeling, the 31st May, 1913.*

D

1125. **Dagli, Vadilal** (*Ed.*) : 1970 : *Infrastructure for the Indian Economy*. Bombay, Voca & Co.: 219-25 (Tripura).

1126. ——— (*Ed.*) : 1974 : *A Regional Profile of Indian Agriculture*. Bombay, Vora & Co., 311p.

1127. **Dainik Sambad** : 1986 : Tripura. *Dainik Sambad* (Agartala), Sept. 10.

1128. **Dalton, E.T.** : 1872 : *Descriptive Ethnology of Bengal*. Calcutta, Supdt. Govt. Printing: 109-11 (*Reprinted* in 1960 by Indian Studies : Past and Present Calcutta : 106-17).

1129. ——— : 1973: *Tribal History of Eastern India*. Delhi, Cosmo Publications (This is the *Reprint* of the book "*Descriptive Ethnology of Bengal*").

1130. **Dam, Marcus** : 1988 : CM's address aimed at wooing tribal voters. *Statesman*, Feb. 11: 16(3-4).

1131. **Das, Amal Kumar** : 1968 : An Analysis of Social System of Chakma Community (Abstract). *Proceedings of Indian Science Congress*, 55th session, part III: 536.

1132. **Das, A.K., Chaudhuri,** M.K. *and* Basu, S. : 1982 : Anthropology of Development : Socio Economic Condition of the Scheduled Tribes and Scheduled Castes of Eastern India (*In*) *Tribal Development in India : Problems and Prospects (Ed)* by Buddhadeb Choudhuri. Delhi, Inter India Publications: 353-70.

1133. **Das, Asim Ranjan** : 1985 : Faunal Resources (*An Anthology of Tripura (Ed)* by Jagadis Gan-Choudhuri. New Delhi, Inter India Publications: 21-27.

1134. **Das, Biplab** : 1986: The Uchais of Tripura. *Folklore*, 27 (8). Aug. : 171-76.

1135. ——— : 1986 : The Uchai of Tripura: An Ethnographic Note. *Human Science* (Anth. Survey of India, Calcutta), 35 (3), Sept.: 241-246.

1136. **Das, Dasarath** : 1979 : Uplift of Scheduled Castes and Tribes. *Economic Times*, Jan. 5: 4(1).

1137. **Das, Durga** : 1973 : *Sardar Patel's Correspondence*, vol. 5 and 8. Delhi, Govt. of India.

1138. **Das, Jogendra Chandra** : 1987 : Establishment of Tripura Government Law College. *Proceedings of NEIHA* (Kohima), vol. 8: 571-73.

1139. ——— : 1989 : Population education in Tripura. *Proceedings of NEIHA* (Shillong), Xth (Annual) Session. Shillong, North Eastern Hill University, History Deptt. 389-392.

1140. **Das, Jogesh** : 1972 : *Folklore of Assam* (Folklore of India series). New Delhi, National Book Trust, India: 5,34,35.

1141. **Das, J.N.** : 1986 : Land, Land-relations and Land reforms in the plains and valleys of North-East India *(In) Land Reforms and Peasant Movement : A Study of North East India, (Ed)* by Atul Goswami. New Delhi, Omsons Publications: 11-14.

1142. ——— : 1990 : *A Study of the land system of Tripura*. Gauhati, Law Research Institute (Sponsored by NEC, Shillong), 196p.

1143. ——— : 1990 : *A Study of administration of justice among the tribes and races of North Eastern Region (excluding Nagaland and Meghalaya)*. Gauhati, Law Research Institute, Eastern Region (1987). 627p.

1144. **Das, K.L.** : 1939 : Note on the geology of Tripura State. *(in Bengali). Quart. Jour. Geol. Min. Met. Soc. Ind.*, vol. 2(3) : 119-22.

1145. **Das, M.T.** : 1979 : On making the single teacher schools of Tripura Viable Educational Institutions. *Jour. Ind. Education*, 4(6), March: 44-8.

1146. **Das, N.C.** : 1984 : Problems of marketing of handloom products in north eastern region with special reference to Assam, *(In) Marketing in North East India, (Ed)* by J.B. Ganguly. Gauhati, Omsons Publications: 119-131.

1147. **Das, N.K.** : 1989 : *Ethnicity and Social Stratification in North East India*. New Delhi, Inter India Publications.

1148. **Das, R.** : 1977 : Variation in later spaces of the foot in certain populations of North East India. *Man in India,* 57(3) : 263-68.

1149. **Das, Rabindranath** : 1974 : Prachin Tripura Mudra tattye Mat O Murti. *(in Bengali). Ajanta,* 1st year, vol. VI (Agartala) : 3.

1150. ——— : 1986 : Tulanamulak Bhasatatter Dristite Kok-Borok Sabdasambhar. *(in Bengali). Tirthamukh* (Agartala), vol. II: 13.

1151. **Das, Ratna** : 1975 : Pratna Upakarane Prachin Tripura *(In) Tripura Prasanga (in Bengali) (Ed)* by Swapan Sengupta. Agartala, Directorate of Public Relations & Tourism : 11-18.

1152. ——— : 1977: Tripurar Puratatwick Silpa *(in Bengali). Samachar* (Agartala) : 168-77.

1153. ——— : 1979: Art in Tripura coinage. *Jour.N.S.I.,* XLI, pt. I & II. 116.

1154. ——— : 1985 : Socio-Religious Background of Art Heritage, *(In) An Anthology of Tripura (Ed)* by Jagadis Gan Choudhuri. New Delhi, Inter-India Publications : 29-35.

1155. **Das, S.B.** : 1975 : Gas strike in Tripura : Marketing problem. *Economic Times,* March 9: 5 (5).

1156. **Das, Sarat Chandra**: 1898 : Note on the antiquity of Chittagong (based on Tibetan Records). *Jour. Royal Asiatic Society of Bengal,* pt. I, page 20.

1157. **Das, S.M.** :1967: A Brief scheme for formation of Hills States *(In) A Common Perspective for North East India, (Eds)* by R. Mitra *and* B. Das Gupta. Calcutta, Pannalal Das Gupta : 138-40.

1158. **Das, S.T.** : 1986 : *Tribal Life of North Eastern India.* Delhi, Gyan Publishing House.

1159. **Das, Tarak Chandra** :1955 : Social organisation *(In) The Adivasis* by Publication Division. Delhi, Ministry of Information and Broadcasting, Govt. of India (December, 1955) : 99-117.

1160. **Das, T.C.** : 1963 : Aspects of Tribal culture under modern impact in Eastern India *(In) Anthropology on the March, (Ed)* by Bala Ratnam. Madras, The Book Centre : 137-54.

1161. **Das, Tapan Kumar** : 1986 : Eastern States need massive fertiliser drive. *Amrita Bazar Patrika*, Nov. 24 : 5 (1).

1162. **Das, Umakanta** : 1887 : *Letter from Babu Umakanta Das, Asstt. Political Agent of Hill Tipperah, to Babu Harcharan Nandi, Dewan in Charge of H.H. the Maharajah's English Officer*, No. 1066, dated Agartala, the 7th January, 1887.

1163. **Das Chaudhuri, A.B.** :1991: Primate studies in India—A Review. *Man in India*, 71 (1), March, *Spl. Issue*: 241-277.

1164. **Das Gupta, Barun** :1988: Tripura Scene : Peace prospects before poll brighter. *Shillong Times*, Jan. 18: 2(3-6), 3 (1-3).

1165. ——— : 1988: Tripura: An uneasy alliance. *Shillong Times*, Feb. 18: 2(3-6), 3(5-6).

1166. ——— : 1990: Funds held back, says Tripura Tribal District Council. *Shillong Times*, Feb. 23: 2(3-6).

1167. ——— : 1990: Tripura CPI (M) echoes TSF demand over 'Inner Line'. *Amrita Bazar Patrika*, Feb 28: 7(1-7).

1168. **Das Gupta, K.R.** :1983: Need for agricultural resource planning in the North Eastern Region with a view to boosting agricultural production. *Social Research : Jour. of Institute of Social Research* (Shillong), 3(3-4), July-Dec.: 13-22.

1169. ——— : 1985: An Introspection on achievement in food grains production in the North Eastern Region during the plan era 1950-'51 to 1980-'81. *(In) Planning in North East India, (Ed)* K. Alam. New Delhi, Omsons Pubs : 207-13.

1170. **Das Gupta, Malabika** :1981: Comments on a model of Technological change in Agriculture. *Jour. NEICSSR*, V(II), Oct. : 27-31.

1171. ——— : 1983 : Anatomy of a Jhum failure : Some extensions. *Jour. NEICSSR*, 7 (1), April : 19-25.

1172. ——— : 1983 : Panchayat level planning in Tripura : A case study. Proceedings of a Seminar on *"Planning in North East India: Retrospective and Perspective"*, April 21-23 by NEICSSR, Shillong.

1173. **Das Gupta, Malabika** : 1985 : Panchayat level Planning in Tripura : A Case Study, *(In) Planning in North*

East India. (Ed) by K. Alam. New Delhi, Omsons Pubs. : 173-80.

1174. ——— : 1985 : Class formation among the Mogs of Tripura : A Preliminary Exploration in two villages in South Tripura District. Proceedings of a Seminar on *"Sequences in Development in North East India (A Study of Tradition, Continuity and Change)"*, held on 9-10 Dec. 1985, organised by NEICSSR, Shillong.

1175. ——— : 1986: North East : Regional imbalances and seventh plan Economic and Political *Weekly*, XXI, March 29: 528-29.

1176. ———: 1986: Greater Mizoram issue and Tripura. *Ecomomic and Political Weekly*, XXI, Sept. 13: 1629-30.

1177. ——— : 1986: The Jhumias of Tripura. *Economic and Political Weekly*, XXI (44-45), Nov. 1-8: 1955-1960.

1178. ———: 1986: Some empirical evidence on the changing marriage system among the Reangs of Tripura. *Proceedings of NEIHA* (Pasighat), vol. 7: 301-08.

1179. ———: 1986: *Then and Now : Planning and Plan Implementation in Tripura*. Agartala, Govt. of Tripura, 7p.

1180. ——— : 1986: Nationalities, Ethnicity and Cultural Identity: A case study of the Mizos of Tripura. Proceedings of a Seminar of *"Questions of Nationalities, Ethnicity and Cultural Identity in the context of North East India"*, 5-6 Dec.1986 by NEICSSR, Shillong: 10p *(Mimeo)*.

1181. ———: 1986: The Jhumias of Tripura in the past and at present, *(In) Tribes of Tripura, (Ed)* by Sudhanshu Bikash Saha. Agartala, Rupali Book Store: 93-114.

1182. ———: 1986 : Geology with special reference to forests, the N-E in 2000 AD (Perspective for futurology; A Social Scientist's a point of view). Proceedings of a Seminar on *"North East India 2000 AD: Perspective for Futurology"*, held on 3-5 April, 1986 by NEICSSR, Shillong.

1183. **Das Gupta, Malabika** : 1987: The Impact of LAMPS on the marketing of oranges in Tripura. *Jour NEICSSR*, XI (1), April:23-8.

1184. ——— : 1987: Will the creation of small farms through land reforms solve Tripura's agrarian problems ? The search for an alternative solution. Proceedings of a Seminar on *"Impact of Land Reforms on North East India*, held on 24-25 April, 1987, by NEICSSR, Shillong.

1185. ——— : 1987: Land alienation and social discontent in Tripura : A Preliminary Hypothesis. *(In) Land Relating in North East India, (Ed)* by B.B. Dutta *and* M.N. Karna. New Delhi, Peoples Publishing House: 234-242.

1186. ——— : 1988 : Congress (I) moves misfire pre-election scene in Tripura. *Economic and Political Weekly,* XXIII (4), Jan. 23: 119-121.

1187. ——— : 1988 : Rehabilitations Jhumias on Rubber plantations: An Assessment of the Tripura Experiment. Proceedings of a Seminar on *"Review and Re-Appraisal Seminar on Shifting Cultivation in North East India"*, held on 13-14 May 1988 by NEICSSR, Shillong.

1188. ——— : 1989-'91 : *The Alienation of Tribal Lands in Tripura* (Research Project grant by Ministry of Agriculture, Deptt. of Rural Development, Govt. of India).

1189. ——— : 1989 : Development and Ecology: Case Study of Gumti river in Tripura. *Economic & Political Weekly,* XXIV (40), Oct. 7: 2267-70.

1190. ——— : 1989 : Class formation among the Mogs of Tripura : A Preliminary Exploration in two villages in South Tripura District, *(In) Sequences of Development in North East India, (Ed)* by J.B. Bhattacharjee. New Delhi, Omsons Pubs. : 223-33.

1191. ——— : 1989 : Bride price and the status of Riang women in Tripura. Proceedings of a seminar on *"Status of Women in the Tribal Societies of Tripura"*, sponsored by the ICSSR (NERC), held at Agartala on Jan. 14,1989 in Tripura University *(Mimeo.)*.

1192. **Das Gupta, Malabika** : 1990 : Nationalities, Ethnicities and Cultural Identity: A case study of the Mizos of Tripura, *(In) Nationality, Ethnicity and Cultural*

Identity in North East India, (Ed). by B. Pakem. New Delhi, Omsons Pubs.: 365-76.

1193. ——— : 1991 : Land alienation among Tripura Tribals. *Economic and Political Weekly*, XXVI (36), Sept. 7: 2113-18.

1194. ——— : 1991 : Rehabiliting Jhumiyas on Rubber Plantations : An account of the Tripura experiment, *(In) Shifting Cultivation in North East India, (Ed)* by D.N. Majumdar. New Delhi, Omsons Pubs. : 308-11.

1195. **Das Gupta, Malabika** *and* **Banerjee, Asis** : 1984 : Jhuming as the way of life of the Jhumias : An analysis of data from Tripura. *Jour. NEICSSR*, 8(1), April : 17-25.

1196. **Das Gupta, M., Gangopadhyay, A.K., Bhattacharya, T.** *and* **Chakraborti, M.** *(Eds.)* : 1986 : *Forestry Development in North East India*. Guwahati, Omsons Pubs., 269p. (Seminar papers on *"Planning for Forestry Development in North East Region,"* organised by the Deptt. on Analytical and Applied Economics of Calcutta University Post Graduate Centre with colaboration of NEICSSR, Shillong on Feb. 27, 1984).

1197. **Das Gupta, Nalini Kanta** : ? : Banglaye Boudha Dharma *(in Bengali)*.

1198. **Das Gupta, Prakash**: 1976 : Tripura : A confluence of many cultures. *North Eastern Review*, November issue.

1199. **Das Gupta, Shashibhushan: ?** : *Obscure Religious Cults*. Agartala.

1200. **Das Gupta, Tamonash Chandra: ?** : *Prachin Bangla Sahityer Itihas*.

1201. **Das Gupta, Tarit Mohan** : 1963 : Tripuraye Ganatantrik Andolaner Itikatha (History of the Democratic Movement in Tripura). *(in Bengali). Nagrik (Agartala), 5 (23), July 1.*

1202. ——— : 1972: Swadhinata Andolan O Tripura. *(in Bengali). Uditi*, Kartik-Chaitra, 1379 (Bengali era): 232.

1203. **Das Gupta, Tarit Mohan** : 1974 : Ratanmani and the Reang Revolt. *(Gomati*, August 15:21.

1204. ——— : 1975 : Riang Vidroha, 1943. *(In) Tripura Prasanga (in Begali), (Ed)* by Swapan Sen Gupta. Agartala, Directorate of Public Relation and Tourism: 36-68.

1205. ——— : 1986 : State Congress and participation of Tribal people, *(In) Tribes of Tripura, (Ed)* by Sudhanshu Bikash Saha. Agartala, Rupali Book Store: 25-30.

1206. **Das Shastri, Rabindranath** *(Ed)* :1980: *Tirtha Mukh*. Agartala, Pub. by the editor.

1207. ——— : 1985 : Sanskritic culture in Tripura. *Proceedings of NEIHA* (Agartala), vol. 6: 69-76.

1208. ——— : 1985 : A Survey of Sanskrit Studies, *(In) An Anthology of Tripura, (Ed)* by Jagadis Gan Choudhuri. New Delhi, Inter-India Pubs.:113-25.

1209. ——— : 1986 : Influence of Sanskrit on the people of princely Tripura, *(In) Tribes of Tripura (Ed)* by Sudhanshu Bikash Saha. Agartala, Rupali Book Store : 39-53.

1210. **Datta, Biren** :1952 : Tripurar Janatar Ganatantrick Andolaner Rup-O-Nirbachanottar Tripura. *(in Bengali). Tripurar Katha,* Aswin, 1359 *(Bengali era)* : 20.

1211. **Datta, Biren** : 1982 : Amar smritite Tripurar Communist O Ganatantrick Andolaner Patabhumika *(in Bengali)*. Calcutta, (September), 39p.

1212. ——— : 1986 : Communist Movement and its Influence Among the Tribals, *In Tribes of Tripura, (Ed)* by Sudhanshu Bikash Saha. Agartala, Rupali Book Store : 31-8.

1213. **Datta, B.B.** :1984: "Tradition *v.* modernity". Proceedings of a Seminar on *"Planning for Forestry Development."* organised by Calcutta University Post Graduate Centre, Agartala with colaboration of NEICSSR, Shillong on Feb. 27.

1214. **Datta, Brajendra Chandra** : 1931 : Udaipur Bibaran (An Account of Udaipur) *(in Bengali)*. Agartala, Govt. Press, 44p.

1215. ——— : ? : *Dharmanagar Bibaran*. Agartala, Govt Press.

1216. **Datta, D.C.** *and* **Banerjee, S.** (Eds) :1976 : *Rajgi, Tripurar Sarkari Bangla*. Agartala, Directorate of Education (Tripura) : 184-85.

1217. **Datta, Jyotirmay** : 1978 : Emergence and role of Middle Class in Tripura. Proceedings of a Seminar on *"Emergence of Middle Class in North East India"*, held on 4-5 Dec. by NEICSSR, Shillong.

1218. ——— : 1980 : Tripuri tribe : A Social and anthropological study. Proceedings of a Seminar on *"Tribes of North East India,"* held on 22-24 September by Sacred Heart Theological College, Shillong collaboration with NEICSSR, Shillong.

1219. ——— : 1981 : Land and land Relations in Tripura. Proceedings of a Seminar on *"Land and Land Relations in the Hills of North East India,"* held on 28-30 May, by NEICSSR, Shillong.

1220. ——— : 1983 : The emergence and role of tribal middle class in Tripura *(In) The Emergence and Role of Middle Class in North East India (Ed)* by B. Dutta Roy. New Delhi, Uppal Publishing House : 193-97.

1221. **Datta, Jyotirmay** : 1987 : *Land and Land Relations on North East India (Ed)* by B.B. Dutta *and* M.N. Karna. New Delhi, Peoples Publishing House : 213-220.

1222. **Datta, J.C.** : 1985 : Inscriptions on land grants *(In) An Anthology of Tripura (Ed)* by Jagadis Gan Choudhuri. New Delhi, Inter India Publications : 37-43.

1223. **Datta, K.P.** :1984 : Tripura tribal extremism: Genesis and growth. *Mainstream*, 22(51), August 18: 31-3.

1224. **Datta, M.S.** and **Nandi, S.B.** : 1988 : Tribes in Eastern India : Selection of mates and trends in marriage *(In) Marriage in India (Eds)* by B.B. Goswami, J. Sarkar *and* D. Danda. Calcutta, Anthropological Survey of India : 34-40.

1225. **Datta, Narendra Chandra** :1980 : Land Reform *(In) Tripura : The Land and its People (Ed)* by Jagadis Gan Chaudhuri. Delhi, Leeladevi Publications : 115-123.

1226. **Datta, P.S.** : 1988 : Shifting Cultivation of North East : A Case for reassessment. *Proceedings of a Seminar of IASSI*, Nov. 1-3, New Delhi *(Mimeo.)*.

1227. **Datta, Rama Prasad** : 1985 : Development of Bengali Newspapers in Tripura. *Proceedings of NEIHA* (Agartala), vol. 6: 341-46.

1228. **Datta, Sekhar** :1990 : Identity cards to check influx : Tripura. *The Telegraph, June 7.*

1229. **Datta Roy, B.** (Ed) : 1978 : *Social and Economic Profile of North East India.* Delhi, B.R. Publishing Corporation.

1230. ——— : 1989 : *Tribal Identity and tension in North East India.* New Delhi, Omsons Publications : 26-7, 45-6.

1231. **Datta Ray, Sunanda K.** 1988 : Tripura's gift to Rajiv : No card left for opposition ? *Statesman,* Feb. 7 : 8 (4-6).

1232. **Dattatreya** : 1965 : *Tripura — rahasyai (jnanakhanda)* (English translation: "Comparative study of the process of individuation"], Varanasi, Chowkhamba Sanskrit Series Office, 1965, 198p.

1233. **David, A.W.** : 1894 : *Gazeetteer of the North Lushai Hills.* Shillong, Assam Secretariat Printing Office.

1234. **De, Ranjit** : ? : *Tripurar Loka Jiban O Loka Sanskriti (in Bengali).* Agartala, 20p.

1235. **De, Ranjit Kumar** : 1985 : Terrorist activities in Tripura. *Proceedings of NEIHA* (Agartala), Vol. 6: 371-82.

1236. **De, Ranjit Kumar** : 1986 : Impact of Non-Cooperation movement on Tripura (1920-'21). *Proceedings of NEIHA* (Pasighat), vol. 7: 465-73.

1237. ——— : 1987 : Congress in Tripura in its formation. *Proceedings of NEIHA* (Pasighat), vol. 7.

1238. ——— : 1987 : Formation of the Tripura Congress Committee and its work, 1939-1942. *Proceedings of NEIHA* (Kohima). vol. 8 : 451-63.

1239. ——— : 1988 : Tripura Rajya Jana Siksha Samiti : Its origin and activities. *Proceedings of NEIHA* (Guwahati), vol. 9: 373-78.

1240. ——— : 1989 : The Reang Rebellion. *Proceedings of NEIHA,* Xth Annual Session, Oct. 12-14 (Shillong).

1241. **Deb, Dasarath** 1977 : Kok Borok. *Chauraung* (Agartala).

1242. ——— : 1979 : Uplift of Scheduled Tribes and Castes. *Economic Times,* Jan. 5: 4(1).

1243. **Deb, Dasarath** : 1981 : Seminar on *"National Integration".* Pub. by Deptt. of Information and Culture, Govt. of Tripura, Agartala.

1244. ——— : 1986 : Evolution and activities of the Gana Mukti Parishad *(In) Tribes of Tripura (Ed)* by Sudhanshu Bikash Saha. Agartala, Rupali Book Store : 19-24.

1245. **Deb, D.B.** : 1960 : Effect of Jhum cultivation in Tripura Territory. *Unpub.* manuscript.

1246. ——— : 1963 : Bibliographical review on the botanical studies in Tripura. *Bulletin of the Botanical Survey of India, 5(1) : 49-59.*

1247. ——— : 1975 : Flora of Tripura *(In Tripura District Gazetteers (Ed)* by K.D. Menon. Agartala.

1248. ——— : 1975 : Economic Plants of Tripura State—Timber Yielding Plants (Miscellaneous Uses). *Indian Forest,* 101 (6) : 328-36.

1249. **Deb, D.B.** : 1976 : Economic Plants of Tripura State—Pasture and Fodder. *Indian Forest,* 104(4) : 275-81.

1250. ——— : 1981 : *Flora of Tripura, vol.I.* Today and Tomorrow Printers and Publications, New Delhi.

1251. ——— : 1968 : Medicinal Plants of Tripura State. *Indian Forest 94 (10) : 733-65.*

1252. **Deb, Ramnarayan** : 1967 : *Rajmala.* Education Deptt., Govt of Tripura.

1253. **Deb, Ranendranath** : ? : *Srihatta Parichay (in Bengali).* Dacca, 40p.

1254. **Deb Barma, Aghore** : 1954 : Riang Krishak Bidroha-O-Sahid Sri Ratanmoni (Riang Peasants Revolution and Martyr Sri Ratanmoni). *Tripurar Katha* (Agartala), *Saradiya Issue,* 1361 B.S.

1255. ——— : 1986 : Tripura Raja, Communist Party O Ganatantrik andolaner prathamik star *(in Bengali).* Agartala : 22-3.

1256. **Deb Barman, Aghore** :1986 : Praja Mandal, its activities among the tribals *(In) Tribes of Tripura (Ed)* by Sudhanshu Bikash Saha. Agartala, Rupali Book Store : 153-58.

1257. ——— : 1986 : *Primary stage of the Democratic and Communist Movement in Tripura.* Agartala. : 24-5.

1258. **Deb Barman, Aghore** : 1987 : Tripura. Proceedings of a Seminar on *"Impact of Land Reforms on North*

East India", 24-25 April, 1987, organised by NEICSSR, Shillong.

1259. **Deb Barma, Ajay** : 1374B.S. : **Tripurár Rupkatha** *(In) Bhaskar*, vol. II. Agartala (1967).

1260. **Deb Barma, Ajit Bandhu** : 1967 : *Kok-Ravam (English-Tripuri Dictionary)*. Agartala, Pub. by the author, 71p.

1261. ——— : ? : *Kok-surunma, Part I and II*. Agartala, Education Directorate (Tripura).

1262. **Deb Barman, Brajendra Kishor** :1975 : Rabindra Sannidhe *(in Bengali) (In) Tripura Prasanga (Ed)* by Swapan Sengupta. Agartala, Directorate of Public Relation & Tourism : 135-47.

1263. **Deb Barman, D.** 1983 : *Treatise on traditional social Institutions of the Tripuri Communities*. Agartala, Directorate of Research, Govt. of Tripura.

1264. **Deb Barma, Dasarath** : 1948 : Tripura Rajyee Bangal Kheda Andolan *(In) Tripura Rajyer Katha (In Bengali)*, no. 47, April : 1-2.

1265. ——— : 1953 : Tripura *(in Bengali). (In) Tripurar Katha* (Agartala), 3rd year, 2nd issue, May 25.

1266. **Deb Barma, Dhabal Krishna** : 1975 : Tripuraye Mishra Sanskritir Rup Rekha *(In Bengali) (In) Tripura Prasanga (Ed)* by Swapan Sengupta. Agartala, Directorate of Pub. Rel. and Tourism : 57-71.

1267. **Deb Barman, Dhirendra Krishna** : 1975 : Tripurar Shilper Itibrittya *(In) Tripura Prasanga (Ed)* by Swapan Sengupta. Agartala, Dir. of Pub. Rel. and Tourism : 5-16 *(In Benglai)*.

1268. **Deb Barma, D.P.** : 1983 : *Treatise on Traditional Institutions of the Tripuri Community*. Directorate of Research. Deptt. of Welfare of Sch. Tribes and Sch. Castes, Govt, of Tripura, 108p.

1269. **Deb Barma, Harendra Kishore** : 1973 : Tripuraye Riang Bidroha-O-Ratanmanir Andolan *(In Bengali). Saptahik Basumati* (Calcutta), Nov. 11 and 18, 1973.

1270. ——— : 1974 : Ratanmoni-O-Riang Bidroha *(in Bengali). Gomati, Sarat Sankalan*, Oct. 15, 1974.

1271. **Deb Barman, Jitendra Mohan** : 1958 : Origin of Tripura and Its People. *Vanyajati,* 6 (3), Jul.: 108-16.

1272. **Deb Barma, Mahendra** : 1967 : Tripurye Sangeet-O-Nritya *(in Bengali). Bhaskar,* vol. II 1374 B.S.

1273. **Deb Barma, Monimay** : 1977-'78 : Tripurar Praja Andolan, Kichu Tathya. *(in Bengali). Dainik Sangbad* (Agartala), December 14,19,24,25 of 1977; January 30, February 5.6.7; March 31; April 1, 27; July 8 of 1978.

1274. ——— : 1979 : *Bidrohi Riang Neta Ratanmoni.* Agartala, Pub. by the author.

1275. **Deb Barman, Mrinal** : 1976 : Chuak : A drink for tribals in Tripura. *Folklore,* 17(11) : 347-51.

1276. **Deb Barman, Mrinal** : 1978 : Musical duel of Riangs. *Folklore, 19(1), January : 28-31.*

1277. ——— : 1978 : Some Kok-Borok (Tripuri) proverbs with illustrations. *Folklore,* 19(2), February: 52-6.

1278. **Deb Barma, N.C.** : 1985 : *A Hand Book of Spoken Kok Borok.* Agartala, Directorate of Research (Tripura), 84p.

1279. ——— : 1985 : *Compilation of Tripuri Folk Songs.* Agartala, Directorate of Research, 80p.

1280. **Deb Barma, Radhamohan** : 1966 : *Kok-Borok-Ma : Tripuri Vyakaran.* Agartala, Education Directorate (Tripura).

1281. ——— : 1968 : *Tripurar Kathamala.* Agartala, Education Directorate.

1282. **Deb Barman, Samarendra Chandra** : 1927 : *Tripurar Smiti (in Bengali).* Agartala, Pub. by the author, 20p. (Reprinted in 1983).

1283. ——— : 1933 : *1340 Tripurabder Census Bibarani (in Bengali).* Agartala, Tripura Govt. Press, 22p. [It contains information about the census conducted in Tripura between the period 1872 to 1931].

1284. **Deb Barma, Sudhir Krishna** : ? : *Surungma Yakhli.* Agartala.

1285. **Deb Barman, Suren** : 1990 : Tagore's Life-long ties with Tripura. *Amrita Bazar Patrika (Sunday Magazine), Oct. 21 : I (1-8).*

1286. **Deb Barma, S.L.** : 1983 : *Sadharan Samikshar Aloke Uchai.* Agartala, Dir. of Research, 46p.

1287. **Deb Barman, Thakur Hriday Ranjan** : 1930-'31 : *Tripurabder Memo Circularadi Sangraha (in Bengali).* Agartala, 1340 T.E. (1302). .

1288. **Deb Barma, Thakur Mahim Chandra** : ? : *Deshiya Rajye.* Agartala, Govt. Press : 133, 167, 186, 199, 208, 228, 244, 250, 260.

1289. **Deb Barma, Thakur Samendra Chandra** : 1930 : *Tripura Rajyer Census Bibarani (in Bengali).* Agartala, Census Deptt., 37p.

1290. **Deb Bharati, Tarak** : 1973 : Eastern Indian Handicrafts : A Preliminary Survey. *Folklore,* XIX(9), Sept. : 354-59.

1291. **Deb Barman, Bijoy Kumar** : 1976 : Tripuraye Kharchi O Ker Puja. *Gomati,* August, Spl, issue.

1292. **Deb Choudhury, Charu Bhusan** : 1940 : *Ancient Tripura and its modern rulers.* Coomilla, Uttara Kutir, 25p.

1293. **Deb Nath, K.R.** : 1985 : Demographic aspects of Development Planning in the North Eastern Region. *Jour. of the North Eastern Council,* 6(1-4), Jan.-April : 23-8.

1294. ——— : 1986 : Demographic aspects of development planning in the North Eastern Region *(In) The Pattern and Problems of Population in North East India (Ed)* by B. Datta Ray. New Delhi. Uppal Publishing House : 1-21.

1295. **Department of Agriculture** : 1977 : *A Guide to Tripura Agriculture.* Agartala, Deptt. of Agriculture (Tripura).

1296. **Department of Analytical** : ? : *Evaluation of Jhumia Rehabilitation (Scheme Report).* Agartala, Deptt. of Analytical and Applied Economics, Calcutta post Graduate Centre.

1297. **Department of Satistics** : 1966 : *Bulletin of Tea Statistics.* Agartala, Deptt. of Statistics, Govt. of Tripura.

1298. ——— : 1978 : *Bulletin of Tea Statistics.* Agartala, Deptt. of Statistics, Govt. of Tripura *(Mimeo.).*

1299. **Department of Welfare** : 1979 : *Compendium of various memoranda/instructions/ circulars/ rules / schemes on welfare of Scheduled Castes and Scheduled Tribes.* Agartala, Deptt. of Welfare for Sch. Caste and Sch. Tribes, 199p.

1300. **Devi, Amiya** : 1989 : *Letters to the Editor* : TV Feature on Tripura. *Assam Tribune,* Feb, 27 : 4 (5-6).

1301. **Dev, Chittaranjan** : 1970 : Tripura aur ushke adivashi *(in Hindi). Vanyajati,* XVIII (2), April : 30-31.

1302. **Dev, Dasarath** : 1981 : Proceedings of a Seminar on *"National Integration"* held in Agartala by Deptt. of Information and Culture, Govt. of Tripura.

1303. ——— : 1987 : *Mukti Parishader iti katha (in Bengali).* Calcutta, February, 14p.

1304. **Dev Burman, Kirit Vikram** : 1968 : *Letters to the Editor* : Spot light on Tripura. *Indian Express,* may 20 : 6(3) and may 21 : 6(3).

1305. ——— : 1968 : *Letters to the Editor* : Tribal Discontent. *Statesman,* June 2 : 8 (8).

1306. **Dev Barman, R.M.** : 1933 : *Tripur Kshatriya Samaj Sankranta Vivaran Sangraha.* Agartala, Pub. by the author, 57p.

1307. **Dev Barman, S.** : 1953 : *CPI (Tripura), Part 1.* Agartala, Pub. by the author 80 p.

1308. **Dev Sharma, J.N.** *and* **Kukis, J.M.** : 1958 : Origin of Tripura and its people. *Vanyajati,* 6(3) : 108-16.

1309. **Dev Varman, S.B.K.** : 1971 : *A Study over the jhum and jhumia : Rehabilitation in the Union Territory of Tripura.* Agartala, Directorate of Research, 27p.

1310. ——— : 1971 : *The Tribes of Tripura : A Dissertation.* Agartala, Directorate of Tribal Research, Govt. of Tripura. 52p *(Reprinted* in 1978, 1986 *and* 1987).

1311. ——— : 1972 : *Privileges and concessions provided for the Schedule Tribes of Tripura.* Agartala. Directorate of Tribal Research, Govt. of Tripura *(Special series).*

1312. ——— : 1972 : *A Study over the jhum and jhumia rehabilitation in the Union Territory of Tripura.* Agartala, Dir. of Research, Deptt. of Welfare for Sch. Tribes and Sch. Castes, Govt. of Tripura, 44p (*2nd edition* pub. in 1978).

1313. **Dev Varman, S.B.K : 1972 :** *Irrijock* (i.e. Folklore, *in Bengali*). Agartala, Dir. of Tribal Research, 50p.

1314. ——— : 1973 : *Nakapilini Hamjag ma* (i.e. Folklore, *in Bengali*). Agartala, Dir. of Tribal Research (*Special series*).

1315. ——— : 1973 : *Thakugnmi* (i.e. Folklore, *in Bengali*). Agartala, Dir. of Tribal Research, 47p.

1316. ——— : 1974 : *Chhengthungfa Naithakbi* (i.e. Folklore, *in Bengali*). Agartala, Dir. of Research, 42p.

1317. ——— : 1974 : Chuak—A Drink for Tribals in Tripura. *Bulletin*, 1 (part III) : 26-35 (Dir. of Tribal Research, Agartala).

1318. ——— : 1974 : Village Economy Survey. *Bulletin* of Directorate of Tribal Research (Agartala), I (part II) : 15-25.

1319. ——— : 1974 : *Kokthun*. Agartala, Dir. of Research, 55p.

1320. ——— : n.m. : *The Tribes of Tripura*. Agartala, Dir. of Research. 32p.

1321. ——— : 1974 : Indebtedness and land alienation survey of Tribal family under Mohanpur Block. *Bulletin* of Directorate of Research (Agartala), I, (part I) : 1-14.

1322. ——— : 1976 : *Garia Puja*. Agartala, Dir. of Research, 32 p.

1323. ——— : 1978 : *A Study over the jhum and jhumia rehabilitation in the Union Territory of Tripura*. Agartala, Tribal Research Institute.

1324. **Dewan, A.Q.S.** : 1989 : *Letters to the Editor* : Weekday Post : Chakma Problem. *Amrita Bazar Patrika*, Jan. 25 : 6 (3-4).

1325. **Dewan, Biraj Mohan** : 1969 : *Chakma jatir Itibrittya (in Bengali)*. New Rangamati (Bangladesh), Pub. by the author, Hill Chittagong (1390 T.D.)

1326. **Dewan, Vijay Kumar** : 1976 : *North Eastern Region : Local Acts of Assam, Nagaland, Meghalaya, Manipur, Tripura, Mizoram and Arunachal Pradesh, Vol. 7*. Allahabad, Orient Law House, 784p.

1327. ——— : 1978 : *The North Eastern Region : Forest Acts and Rules with Indian Forest Acts, 1927*. Allahabad, Orient Law House, 360p.

1328. **Dewan, Vijay Kumar** : 1985 : *Commentary on the Assam urban areas Rent Control Act 1972 with Meghalaya, Tripura and Mizoram Act with Supplement.* Allahabad, Orient Law House.

1329. ———: 1986 : *North Eastern Regional Local Acts and Rules in 12 vols.* [Encyclopaedia of Local Acts and Rules on Assam, Nagaland, Meghalaya, Manipur, Tripura, Mizoram and Arunachal Pradesh, (1984-'86), 2nd edition].

1330. **Dey, B.** : 1979 : Cooperative achievements in Tripura. *Khadi Gramodyog,* 21 (2) : 136-40.

1331. **Dey, Jatin** : 1967 : A scheme for a zonal Government in the Eastern Region. *(In) A Common Perspective for North East India, (Eds)* by R. Mitra *and* B. Das Gupta. Calcutta, Pannalal Das Gupta : 148-52.

1332. **Dey, Sudhin** : 1979 : Void that helps Amra Bengali. *Statesman,* June 17 : 5(2).

1333. ——— : 1979 : Tripura concerned over missionaries activities. *Statesman,* June 19.

1334. **Dhar, Biman Behari** : 1973 : Tritiya-O-Chaturtha Dashake Tripuraye Riang Praja Bidroha. *(in Bengali). Jwala* (Agartala), 3(2-3), Jan,-Feb.

1335. **Dhar, Prabhas C.** : 1983 : *Kok Borok Swroungma* (A grammar of spoken Kakbarak). Agartala, Directorate of Research, 134p.

1336. ———: 1986 : Kakbarak : Problems and Prospects, *(In) Tribes of Tripura, (Ed)* by Sudhanshu Bikash Saha. Agartala Rupali Book Store : 115-127.

1337. **Dibrugarh University** : 1975 : Seminar on *"Sociological Perspective on North Eastern India and the Second Annual Conference of the North East India (Sociological Association)."* Dibrugarh University, Deptt. of Sociology (March 10-12, 1975).

1338. **Dikshit, Moreswar G.** : 1955 : *Tripuri — 1952, being the account of the excavation at Tripuri.* Nagpur, Govt. of M.P. 139p.

1339. **Directorate of Economics** : 1976 : *Statistical Hand book of Tripura.* Agartala, Directorate of Economics and Statistics.

1340. **Directorate of Education** : 1961 : *First Year book of Education (Review of Education in India : 1947-1961) Tripura.* Agartala, Deptt. of Education : 728-738.

1341. ——— : 1975 : *Chakma.* Agartala, Direc. of Education (Tripura).

1342. ——— : 1978-'82 : *Educational Miscellany,* Vol, XII, July, 1978 to June, 1982, *Special Issue.* Agartala, Direc. of Education (Tripura).

1343. ——— : 1987 : *Advancement in Education in Tripura—Some useful informations.* (Booklet, *in Bengali*). Agartala, Statistics and Survey Organisation of the Directorate of Education, Tripura, 26th January.

1344. **Director General** : 1952 : *Inspection Note of the Director-General of Archaeology.* Agartala, Govt. of Tripura, 3p.

1345. **Directorate of Industries** : 1959 : *Handicraft in Tripura.* Agartala, Directorate of Industries (Tripura).

1346. **Directorate of Information** : ? : *Wave of Development in Tripura.* Agartala, Direc. of Infor. and Cultural Affairs, Tourism, Govt. of Tripura, 98 p.

1347. ——— : 1982 : *Four Years of Left Front Government in Tripura (in Bengali).* Agartala, Direc. of Infor. and Tourism, Govt. of Tripura, 65p.

1348. **Directorate of Land** : 1971 : *State Report on World Agricultural Census (1970-'71) in Tripura.* Agartala, Direc. of Land Records and Settlement (Tripura).

1349. ——— : 1977 : *State Report on Agricultural Census (1976-'77) in Tripura.* Agartala, Direc. of Land Records and Settlement.

1350. ——— : 1978 : *General Instructions for Revision of Records-of-rights (Organisation and Methodology).* Agartala, Directorate of Land Records and Settlement.

1351. **Director of Public Relations** : 1972 : *Tripura Review.* Agartala, Director of Public Relations and Tourism, 52p.

1352. **Director of Public Relations** : 1976 : *A Decade of development : Tripura.* Agartala, Govt. of Tripura, Direc. of Public Relations and Tourism, 57p.

1353. **Directorate of Research** : 1983 : *Upajati unnayene grihita bivinna karmasuchi.* Agartala, Direc. of Research, 22p.

1354. ——— : 1990 (?) : *The Lushais of Jampui Hills in Tripura.* Agartala, Direc, of Research.

1355. Directorate of Statistics : 1977 : *The National Sample Survey: Jhum Cultivation in Tripura (31st Round, July 1976 to June 1977).* Agartala, Direc. of Statistics and Evaluation.

1356. ——— : 1978 : *Statistical Abstract, Tripura.* Agartala, Direc. of Stat. and Evaluation.

1357. ——— : 1981 : *Some Basic Statistics of Tripura.* Agartala, Direc. of Stat. and Evaluation.

1358. ——— : 1983 : *Some Basic Statistics of Tripura.* Agartala, Direc. of Stat. and Evaluation.

1359. ——— : 1985 : *Some Basic Statistics of Tripura.* Agartala, Direc. of Statistics, Govt. of Tripura.

1360. ——— : 1988 : *Socio-Economic Indicators of Development.* Agartala, Direc. of Statistics, Govt. of Tripura.

1361. **District Council** : 1988 : *Tripura tribal area autonomous district Council (Third Year of Advancement, 1987-'88).* Agartala, District Council.

1362. **District Gazetteer** : 1914 : *Bengal District Gazetteer : Tippera District Statistics 1900-1901 to 1910-1911.* Calcutta, The Bengal.

1363. **Dube, Leela** : 1974 : Sociology of kinship : A trend report *(In) A Survey of Research in Sociology and Social Anthropology, vol. II* by ICSSR. Bombay, Popular Prakashan : 233-366.

1364. **Dubey, S.M.** *(Ed)* : 1978 : *North East India : A Sociological Study.* Delhi, Concept Pub. Company.

1365. **Duft, Mabel C.** : 1972 : *The Chronology of Indian History.* Delhi, Cosmo Publications.

1366. **Dutta, Aloke Kumar** : 1969 : Present trend of marriages and its implications among the aboriginal tribes of Tripura *(In) Trends of Socio-Economic Change in India (Ed)* by M.K. Chaudhuri. Simla, Prem Printing Press, 811p.

1367. **Dutta, Aloke Kumar** : 1969 : Present trend of marriages and its implications among the aboriginal tribes of Tripura. *(In) Transactions* by Indian Institute of Advance Studies. Simla, Indian Inst. of Adv. Studies : 65-77.

1368. **Dutta, Aloke Kumar** *and* **Ray, Biswanath** : 1974 : Tribal housing and its problems in rural Tripura. *Bulletin of the Cultural Research Institute* (Calcutta), 10(3-4) : 102-112.

1369. **Dutta, Aloke K.** *and* **Dutta, Manjusri** : 1976 : Variation in sex ratio in Tripura *(In) Biosocial studies in India (Eds)* by Kanti B. Pakrasi, Amulya R. Banerjee *and* Amal K. Das. Calcutta, Edition India : 668.

1370. **Dutta, Amitava** : 1970 : Pros and cons grant of Statehood of Tripura. *Tripura Times,* Puja No. (1377B.S) : 17-24.

1371. **Dutta, B.B.** *(Ed.)* : 1986 : *Land use pattern in North East India.* Ludhiana, Gagan Publications.

1372. **Dutta, Brojendra Chandra** : 1972 : *Tripura Rajye Trish Batsar, Khowai Bibhag.* Agartala, Education Directorate *(in Bengali).*

1373. ——— : 1933 : *Udaypur Bibaran.* Agartala, Education Directorate (1340B.S.).

1374. **Dutta, Dwijendra Chandra** : 1975 : Surer jharna tale : Tripura *(In) Tripura Prasanga (Ed)* by Swapan Sengupta. Agartala, Direc. of Public Relations and Tourism : 72-99 *(in Bengali).*

1375. **Dutta, Dwijendranath** *and* **Bandopadhyaya,** *(Eds.)* : 1976 : Bharater Swadhinata Dibas Upalakhsye 'Regent' Srimati Maharani Rajmatar Bani (In) Rajgi Tripurar Sarkari Bangla (Eds) by Dwijendranath Dutta *and* Suprasanna Bandopadhyaya. *Evidence,* No. 94 : 85. *(in Bengali).*

1376. **Dutta, Gita** *and* **Dutta, Mrinal** *(Guide)* : 1982 : *Vraman Sangi.* Calcutta, Asia Publishing Company : 437-443.

1377. **Dutta, G.N.** : 1973 : *Geological structure of Tripura Rocks, East of Kailasahar, Tripura State.* Abst. Proc., Indian Science Congress, 130p.

1378. ——— : 1974 : *Some Geomorphological Aspects of Tripura State. Absts. Indian Science Congress.*

1379. **Dutta, Jyotish Chandra** : 1972-'73 : Tripuraye Riang Bidroha (Riang Revolution in Tripura). *Uditi* (Agartala), 6(3-4), *Kartik* to *Chaitra*, 1379 B.S. *(in Bengali)*.

1380. **Dutta, J.C.** : 1982 : The Revenue Administration of Tripura State During The Late Manikya (1862-1947). *Unpublished* Ph.D. Thesis, University of Calcutta.

1381. ——— : 1984 : *The History of Tripura*. Calcutta.

1382. ——— : 1985 : Tenurial system of Tripura : A Historical Survey till 1947 *(In) Educational Miscellany, Special Issue*, vol. XIII, July 1982-June 1984 : 21-22.

1383. ——— : 1986 : Ghar chukti kar (House Tax) : A Study in the land system of Tripura in the hills *(In) Tribes of Tripura (Ed)* by Sudhanshu Bikash Saha. Agartala, Rupali Book Store : 139-152.

1384. ——— : 1986 : Tea cultivation in Tripura (1917-'47) : A Study in the land settlement and its revenue potential. *Proceedings of NEIHA* (Pasighat), vol. 7 : 421-26.

1385. ——— : *(Ed)* : 1987 : *Editorial : Bhumi-Lekhyapatrer aloke Tripurar Bhumi Vyabastha (1458-1850) (in Bengali)*. Agartala, Deptt. of Higher Education, Govt. of Tripura.

1386. ——— : 1987 : Kaziana : A Communal Tax upon the Muslim subjects of Tripura. *Proceedings of NEIHA* (Kohima), vol. 8 : 214-21.

1387. ——— : 1989 : A Study into the Awabs as in practice in Hill Tipperah and its attached Zamindaris in Chakla Roshonabad. *Proceedings of NEIHA* (Shillong), Xth (Annual) Session, Shillong, History Deptt., NEHU : 293-299.

1388. **Dutta, Krishnapada** : 1975 : Tripurar Abrita Itihas : Engraj-Parba. *(In) Tripura Prasanga (Ed)* by Swapan Sengupta. Agartala, Direc. of Public Relation and Tourism : 19-27 *(in Bengali)*.

1389. **Dutta, Nilmani** : 1975 : Tripuraye Manipuri Nritya Charcha *(In) Tripura Prasanga (Ed)* by Swapan Sengupta. Agartala, Direc. of Pub. Rel. and Tourism. : 100-112 *(in Bengali)*.

1390. **Dutta, N.C.** : 1961 : Land Reforms and Agrarian Relations in Tripura, *(In) Census of India 1971, Tripura, series 20*. Agartala, Tripura Census Operation : 8-10.

1391. **Dutta, N.C.** : 1975 : *Land Reforms and Agrarian Relation in Tripura.* Agartala, Direc. of Census Operations, 9p.

1392. **Dutta, N.C.** : 1984 : Land Reforms in Tripura. Proceedings of a Seminar on *"Land and Land Relations and Land Reforms in North East India"*, held on 17-18 April by NEICSSR, Shillong.

1393. **Dutta, N.C.** : 1986 : Land Reforms in Tripura *(In) Land Reforms and Peasant Movement : A Study of North East India (Ed)* by Atul Goswami. New Delhi, Omsons Publications : 130-144.

1394. ——— : 1987 : Land Reforms in North East India : A case study of Tripura. Proceedings of a Seminar on *"Impact of Land Reforms on North East India"*, held on 24-25 April by NEICSSR, Shillong.

1395. ——— : 1990 : Public sector undertakings in Tripura : A study of their performance. *Jr. NEICSSR* (Shillong), 14(1), April : 54-61.

1396. **Dutta, N.K.** : 1979 : Adequate scope for industrial growth. *Economic Times*, Jan. 5 : 4(5).

1397. **Dutta, Nani Ranjan** : 1986 : Assessment of forestry planning in Tripura during the five year plans, *(In Forestry Development in North East India (Eds)* by M. Das gupta *et al.* Guwahati, Omsons Publications : 110-19.

1398. **Dutta, Rama Prasad** : 1975 : Bibhinna Pustake Tripura Sambandhiya Tathya Panji *(In) Tripura Prasanga (Ed)* by Swapan Sengupta. Agartala, Dir. of Pub. Rel. and Tourism : 205-216.

1399. **Dutta, Rama Prasad** : 1980 : *Tripura Lusai Kukider Itikatha (in Bengali).* Agartala, Dir. of Research, Sch. Caste and Sch Tribe Welfare Division, Govt. of Tripura, 63p.

1400. **Dutt, R.P.** : 1986 : Tripura. *India Today*, April : 446.

1401. **Dutt, Shosee Chunder** : 1984 : *The Wild Tribes of India.* New Delhi. Cosmo Publications (*Reprinted*, 1st Published in 1884) : 170-72.

1402. **Dutta, S.K.** : 1981 : Tripura tea industry : Need for rehabilitation. *Economic Times*, Sept. 5 : 5.

1403. **Dutta, Upali** : 1987 : Ear-lobe type among the Jugi of West Tripura. *Vanyajati*, XXXV(4), Oct. : 4-14.

1404. **Dutta, Upali** *and* **Ghosh, G.C.** : 1988 : A Study of hand clasping and arm folding among the Jugi of Tripura. *Man in India*, 68(2-3), June-Sept. : 211-15.

1405. **Dutta Bhaumik, B.** : 1972 : Cong (N) infighting will mar. chances in Tripura. *Hindustan Times*, Feb. 28 : 6(5).

1406. ——— : 1980 : Parties exploit tribal Fears. *Hindustan Times*, Jan. 5.

1407. **Dutt Majumdar, Niharendu** : 1987 : *Letter to the Editor* : Save the Chakmas. *Amrita Bazar Patrika*, Jan. 10 : 4(3-4).

1408. ——— : 1990 : *Letters to the Editor* : Chakma Plight. *Statesman*, December 9 : 8(5).

1409. **Dwija, Bangachandra** : n.p. : Tripura Bangshabali. (*Unpublished mss. in Bengali*) [Kept in Rajamala Library and thereafter in M.B.B. College Library].

E

1410. **Economic** *and* **Political Weekly** : 1979 : Tripura : Early solution. *Economic and Political Weekly,* XIV (2), Jan 13 : 43-44.

1411. ——— : 1980 : Editorial : Tragic Aftermath in Tripura. *Eco. & Pol. Weekly,* XV (16), April 19 : 1566-1567.

1412. ——— : 1980 : Tripura : Depth of alienation. *Eco. & Pol. Weekly,* June 14 : 1634-35.

1413. ——— : 1986 : Tripura : Refugee Influx. *Eco. & Pol. Weekly,* XXI (38-39), Sept, 20-27 : 1664.

1414. ——— : 1988 : Deal in Tripura. *Eco. & Pol. Weekly,* XXIII (34), Aug. 20 : 1711.

1415. ——— : 1988 : Tripura : 'Security' for the Government. *Eco. & Pol. Weekly, XXIII(39), Sept. 24 : 1980.*

1416. ——— : 1988 : Tripura : On whose hands is this, blood ? *Eco. & Pol. Weekly,* XXIII(40), Oct. 1 : 2028.

1417. ——— : 1989 : Parliamentary Elections : Tripura style. *Eco. & Pol. Weekly,* XXIV(50), Dec. 16 : 2757-58.

1418. ——— : 1990 : Tripura : Upstaging TUJS. *Eco. & Pol. Weekly,* XXV(15), April 14 : 749(col. 3) and 750(1-2).

1419. ——— : 1990 : Tripura : Government flouts court order. *Eco. & Pol. Weekly,* XXV(17), April 28 : 933.

1420. ——— : 1990 : Tripura tribal areas autonomous district council elections. *Eco. & Pol. Weekly,* XXV(30), July 28 : 1627-29.

1421. ——— : 1991 : Tripura and election commission : A Correspondent. *Eco. & Pol. Weekly,* XXVI(19), May 11 : 1203-04.

1422. **Economic Times** : 1975 : Focus on land reforms : Tripura land rights for tribals. *Economic Times,* Jul. 18 : 3(4).

1423. ——— : 1975 : Tripura plan to raise rubber. *Economic Times,* July 30 : 8(5).

1424. **Education Deptt.** : 1950 (?) *Tripura Gazettee Sankalan : 1903-1949*. Agartala, Education Deptt., 26p.

1425. ——— : 1972 : *Unakoti*. Agartala, Education Deptt., Govt. of Tripura.

1426. **Education Directorate** : 1967 : *Rajamala (Bangiya Sahitya Parishad version)*. Agartala, Directorate of Education, 21p.

1427. **Elliot, H.M.** : 1869 : *The Races of the North West Provinces of India*. London. (vol. I : 35, 287, 325 ; vol. II : 10).

1428. **Encyclopaedia Britanica** : 1964 : *A Short Description of Tripura, vol. XXII*. London, Ency. Bri. : 485.

1429. ——— : 1977 : *The New Britanica (Macropaedia), vol. 18*. 15th edition. Chicago, Encyclopaedia Britanica Inc. : 714.

1430. **Endle, Sydney** : 1911 : *The Kacharis with an introduction by J.D. Anderson*. London, Macmillan & Co., 121p (Reference on Tripura Bodos).

1431. **Englishman** : 1918 : Tripura. *The Englishman* (Calcutta), March 12.

F

1432. **Financial Express** : 1970 : Tribal unrest in Tripura region. *Financial Express*, July 15 : 4(3).

1433. ——— : 1970 : Tripura's Economy needs big push for take off. *Financial Express*, Sept. 6 : 5(6).

1434. **Flynn, Dorris** : 1971 : *Costumes of India.* Calcutta, 13H. Publishing Company (Tripura girl : 26p).

1435. **Forest Deptt.** : ? : *Project Report for Rehabilitation of Primitive Group, Tribe Residing in Reserve Forests.* Agartala, Forest Deptt., Govt. of Tripura.

1436. ——— : 1973 : *Jhuming in Tripura and future approach to the problem* Agartala, Forest Deptt., Govt. of Tripura.

1437. ——— : 1342 T.E. : *Swadhin Tripurar Banaja bastu sankranta bidhi (in Bengali),* Act I of 1313 T.E., 3rd edition. Agartala, Forest Deptt.

1438. **FAO** : 1980 : *Population Data regarding forestry communities practising shifting cultivation, Report of India.* FAO/JNFPA.

1439. **Forter, Nelson** : 1988 : Tribal Buddhists struggle for life in Bangladesh *(In) The Chakmas* by S.P. Talukdar. Delhi, Gyan Publishing House : 169-71.

1440. **Frontier** : 1974 : Tripura : The ordeal of the tribals. *Frontier,* Feb. 23 : 4-5.

1441. ——— : 1975 : Tripura Strike. *Frontier,* May 3 : 3-5.

1442. ——— : 1979 : Tripura Turmoil. *Frontier,* June 23 : 1-2.

1443. **Fuchs, Stephen** : 1973 : *The Aboriginal Tribes of India : The Tribes of Eastern India.* Delhi, The Macmillan Company : 201-41 (Regarding Mizo).

1444. **Furer-Haimendorf, C. von** : 1982 : *Tribes of India : The struggle for survival.* New York, Oxford University Press (1st Indian Impression from Oxford University Press, New Delhi in 1985) : 313-22.

G

1445. **Gait, E.A.** : 1902 : *Census of India, 1901 vol. VI : The Lower Provinces of Bengal and their feudatories, Part I Report*. Calcutta, Govt. Press : 137, 413.

1446. ——— : 1926 : *History of Assam*. Calcutta. Thacker & Spink, 366 p (*Reprinted* in 1963 from Calcutta by Thacker Spink which revised and enlarged by B. K. Barua *and* H.V.S. Murthy [3rd revised edition], 449 p *and* again *reprinted* in 1981 from Gauhati by LBS Publications).

1447. **Gan-Chaudhury** G.P. : *Regional Employment Exchange, Tripura*. Agartala (Circulated on the basis of the information obtained).

1448. **Gan-Chaudhury, Jagadis** : n.p. : *The Tipras of Tripura. Unpublished* mss.

1449. ——— : n.p. *Folk Deities of Tripura. Unpublished* mss.

1450. ——— : 1972 : Uchai of Tripura. *Vivekananda Kendra Patrika*, 1(2) : 348-52.

1451. ——— : 1974 : Village Administration and Justice in old Tripura. *Quarterly Review of Historical Studies* (Calcutta), October : 159-60, 163.

1452. ——— : 1975 : Changing Pattern of tribal womanhood in North East India. *Vivekananda Kendra Patrika*, 4(2), Aug. : 166.

1453. ——— : 1976 : Upajatiya Tripuri : Brittibhog. *Bhaskar* (Tripura Rabindra Parishad, Agartala), vol. III.

1454. ——— : 1976 : *The Tipras of Tripura*. Calcutta Ph.D Thesis, Calcutta University.

1455. ——— : 1977 : Marriage among the Tipras of Tripura. Proceedings of a Seminar on "*Social and Political Institutions of the Hill People of North East India*", organised jointly by Anthropolgical Survey of India *and* NEICSSR Shillong on 4-5 July, 1977.

1456. **Gan-Chaudhury, Jagadis** : 1978 : Emergence and role of the tribal middle class in Tripura. Proceedings of a Seminar on "*Emergence of Middle Class in North East India*, Held on Dec. 4-5, by NEICSSR, Shillong.

1457. **Gan-Chaudhury, Jagadis** : (*Ed*) : 1980 : *Tripura : The Land and its People*. Delhi, Leeladevi Publication, 186p.

1458. ——— : (*Ed*) : 1980 : Tripuri Folklore *(In) Tripura : The Land and its People (Ed)* by Jagadish Gan Choudhuri. Delhi, Leeladevi Publications : 159-81.

1459. ——— : 1980 : Tripuri Political Consciousness *(In) Tripura : The Land and its People (Ed)* by Jagadish Gan Choudhuri. Delhi, Leeladevi Publications : 153-58.

1460. ——— : 1980 : Local Government *(In) Tripura : The Land and its People (Ed)* by Jagadish Gan Choudhuri. Delhi, Leela Devi Publication : 141-52.

1461. ——— : 1980 : The Electoral System *(In) Tripura : The Land and its People (Ed)* by Jagadish Gan Choudhuri. Delhi, Leela Devi Publications : 124-40.

1462. ——— : 1980 : The Perennially charming Tripura *(In) Tripura : The Land and its People (Ed)* by Jagadish Gan Choudhuri. Delhi, Leeladevi Publications : 1-12

1463. ——— : 1982 : Tripuri folktales : A study in their motifs. Proceedings of a Seminar on "*Folklore in North East India*", Nov. 17-18, by NEICSSR, Shillong.

1464. ——— : 1982 : Tha Halams : A Study of a tribal community of Tripura, *Jour. of Educational Miscellany*, 12 : 17-38.

1465. ——— : 1983 : *The Riangs of Tripura*. Agartala, Directorate of Research, Deptt. of Welfare for Schedule Tribes and Schedule Castes, Govt. of Tripura, 87p.

1466. ——— : 1983 : Place names of Tripura. *Jour. of NEICSSR* (Shillong), 7(2), Oct. : 16-22.

1467. ——— : 1983 : The emergence and role of tribal middle class in Tripura *(In) The Emergence and role of Middle class in North East India (Ed)* by B. Dutta Ray. New Delhi, Uppal Publishing House : 199-210.

1468. ——— : 1983 : Politics of elections in Tripura. Proceedings of a Seminar on "*Electoral Politics in North East India*", held on Dec. 14-15, by NEICSSR, Shillong.

1469. ——— : 1984 : Demographic Features of Tripura. Proceedings of a Seminar on "*Pattern and problems of population in North East India : A Multidimensional study"*, held on 7-8 Dec. 1984 by NEICSSR, Shillong.

1470. **Gan-Chaudhury, Jagadis** : 1984 : Pilgrim centres in Tripura. *Vivekananda Kendra Patrika*, Feb. 3, 1 : 270-75.

1471. ——— : 1984 : The Marchom community of Tripura. *Social Mirror*, Oct.-Dec. : 7-17.

1472. ——— : 1985 : Traditional Tribal Panchayat *(In) An Anthology of Tripura (Ed)* by Jagadish Gan Choudhuri. New Delhi, Inter India Publications : 79-91.

1473. ——— : 1985 : Demographic Features *(In) An Anthology of Tripura (Ed)* By Jagadis Gan Choudhuri. New Delhi, Inter India Publications : 105-112.

1474. ——— *(Ed)* : 1985 : *An Anthology of Tripura*. New Delhi, Inter India Publications, 131p.

1475. ——— : 1985 : Place Names *(In) An Anthology of Tripura (Ed)* by Jagadish Gan Chouduri, New Delhi, Inter India publications : 93-103.

1476. ——— : 1885 : Trends of Urbanisation *(In) An Anthology of Tripura (Ed)* by Jagadis Gan Choudhuri. New Delhi, Inter India Publications : 65-77.

1477. ——— : 1985 : Tripuri Folktales *(In) Folklore in North East India (Ed)* by Soumen Sen. New Delhi, Omsons Publication : 195-201.

1478. ——— : 1985 : A survey of the tea garden labourers in Tripura. Proceedings of a Seminar on *"Tea Garden Labourers in North East India : A Multi- Dimensional Study"*, organised by NEICSSR, Shillong in collaboration with Sacred Heart Theological College on 25- 27 Feb., 1985.

1479. ——— : 1985 : *Political History of Tripura*. New Delhi Inter India Publications 92p.

1480. ——— : 1986 : Politics of Elections in Tripura *(In) Electoral Politics in North East India (Ed)* by P.S. Dutta. New Delhi, Omsons Publications, : 197- 206.

1481. ——— : 1986 : Demographic features of Tripura *(In) The Pattern and Problems of Population in North East India (Ed)* by B. Datta Ray. New Delhi, Uppal Publishing House : 367-75.

1482. **Gan-Chaudhury, Jagadis** : 1990 : Marriage among the Tipras of Tripura *(In) Social and Political Institutions of the Hill People of North East India (Eds)* by Jayanta Sarkar *and* B. Datta Ray. Calcutta, Anthropological Survey of India : 183-89.

1483. ——— : *(Ed)* : 1990 : *A Corpus of Tripura*. New Delhi, Inter India Publications, 154p.

1484. **Gangopadhyay, Arun Kumar** : 1980 : Planned Economic Development *(In) Tripura : The Land and its People (Ed)* by Jagadis Gan Chouduri. Delhi, Leeladevi Publications : 89-104.

1485. ——— : 1981 : The case for village and small scale industries in Tripura *(In) North Eastern Hill Regions of India, Problems and prospects of development (Ed)* by T. Mathew. New Delhi, Agricole Publishing Academy : 158-64.

1486. **Gangopadhaya, Ganendra Mohan** : ? : *Bansha Parichaya*. Agartala : 1-23, 24-6, 27-30, 31-9, 40-4.

1487. **Ganguly, J.B.** : 1962 : *Economic Problems of the Jhumis of Tripura : A Socio Economic Study of the system of shifting cultivation in transition*. Calcutta University, Ph.D. Thesis.

1488. ——— : 1966 : Land Carrying capacity under jhuming in Tripura. *Educational Miscellany* (jour. Directorate of Education, Agartala), 3(1-2).

1489. ——— : 1967 : Economic Development of Tribal areas *(In A Common Perspective for North East India, (Ed)* By R. Mitra *and* B. Das Gupta. Calcutta. Pannalal Das Gupta: 191-93.

1490. **Ganguly, J.B.** : 1968 : *Economic Problems of the jhumias of Tripura: A Socio-Economic study of the system of shifting cultivation of transition*. Calcutta, Bookland Pvt. Ltd, 129p.

1491. ——— : 1970 : Jhumia resettlement and social change in Tripura. *North Eastern Research Bulletin* (Dibrugarh University), I, Summer: 11-9.

1492. ——— : 1973 : Two decades of development performance. *Link* [Special Supplement on Tripura], March 11: 42-7.

1493. **Ganguly, J.B.** : 1974 : Problems and prospects of economic development of Tripura. *North Eastern Research Bulletin* (Dib. Uni.) 5, Summer: 25-35.

1494. ——— : 1975 : Tripuraye Bhumi Samashya O Bhumi Shanskar *(in Bengali) (In) Tripura Prasanga (Ed)* by Swapan Sengupta. Agartala, Directorate of Public Relations and Tourism : 1971-85.

1495. ——— : 1976 : Prospects of integrated development of North Eastern Region. *North Eastern Affairs* (Shillong), 5(1-2).

1496. ——— : 1976 : Socio-Economic Problems of Transition for shifting to sedentary culture in North East India *(In) Shifting Cultivation in North East India (Ed)* by B. Datta Ray. Shillong, NEICSSR : 28-36.

1497. ——— : 1978 : Role of the North Eastern Council in Economic Development of North East India *(In) North East India (Ed)* By S.M. Dubey Delhi, Concept Publishing Company : 349-95.

1498. ——— : 1978 : Problems and Prospects of Economic develpment of Tripura *(In) North East India (Ed)* by S.M. Dubey. Delhi, Concept Publishing Company : 367-79.

1499. ——— : 1980 : The Rich Resources of Tripura *(In) Tripura : The Land and its People (Ed)* by Jagadis Gan Choudhuri. Delhi, Leeladevi Publications: 71-88.

1500. ——— : 1981 : Progress of Jhumia Rehabilitation in Tripura : A Critical review *(In) North Eastern Hill Regions of India, a problems and prospects of development (Ed)* by T. Mathew. New Delhi, Agricole Publishing Academy: 47: 47-58.

1501. ——— : 1981 : Problem of tribal landlessness in Tripura. Proceedings of a Seminar on *"Land and Land Relations in the Hills of North East India"*, May 28-29 by NEICSSR, Shillong.

1502. ——— : 1982 : Vulnerability of Jhuming as a closed systems to natural calamities, *Jour. of NEICSSR*, VI(II), Oct.: 9-13.

1503. ——— : 1983 : *The Benign Hills : A study in Tripura's population growth and problems* Agartala, Tripura Darpan Prakashani, 64p.

1504. **Ganguly, J.B.** : 1983 : Operation of the Jhum Model. *Jour. of North East Indian Council for Social Science Research*, 7(2) : 13-22.

1505. ——— : 1983 : *The High Hills : A Study in Tripura's population growth and problems.* Agartala, Darpan Prakashani, 28p.

1506. ——— : 1984 : Economic development and social tension in the North Eastern Region *(In) Northeast Region : Problems and Prospects of development (Ed)* by B.L. Abbi. Chandigarh, Centre for Research in rural and Industrial Development ; 99-110.

1507. ——— : 1985 : Pattern of occupational structure of the Tribal population in Tripura. *Purisankhyan Barta* (Agartala) Directorate of Statistics and Evaluation, I(2), April-Sept: 15.

1508. ——— : 1985 : Economic content of the State Formation process in Medieval Tripura. *Proceedings of NEIHA* (Agartala), number 6 : 146-59.

1509. ——— : 1985 : A strategy for the development of the rural sector of the North Eastern Region, Proceedings of a Seminar on "*Economic environment of the North East India*", organised by North East India Institute of Bank Management in 1985.

1510. ——— : 1985 : Economics of development of the Tribal villages of North East India, Proceedings of a Seminar on "*Sequences in Development in North East India (A Study of Tradition, Continuity and Change)*", held on 9-10 Dec., 1985, organised by NEICSSR, Shillong.

1511. ——— : 1986 : Problem of tribal landlessness in Tripura *(In) Land use pattern in North East India (Ed) by* B.B. Dutta. Ludhiana, Gagan Publications.

1512. ——— : 1986 : Presidential Address. *Procedings of NEIHA* (Pasighat), Vol. 7 : 1-16.

1513. ——— : 1986 : Tripura tribals and mainstream of Tripura politics. Symposium on "*Ethnicity in Asian context*". Calcutta, Netaji Institute for Asian Studies.

1514. ——— : 1986 : Planning for forestry development in the North Eastern Region : An Approach *(In) Forestry*

Development in North East India (Eds) by M. Das Gupta *et al* Guwahati, Omsons Publications : 120-32.

1515. **Ganguly, J.B.** : The role of the autonomous District Council in fulfilling the tribal aspirations for development in Tripura. Proceedings of a Seminar on *"Rural Development in Eastern and North Eastern India"*, held at the Indian Institute of Management, Calcutta from 8-10 May, 1986.

1516. ——— : 1986 : The Economic conditions and change in North East India *(In) Changing North East India (Ed)* by A.P. Sinha. Ludhiana, Gagan Publishers : 1-28.

1517. ——— : 1987 : The Problem of tribal landlessness in Tripura *(In) Land Relations in North East India (Eds)* by B.B. Dutta *and* M.N. Karna. New Delhi, Peoples Publishing House : 221-33.

1518. ——— : 1988 : The role of the autonomous district council in fulfilling the tribal aspirations for development in Tripura *(In) Social Science and Social Concern : Felicitation volume in Honour of Professor B.K. Roy Burman (Ed) by S.B. Chakrabarti. Delhi, Mittal Publications : 62-74.*

1519. **Ganguly, J.B.** : 1989 : Nehru and the evolution of the policies and programmes of development of tribal areas in the north east. Proceedings of a Seminar on *"Jawaharlal Nehru and the disadvantages: A birth century tribute"* sponsored by Deptt. of parliamentary Affairs, Govt. of Meghalaya, Shillong, 25-26 Sept., 1989 organised by NEICSSR, Shillong.

1520. ——— : 1989 : Development of a viable alternative to jhuming in Tripura. *Himalaya : Man and Nature*, XIII(5), Oct : 15-6.

1521. ——— : 1990 : Problems of Social Science Research in North East India. *Jour. of NEICSSR*, 14(2), Oct. : 16-20.

1522. ——— : 1991 : The problem of tribal landlessness *(In) The Impact of Land Reforms in North East India (Ed)* by Malabika Das Gupta (in Press).

1523. **Gantuli, P.** *and* **Bhowmic, D.C. : 1985** Urbanization in North East India : Its Implications for Planning.

(In) Planning in North East India (Ed) by K. Alam, New Delhi, Omsons Publications : 253-59.

1524. **Gantzer, Hugh** *and* **Colleen : 1987 :** The Warmth of Agartala. *Statesman (Miscellany Sunday Supplement), Sept. 6.*

1525. **Gauhati Hinh Court** : 1974 : *Souvenir : Silver Jubilee Commemoration Volume, 1948-1973*. Gauhati, High Court, Published by the Souvenir Committee.

1526. **Gazetteer** : c. 1908 : *Provincial Gazetteer of India : Eastern Bengal and Assam*. Oxford, Horace Hart Printer to the University : 217-20, 373-82, 605-12.

1527. **Gazettee** : 1923(?) : *Tripura State Gazette, vol. XIX(12 [1330 T.E.]*

1528. ——— : 1971 : *Tripura State Gazette Sankalan*. Agartala, Publication Division, Govt. Press.

1529. ——— : 1975 : *Tripura District Gazetteer*. Agartala, Pub. Div., Govt. Press; 121 p.

1530. **George, K. Tharian; Haridasan, V.** *and* **Sreekumar, B.** : 1988 : Role of Government and structrual charges in rubber Plantation Industry. *Economic & Political Weekly*, XXIII(48), Nov. 26 : M158-M166.

1531. **Ghatak, I.B.** : 1945-'46 : Ethnology of India. *Quarterly Jour. of the Mythic Society* (Bangalore), 36(1): 24-5.

1532. **Ghate, Muralidhar** : 1968 : Hamara Simanta aur Adivasi *(In Hindi). Vanyajati*, 16(3), April : 116-18.

1533. **Ghosh, A.K.** : 1976 : Forestry. Proceedings of a Seminar on *"People and Forests in the North East India"*, Himalaya Seva Sangh, Shillong, Oct. 18-19, 1976, Plenary Session-I.

1534. ——— : 1979 : Tribal Development. *Himalaya : Man & Nature*, 2(8), Jan.: 18-24.

1535. ——— : 1986 : Shifting cultivation in North East India and its alternatives, with special reference to Tripura. *Himalaya : Man and Nature*, X(1), June : 6-9; X(2), X(3)

1536. **Ghosh, Alok Kumar** : 1990 : Book Review : Verrier Elwin and India's North Eastern Borderlands by Nari K. Rustomji. Shillong, North Eastern Hill University, Pub. in 1988, Rs. 45/-, 82p (foreward by R.K.

Mishra). *Jour. of Indian Anthropological Society, 25(1), March : 96.*

1537. **Ghosh, Bhanu** : 1987 : *Letters to the Editor* : Tripura Politics. *Statesman,* Oct. 20 : 8(5-6).

1538. **Ghosh, B.N.** (Ed) : 1935 : Tripura Lakshmi. *Silver Jubilee Issue,* 58p.

1539. **Ghosh, J. P.** : 1967 : *Letters to the Editor* : Tripura elections. *Now,* April 14, 3(28) : 22.

1540. **Ghosh, Kamalini** : 1984 : *Tribal Insurrection in Tripura* Hyderabad, Booklinks Corporation, 81p.

1541. **Ghosh, Manash** : 1980 : Land, the source of tension in Tripura. *Statesman.* June 24.

1542. ——— : 1980 : Worst riots since independence. *Statesman,* July 2.

1543. ——— : 1980 : Tripura-II : Politicians fanned Tripura Flames. *Statesman,* July 3.

1544. ——— : 1988 : Fallout of Chakma problem. *Statesman,* May 28:1(2-5).

1545. **Ghosh, Manash** : 1991 : Chakma chiefs wistful look at Kurdish 'haven'. *Statesman,* April 21 : 1(1-5), 7(7-8).

1546. **Ghosh, Sukhamoy** : 1967 : The problem of attitudinal adjustments among the tribal and non-tribal people of Tripura. *Educational Miscellany,* 3(3-4) : 51-6.

1547. **Ghosh, S.C.** : 1909 : *Chakma Jati.* Calcutta, Bangya Shahitya Parishad (series 24).

1548. **Ghosh, S.K.** *and* **Chopra, Prabha** : 1980 : *Echoes from North Eastern India.* New Delhi, S.Chand & Company: 95-102.

1549. **Ghosh, S.P.** : 1984 : *Horticulture in North Eastern India.* New Delhi, Associate : Publishing Company, 230p.

1550. **Ghoshal, Subhas C.** : 1986 : A tale of two tribes. *Amrita Bazar Patrika, Sunday Supplement,* Sept. 14 : I(1-8) [The padhar tribe of Gujarat and the Noatia Tribe of Tripura].

1551. **Ghurye, G.S.** : 1980 : *The burning caldron of North East India.* Bombay, Popular Prakashan, 160p.

1552. **Gogai, P.** : 1986 : *The Tai and the Tai Kingdom.* Gauhati, Gauhati University : 158.

1553. **Gohain, Bikash Chandra** : 1977 : *Human Sacrifice and Head Hunting in North Eastern India.* Gauhati, Lawyers' Book Stall.

1554. **Gopalkrishnan, R.** : 1991 : *Political Geography of India's North East.* New Delhi, Vikas Publishing House : 206-222.

1555. **Goswami, B.B.** : 1973 : The Tribes of North East India : A few comments on their Social and Cultural ties with the non-tribes. *North Eastern Research Bulletin, IV, Summer : 41-8.*

1556. ——— : 1979 : *The Mizo unrest : A study of politicisation of culture.* Jaipur, Aalekh Publishers [Chakma. Riang, Tripuri also].

1557. **Goswami, Chidananda** : 1964 : Swadhinata sangrame Tripura *(in Bengali). Saptahik Basumati* (Calcutta), 69(12), Aug. 13.

1558. **Goswami, C.R.** : 1967 : The Languages of Tripura. *(In) A Common Perspective for North East India, (Eds) by* Rathin Mitra *and* Barun Das Gupta. Calcutta, Pannalal Das Gupta : 15-8.

1559. **Goswami, Debabrata** : 1985 : Operations of Hussain Shah against Tripura : Its nature. *Proceedings of NEIHA* (Agartala), vol. 6 : 170-74.

1560. ——— : 1986 : Study on the organisation of Armed Forces of Tripura (1490-1586 A.D.). *Proceedings of NEIHA* (Pasighat), vol. 7 : 175-82.

1561. ——— : 1988 : Tripura during the Second World War. *Proceedings of NEIHA* (Guwahati), vol.9: 282-84.

1562. ——— : 1990 : Geography dictates strategy : Tripura in the context. *Proceedings of NEIHA* (Imphal), vol. 11 : 149-52.

1563. **Goswami, Dhanapati** : 1988 : *Letters to the Editor : How TNV helped Congress(I). Statesman,* Feb. 14 : 8(5-6).

1564. **Goswami, D.N.** : 1985 : Land system of Govinda Manikya as reflected in the land grants, *Proceedings of NEIHA* (Agartala), vol. 6 : 77-84.

1565. ——— : 1989 : The episode of Shuja mosque : A Historical Review. *Proceedings of NEIHA,* (Shillong). vol. 10.

1566. **Goswami, M.C** (*Ed*) : 1982 : *The Customary laws and practices of the Riang of Tripura. Gauhati, Law Research Institute, Eastern Region* (Sponsored by NEC, 83p (*Mimeo*).

1567. **Goswami, P.C.** : 1971 : Shifting Cultivation in the Hills of North Eastern India. *Indian Farming*, XXI(V): 10-13.

1568. ———(*Ed*) : 1972 : *Socio Economic Research in Tribal Areas*. Jorhat, Agro Economic Research Centre for North East India.

1569. ——— : 1987 : The lonely "Seven Sisters". *Times of India* June 28 (*Sunday Review*) : VI (1-5).

1570. **Goswami, P.C.** (*Ed*) : 1987 : *Problems and prospects of Industrialisation : A study of North East India*. Guwahti, Institute of Development Studies.

1571. **Goswami, P.C.** *and* **Saha, N.** : 1969 : *Problems of agricultural development in the hill areas of North East India*. Jorhat, Agro Economic Research Centre.

1572. **Goswami, P.C.** *and* **Saikia, P.D**. : 1970 : Problems of agricultural development in Tribal areas. *Indian Jour. of Agricultural Economics*, 25(3).

1573. **Goswami, Praphulladatta** : 1982 : *Essays on the folklore and culture of North Eastern India*. Gauhati, Spectrum Publications.

1574. **Goswami, Tarun** : 1985 : *Kuki life and lore* Haflong (Assam), North Cachar Hills District Council.

1575. **Govt. of India** : 1955 : *Report of the State Re-organisation Commission*. New Delhi, Govt. of India.

1576. ——— : 1973 : *The Gazetteer of India : Country and People, vol. I* Delhi, Publication Division : 27.

1577. ——— : 1976 : Report of the National Commission on Agriculture, part XV, Agrarian Reforms. New Delhi, Ministry of Agriculture and Irrigation, Govt of India.

1578. **Govt. of Tripura** : ? : *Project Report for Tripura Plantation*. Agartala, Rehabilitation Corporation, 20p.

1579. ——— : ? : *A Study on shifting cultivation in Tripura*. Agartala, Deptt. of Information, Culture and Toursim.

1580. ——— : ? : *Jhumiader natun jiban (in Bengali)*. Agartala, Deptt. of Information. Culture and Toursim.

1581. **Govt. of Tripura** : ? : *A Decade of Development : Tripura.* Agartala, Govt. of Tripura.

1582. ——— : n.d. : *Report and recommendation on the Socio-Economic Development of the Dambur Oustees in Amarpur Sub-Division.* Agartala, Tribal Welfare Deptt., Govt. of Tripura (*Unpublished*).

1583. ———: n.d : *Second Report of the study team on assessment of the present economic conditions of Dumbur Oustee families : Recommendation for revitalising their economy.* Agartala, Tribal Welfare Deptt., Govt. of Tripura (*Unpublished*).

1584. **Govt. of Tripura** : n.d. : *Report of the field level team in Raima Sarma valley.* Agartala, Govt. of Tripura (*Unpublished*).

1585. ——— : 1969 : *Tripura's tie with Tagore.* Agartala, Govt. of Tripura, Directorate of Education.

1586. ——— : 1922 : *Parbatya Prajaganer Ghar chukti Sambandhiya Kar Ain, Act IV of 1329 T.E., Section 5.* Agartala, Revenue Deptt., Govt. of Tripura (1329 T.E.)

1587. ———: 1944 : *Order of the Chief Secretary, No. 596/C, Dated 13 Poush, 1354 T.E.* (i.e. 30 Dec. 1944). Agartala, Govt. of Tripura.

1588. ——— : 1952 : *Scha No. 3567-B/3-88 dated 3/8/52 T.E. of the Forest and Customs Deptt.* Agartala, Govt of Tripura.

1589. ——— : 1960 : *The Tripura Land Revenue and Land Law Department Reform Act, 1960.* Agartala, Govt. of Tripura.

1590. ———: 1969 : *Draft Fourth Five Year Plan.* Agartala, Govt. of Tripura, Deptt. of Planning.

1591. ——— : 1969 : *The National Sample Survey : Indebtedness of Scheduled Tribe Households in Tripura.* Agartala, Govt. of Tripura, Statistical Deptt. (1st Round of NNS).

1592. ———: 1970 : *Tripura on the March* [26th January]. Agartala, Deptt. of Public Relations, Tourism and Publicity, 45p.

1593. **Govt. of Tripura** : 1972 : *Agricultural Development in Tripura during 15 years of Independence*. Agartala, Deptt. of Agriculture, Govt. of Tripura.

1594. ——— : 1976 : *Tripura : The Enchanting land*. Agartala, Govt. of Tripura.

1595. ——— : 1976 : *A Decade of Development*. Agartala, Directorate of Public Relations and Toursim, Govt. of Tripura.

1596. **Govt. of Tripura** : 1977 : *A Guide of Tripura agriculture*. Agartala, Govt. of Tripura, Deptt. of Agriculture.

1597. ——— : 1978 : *The Tripura land tax Act 1978*. Agartala, Govt. of Tripura.

1598. ——— : 1978 : *Report of the tribal bench mark survey*. Agartala, Deptt. of Tribal Welfare, Govt. of Tripura.

1599. ——— : 1979 : *One year of Left Front Government in Tripura*. Agartala, Directorate of Public Relations and Tourism.

1600. ——— : 1979 : *Tripura Tribal areas autonomous district council : Report of the study team on Dumbur Oustee colonies*. Agartala, Govt. of Tripura. (*Unpublished*).

1601. ——— : 1980 : *The Tripura land tax amendment act*. Agartala, Govt. of Tripura.

1602. ——— : 1981 : *Four Years at a Glance 1978-'81*. Agartala, Left Front Govt. in Tripura, 10p.

1603. ——— : 1982 : *Project Report for Tripura Rehabilitation Plantation Corporation Ltd. Agartala,* Deptt. of Welfare for Scheduled Tribes and Scheduled Castes, 10p.

1604. ——— : 1984 : *Tripuraye Bamfront Sarkarer Chhoy Bachar (in Bengali)*. Agartala, Deptt. of Publicity, Culture and Toursim, 58p.

1605. ——— : 1984 : *Draft Annual Plan : 1984-'85 (Mimeo.)* Agartala, Govt. of Tripura.

1606. ——— : 1986 : *Draft Annual Plan, 1987-'88*. Agartala, Govt. of Tripura.

1607 ——— : 1986 : *Eight years of Left Front Government in Tripura*. Agartala, Govt of Tripura.

1608. ——— : 1987 : *Bhumi Sanskar O punarjariper kajer agragati (in Bengali)*. Agartala, Directorate of Land Records and Settlement.

1609. **Govt. of Tripura : 1988** : *A Guide to Tripura Agriculture.* Agartala, Deptt. of Agriculture, Govt. of Tripura.

1610. ——— : 1989 : *Draft Annual Plan, 1988-'89, Tripura.* Agartala, Govt. of Tripura.

1611. ——— : 1989 : *State of Environment of Tripura.* Agaratala, Deptt. of Science, Technology and Environment, Govt. of Tripura.

1612. **Greer, R.T.** : 1891 : *D.O. From R.T. Geer, Esq. the political Agent to Babu Umakanta Das, Rai Bahadur, Minister, Hill Tipperah, Dated Comilla, the 19th September 1891 and the 31st Sept. 1891.*

1613. **Grierson, G.A.** : 1904 : *Linguistic Survey of India, Vol. III, pt. III.* Calcutta, Govt. Printing Press.

1614. ——— : 1927 : *The Linguistic Survey of India, vol. I, part-I.* Calcutta, Govt. Printing Press.

1615. ——— : 1967 : *Linguistic Survey of India, vol. III, pt. II: Tibeto-Burman Family : Bodo Naga and Kachin Groups.* Delhi, Motilal Banarasidass (*Reprinted*) : 109-17.

1616. ——— : 1987 : *Languages of North Eastern India, 2nd vol.* Delhi, Gyan Publications (*Reprinted*) : 369-371.

1617. **Guha, A** : 1982 : The Indian National Question ; A Conceptual Frame. *Economic and Political Weekly,* XVIII(31), July.

1618. **Guha, Amalendu** : 1982 : A Historiographical perspective for North East India. *Man in India,* 62(3) : 221- 33.

1619. ——— : 1988 : Book Review : B.P. Singh : The problem, of change : A Study of North East India, Oxford University Press, Rs. 110/-. *Statesman, Sunday Miscellany,* Feb. 7 : 11(1-5) and 12(1-5).

1620. **Guha, Ashutosh** : 1973 : Industrial Potential. *Economic Times,* Jan. 21 : 10(7).

1621. **Guha, A.S.** : 1986 : Regionalism in the North East : A Potent Force. Social Research (Shillong), 6 (2-3), April-Sept.: 25-30 [Chakma].

1622. **Guha, B.S.** : 1951 : The Indian aborigines and the administration *Jour. of the Asiatic Society of Bengal,* 17.

1623. **Guha, Upendra Chandra** : 1971 : *Cacharer Itibritya.* Gauhati, Asom Prakashan Parishad : 20-28.

1624. **Guha Thakurta, S.N.**: 1970 : Employment in the construction industry : Does it have to be so unstable ? *Economic & Political Weekly,* March 21 : 521-27.

1625. ——— : 1978 : Tripura : Towards a composite culture. *Jour. of NEICSSR,* II(II), Oct. : 13-14.

1626. ——— : 1980 : *Contract labour in construction industry : An empirical study with reference to Tripura.* Calcutta, Firma KLM, 131p [Revised version of the thesis submitted to the University of Calcutta for Ph.D. in 1972].

1627. ——— : 1986 : *Tripura.* New Delhi, National Book Trust (India), 123p.

1628. **Guide (Dutta, Gita** *and* **Dutta, Mrinal)** : 1982 *Vraman Sangi (in Bengali).* Calcutta, Asia Publishing Company ; 437-43.

1629. **Gupta, Aniruddha** : 1979 : Tripura, towards prosperity. *Economic Times,* Feb, 20 ; 5 (6).

1630. **Gupta, A.K.** : 1990 : *Letters to the Editor : Tripura wild life. Hindustan Times,* Sept. 17 : 11(4-5).

1631. **Gupta, D.N.** : 1982 : *Strength of achievement motivation and Personality of two cultural groups in Tripura.* Agartala, Directorate of Research, 68p. XXVIII.

1632. **Gupta G.P.** : 1976 : Shifting cultivation : Maladies and remedies *(In) Shifting cultivation in North East India (Ed) by* B. Datta Ray Shillong, NEICSSR : 131-32.

1633. **Gupta I.C.** *and* **Pahawa, K.N.** : ? : *Tripura : Its History and culture.* Calcutta.

1634. **Gupta, Jogendra Nath** : ? : *Asamer Itihas (in Bengali).* Calcutta : 111-21.

1635. ——— : ? : *Banger Mahila Kabi (Rajkumari Ananga Mohini Devi).* Calcutta. : 295-301.

1636. **Gupta, Joydeep** : 1988 : Chakma exodus after Islamization. *Statesman,* June 28 : 12(3-4).

1637. **Gupta, Kamalakanta** : 1967 : *Copper plate of Sylhet, vol. I.* Sylhet, Pub. by the author, 74p.

1638. **Gupta, Krishna Murti** : 1979 : A brief account of visits to Tripura and Mizoram, *Himalaya : Man and Nature,* 1(5-6), Oct.-Nov. : 31-9.

1639. ——— : 1980 : Ashanta Tripura (*in Hindi*). *Himalaya : Man and Nature,* 4(3), Aug.; 33-6.

1640. **G.P.** : 1977 : Tipperah : The ancient hill kingdom. *The North Eastern Spectrum,* 1(11-12), May-June : 24-33.

1641. **Gupta, Pabitra,** *and* **Dutta, Pratap C.** : 1966 : *Anthropometry In India 1868-1961), Memoir No. 10, 1962.* Calcutta, Anthropological Survey of India.

1642. **Gupta, P** *and* **Gupta, A.** : 1967 : Limb and body proportions of the Riang of Tripura : A study in intratribal variations. *Bulletin of Anthropological Survey of India,* XVI (3-4), July-Dec.; 379-426.

1643. **Gupta, Paramesswari Lal** : ? : *Coins* (in Chapter XV-Assam). : 129-30.

1644. **Gupta, Satya Prakash** : 1955 : Riang shradh. *Vanyajati,* 3(1) : 6-9.

1645. **Gupta, S.P.** : 1958 : ABO blood groups in Tripura (North East India). *Jour. of the Royal Anthropological Institute of Great Britain and Ireland,* 88(1), Jan.-June : 109-11.

1646. ——— : 1968 : Palmar Dermatoglyphics of Riangs and Tippras in Tripura State. *Proceedings Volume of International Symposium on Dermatoglyph (Delhi) : 271-78.*

H

1647. **Haksar, P.N.** : 1984 : Problems of Building a diverse society *(In) North East Region : Problems and Prospects of Development (Ed)* by B.L. Abbi. Chandigarh, Centre for Research in Rural and Industrial Development: 31-2.

1648. **Halder, Gopal Ch.** : 1983 : *Economic Problems of Tripura with special reference to its population since 1947.* University of North Bengal, Ph.D. Thesis.

1649. **Haldar, Rakhal Das** : 1925 : A Kurmi marriage. *Man in India,* 5 : 255-58.

1650. **Haldipur, R.N.** : 1975 : Policy towards and administration of the tribes of North East India. *Vanyajati,* 23(3-4) : 8-15.

1651. **Hazarika, M.P.** : 1988 : Jhuming : Perennial problem in North East. *Assam Tribune,* July 10 : 4 (3-6), 5(4-5).

1652. **Hiernaux, J.**: 1980 : Human Biological variations in Asia with special reference to India *(In) La Diversite Biologique Humaine : Human Biological Diversity (Collection d'Anthropologie Physique).* Paris, Masson de Montreal : 197-273.

1653. **Himalaya** : 1976 : Tripura : All India Chakma conference held. *Himalaya,* 5(3), March : 14.

1654. **Hindu** : 1967 : Wide spectrum of popular unrest. *Hindu,* Sept. 4,6(5).

1655. ——— : 1981 : Tribal influx into Tripura continues. *Hindu,* Aug. 15.

1656. ——— : 1981 : Tribals' hour of travail. *Hindu,* Oct. 4.

1657. ——— : 1982 : Tripura poll results show TUJS. *Hindu,* Jan. 12.

1658. **Hindustan Standard** : 1974 : Tribal people being made hostile towards India. *Hindustan Standard, Nov. 28.*

1659. **Hindustan Times** : 1974 : Editorial : Vizol seeks initiative. *Hindustan Times,* June 28: 5(1).

1660. **Hindustan Times** : 1974 : Tribal stir aimed at new State. *Hind. Times* Nov. 24.

1661. ——— : 1975 : Editorial Tripura Tremors. *Hind. Times,* March 27 : 7(1).

1662. ——— : 1980 : tribal women on dharna near Agartala. *Hind. Times,* Aug. 13.

1663. ——— : 1980 : Tripura Tribals demand to implement act. *Hind. Times,* Oct. 11.

1664. ——— : 1981 : Tribal D.P. s enter India. *Hind. Times,* Sept. 21.

1665. ——— : 1982 : Tribal extremists fire on patrol. *Hind. Times,* Dec. 31.

1666. ——— : 1989 : Chakmas face uncertain future. *Hind. Times* (New Delhi), Dec. 26 : 6(6-7).

1667. ——— : 1990 : New rail links in north east. *Hind. Times,* January 2: 9(1-3).

1668. ——— : 1990 : Tripura assurance to press council *Hind. Times.* April 3 : 9(2-3).

1669. ——— : 1990 : Tribal Council poll in Tripura by July. *Hind.Times,* April 18:3(2-3).

1670. ——— : 1990 : Tripura announces industrial policy. *Hind.Times,* April 30 : 7 (5-6).

1671. ——— : 1990 : Tripura seeks central forces. *Hind.Times,* May 3:3(2-3),

1672. ——— : 1990 : Chakma issue discussed with Bangla : Lok Sabha Questions. *Hind.Times,* May 4 : 9(1).

1673. ——— : 1990 : Tripura tea industry in shambles. *Hind.Times,* May 21 : 16(5-8).

1674. ——— : 1990 : Tripura campaign in full swing. *Hind.Times,* July 4 : 9(1-2).

1675. ——— : 1990 : Tripura goes to polls today. *Hind Times,* 8 : 9(4-6).

1676. ——— : 1990 : 10 killed in Tripura poll violence. *Hind.Times,* July 9: 1(2-3).

1677. ——— : 1990 : Tripura areas tense. *Hind.Times,* July 10 : 4(6).

1678. ——— : 1990 : Debbarma Tripura ADC chief. *Hind.Times,* July 16 : 10(1).

1679. ——— : Dispute on Tripura-Bangla border. *Hind. Times,* July 31 : 6(5).

1680. **Hindustan Times : 1990 : Bedlam in Tripura Assembly.** *Hind.Times*, Aug. 1 : 9(1).

1681. ——— : 1990 : Ire over Tripura poll probe. *Hind.Times*, Aug. 6 : 7(1-3)

1682. ——— : 1990 : TUJS to serve links with TNV. *Hind.Times*, Aug. 27 : 4(6-7).

1683. ——— : 1990 : TUJS follow-up action soon. *Hind.Times*, Oct. 5: 4(6).

1684. ——— : 1990 : Tripura C.M. asks for extra forces. *Hind.Times*, Dec. 4 : 9(3)

1685. ——— : 1990 : Red alert on Tripura Border. *Hind.Times*, Dec. 5 : 7(5).

1686. ——— : 1990 : Chakma camp woes don't scare cupid. *Hind.Times*, Dec. 11: 3(1-4).

1687. ——— : 1990 : Tripura seeks more aid from Centre. *Hind Times*, Dec. 14 : 7(1-2).

1688. ——— : 1991 : Editorial : Insurgency in the North East. *Hind. Times* Jan. 1 : 13(1-2).

1689. ——— : 1991 : Chakmas deserting camps in Tripura. *Hind.Times*, Feb. 25 : 6(4-7).

1690. ——— : 1991 : Water scarcity hits N-E tribals. *Hind.Times*, Feb. 16 : 3(4-5) [Tripura Jampui].

1691. ——— : 1991 : Assembly poll likely in Tripura. *Hind.Times*, March 25 : 1(3).

1692. ——— : 1991 : Influx hits Tripura economic growth. *Hind. Times*, April 8 : 6(6-7).

1693. ——— : 1991 : RSP to support CPM in Tripura. *Hind. Times*, April 9: 10(5-8).

1694. ——— : 1991 : Stir to postpone Tripura poll. *Hind. Times*, June 6 : 4(6-8).

1695. ——— : 1991 : Editorial : Polls in Tripura. *Hind.Times*, June 10 : 11(1-2).

1696. ——— : 1991 : Tripura C.M. blames ATTF for violence. *Hind.Times*, July 5 : 6(1-2).

1697. ——— : 1991 : Extension of Rly network in Tripura. *Hind. Times*, July 22 : 7(1-2).

1698. ——— : 1991 : Editorial : Tussle in Tripura. *Hind. Times*, Sept. 11 : 11 (1-2).

1699. ——— : 1991 : Tension grips W. Tripura sub-division. *Hind.Times*, Sept. 28 : 22(1).

1700. **Hrangkhawl, B.K.** : 1988 : Letter to Mr. S.R. Bhattacharjee *(In) Tribal Insurgency in Tripura* by S.R. Bhattacharjee. New Delhi, Inter-India Publications (1989) : 206-07.

1701. **Human Resource** : ? : *Gazetteers of Tripura*. New Delhi, Ministry of Human Resource Development, Deptt. of Education.

1702. **Hunter, W.W.** : 1868 : *The Annals of Rural Bengal*. London.

1703. ——— : 1876 : *A Statistical Account of Bengal, Vol. VI. Chittagong Hill Tracts, Chittagong, Noakhali, Tipperah, Hill Tipperah*. London, Trubner & Co: 355-522 [Reprinted by D.K. Publishing House in 1973, Delhi: 39-43, 45-49, 51-53, 482-488].

1704. **Hutchinson, R.H. Sneyd** : 1906: *An Account of the Chittagong Hill Tracts* Calcutta, Bengal Secretariat [*Reprinted* by Vivek Publishing Company in 1978, Delhi: 15-23, 29-35, 36-38, 92-96].

1705. ——— : 1909 : *Eastern Bengal and Assam District Gazetteer*. Allahabad, Govt. Press.

1706. **Hutton, J.H.** (*Ed*) : 1935 : Notes on Moghs of Cox's Bazar *(In) Census of India 1931, vol. I, India, Part II, Ethnographical*. Simla, Govt. Press : B 124-25., [*Reprinted* by Gyan Publishing House in 1986, Delhi : 118-125].

1707. ——— : 1951 : Chakma *(In) Caste in India* by J.H. Hutton, Bombay, Oxford University Press : 277.

I

1708. **India** : 1954 : *Census of India 1951, paper no. 1, Language.* New Delhi, Govt. of India Press.
1709. **Indian Archaeology** : 1957 - 58 : *Indian Archaeology : A Review.* Udaipur (Tripura), Deptt. of Chaturdasa Devata Temple, 88p.
1710. ——— : 1958-'59 : *Indian Archaeology: A Review.* Udaipur (Tripura), Deptt. of Gunavati Group of Temples, 89p.
1711. ——— : 1959-'60 : *Indian Archaeology : A Review.* Udaipur (Tripura), Deptt. of Gunavati Group of Temples, 91p.
1712. ——— : 1960-'61 : *Indian Archaeology : A Review.* Udaipur (Tripura), Deptt. of Bhubaneswari Temple, 82p.
1713. ——— : 1961-'62 : *Indian Archaeology : A Review.* Udaipur (Tripura), Deptt. of Bhubaneswari, Chaturdasa and Gunavati Temple : 119-20.
1714. **Indian Council** : ? : *A Survey of Research in Sociology and Social Anthropology, vol. III.* Bombay, Popular Prakashan on behalf of Indian Council of Social Science Research : 11, 53.
1715. **Indian Express** : 1970 : Unending flow of refugees. *Ind. Exp.*, July 6 : 2(6).
1716. ——— : 1980 : Now Tripura too. *Indian Express* (Bombay), June 14.
1717. **Indian Finance** : 1970 : Tripura and Manipur. *Ind. Finance*, Sept. 19 : 312.
1718. **India Govt.** : 1966 : *Report of the Commissioner on the Hill areas of Assam, 1965-'66.* New Delhi, Ministry of Home Affairs.
1719. **India Tea Board** : 1962 : *Survey of the living condition of labour in Tripura.* Calcutta, India Tea Board, 43p.
1720. ——— : 1983 : *Techno Economic Survey of the tea industry in Tripura.* Calcutta, India Tea Board, 46p.
1721. **Indo African Trade** : 1973 : *Tripura : Industrial progress. Jour. of Indo African Trade*, Sept. 9 : 9(19-20).

1722. **IDBI** : 1970 : *Industrial Potential Survey of Tripura*. Bombay, IDBI, RBI, ICICI and IFCI, IDBI.

1723. ——— : 1972 : *Industrial Survey of Arunachal Pradesh, Assam, Manipur, Nagaland and Tripura*. Bombay, Industrial Development Bank of India.

1724. **Information, Cultural Affairs** : n.d. : *Tripura calling Sepahijala*. Agartala, Information, Cultural Affairs and Tourism.

1725. **Information and Public Relation** : 1967 : *Tripura on the March*. Agartala, Inf. and Pub. Rel., 33p.

1726. **Information Wing** : 1986 : *Tripura Tribal Autonomous District Council : Structure and Function*. Agartala, TTADC, Govt. of Tripura, 16p.

1727. **Islam, Antiqual** : 1967 : Tripura in the grip of acute food crisis. *New Age*, 15(25), June 18 : 11.

1728. ——— : 1967 : Tribal conference demands implements the fifth Schedule.: Seventh Annual Conference of Gana Mukti Parishad. *New Age*, 15, Dec. 10 : 10-11.

1729. ———: 1968 : Tripura tribals anxiety. *Mainstream*, March 9 : 22-25.

1730. **Iyer, L.A. Krishna** *and* Ratnam, L.K. Bala : 1961 : *Anthropology in India*. Bombay, Baratiya Vidya Bhavan : 43, 48, 49.

J

1731. **Jafa, Jyoti** : 1986 : Keep the army out. *Seminar* (Delhi), 326, October : 29-31 *and* also in *Statesman*, August 19.

1732. **Jafri, S.S.A.** : 1980 : Industrial classification and Hierarchical order of towns in North Eastern Region of India. *Jour. of NEICSSR* (Shillong), IV(II), Oct. : 19-25.

1733. **Jagannathan, S.** : 1961 : The tribes of Tripura.*Vanyajati*, IX(2) April : 57-65.

1734. **Jahangir, B.K.** : 1979 : Tribal peasants in transition : Chittagong Hill Tracts. *Economic & Political Weekly*, 14(11), March 17 : 597-608.

1735. **Jana Siksha Samiti** : 1946 :*Leaflet of Tripura Jana Siksha Samiti*. Agartala, Jana Siksha Samiti (29th Bhadra 1356 T.E).

1736. **Jaswal, I.J.S.** : 1979 : Physical Anthropology and the study of population Arunachal, Tripura and Meghalaya. Proceedings of a Seminar on *"The History and Culture of North East India"*, 26th-28th April, 1979, Deptt. of History, NEHU, Shillong.

1737. ——— : 1984 : Book Review : The Bening Hills : A Study in Tripura's Population Growth and Problems by J.B. Ganguli, Tripura Darpan Prakashani, Agartala, 1983, 64p, Rs. 25/-. *Jour.of NEICSSR*, 8(1), April : 53.

1738. **Jha, M.N. ; Pandey, P.** *and* **Pathak, T.C.** : 1979 : Studies on the changes in the physico-chemical properties of Tripura soils as a result of Jhuming. *Indian Forester*, 105(6) : 436.

1739. **Jha, S.D.** : 1985: A Perspective view of Appropriate Technology with respect to N.E. Region *(In) Planning in North East India, (Ed)* by K. Alam. New Delhi, Omsons Publications: 288-96.

1740. **Journl Asiatic** : 1951 : Tripura. *Jour. of Asiatic Society, Letters*, XVIII(2) : 73-82.

1741. ——— : ? : Tripura. *Jour. of Asiatic society* (Calcutta), XLII, pt. I : 214-34.

1742. **Jugantar** : 1987 : Chakma : Antorjatic issue karte chan Nripenbabu *(in Bengali)*. *Jugantar*, Aug. 2 : 5(3-4).

K

1743. **Kabiraj, Shibnarayan** : 1988 : Agitation for Jharkhand State in West Bengal: Some observation and remarks on the development of movement. *Folklore*, 29(7), July : 162-63 [TNV].

1744. **Kabui, Gangmumei** : 1989 : Tribes in North East India in Historical perspective : The emerging pattern and the perspective for the future. *Vanyajati*, XXXVII(4). Oct. : 12-19.

1745. **Kakati, Satis Ch.** : 1986 : Seven sisters of N.E. Region, *Assam Tribune*, Dec. 18: 4(3-6), 6(6).

1746. ——— : 1988 : Poll outcome in Tripura and Meghalaya. *Assam Tribune*, Feb. 10 : 4(3-8).

1747. ——— : 1988 : Thumb-nail profile of Tripura. *Assam Tribune*, Aug. 20.

1748. **Kalla, A.K.** *and* Singh, K.S. (*Eds*) : 1987 : *Anthropology development and nation building*. New Delhi, Concept Publishing Company.

1749. **Kandali, Ratna Sarma** *and* **Das Bairagi, Arjun** : 1938 : *Tripura Buranji (Ed)* by S.K. Bhuyan, Gauhati, Historical and Antiquarian studies ((originally it was written in *Assamese* in 1724 by the authors).

1750. **Kandali, Ranta** *and* **Das, Arjun** : 1960 *Tripura Deser Katha (1626-1715 A.D.) (Ed)* by T.C. Sen. Agartala : 22.

1751. **Kar, Biman** : 1975 : *Economic Development of Tripura from 1951-66 A critical study. Gauhati University, Ph.D. Thesis (unpublished).*

1752. ——— : 1977 : Tripura and Assam : Cultural Bonds, migrations and acculturation. *North Eastern Spectrum*, 1(6), 1976-'77, Dec. : 60-1.

1753. ——— : 1977 : Tripuri and their kingdom *North Eastern Spectrum*, 1(6), 1976-1977 : 61-62.

1754. ——— : 1983 : The immigrant middle class and North East India. : Some observations *(In) The Emergence and Role of Middle Class (Ed)* by B. Datta

Ray. New Delhi, Uppal Publishing House: 245-57.

1755. **Kar, B.C.** :1958 : The Method and Contents of Tribal Education. *Jour. of Gauhati University.* IX (1).

1756. **Kar, P.K.** : 1986 : Rehabilitation of Jhumias : A New Horizon, *(In) Tribes of Tripura (Ed)* by Sudhanshu Bikash Saha. Agartala, Rupali Book Store : 69-76.

1757. **Kar, R. K.** : 1990 : The People of North East India : An Appraisal. *Vanyajati,* 38(1), Jan. : 11-19.

1758. **Karapurkar, Pushpa** : 1972 : *Tripuri Phonetic Reader.* Mysore, C.I.I.L.. (Ed) by H.S. Biligiri *and* E. Annamalai, 64p.

1759. **Kataki, Ratna Kandali Sarma** *and* Kataki, Arjun Das Bairagi : ? : *Tripura Deshar Kathar Lekha, 1724 A. D..* Agartala.

1760. **Kaviraj, Chiranjib** : 1969 : *Tripura's ties with Tagore.* Agartala, Publication Unit, Education Directorate, 69p.

1761. **Kendriya Sabha** : 1933 : *Tripura Kshatriya Samaj Sankranta Bibaran Sangraha.* Agartala, Kendriya Sabha of the Tripura Khatriya Samaj, 1343 T.E.

1762. **Khan , Abdul Majed** : 1969 : *The Transition in Bengal (1756-1775).*

1763. **Khan, F.A.** : 1963 : *Mainamati.* Karachi, Deptt. of Archaeology, Govt. of Pakistan, 38p.

1764. **Khandpur, Swarn** : 1971 : *Our Country Series : India, the land and its people.* Bombay, Ratnabharati : 116-19.

1765. **Khanna, S.N.** : 1979 : Act aim at 'dividing people'. *Hindustan Times, Oct. 17.*

1766. ——— : 1979 : Upsurge of a sectarian party. *Hindustan Times,* Oct. 22.

1767. **Kharmih. L.** : 1980 : Role of banking in the economic development of Tribal areas in North Eastern India *(In) Tribal Economy of North Eastern Region (Ed)* by T. Mathew. Gauhati, Spectrum Publications : 206-09.

1768. **Khound, H.P.** : 1972 : Problems of field Research : The case of a Jhumia colony in Tripura *(In) Socio Economic Research in Tribal Areas (Ed)* by P.C. Goswami. Jorhat, AERC, NEI : 68-70.

1769. **Khound, H.P.** *and* **Dutta, P.C.** : 1970 : *Case Study of Jhumia Colony in Tripura : Kathaliacherra.* Jorhat, AERC, NEI.

1770. **Koloi, Gopal Singh** : ? : *Koloi Sampradayer Niyamaboli (in Bengali).* Agartala, Directorate of Research.

1771. **Kriesel, Melvin E.** *(Jr)* : 1976 : Kuki disturbances in Tripura, 1860-'61 (Notes). *Social Scientist,* 4(9), April : 60-65.

1772. **Kumar, Braj Bihari** *and* Chakraborty, Shantimoy : 1976: *Hindi Tripuri Dictionary.* Kohima, Nagaland Bhasha Parishad, 94p.

1773. **Kumar, Narendra : n.p.** : *Blood Groups among Maghs from Tripura State : A Short Note.* Calcutta, Anthropological Survey of India *(unpublished Report).*

1774. ——— : 1958 : ABO Blood Groups and Secretor Factor Distribution Among the Noatia : A Mongoloid tribe of Tripura State. *The Anthropologist,* V (1-2). March-Aug. : 42-46.

1775. **Kumar, Narendra** *and* **Sastry, D.B.** :1961 : A Genetic Survey among the Riang, a Mongoloid tribe of Tripura. *Zeitschrift fur Morphologie und Anthropologie* (Stuttgart), 51 (3) : 346-55.

L

1776. **Labour Bureau Publication** : 1964 : *Family living of the tea plantation workers in Tripura (Labour Bureau Publication No. 64).* Delhi, Manager of Publications, 92p.

1777. **Lariri, A.N.** : 1986 : *Tripura coins of Iconographic interest : A source book of the Numismatic Studies in North East India.* Guwahati, 169p.

1778. **Lahiry, Kartick** : 1971 : Temple architecture in Tripura. *Pine* (Shillong), 1(1), March : 93-97.

1779. **Lahiri, Kartik** : 1975 : Rabindra Nathen Pocket Books Jadu Bhatter Gan O Tatprasangik *(in Bengali). (In) Tripura Prasanga (Ed)* by Swapan Sengupta. Agartala, Direc, of Public Relations & Tourism : 17-28.

1780. **Lahiri, R.K.** : 1973 : Managerial problems of co-operative forms in Tripura. *Indian Jour. of Commerce,* 26 (4) : 688-94.

1781. **Lahiri, Ranjan Kr.** : 1976 : *Family farming in a developing economy : A Study based on farm management Survey of Tripura.* Kalyani University, Ph. D. Thesis.

1782. ——— : 1978 : Technological transformation and psychological constraints (A Study of the Farmers of Tripura). Proceedings of a Seminar on *"North East in Transition"* (NEHU, Shillong), 2nd Oct., 1978.

1783. ——— : 1979 : *Family farming in a developing economy : A study based on farm management survey of Tripura.* New Delhi, Concept Publishing House, 132p.

1784. ——— : 1979 : Family farming in a developing economy. *Indian Jour. of Agri. Eco.,* 34(2), April-June.

1785. ——— : 1985 : Family Farming *(In) An Anthology of Tripura (Ed) by* Jagadis Gan Choudhuri. New Delhi, Inter India Publication : 51-56.

1786. **Lahiri, T.B.** : 1989 : Strategy for rural development in North East India. Proceedings of a Seminar on *"Perspective, Issues and Experiences of Rural*

Development in North East India" held on 26-27 May by NEICSSR, Shillong.

1787. **Lalchungnunga, K.** : 1991 : *A Mizo village its socio, economic, cultural, religious and administrative aspect,* Gauhati University, Ph.D. Thesis (*Unpublished*).

1788. **Lal Dena** : 1978 : Patterns of leadership in a changing Human society *(In) Cultural and Biological Adaptability of Man with Special Reference to North East India, (Ed)* by A.C. Bhagabati *and* R.K. Kar (*Bulletin of Anthropology Deptt.,* Dibrugarh University, Vol. 6, 1977). Dibrugarh University, Deptt. of Anth.: 86-95.

1789. **Lal, PVSM Mohan** : 1984 : Harmony among peoples of the North-eastern Region and between it and the rest of India *(In) North-east Region : Problems and Prospects of Development (Ed)* by B.L. Abbi. Chandigarh, Centre for Research in Rural and Industrial Development: 202-214.

1790. **Law Deptt.** : 1979 : *Tripura Tribal Areas Autonomous District Council Act, 1979 (Tripura Act 12 of 1979).* Agartala, Law Deptt.

1791. **Law Research Institute** : 1984 : *A Study of the land systems of North Eastern Region, Vol. III : Tripura* Gauhati, Gauhati High Court, Law Research Institute.

1792. **Lewin, T.H.** : 1869 : *Progress colloquial exercised in the Lushai Dialect of Dzo or Kuki Language.* Calcutta.

1793. ——— : 1870 : *Wild Races of South Eastern India.* London, W.H. Allen & Co. [*Reprinted* by T.R.I., Aizawl in 1978 through Firma K.L.M. Pvt. Ltd, Calcutta] : 85-101, 102-116.

1794. ——— : 1869 : *The Hill Tracts of Chittagong and the Dwellers therein.* Calcutta, Bengal Printing Co. 100p.

1795. ——— : 1943 : Anthology of marriage : Chakma of Chittagong. *Man in India,* 23(2) : 106-110.

1796. **Lillingston, E.G.** : 1874 : *Letter from Captain E.G. Lillingston, officiating Political Agent to the Rajah of Hill Tipperah, no. 60, dated Agartala, the 3rd March, 1874.*

1797. **Link** : 1969 : Manipur, Tripura problems. *Link*, Oct. 5:8.

1798. ——— : 1970 : Tribulation of Tripura. *Link*. Sept. 13: 23.

1799. **Lloyd, G.T** : 1923 : Triputa *(In) Census of India 1921, vol. III, Assam*, Pt. I, Report. Shillong, Govt. Press : 148.

1800. **Lodh, A.K.** : ? : Tripurar Bhubashan Itihas (*in Bengali*). *Bhaskar*, II: 11.

1801. **Loffler, L.G.** : 1964 : Chakma and Sak. *International Archiv fur Ethnogra.*

1802. **Lok Sabha Secretariat** : 1960 : *India : Joint Committee on Tripura land revenue and land reforms bill 1959 (Report)*. Delhi, Lok Sabha Secretariat, 93p.

1803. **Long, James** : 1851 : Analysis of Bengali poem Rajamala or chronicles of Tripura. *Jour. Asiatic Society of Bengal*, XIX : 533-57.

1804. ——— : 1978 : *Rajamala or an analysis of the chronicles of the Kings of Tripura : 1814-1887. Revised Edition* by S. Chaudhuri. Calcutta, Firma K.L.M. Pvt. Ltd.

1805. **Lowis, O.O.** : 1902 : The Riang or Yin *(In) Census of India 1901, vol. XIII, Burma, Pt. I Report*. Rangoon, Govt. Press : 130.

M

1806. **Mackenzie, Alexander** : 1969 : *Memorandum on the North Eastern Frontier of Bengal.* Calcutta, Bengal Secretariat Press, 78p.

1807. ——— : 1884 : *History of the Relations of the Government with the Hill Tribes of the North East Frontier of Bengal.* Calcutta, Home Deptt. Press [*Reprinted* in 1989].

1808. ——— : 1989 : *The North East Frontier of India.* Delhi, Mittal Publications: 269-286, 561-62 (3rd time *reprinted,* the original title was: *"History of the relations of government with the Hill Tribes of the North East Frontier of Bengal"* (1884).

1809. **Mahadev, G.** : 1975 : *Letters to the Editor:* Rubber export plan. *Hindu,* Oct. 30; 6 (6).

1810. **Mahajan, V.S.** (*Ed*) : 1988 : *Emerging pattern of North Eastern Economy.* New Delhi, Deep & Deep Publications.

1811. **Maharaja** : 1874 : *Maharaja Birendra Manikya's letter to the Political Agent, Hill Tipperah, No. 21 dated Agartala, the 9th Feb. 1874.*

1812. **Mahato, P.P.** : 1983 : Uttar Bango Assamer lok Sanskriti O Tripurar Ganotantra (Review) (*in Bengali*). *Desh* (Calcutta), Dec. 17.

1813. **Mahato, Pashupati Prasad** : 1986 : Ethnicity, Cultural Identity and Nationality Formation: A case study of the tribals of Tripura. Proceedings of a Seminar on *"Questions of Nationalities, Ethnicity and Cultural Identity in the context of North East India",* 5-6 Dec. by NEICSSR, Shillong.

1814. ——— : 1990 : Ethnicity, Cultural Identity and Nationality Formation: A case study of the Tribals of Tripura *(In) Nationality, Ethnicity and Cultural Identity in North East India (Ed)* by B.

Pakem. New Delhi, Omsons Publications: 349-364.

1815. **Maitra, S.** : 1970 : Bachelor's dormitories of the tribes of eastern India. *Bulletin of Anthropological Survey of India*, 19 (2): 61-5.

1816. **Majumdar, A.** : 1985 : Letters to the Editor : Alternative Rail Link-up to Cachar-Tripura-Mizoram. *Shillong Times*, July 27 : 2 (3-5).

1817. **Majumdar, B.** : 1973 : States' planned steps for economic development. *Economic Times*, Jan. 21 : 13 (1).

1818. ——— : 1977 : Tribe and politics in Tripura: Past and present. *Social Perspective*, 5 (1), June: 21-35.

1819. ——— : 1979 : Many milestones to cross for Left Front Govt. *Economic Times*, Jan. 5: 11 (1).

1820. **Majumdar, Benimadhab** : 1985 : Struggle for responsible Government in Tripura (1947-1956). *Proceedings of NEIHA* (Agartala), No. 6 : 417-24.

1821. **Majumdar, Binapani** : 1985 : Status and Education of women in Tripura. *Proceedings of NEIHA* (Agartala), No. 6: 482-91.

1822. ——— : 1986 : From tradition to modernity: Changing position of women in Tripura. *Proceedings of NEIHA* (Pasighat), No. 7: 309-14.

1823. **Majumdar, Diptosh** : 1991 : An island of peace in turbulent North-East. *Statesman*, Feb. 21: 16 (3-5).

1824. **Majumdar, D.N.** : 1969 : An appraisal of administrative policies for economic development of the people of the hill areas of North East India. *Tribe*, VI (1), June : 24-31.

1825. ——— : 1973 : Size-shape categories in the languages of North East India : An Exploration of the Sapir-Whorf hypothesis. *Bulletin of the Deptt. of Anthropology, Gauhati University*, 2 : 41-61.

1826. ——— : 1980 : North East India : A Profile. (*In*) *Eastern Himalayas : A Study on Anthropology and Tribalism (Eds.)* by T.C. Sharma *and* D.N. Majumdar. New Delhi, Cosmo Publications: 23-62.

1827. **Majumdar, D.N.** : 1983 : The Tribes and their problems in North East India *(In) Souvenir : Anthropological Society of North East India (Eds.)* by H.C. Sharma *and* B. Choudhury. Gauhati, Anth. Deptt., Gauhati University: 12-7.

1828. ——— : 1984 : Shifting cultivation in North East India: A Short account of the land and the people *(In) Socio Economic aspects in Soil Conservation Activities with special Reference to North Eastern Region* by Soil Conservation Deptt. Shillong, Soil Conservation Deptt., Govt. of Meghalaya : 12-24 (Seminar held at Tura on 17-20 June, 1981).

1829. ——— : 1988 : Dress and ornaments of the people of North-East India. Tokya (Japan), National Museum of Ethnology (*Unpublished).*

1830. ——— : 1991 : *Shifting Cultivation in North East India.* New Delhi, Omsons Publications, 341p.

1831. **Majumdar, H.** (*Ed.) : 1979 : India, Census 1971, Tripura, pt. II-D, Migration Tables.* Delhi, Controller of Publications, 245p.

1832. **Malakar, Dilip** : ? : *Nanan Desher nanan samaj : Tripura (in Bengali).* Agartala, Pub. by the author, 63p.

1833. **Malhotra, R.** : 1985 : Tribal groups in India : Their Problems and Development. *Vanyajati,* 33 (2), April: 9-17.

1834. **Mamdani, Mahmood** : 1984 : Nationality question in a neo-colony: A Historical perspective. *Economic and Political Weekly,* XIX (27): 1046-1054.

1835. **Mandal, Debabrata** : 1974 : Some gods and goddesses among the Jamatia. *Folklore,* 19 (8) : 229-33.

1836. ——— : 1978 : The Tripuri : A Tribe in Transition. *Jour. of NEICSSR,* II (II), Oct.: 11-2.

1837. ——— : 1978 : The Jamatia : A Short Ethnographic Note. *Vanyajati,* 26 (1): 19-23.

1838. ——— : 1979 : Tribal welfare in Tripura. *Vanyajati,* XXVII (1), January: 18-23.

1839. ——— : 1981 : Political organization of Jamatia. *Jr. Indian Anth. Society* (Calcutta), 16 (3) : 275-77.

1840. **Mandal, Sushila** : ? : *Banga Desher Itihas* (Middle Age, 1st Part): 283-91.

1841. **M.D.G.** : 1988 : Problem-Ridden Accord in Tripura. *Economic and Political Weekly*, XXIII (36), Sept. 3 : 1833-34.

1842. **Mann, R.S.** : 1984 : Research ventures and trends : Case of tribal North East India. Proceedings of a Seminar on *"Tribal Research in North Eastern Region"*, organised by North Eastern Council Secretariat, Shillong.

1843. **Maretina, S.A.** : 1971 : Relations between natural conditions of labour economy and social order of mountain peoples of North East India. *Peoples of Asia and Africa*, No. 6: 46-67.

1844. **Mathew, K.M.** (*Ed*) : 1983 : *Manorama Year Book, 1983*. Kerala, Manorama Publishing House: 659-62.

1845. **Mc Gindle** : 1927 : *Ancient India : As described by Potlemy*. Calcutta, Chakraborty-Chatterjee & Co. : 232-34 (Reference of Early Tripura).

1846. **Mc Swiney, J.** : 1912 : Chakma. *(In) Census of India 1911, vol. III: Assam, Part-I, Report*. Shillong, Govt. Press, 129 p.

1847. **Medhi, Surendra Nath** : 1990 : Article 244A should be omitted. *Assam Tribune*, Aug. 31: 4 (3-6), 7 (1).

1848. **Mehrotra, Prakash** : 1982 : Ecological equilibrium in North Eastern Region. *Shillong Times*, May 15: 2 (3-5), 5 (1-5).

1849. **Menon, K.D.** (*Ed.*) : 1975 : *Tripura District Gazetteers*. Agartala, Govt. of Tripura, 504p.

1850. **Menon, V.P.** : ? : *The Story of the integration of the Indian States*: 287-88 (Tripura).

1851. **Mills, J.P.** : 1935 : Tipperas *(In) Notes on a tour in the Chittagong Hill Tracts in 1926. Census of India 1931, India, Pt. III, vol. Ethnographical*. Simla, Govt. Press: B 121-22.

1852. **Minister** : 1891 : *D.O. from the Minister, Tipperah State to the Political Agent of Hill Tipperah dated Agartala, the 11th Oct., 1891.*

1853. **Minister** : 1905 : *Representation of the Minister, Tipperah State, to the Political Agent, No. 50-XI-1, dated Agartala, 26th May, 1905, Supplement No. 119-XI-1, dated Agartala the 21st July, 1905.*

1854. **Ministry of Education** : 1978-1979 : *Tripura*. New Delhi, Ministry of Education and Social Welfare. (Price Rs. 53, 50p.)

1855. **Ministry of Human Resource** : ? : *District Gazetteers of Tripura*. New Delhi, Ministry of Human Resources (Development), Deptt. of Education.

1856. **Mirchandani, T.J.** : 1971 : *Investigation into methods and practices of farming in various States*. Delhi, Indian Council of Agricultural Research: 504-15.

1857. **Misra, Baniprasanna** : 1976 : The Positive Approach to the Problem of shifting cultivation in Eastern India and a few suggestions to the Policy makers *(In) Shifting Cultivation in North East India. (Ed)* by B. Datta Ray. Shillong, NEICSSR : 106-21.

1858. **Misra, Baniprasanna** : : 1976 : *Socio-Economic Adjustments of Tribals: Case-Study of Tripura Jhumias*. New Delhi, People's Publishing House, 137p.

1859. ——— : 1972 : *Socio-Economic Adjustment of Tribals: A Case Study of Tripura Jhumias*. Ph.D. Thesis, Poona (1968-'72).

1860. ——— : 1982 : Kirata Karyokinesis : An Introduction to the Political Economy of Tribal Societies in North East India. *(In) Economies of the Tribes and their transformation, (Ed)* by K.S.Singh. New Delhi, Concept Publishing Company : 43-62.

1861. **Mishra, B.K.** *and* **Ramakrishnan, P.S.** : 1983 : Slash and burn agriculture in high elevations in North East India. *Agriculctural Eco. Systems & Environment*, 9 : 69-80.

1862. **Misra, Promode Kumar** : 1977 : Patterns of Inter-Tribal Relations *(In) Tribal Heritage of India, vol. I : Ethnicity, Identity and Interaction (Ed)* by S.C. Dube. New Delhi, Vikas Publishing House : 88-95.

1863. **Misra, Udayon** : 1988 : *North East India : Quest for Identity (A Collection of Essays on Socio-Political topics)..* Guwahati, Omsons Publication, 189p.

1864. ——— : 1989 : Letters to the Editor : Delhi's hand in Assam? *Statesman,* Feb. 25: 8(4). [Bodo, T.N.V.].

1865. **Mitra, A.** : 1964 : *Census of India 1961, vol.I, India, Pt.II-C(ii) : Language Tables.* Delhi, Managers of Publications, 534p (2nd edition published in 1967, 554p.)

1866. **Mitra, A.K.** : 1956 : *Anthropometry of Kaipeng and Tipra of Tripura.* Calcutta, Anthropological Survey of India (*Unpublished*).

1867. ——— : 1962 : The Riang of Tripura. *Bull. Anth. Survey of India,* V(2), July (1956) : 21-120.

1868. **Mitra, D.** : 1976 : Antiquities of Pilak and Jalaibari, Tripura. *Jour. Asiatic Society,* 18 (1-4) : 56-77.

1869. **Mitra, Nikhilesh** : 1990 : N.F. Railway : Tracts of Progress. *Assam Tribune,* April 11 : 4(3-6), 7(3-4).

1870. **Mitra, Prabhat** : 1973 : Tripura on the March. *Economic Times,* Jan. 21 : 9(1).

1871. **Mitra, R.** *and* **Das Gupta, B.** (Eds) : 1967 : *A Common Perspective for North East India.* Calcutta, Pannalal Das Gupta.

1872. **Mitra, Satis Chandra** :? : *Jashohar, Khulnar Itihas,* 1st part. (*in Bengali*). : 88, 90 (Tipariya).

1873. **Mittal Publication : 1984** : *Report on the Administration of North East India (Reprinted).* Delhi, Mittal Publications, 136p. (Original Title was *"Report on the Administration of Assam for the year 1921-'22"*).

1874. **Mohan, Vishwa : 1964** : Remmants of shifting cultivation. *Eastern Anthropologist,* 17(1) : 31-8.

1875. **Mohanta, Bijan** : 1885 : Status of Princely Tripura during British Rule. *Proceedings of NEIHA* (Agartala), No.6: 285- 94.

1876. **Mookherjee, Radhakumod** : ? : *The Gupta Empire* : 10, 106, 123, 136 (Tripperah).

1877. **Mukherjee, Bhabananda** : 1954-'55 : Note on the Residence in wife's house among the Riang of Tripura. *Adibasi* (Orissa). 3(3-4) : 2.

1878. ——— : 1959 : The cult of the dead and funerary customs of the Riang. *Bulletin of the Deptt. of Anthropology* (Anth. Survey of India), 4(2), July : 111-20 (1955).

1879. ——— : 1956 : A Few Riang Tales. *Indian Folk-Lore,* 1(1) : 17-21.

1880. ——— : 1956 : A Riang Myth. *Indian Folk-Lore,* I(2), Sept. Dec. : 69-72.

1881. ——— : 1957 : Tales of orphan Boys. *Indian Folk-Lore,* 2(1) : 13-7

1882. ——— : 1957 : Riang Folk Tales *Indian Folk Lore,* 2(2), Oct. Dec. : 39-45.

1883. ——— : 1957 : Riang Culture and Historical Changes. *Indian Science Congress Bulletin,* pt. III : 337-38.

1884. ——— : 1958 : Kinship and Marriage of the Riang of Tripura. *Procedings of Forty Fifth Session, Indian Science Congress, 3p.*

1885. ——— : 1958 : Residence in Wife's House among the Riang of Tripura. *Indian Science Congress Bulletin:* 407.

1886. ——— : 1970 : The Riang. *Bulletin of Anth. Survey of India,* 8(1), January : 1-107 (1959).

1887. ——— : 1960 : Trends of changes in the Riang culture since Independence. *Bulletin of Anth. Survey of India,* VIII(2), July (1959) : 103-08.

1888. ——— : 1960 : Cross Cousin Marriage among the Riang. *Anthropos,* 55(5-6) : 734-38.

1889. ——— : 1960 : Cross cousin marriage among the Riang. *The Anthropologist,* V : 386.

1890. ——— : 1961 : Consequences of the adoption of settled cultivation in place of shifting cultivation, *Bulletin Deptt. of Anth.* (Anth. Survey of India), 10(2), July : 52-55.

1891 ——— : 1962 : Riang Economy. *Bulletin of Anth. Survey of India,* V(1), Jan (1956) : 61-6.

1892. ——— : 1969 : Riang. *Educational Miscellany.* 5(3-4) : 62-6.

1893. **Mukkherjee, Bhabananda** : 1973 : Kinship Terminology. *Jour. of Indian Anth. Society 8(1), April : 45-59* [mixed-article with the Naga, Khasi, etc.]

1894. ——— : 1980 : Tribal Situation and development problems in Tripura. *Bulletin of Anth. Survey of India*, 22(3-4), July-Dec. 1973) : 16-31.

1895. ——— : 1981 : Tribalism and Extremism in Tripura. *Jour. of Indian Anth. Society,* 16(2), July : 145-48.

1896. ——— : 1983 ; The future of the traditional tribal culture of Tripura *Bull. Anth. Survey of India,*, 24(3-4, July-Dec: 1-6(1975).

1897. ——— : 1983 : Book Review : Folk tales and myths of Riang and Tripuri communities by Tushar K. Niyogi, Pub. by Anthropological Survey of India, Calcutta 1983 *Human Science,* 32(4), Dec.: 313-15.

1898. ——— : 1984 : Riang *(In) Tribal Education in India (Eds)* by Biman K. Das Gupta *and* Ajit K. Danda. Calcutta, Anth. Survey of India: 29.

1899. ——— : 1990 : Social *and Political* Institution of the Riang of Tripura *(In) Social and Political Institutions of the Hill People of North East India (Eds)* by Jayanta Sarkar *and* B. Datta Ray. Calcutta, Anthropological Survey of India : 190-202 (It was a Seminar paper about *"Social and Political Institutions of the Hill People of North East India"* organised jointly by Anth, Survey of India *and* NEICSSR, Shillong on 4-5 July, 1977.)

1900. **Mukherjee, Bhabanada** *and* **Singh, K.S.** : 1982 : Tribal Movements in Tripura *(In Tribal Movements in India, vol.I (Ed)* by K.S. Singh New Delhi, Manohar Publications : 317-37.

1901. **Mukherjee, Malina** : 1988 : Demographic Profile of the Himalayan Region in India with special reference to the Eastern and North Eastern Sub-Sector *(In Current Anthropological and Archaeological Perspective : High Altitude Anthropoloy, vol. IV (Ed)* by K.L. Bhowmik. New Delhi, Inter-India Publications : 39-79.

1902. **Mukherjee, Mihir** : 1991 : Chakmas grateful for BSF security. *Statesman* Aug. 13 : 4(4-5).

1903. **Mukherji, Ranjit** : 1974 : Problems of shifting cultivation. *North Eastern Affairs*, 3(1), April-June : 47-54, 57.

1904. ——— : 1975 : Some social constraints to Agricultural development in North Eastern India, *North Eastern Affairs, Annual Number*, 4(1), : 43-50.

1905. **Mukherjee, R.P.** : 1977 : Rhesus and other monkeys of Tripura. *Newsletter Zoological Survey of India*, 3(3) : 111.

1906. ——— : 1979 : Phayre's Leaf monkeys (Presbytis phayrie Blyth, 1874) of Tripura. *8th Cong. Int. Primat. Soc.* Abstract).

1907. ——— : 1982 : Pharey leaf monkey (Presbytis phayrie Blyth, 1847 : of Tripura, *Jour. Bombay National Historical Society*, 79(1) : 47-56.

1908. ——— : 1982 : Survey of non-human primates of Tripura. *Jour Zool. Soc. India, 34 (1-2) : 70-9.*

1909. **Mukhopadhay, A.** : 1984 ; A peace loving tribe on the war path. *Indian Express* (New Delhi) July 17.

1910. **Mukhopadhyay, Prabhat Kumar** : 1960 : *Bengali Sakabda : Rabindra Jibani-O-Rabindra Sahitya Prabeshak* (1st part, B.S. 1367). Calcutta, Rabindra Bharati ; 195, 196, 463, 465, 467.

1911. ——— : ? : *Naba gyan Bharati.* Calcutta, Rabindra Bharati; 10, 23, 83, 104, 203, 328, 406, 597.

1912. **Mukhopadhyay, Sudarshan** : 1967 Tripuraye Vaishnav dharama Prasar *(In) Bhaskar* (Agartala), vol;. II *(In Bengali).*

1913. **Mukhopadhyay, Sukhamoy** : 1966 : *Bangala Itihaser Duso Bachar : Sultander amal (1338-1538 A.D.), 2nd edition : 313-336 (in Bengali)* [about "Tripurar Sange Hosen Shaher judhan"].

N

1914. **Naba Bharat Times** : 1986 : Tripura men 14 logon ki hattya *(In Hindi) Naba Bhara Times,* Aug. 31: 1(8).

1915. ——— : 1986 : Tripura men aatankvadiyon ki gati vidiya tej *Naba Bharat Times,* Sept. 16 : 1(1-3).

1916. ——— : 1986 : Tripura ke aatankavadiyon ke adde Bangladesh men N.B.T., Dec. 16 : 1(2-3).

1917. ——— : 1986 : Tripura Bandh : Bipakhya Bidhansava se bahar *N.B.T.., Dec. 25 : 1(4-5).*

1918. ——— : 1986 : Tripura men chapamaron ka phir hamla, char mare. *N.B.T.* Dec. 26 : 1(3-5).

1919. ——— : 1986 : Tripura men ek ghar ke ath sadashyon ki hatta : Ugravadiyon dwara tin din men 23 hattayen. *N.B.T.,* Dec. 27 : 1(1-3), 4(7-8).

1920. ——— : 1987 : Nripen Chakravarti ki T.N.V. ko chetavani *N.B.T.,* Jan. 17 : 3(1-2).

1921. ——— : 1987 : Chakma Bangladesh quen nahi jana Chahate ? *N.B.T., Jan. 23 : 5(2-3).*

1922. ——— : 1987 : Tripura ke Tin Jiolon men Vyapak dharpakar, *N.B.T., Jan 23 : 10 (5-6).*

1923. ——— : 1987 : Tripura men ek parivar ke sat logon ki hattya. *N.B.T., Jan 25 : 1(1-2).*

1924. ——— : 1987 : Char sou aur sharanarthi Tripura men dakhil. *N.B.T., Feb. 9 : 10 (3-4).*

1925. ——— : 1987 : Editorial ; Chakma Adivasi. *N.B.T., March 10 : 4(1-2).*

1926. ——— : 1988 : Editorial ; Tripura men samjhota. *N.B.T.,* Aug. 15 : 6(1-2).

1927. ——— : 1'989 : Tripura Divas Parishisth. *N.B.T.,* March 26 : 5(1-8).

1928. ——— : 1989 : Chakma adivasi apne bhabishya ke prati shankit. *N.B.T., may 9 : 4(8).*

1929. **Naba Bharat Times** : 1989 : Tripura men 63 hazar Chakma sharanarthi. *N.B.T., June 29 : 5(1-2).*

1930. ——— : 1989 : Editorial Tripura men Congress gutbaji. *N.B.T.*, June 24 : 4(1-2).

1931. ——— : 1989 : Chakma Sharanarthiyon se Tripura men bhari sankat. *N.B.T., July 10 : (7-8).*

1932. **Nag, Amit** : 1986 : Tripura also faces Tribal discontent . *Statesman*, May 11 and 15 : 7.

1933. **Nag, A.K.** : 1973 : Christinanity and role of church in Mizoram. *North Eastern Affairs* (Shillong), 2(1).

1934. **Nag, Amit Kumar** : 1975 : paper on "Problems of Economically weaker tea estates with particular reference to those of Tripura". For Seminar on *"Problems of Tea Plantation Industry,*: Nov. 22-23 by NEICSSR.

1935. ——— : 1979 : Tea in Tripura : Languishing estates need assistance. *Capital*, March 29 : 312.

1936. ——— : 1981 : Problems of economically weaker Tea estates with particular reference to those of Tripura *(In) Problems of Tea Industry in North East India*, (Ed) by NEICSSR. Calcutta, Research India Publications : 129-39.

1937. ——— : 1990 : Tripura wants allocations for annual plan raised. *Amrita Bazar Patrika*, May 9 : 7(5-8).

1938. ——— : 1990 : Chittagong tribal's distress yet to get proper attention. *Amrita Bazar Patrika*, July 27 : 5(1-6).

1939. **Nag, Ranan** : 1973 : Farm Development. *Economic Times*, Jan. 21 : 11(1).

1940. **Nag, Sajal** : 1990 : *Roots of ethnic conflict : Nationality Question in North East India*. New Delhi, Manohar Publications, 193p.

1941. **Nagaland Bhasha Parishand** : 1984 : *Tripuri Folk Tales*, Kohima, N.B.P.

1942. ——— : ? : *Hindi Tripuri Dictionary*, Kohima, N.B.P.

1943. **Nakane, Chie** : 1954 : Ethnological Survey of the aboriginals in the State of Tripura. *Japan. J. of Ethnology*, 19(1): 58-99.

1944. **Nandi, M.** : 1974 : The Relation of Agartala Floods to the Haora River Catchment, Tripura State, *Records G.S.I., Vol. 108, Pt. 2 : 149-52.*

1945. ——— : 1974 : Agricultural aspects of Tripura. *Indian Geographical Studies : Research Bulletin* (Patna), No. 2 : 76.

1946. ——— : 1975 : Geographical Review of the Gumti H.E. Project, Tripura State, *Geog. Rev. Ind.: Geo. Soc. Ind., Vol. 37(4): 382.*

1947. ——— : 1977 : Physiography of Tripura State. *Geog. Rev. India : Geog. Soc. India,* vol. 39(4) : 367-73.

1948. ——— : 1984 : *Land form development of Tripura (West Baramura Range and North of Sonamura-Udaipur-Amarpura towns).* Ph.D. Thesis, Calcutta University (*Unpublished*).

1949. **Nandi, Manika** : 1985 : Geographical Account *(In) An Anthology of Tripura (Ed) by Jagadis Gan Choudhuri. New Delhi, Inter-India Publications : 1-9.*

1950. **Narayanaswami, S.** : 1964 : Mineral potentialities of Assam, Manipur and Tripura region *(In) Mineral Development of Assam.* Shillong Govt. of Assam, : 58.

1951. **Natarajan, Nalini** : 1966 : Marriage in Chakma society. *Social Welfare,* 13(1), April : 13-4.

1952. ——— : 1970 : Mizos : Social Institutions and practices *Social Welfare,* 16(2), March: 32.

1953. ——— : 1973 : The Chakmas. *North Eastern Affairs,* vol.2.

1954. **Nath, H.C.** : 1974 : Tripura -"Judiciary in Tripura" *(In) Souvenir of Gauhati High Court, 1948-1973, Silver Jubilee Commemoration Volume* by Souvenir Committee, Gauhati High Court : 154.

1955. **Nath, Lal Mohan** : 1978 : Dasda peace centre (Tripura State). *Himalaya : Man and Nature,* 2(2), July : 25-6.

1956. ——— : 1982 : Social work in Tripura-Mizo Border Hill Area. *Himalaya : Man and Nature,* 6(7), Dec. : 11.

1957. ——— : 1985 : Dasda Sarvodaya Santi Kendra, Tripura (N). *Himalaya Man and Nature,* VIII(9-10), Feb-March : 12-3.

1958. **Nath, Lal Mohan** : 1987: Dasda sarvodaya Shanti Kendra, Tripura *Himalaya : Man and Nature,* X (10), March : 15-6.

1959. **Nath, N.C.** : 1985 : History of Vanga-Loka in Tripura. *Proceedings of NEIHA* (Agartala), *No. 6 : 261-64.*

1960. **Nath, R.M.** : 1948 : *The Background of Assamese culture.* Shillong, A.K. Nath, 1948 (Chapter XIV: The Tipperahs).

1961. **Nath, S.C.** *and* **Bordoloi, D.N.** : 1988 : North East India : An Ethnobotanic Survey. *Himalaya : Man and Nature,* XI (8- 9), Jan. Feb.: 2-6.

1962. **NCAER** : 1961 : *Techno Economic Survey of Tripura.* New Delhi, National Council of Applied Economic Research, 163p.

1963. **National Institute** : 1990 : Seminar on *"Agrarian structrure and land relations in North Eastern Region",* organised by the National Institute of Rural Development, North Eastern Regional Centre, Guwahati.

1964. **National Sample Survey** : 1977 : *Jhum cultivation in Tripura.* Agartala, Directorate of Statistics, and Evaluation, Govt. of Tripura (July 1976 to June 1977, 31st round).

1965. **Nawari, N.P.** : 1973 : Socio-Economic Problems of tribal life. *Link, 11 March : 47-51.*

1966. **Nayak, Chhayakanta** : 1990 : Chakma refuges face uncertain future. *Assam Tribune,* Feb. 26 : 4(7-8).

1967. **Negi, Balbir Singh** : 1964 : Tribes of the North East Frontier Region. *(In) Anthropogeography : A Study of Races and People of the World Geographical Series No. 1).* Allahabad, Kitab Mahal : 237-69.

1968. **Nehru, Jawaharlal** : 1945 : *Letter from Pandit Jawaharlal Nehru, dated 9th December. File No. 1945, B 52/S-9A3, Administrative Deptt.* (*Unpublished*).

1969. ——— : 1964 : Speech on return from a tour of North East Frontier in 1952. *Vanyajati,* 12(3): 127-28.

1970. **Niyogi, Tusher Kanti** : 1974 : A Study of Tripura proverbs. *Folklore* XV(1), Jan.: 19-24.

1971. **Niyogi, Tusher Kanti** : 1983 : Folk tales and myths of Riang and Tripuri communities (*Folklore Series No.* 2). Calcutta, Anthropological Survey of India, 200p.

1972. **North Eastern Council** : 1980 : *Basic Statistics of North Eastern Region 1980.* Shillong, North Eastern Council Secretariat, 243p.

1973. **North Eastern Hill University** : 1986 : *Studies in the History of North East India (H.L. Barpujari Felicitation volume).* Shillong North Eastern Hill University.

1974. **North Eastern Spectrum** : 1976 : Tripura Newsletter. *North Eastern Spectrum,* (1), July: 47 : 1(8-10), Feb. -April : 54-5; 1(5) Nov. : 76 : 1(6) Dec. : 60-2.

1975. **Notification** : 1990: Government notification laying down the new rules and regulations for the administration of Chittagong Hill Tracts to come into effect from 1st May, 1990 *(In) The Chakma* by S.P., Talukdar. Delhi, Gyan Publishing House 1988 : 143-58.

1976. **Now** : 1967 : Tripura (on election-eve) *Now,* Feb. 103 (19): 12.

1977. ——— : 1967 : Tripura delacle, Now, March 31, 3(26) : 14.

1978. ——— : 1967 : Tripura *Now, 3(32), May 12 : 22.*

1979. ———: 1967 : Tripura : The Naxal bari way ? *Now,* 3 (40), July 7 : 11-2.

1980. ——— : 1967 : Tripura : Forest fires *Now*, Sept. 15,3(50) : 11-2

O

1981. **Odhikari, O.S.** : 1980 : *The problems of indebtedness amongst the tribals in Sadar Sub-Division in Tripura.* Agartala, Directorate of Research, Deptt. of Sch Tribe and Sch. Caste, Govt. of Tripura.

1982. **O'Donel, J.H.** : 1968 : Notes on Tribes of the Eastern Frontier. *Jour. Asiatic Soc. Bengal.*

P

1983. **Pai (Karapurkar), Pushpa**: 1976 : *Kokborok Grammar.* Mysore, Central Institute of Indian Language (*Ed*) by E. Annamalai 144p.

1984. **Pakem, B** : 1986 : Political development and change in North East India *(In) Changing North East India (Ed)* by A.P. Sinha. Ludhiana, Gagan Publications : 29-64.

1985. ——— : 1989 : Polity-Formation in Pre-Colonial Biate chieftancy proceedings of NEIHA (Shillong) Xth Annual session.

1986. **Pakyntein, E.H.** : 1965 : *Census of India 1961, vol. III : Assam, pt. V-A Scheduled Tribes and Scheduled Castes (Reprints from old Census Reports and Special Tables).* Delhi, Manager of Publications, 148p.

1987. **Pal, Hmansu** : 1985 : Students' Movements in Tripura (1950- '70) *Proceedings of NEIHA* (Agartala), *No. 6 : 425-32.*

1988. **Pandey, Laksmikanta** : 1990 : Book Review: Sashastra Gatibidhiyon ki jao hai Asaman vikas : Tripura. *[Tribal Insurgency in Tripura* by S.R. Bhattacharjee, Inter-India Publications, New Delhi]. Purbanchal Prabhari May 13 : 4(3- 7) [*in Hindi*].

1989. **Pandit, C.S,** : 1988 : Political victory in Tripura *Amrita Bazar Patrika,* Feb. 11 : 6(3-6).

1990. **Pardeshi, Ghanshyam** ; 1987 : Problems of Industrialisation in N-E region, *Shillong Times, Sept. 19 : 2(3-6), 3(5-6).*

1991. ——— : 1987 : TNV violence against civilians. *Shillong Times,* Nov. 4 : 2(3-6)

1992. ———: 1988 : Tripura Government on razor's edge, *Amrita Bazar Patrika Feb. 23 : 7(1-4).*

1993. **Pardeshi, Ghanshyam** : 1988 : Changing scenario in North-East plus in Tripura, minus in Nagaland. *Shillong Times*, Aug. 24:3(1-4).

1994. **Pathachari** : 1973 : Agony of Tripura. *Frontier*, May 12 : 6.

1995. **Paul, B.K.** :1991 : 'Essential oil' rich North-East *Assam Tribune*, March 3 : 4(3-6).

1996. **Paul, C.R.** *(Ed)* : **1962** : *Census of India 1961, vol. XXVI, Tripura*. Delhi, Controller of Publications.

1997. ——— (*Ed*) : 1962 : *Census of India 1961, vol. XXVI, Tripura District* Census Handbook Delhi, Controller of Publications.

1998. ——— (*Ed*) : 1965 : *Census of India 1961, Tripura, vol. XXVI, pt. VI, Village Survey Monographs: Dwarika Talukdar Para village (Ghorakuppa Tehsil, Sabroom Sub Division)*. Delhi, Manager of Publications.

1999. ——— : 1964 : *Census of India 1961, Tripura, vol. XXVI, pt. VI, Village Survey Monograph on Sekerkot (Insanchanadranagar Tehsil, Tribpura District)*. Delhi, Controller of Publications.

2000. ——— : (*Ed*) : 1964 : *Census of India 1961, Tripura, vol. XXVI, pt. VIII-A : Administrative Report (Enumeration)* Delhi Controller of Publications.

2001. ——— : (*Ed*) 1967 : *Census of India 1961, Tripura, vol. XXVI, pt. II-C : Cultural and Migration Tables*. Delhi, Manager of Publications., 306 p.

2002. ——— (*Ed*) : *Census of India 1961, Tripura, vol. XXVI, pt. IV Report on Housing and Establishments*. Delhi, Manager of Publications.

2003. ——— (*Ed*) : 1966 : *Census of India, 1961, Tripura, vol. XXVI, pt. VI, Villages Survey Monograph on Kamalghat (Bamutia Tehsil, Sadar Sub-Division)*. New Delhi, manager of Publications, 68p.

2004. ——— (*Ed*) : 1966 : *Census of India 1961, Tripura, vol. XXVI, Pt. 11(i): General Population Tables and General Economic Tables*. Delhi, Manager of Publications, 485p.

2005. **Paul, C.R.** (*Ed*) : 1966 : *Census of India 1861, Tripura, vol. XXVI pt. VI, Village Survey Monographs, No. 3 : Rudijala (Sonamura Tehsil, Sonamura Sub-Division).* Delhi, Manager of Publications, 61p.

2006. ——— (*Ed*) : 1966 : *Census of India 1961, Tripura : Fairs and Festivals of Tripura.* Delhi, Manager of Publications, 123p.

2007. ——— (*Ed*) : 1967 : *Census of India 1961, Tripura, Vol. XXVI : Household Economic Tables and Special Tables for Scheduled Castes and Scheduled Tribes.* Delhi, Manager of Publications.

2008. **Paul, C.R.** (*Ed*) : 1967 : *Census of India 1961, Tripura, vol XXVI, pt. I-C Subsidiary Tables.* Delhi, Manager of Publications.

2009. **Paul, P.K.** : ? *Horticultural Bio-Resource of Tripura.* Paper submitted in a symposium.

2010. **Peoples; Democracy** : 1967 : Tripura-Demand for Scheduled Tribal Area *Peoples' Democracy* (Agartala), 3(30), July 23 : 5.

2011. ——— : 1971 : Tripura under President's rule. *Peoples' Democracy,* Nov. 14 : 2.

2012. **Phayre, A.** :1841 : Account of Arakan *Jour. of Asiatic Soc. of Beng., 10(2) : 711.*

2013. **Phookan, Prosenjit** : 1986 : Letters to the Editor : Tripuris in Tripura. *Assam Tribune,* Feb. 25, Tuesday : 4 (3).

2014. **Phukan J.N.** (*Ed*) : 1986 : *The Journal of the Assam Research Society : Professor Dibakar Goswami Commemoration vol. XXVIII, 1984-'85.* Guwahati, Kamarupa Anusandhan Samiti (Assam Research Society. 1984).

2015. **Planning Commission** : 1966 : *India : Report of the study team on tribal development Programmes.* Delhi, Planning Commission of India, 94p.

2016. **Planning** *and* **Co-Orderation Deptt.** : ? : *Fifth Five Year Plan proposal, vol* 2. Agartala, Govt. of Tripura, Planning and Co-ordination Deptt.

2017. **Poddar, B.C.** *and* **Ramesh, N.R.** : 1983 : Spot Lingh on Pre-history of Tripura *Geological Survey of India (N.E.R.) Newsletter* (1): 1-4.

2018. **Political Agent** : 1921 : Letter No. 877-P/VII-11 of the Political Agent, Tripura, to the Minister of Tripura, Dated 11th June, 1921 (*Unpublished*).

2019. **Porter, A.E.** : 1933 : *Census of India 1931, vol. V : Bengal & Sikkim, pt. I, Report*, Calcutta, Govt. Press : 486-87, 518-19 (Tippera).

2020. **Prabhakara, M.S.** : 1989 : An end to Tripura insurgency. *Hindu*, April 13.

2021. **P., M.S. (Prabhakara, M.S.)** : 1990 : In the thick of it. *Frontline* (Madras), May 12-25 : 33-41.

2022. **Prasad, R.N.; Varma, Arun** *and* **Singh, A.** : 1988 : Shifting cultivations problems, solutions and myths. Proceedings of a Seminar on *'Eco-Development of North Eastern Region'* Shillong, Dec. 2nd 1988, North Eastern Council.

2023. **Publicity Deptt.** : ? : *The Profile of Tripura*. Agartala, Publicity Deptt., 7p.

2024. ——— : ? : *This is Tripura*. Agartala, Tripura Publicity Deptt., 46p.

2025. ——— : 1957 : *Refugee Rehabilitation in Tripura. Republic Day Souvenir* (Agartala, Deptt. of Publicity), 8p.

2026. ——— : 1958 : *Tripura Marches Ahead*. Agartala. Tripura Publicity Deptt., 75p.

2027. ——— : 1961 : *Tripura on the march*. Agartala, District Publicity Deptt., 52p.

2028. **Purbanchal Prahari** : 1990 : Agartala men passport daftar ka shibir. *Pur. Pra.* (*Hindi* Daily, Guwahati), March 1 : 2(3).

2029. ——— : 1990 : Purbottar ke savi rajyon ke liye dhara 370 ki mang. *Pur. Pra.*, May 4 : 3(3-5).

2030. ——— : 1990 : Jel varo andolan ke douran chitput hinsa, do mare gaye. *Pur. Pra., May 5: 1(7-8).*

2031. ——— : 1990 : Chakma Sharanarthi - Surakshabalmidantamen 3 mare. *Pur. Pra.*, May: 1(5).

2032. ——— : 1990 : Chakma Samashya par tripakshya barta ki mang. *Pur. Pra.*, May 14 : 1(1).

2033. ——— : 1990 : Sharanarthiyon ka masala nahi suljhane say tanav : Tripura. *Pur. Pra.*, May 15 : 7(7-8).

2034. ——— : 1990 : Aswasanon ka "Lanli Panp" chus rahe hain Chakma sharanarthi : Shibiron men dhandhli ka arop *Pur. Pra.*, June 2 : 7(3-6).

2035. ——— : 1990 : Chakma : Chakmaon ki bhapsi ke liye tripakhiya Barata Jaruri, *Pur. Pra.*, June 5 : 3(5-6).

2036. ——— : 1990 : Pechish Leel rahi hai Jampui ko *Pur. Pra.*, June 5 : 1(1-8)

2037. ——— : 1990 : Aoth July ko Tripura ki swashasita jila parishad ka chunav. *Pur. Pra.*, June 13: 1(3).

2038. ——— : 1990 : Tripura men edici ka chunavi samikaran sposta *Pur. Pra.*, June 16 : 3(4-6).

2039. ——— : 1990 : Bhoot se peecha nahin chut raha Mondeibalon ka. *Pur. Pra.*, June 18: 2(1-3).

2040. **Purbanchal Prahari** : 1990 : Zila Parishad chunav nirnayak dour men (Tripura). *Pur. Pra.*, July 2: 3(4-6).

2041. **Purbanchal Prahari** : 1990 : janajatiya swayatta zila parishad chunab : Tripura men matdan ke douran hinsa, 10 mare *Pur.Pra.*, July 9: 1(2-3).

2042. ——— : 1990 : Tripura : Hingsagrastha Ilakayon men tanab bapta *Pur. Pra.*, July 10 : 1(2-4).

2043. ——— : 1990 : Manjhdhar me adhar talashate Chakma sharanarthi *Pur. Pra.*, Aug. 6 : 5(1-8).

2044. ——— : 1990 : "Meri Sarkar giraye to uttar purb men Kashmir benega. *Pur. Pra.*, Aug. 22 : 1(7-8).

2045. ——— : 1990 : Chashma Bandar Tripurase Asom ko bhage. *Pur. Pra.*, Aug. 28 : 1(5).

2046. ——— : 1990 : Tripura men hinsa : Tal-Matol kee rajniti. *Pur. Pra.*, Oct. 24 : 7(1-3).

2047. ——— : 1990 : Chakma sharanarthi : Uttar Purba Rajyon ke toe pran sansan men hai. *Pur. Pra.*, Oct. 24 7(2-7).

2048. ——— : 1990 : Uttar Tripura men muthbher, 3 jakhmee. *Pur. Pra.*, Dec. 25 : 1(3-4).

2049. ——— : 1991 : Tripura men ATTAF ke 32 ugrabadiyon ne hatiyar dale. *Pur. Pra.*, March 31 : 1(5-6).

2050. ——— : 1991 : Tripura ki Dayeri : Makpa ke math par jamee vaithee hai Congress. *Pur. Pra.*, April 3 : 4(3-8).

2051. ——— : 1991 : Editorial : Tripura men bahishkar. *Pur. Pra.*, June 10 : 4(1-2).

2052. ——— : 1991 : ULFA-ATTF ki gupta yojana ka vhanda phuta. *Pur. Pra.*, Aug. 11: 1(6-7).

2053. **Puri, Rakshat** : 1972 : Towards Security in the North East : Transportation and nationalism. *(In) Tribal Situation in India : Proceedings of a Seminar, (Ed)* by K. Suresh Singh, Simla, Indian Institute of Advanced Study : 98-109

2054. **Purkayastha, Mohit** : 1958 : *Tripurar Bangla Bhasa O Sahitya*. Calcutta. Firma K.L. Mukhopadhya, 244p.

2055. **Purkayastha, Rakhal** *and* **Chakraborty, A. B.** : 1989 ; Book Review : Emerging Pattern of North Eastern Economy, (*Ed*) by V.S. Mahajan. New Delhi, Deep and Deep Publications. *Jour. NEICSSR (Shillong), 13(1), April : 56-60.*

R

2056. **Radio Bangladesh** : 1986 : Radio Magazine (Uttoran : Tipra. *Radio Bangladesh*, Oct. 23(8'45pm) [Radio Talk].

2057. ——— : 1986 : Radio Magazine (Uttoran) : Aronya Chayai Chakma *Radio Talk from Bangladesh* on 2nd, 9th, 16th, 23rd, 30th, April, 21st, 28th May and 4th June 1988 (*In Bengali*).

2058. **Raghavan, B.S.** : 1976 : Handicrafts of Tripura. *North Eastern Spectrum*, 1(3-4), Sept-Oct.; 14-5.

2059. **Raha M.K.** : 1990: Book Review : The Chakmas : Life and struggle by S.P. Talukdar. Delhi, Gian Publishing House, 1988. Rs. 150/-. *Jour. of the Indian Anthropological Society*, 25(1), March : 96-7.

2060. **Raha, Manis Kr.** *and* **Coomar, Palash Kr.**: 1985 : Book Review : Folk tales and myths of Riang Tripuri Communities by Tushar Kr. Niyogi, Anthropological Survey of India, 1983, price not mentioned pp. vi+1200 with plates. *Man in India*, 11(1-2), Jan.-June : 119-20.

2061. **Rahman, F.** : 1969 : Tripura. *(In) Tribes of Assam (Comp)* by S. Barkataki. New Delhi, National Book Trust (India) : 156-59 (only in the *Ist edition* of this book).

2062. **Rahaman, Mizanur** : 1988 : Letters to the Editor : Election in Tripura, Meghalaya. *Assam Tribune*, Feb. 19 : 4(5- 6).

2063. **Rajkhowah, J.B.** : 1971 : Traces of early History of North Eastern India in Kachari, Dimacha and Tipra languages. *Pine* (Shillong), 1(1), March : 39-45.

2064. **Ramnarayandev** : 1967 : *Rajmala*. Agartala, Education Deptt., Govt. of Tripura.

2065. **Ramunny, M.** : 1977 : Manipur, Nagaland, Tripura. *Illustrated Weekly of India, Annual No.* : 136-41.

2066. **Ramunny, Murkot** : 1988 : Changing face of Tripura. *Economic and Political Weekly,* XXIII(37), Sept. 10: 1879-1880.

2067. **Rana, Anil** : 1991 : CPI(M) wants polls deferred in Tripura. *Statesman,* May 28 : 12(4-5).

2068. **Rana, Bodhjung** : 1929 : *Report of the tour of the Chief Secretary in Dhalai and Mana Valleys.* Agartala, Govt. Press.

2069. **Randhawa, M.S.** : Mitra, Asok *and* Mehta, Gisela : 1964 : *Farmers of India, vol. III,* New Delhi, Indian Council of Agricultural Research : 387-88.

2070. **Rangkhawal, B.** : 1975 : *Karam, vol.2(20)* Agartala, June 2.

2071. **Rao, B. Bhaskara** : 1971 : Khas land and development values. *Economic Times, Dec. 28 : 18(5).*

2072. **Rao, Narasimha** *and* Prasad, K.K. : **1978** : *Hydrogeology and ground water development potential of Tripura.* Gauhati, North Eastern Region.

2073. **Rao, Vijayendra Kasturi Ranga V** : 1955 : *A Economic review of refugee rehabilitation in India : A Study of Tripuri Township.* Delhi, School of Economics, University of Delhi, 68p.

2074. **Rao, V. Venkata** : 1968 : Assam State Politics 1947-1967. *Jour. of Gauhati University,* XXI(1), Arts : 1-54.

2075. ——— : 1974 : North East India : Problems and suggestions. *North Eastern Research Bulletin,* 5 : 12-24.

2076. ——— : 1976 : *A Century of Tribal Politics in North East India, 1874-1974.* New Delhi, S. Chand & Company.

2077. ——— : 1989 : Trends in consumption and proverty in Rural North Eastern India. Proceedings of a Seminar on *"Perspective, Issues and Experiences of Rural Development in North East India"* held on 26-27 May '89 by NIECSSR, Shillong.

2078. **Rao, V. Venkata** *and* Hazarika, Niru : *1983 : A Century of Government and politics in North East India.* New Delhi, S. Chand.

2079. **Rawlings, John** : 1792 : On the manners, religion and laws of the cu'ci's or Mountaineers of Tipra. *Asiatick Researches,* II(XII) : 187-93. (*Reprinted* by Cosmo Publications, New Delhi, in 1978, 144p).

2080. **Ray, Jagat Jyoti** : 1988 : Tripura Upajati Juba Samity : A Regional Political Party. Proceedings of a Seminar on *"Regional Political Parties in North East India,"* 9-10 Dec. 1988, by NEICSSR, Shillong.

2081. **Ray, Ram Bahadur** : 1988 : Tripura chunav men Congress ka palla vari. *Naba Bharat Times (in Hindi),* Jan. 28 : 1(2-5), 8(2).

2082. **Ray, Ram Bahadur** : 1988: Pradhanmantri ka Tripura sarkar par arop. *Naba Bharat Times,* Jan. 30: 1(6-7), 12(4-5).

2083. ——— : 1988 : T.N.V. ka atankbad sabse bori chunouti. *Naba Bharat Times,* March 1: 3(1-5).

2084. ——— : Uttar-Purb men phir sulog rahi hai ugravad ki aag. *Naba Bharat Times,* April 19 : 3(1-6).

2085. ——— : 1989 : Chakma samashya : Vivajan ka nasur. *Naba Bharat Times,* June 28: 8(3-7).

2086. ——— : 1988 : Loktantra Bajuon ke bol par koyed hai : Tripura. *Naba Bharat Times,* May 3 : 3(4-6).

2087. **Ray, Shantanu** : 1987 : Chakmas : Beleagured Buddists of Bangladesh. *Shillong Times,* Sept. 27 : 2(5-6) & 3(1-6).

2088. **Ray, Siddhartha** : 1989 : In the CHT guerilla den - 1 : Genocide of an ethnic minority. *Amrita Bazar Patrika,* Jan. 16: 1(2-4), 12(1-2). [Chakma].

2089. ——— : 1989 : In the CHT gurella den-II: Torture and extermination of Jummas. *Amrita Bazar Patrika,* Jan. 17 : 1(2- 4), 12(2-3) [Chakma].

2090. ——— : 1989 : In the CHT guerilla den-III : Jummas to continue resistance struggle. *Amrita Bazar Patrika,* Jan. 18 : 1(2-5), 12(2-3).

2091. ——— : 1989 : In the CHT guerilla den-IV : Mill tracts for hillmen. *Amrita Bazar Patrika,* Jan. 19: 1(2-5).

2092. **Ray, Siddhartha** : 1989 : In the CHT guerilla den-V : 'Shanti Bahini is in full command'. *Amrita Bazar Patrika,* Jan 20 : 1(1- 3).

2093. **Ray, S., Sircar, B.** *and* Chakraborti, N.K. : 1986 : Medicinal and Nutritive value of forest products collected by the tribals of Tripura : A Case study of the jamatia Tribe *(In) Forestry Development in North East India (Eds).* by M. Das Gupta *et al.* Guwahati, Omsons Publications : 225-32.

2094. **Raynold, H.J.** : 1868 : Tribes of Eastern Forntier. *Jour. of Asiatic Society of Bengal,* 32 : 407.

2095. **Raza, Moonis** *and* **Ahmad, Aijazuddin** : 1990 : *An Atlas of Tribal India.* New Delhi, Concept Publishing Cor., 472 p.

2096. **Raza, Moonis** and **Nangia, Sudesh** : 1986 : *Atlas of the child in India.* New Delhi, Concept Pub. Cor., 477p.

2097. **Reddy, Brahmananda** : 1975 : Untoward activities by tribals with no help to solve their problems, *Assam Tribune,* Jan. 24 : 3(1-3).

2098. **Reddy, N. Subba** : 1978 : Revolt in Chittagong Hill Tracts. *Economic and Political Weekly,* 13(17).

2099. **Reds, Roouse** : 1968 : Tripura's Tipras. *Enlite,* May 18 : 14-5.

2100. **Reserve Bank of India** : 1976 : *Report on Currency and Finance, vol.II (1975-'76).* New Delhi, Reserve Bank of India.

2101. **Risley, H.H.** : 1891 : *The Tribes and Castes of Bengal.* Calcutta, Bengal Secretariat Press : 52-3, 168-76, 323-27.

2102. ——— : 1903 : Seriations of the Mongoloid type : Chakma, Lepcha and Kasia and Summary of measurement *(In) Census of India 1901, V-1, India, pt.-I, Report : Ethnographic Appendices.* Calcutta, Govt. Press : 31-5.

2103. **Rizvi, S.H.M.** *and* **Roy, Shibani** : 1990 : *Customary Law of North East India.* Delhi, B.R. Publishing House : 95- 101.

2104. **Roche, Michael** : 1988 : The Buddhist Peace Fellowship, *(In) The Chakmas* by S.P. Talukdar. Delhi, Gyan Publishing House : 171-75.

2105. **Roy, Achintya Kumar** : 1973 : Economic and institutional financing. *Link*, 5 March 11: 3.

2106. ——— : 1975 : Sarba Bharatiya Bhog-Prakritir Pariprekshite Tripura *(In) Tripura Prasanga (Ed)*, by Swapan Sengupta. Agartala, Directorate of Pub Rel. and Tourism : 186-94 (*In Bengali*).

2107. **Roy, Ajit** : 1981 : Tripura : CPI(M)'s short sightedness. *Economic and Political Weekly*, XVII(31): 1385-86.

2108. **Roy, Braja Gopal** : 1986 : Our Thoughts on Tribals in Tripura, *Tribes of Tripura (Ed)* by Sudhanshu Bikash Saha. Agartala, Rupali Book Store: 61-8.

2109. **Roy, Devasish** : 1989 : Barbarous killing space, says Chakma Chief. *Statesman*, June 2 : 1(2-7), 7(6-7).

2110. **Roy, Gopal Krishna** : 1988 : Tripura Poll : A Nerve Racking Battle. *Assam Tribune*, Feb. 20 : 4(7-8).

2111. ——— : 1988 : Changing scenario in Tripura. *Assam Tribune*, April 21 : 4(7-8).

2112. **Roy, Hashi** (*Ed*) : 1952 : Editorial : Tripurar Prati Abichar (Injustice to Tripura). *Chinha* My Country, a weekly magazine from Agartala), III(32), Dec. 14(27 Agrahayan, 1362 TE), (*in Bengali*).

2113. **Roy, Jagat Jyoti** : 1985 : *Vidroha, Bibartan O Tripura*. Agartala, Tripura Darpan Prakasani (*in Bengali*).

2114. ——— 1986 : The question of Tribal Identity in Tripura. Proceedings of a Seminar on questions of *Nationalities, Ethnicity and Cultural Identity in the context*" of North East India, 5-6 Dec. 1986 by NEICSSR, Shillong.

2115. ——— : 1986 : Breaking eggs to make omlette *(In) Tribes of Tripura (Ed)* by Sudhanshu Bikash Saha. Agartala, Rupali Book Store : 133-38.

2116. ——— : 1987 : Impact of land reforms in Tripura. Proceedings of a Seminar on *"Impact of Land Reforms on North East India"*, 24-25 April, 1987 by NEICSSR, Shillong.

2117. **Roy, Jagat Jyoti** : 1990 : The Question of Tribal Identity in Tripura *(In) Nationality, Ethnicity and Cultural Identity in North East India (Ed)* by B. Pakem. New Delhi. Omsons Publications : 377-88.

2118. **Roy, J.K.** *and* **Biswas, S.K.** : 1964 : Proteins in the diets of some Indian tribes, *Science and Culture,* 30(3), March : 126-29.

2119. **Roy, P.C.** : 1957 : The Effect of Culture Contact on the Personality Structure of two Indian Tribes: The Riang of Tripura and the Baiga of Madhya Pradesh. *Bull. of Anth. Surv. of India,* VI(2), July : 1-84.

2120. **Roy, Promod Chandra** : 1966 ; Cultural levels and Resulting Psycho-cultural types among the Riang of Tripura. *Bull. of Anth. Surv. of India* : 22-34.

2121. **Roy, Radha Binode** : 1974: Colourful Tripura. *North Eastern Affairs,* 3(2-3), July-Dec : 23-4.

2122. **Roy. R.K.** : 1981: *A Report on the progress of geohydrological investigation in parts of Tripura State (Field Season 1969-'70).* Calcutta, Central Govt. (West Bengal Govt.), 47p

2123. **Roy, Sukumar** : 1967 · Music of the Hill People of North Eastern India, *(In) A Common Perspective for North East India, (Ed)* by Rathin Mitra *and* Burun Das Gupta. Calcutta, Pannalal Das Gupta: 29-40.

2124. **Roy, S.C.** : 1960 : Atur Asram in Tripura. *Social Welfare,* 6(12), March : 33-4.

2125. **Roy. S.K.** : 1975 : Agriculture in Tripura: Present situation and future prospects. Proceedings of a Seminar on *"Integrated development of North East India",* March 14-16, by NEICSSR, Shillong.

2126. ——— : 1978 : Agriculture in Tripura : Present situation and future prospects *(In) Social and Economic Profile of North East India (Ed)* by B. Dutta Roy. Delhi, B.R. Publications : 160-66.

2127. **Roy, Upendra Kumar** : 1971 : Public Accounts Committee in Tripura Legislative Assembly: Its origin, role and achievements *(In) Souvenir 1921-71,*

Golden Jubilee. Delhi, India, Lok Sabha, Secretariat, Public Accounts Committee : 205-15.

2128. **Roy Burman, B.K.** (*Ed*) : n.d. *A Preliminary Appraisal of the Scheduled Tribe*. New Delhi, Office of the Registrar General of India : 135, 192-96, 228, 250, 291-92, 343, 354, 357, (*Cyclostyled*).

2129. ——— : 1966 : Structure of bridge and buffer communities in the Border Areas. *Man in India*, 46(2) : 103-07.

2130. ——— : 1967 : Hillman of North East India and Tensions of Socio-Economic Development. *Vanyajati*, 15(3) : 109-19.

2131. ——— (*Ed*) : 1970 : *Demographic and Socio-Economic Profiles of the Hill Areas of North East India : Census of India 1961*. Delhi, Manager of Publications.

2132. ——— : 1972 : Tribal Demography : A Preliminary Appraisal, (*In*) *Tribal Situation in India : Proceedings of a Seminar*, (*Ed*) by K. Suresh Singh. Simla, Indian Institute of Advanced Study : 39-50.

2133. ——— : 1976 : New age in ageless North East India. *Jour. of Social Research*, 19(1) : 64-7.

2134. ——— : 1977 : Social Process in Hills of North East India : An Ecological Perspective (*In*) *Dimensions of Social Change in India (Ed)* by M.N. Srinivas, S. Seshaiah *and* V.S. Parthasarathy. Bombay, Allied Publishers : 405-18.

2135. ——— : 1980 : Rapid Appraisal of the critical issues relating to the Scheduled Tribes and Scheduled Castes (*In*) *Eastern Himalayas : A Study on Anthropology and Tribalism (Eds)* by T.C. Ṣharma *and* D.N. Majumdar New Delhi, Cosmo Publications : 11-22.

2136. ——— : 1984 : Issues in the North East : An Appraisal, (*In*) *Northeast Region : Problems and Prospects of Development (Ed)* by B.L. Abbi. Chandigarh, Centre for Research in Rural and Industrial Development : 174-180.

2137. ——— : 1986 : *Community land and Institutional finance with reference to the tribal areas of Manipur and*

Tripura. New Delhi Council for Social Development (Project Report, *Mines*).

2138. **Roy Burman, B.K.** : 1986 : Institutional Finance and Tribal Development *Mainstream*, January 19.

2139. ——— : 1988 : Shifting Cultivation in India : An overview. *Mainstream*, Nov. 26.

2140. ——— : 1992 : Issues in land reforms in tribal areas of North East India : A Preliminary Appraisal *(In) The Impact of Land Reforms in North East India (Ed)* by Malabika Das Gupta (*in Press*, 1991).

2141. **Roy Burman, B.K.** *and* **Sharma P.S.** : n.d. : *Development of Agriculture in Tribal Areas : Tribal Agriculture in India*, Delhi Ministry of Home Affairs, Govt. of India (Mimeo).

2142. **Roy Burman J.J.** : 1990: Shifting Cultivation : An Aspect of Tribal exploitation. *Indian Journal of Social Work* (Bombay), LI (91), January : 57-73.

2143. **Roy Choudhury, A.K.** : 1981 : The genetic composition of the people in eastern India. *Jour. of Indian Anth. Society*, 16(2), July : 153-70.

2144. **Roy Choudhury, Dibyendu** : 1957 : Palmar Main lines and configuration types of the Riangs of Tripura. *Bull. Anth. Surv. of India*, VI(1), Jan (1957) : 47-76.

2145. **Roychoudhury, J.; Bhowmik, Atrayee** *and* **Das, P.** 1976 : Economic corelates of tribal fertility in Eastern India. *Bull. Cultural Research Institute* (Calcutta), 12(1-2) : 83-7.

2146. **Roy Choudhury, Kamal** : 1978 : Jana siksha andolan. *Gomati*, No. 79, Nov.

2147. **Roychoudhury, Nalini Ranjan** : ? : Kuki disturbances in Tripura, *(In) Social Scientist* (Monthly Journal of the Indian School of Social Sciences, Trivandrum).

2148. ——— : n.p. : *Tribal Uprisings in Tripura*. Ph.D. Thesis of Rabindra Bharati University, History Deptt., Calcutta.

2149. **Roychoudhury, Nalini Ranjan** : 1971 : *A Short History of Tripura*. Agartala, Bureau of Research and Publications on Tripura.

2150. ——— : 1977 : *Tripura through the Ages : A Short History of Tripura from the earliest times to 1947A.D.*. Agartala, Bureau of Research and Publication, Tripura, 153p.

2151. ——— : 1979 : Towards an understanding of the source materials of the History of Tripura. Proceedings of a Seminar on the *"History and Culture of North East India,"* 26-28 April, 1979, Deptt. of History, Shillong, North Eastern Hill University, 3p (*Mimeo.*)

2152. ——— : 1980 : The Historical Past *(In) Tripura : The Land and its People (Ed)* by Jagadis Gan Choudhuri. Delhi, Leeladevi Publications : 13-43.

2153. ——— : 1981 : Some inscriptions of medieval Tripura. *Proceedings of NEIHA* (Dibrugarh), No. 2 : 34-7.

2154. ——— : 1981 : Causes of the tribal uprisings in Tripura in the Nineteenth century *(In) Proceedings of the North East India History Association (Ed)* by Jayanta Bhusan Bhattacharjee (1980). Shillong. NEIHA, Deptt. of History, NEHU : 105-10.

2155. ——— : 1983 : *Tripura through the ages : A Short History of Tripura from the earliest times to 1947 AD.* New Delhi, Sterling Publishers Pvt. Ltd, 127p.

2156. **Roy Chowdhury, Profulla** : 1986 : *The North East : Roots of Insurgency.* Culcutta, Firma KLM Pvt.Ltd.

2157 **Roy Choudury, R.N.** : 1987 : Letters to the Editor India's moral duty to save Chakmas. *Statesman*, April 24 : 8(4-5).

2158. ——— : 1988 : Letters to the Editor : How TNV helped Congress (1). *Statesman,* Feb. 14 : 8(4).

2159. **Rustomji, Nari** : 1971 : *Enchanted Frontiers : Sikkim, Bhutan and India's North Eastern Border lands*. London, Oxford Univ. Press.

2160. ——— : 1987 : ? : *Verrier Elwin and India's North East Borderlands*. Shillong. North Eastern Hill University.

S

2161. **Sachchidananda** : 1989 : *Shifting cultivation in India*. New Delhi, Concept Publishing Com. : 76-96.

2162. **Sage Publications** : 1981 : *State Elections in India, 1952-'85, vol. 3, The East and Northeast (Including Sikkim)*. New Delhi, Sage Pubs., 702p.

2163. **Saha, Akshay Kumar** : 1990 : Destination, North East. *Amrita Bazar Patrika, Sunday Magazine*, Nov. 4 : I (1- 8).

2164. **Saha, Arunoday** : 1982 : Marketing of bamboo crafts of Tripura : Its problems and Prospects. Proceedings of a Seminar on *"Rural Market and Marketing in North East India"*, Sept. 16-17 by NEICSSR.

2165. ——— : 1984 : The marketing of bamboo crafts of Tripura : Its problems and prospects, *(In) Marketing in North East India (Ed)* by J.B. Ganguly. New Delhi, Omsons Publications : 102-06.

2166. ——— : 1984 : Structural changes in the agricultural holdings in Tripura : Some implications. Proceedings of a Seminar on *"Land, Land Relations and Land Reforms in the Plains and valleys of North East India"*, April 17-18, by NEICSSR, Shillong.

2167. ——— : 1986 : Structural Changes in the agricultural holdings in Tripura : Some implications, *(In) Land Reforms and Peasant Movement : A Study of North East India (Ed)* by Atual Goswami. New Delhi, Omsons Publications. 156-61.

2168. **Saha, J.** : 1985 ; *Statistical outline of Tripura 1983*. Agartala, Directorate of Statistics, 159p.

2169. **Saha, Manik** : 1989 : Letters to the Editor : Jhum Cultivation. *Assam Tribune*, May 29 : 4(3-4).

2170. **Saha, Niranjan** : 1970 : Carrying capacity of shifting cultivation. *Indian Jour. of Agricultural Economics*, XXV(3).

2171. **Saha, Niranjan** : 1973 : *The Economics of shifting cultivation in North East India : Ad-hoc study No. 22.* Jorhat, Agro. Eco. Res. Centre.

2172. ——— : 1973 : Carrying capacity of land under shifting cultivation : Results of a few Surveys. *North Eastern Affairs,* 2(IV) : 33-4.

2173. ——— : 1976 : Levels of production and income under shifting cultivation in North East India *(In) Shifting cultivation in North East India (Ed)* by B. Datta Ray. Shillong, NEICSSR (2nd edition, 1980) : 19-27.

2174. **Saha, Niranjan** *and* **Barkotoky, M.D.** : 1968 : *Hmunpui : A Mizo village* Jorhat, Agro Eco. Res. Centre.

2175. **Saha, Niranjan** *and* **Borgohain, D.K.** : 1969 : *An assessment of colonisation scheme of shifting cultivations in Tripura.* Jorhat, Agro Economic Research Centre, 106p. *(Mimeo).*

2176. ——— : 1970 : Colonisation scheme of shifting cultivators in Tripura : An assessment. *Indian Jour. of Agricultural Economics,* XXV(3).

2177. **Saha, Sudhanshu Bikash** : ? : *Gomati,* (A Bengali novel of a Bengali youth for a *Chakma* demosel). Agartala, Rupali Book Store.

2178. ——— : ? : *Pataute, I love you.* Agartala, Rupali Book Store (A novel on the *Riang* girl).

2179. ——— : ? : *Bisforan.* (A Bengali Novel on the *Kalai* youth). Agartala, Rupali Book Store.

2180. ——— : ? : *Banthangi.* (A Bengali novel on the *Kuki* life). Agartala, Rupali Book Store.

2181. ——— : 1977 : The Chakmas of Tripura. Proceedings of a Seminar on *"Social and Political Institutions of the Hill People of North East India"*, organised jointly by Anthropological Survey of India and NEICSSR, Shillong on 4-5 July, 1977 *(Mimeo).*

2182. ——— : 1978 : *Socio-Economic Survey of the Noatia tribes.* Agartala, Deptt. of Welfare for Sch. Castes and Sch. Tribes (Direc. of Research), 104p.

2183. **Saha, Sudhanshu Bikash** ——— : 1985 : Administrative system of the Garos of Tripura. *(In) Proceedings of North East India History Associaiion, Sixth session, Agartala (Ed.)* by Jayanta Bhusan Bhattacharjee. Shillong, Deptt. of History, North Eastern Hill University : 463-68.

2184. ——— *(Ed)* : 1986) : *Tribes of Tripura : A Historical Survey.* Agartala, Rupali Book Store, 172p.

2185. ——— : 1986 : Dawn of History *(In) Tribes of Tripura (Ed)* by Sudhanshu Bikas Saha. Agartala, Rupali Book Store : 55-68.

2186. ——— : 1986 : Geographical Account *(In) Tribes of Tripura (Ed)* by Sudhanshu Bikash Saha. Agartala, Rupali Book Store : 1-6.

2187. ——— : 1986 : *Socio-Economic Survey of the Noatia tribes* (2nd edition). Agartala, Directorate of Research, 104p.

2188. ——— : 1986 : Social Background *(In) Tribes of Tripura (Ed)* by Sudhanshu Bikash Saha. Agartala, Rupali Book Store: 7-11.

2189. ——— : 1986 : Kolois of Tripura : A Socio Economic study, *(In) Proceedings of North East India History Association, session 7, Pasighat (Ed.)* by Jayanta Bhusan Bhattacharjee : 315-24.

2190. ——— *(Ed)* : 1987 : *Tribes of North East India : Spectrum of changes.* Agartala, Rupali Book Store.

2191. ——— : 1990 : The Chakmas of Tripura *(In) Social and Political Institutions of the Hill People of North East India (Eds)* By Jayanta Sarkar *and* B. Datta Ray. Calcutta, Anthropological Survey of India : 172-82.

2192. **Saha, Tan Kumar** : 1988 : Shifting cultivation among the Riang : A micro study in Tripura. *Journal of Indian Anti. Society,* 28(1), March : 45-55.

2193. **Sahadev, Bikram-Kisor Maharajkumar** *and* **Gan-Chaudhuri, J.** : 1986 : Princely Tripura's Constitution Act, 1941 *(In) Proceedings of North East India History Association, Seventh Session, Pasighat (Ed)* by

Jayanta Bhusan Bhattacharjee. Shillong, Deptt. of History, North Eastern Hill University : 192-200.

2194. **Siagal, Omesh** : 1978 : *Tripura : Its History and Culture.* Delhi, Concept Publishing Company, 164p.

2195. **Saikia, J.P.** : 1972 : Brighter future for Tripura : Access to Bangladesh. *Times of India,* June 11 : 2

2196. **Saikia, J.P.** : 1972 ; Return of rebels likely to aid Congress in Tripura. *Times of India.,* March 1 : 1(2).

2197. **Saikia, P.D.** ; 1970 : Problems of agricultural development in the tribal areas of North East India. *Indian Journal of Agricultural Economics* (Bombay), XXX(3).

2198. ——— : 1982 : Impact of irrigation on small farmers of North East Region. *Yojana,* XXVI (14-15), August 16-31 : 32.

2199. ——— : 1982 : A Note on shifting cultivation in North East India *(In) Economies of the Tribes and their transformation (Ed)* by K.S. Singh. New Delhi, Concept Pub. Com. : 228-39.

2200. **Saikia, P.D.** *and* **Boarah, Durgeswar** : 1988 : Agricultural development in the North East Region. *Himalaya : Man & Nature, XI(10), March : 7-10.*

2201. **Saikia, P.D., Saha, N.** *and* **Sarma, J.N.** : 1962 : *Report on the Socio-Economic Survey of Govt. sponsored jhumia colony in Tripura : Kathaliacherra.* Jorhat, Agro Economic Research Centre, 143p. *(typed mss).*

2202. **Samanta, R.K.** : 1980 : Reangs of Tripura : Their Socio-Cultural and agro-economic changes. Seminar on the *"Tribes of North East India",* Sept. 22-24, by NEICSSR with S.H.T.C. (Vendrame Missiological Institute), Shillong.

2203. ——— : 1980 : Notes on Hill Tribes of North East India. *Man in India,* 60(1-2), June : 129-34.

2204. ——— : 1981 : Reangs of Tripura : Socio-cultural and agro economic changes. *Social Scientist.* 9(5-6), Dec.-Jan., 1980-81 : 44-54.

2205. **Samanta, R.K.** : 1981 : Shifting to settled cultivation : A Case Study of Tripura villages. *Social Research*, 1(2), April : 50-7.

2206. ——— : 1982 : Shifting cultivation : Perception of tribal farmers in Tripura. *Man in India*, 62(2) : 186-90.

2207. ——— : 1984 : The Reangs of Tripura : Their Socio-cultural and Agro-Economic changes *(In) The Tribes of North East India, (Ed)* by S. Karotemprel. Calcutta , Firma K.L.M. Pvt. Ltd. : 184-95.

2208. ——— : 1987 : Extension training and education need for effective transfer of technology in North Eastern Hills Region. *Journal NEICSSR, 11(1)*, April : 29-32.

2209. **Samanta, R.K.** *(Ed)* : 1991 : *Rural development in North East India*. New Delhi, Uppal Pub. House, 336p.

2210. **Samanta, R.K.** *and* **Mukherjee, K.K.** : 1980 : Rural Development and Socio Economic Status of tribal farmers in a Tripura village. *Man & life*, 6(3-4), July- Dec. : 187-90.

2211. **Sandys, E.F.** ; 1915 : *History of Tripura*. Agartala, Tripura State Govt.

2212. ——— : 1917 : The Tripura (Hill Trippera) State, *(In) Bengal and Assam, Bihar and Orissa : Their History , People, Commerce and Industrial Resources (Comp.)* by Somerset Playne : 436-64.

2213. **Sankalan** : 1971 : Tripura State Gazettee, 1971. *Sankalan*, 311p.

2214. **Sankaranarayan, R.** : 1971 : Land Revenue system and land reforms measures in Tripura *(In) Census of India 1971, series 20, Tripura, Seminar Papers on Social, Economic and Cultural Aspects of Tripura.* Agartala, Govt. Publications : 28-9.

2215. **Sankrityayan, Kamla** : 1973 : *Manipur, Tripura*. Delhi, Rajpal Publications, 94p.

2216. **Sanwal, B.D.** : 1981 : Book Reviews : Tripura : The Land and its People, *Ed* by Jagadis Gan Chaudhauri. Delhi, Leeladevi Publications, 1979. *Eastern Anthropologists, 34(1), Jan-March : 75-6.*

2217. **Sanyal, Girija Mohan** : 1930 : The cultivation in Tripura. *Chunta Prakash* (Agartala), January 16.

2218. **Saptasetu** : 1991 : Tripura : Aparadho ke barne ankaren *(in Hindi). Saptasetu* (Purbanchal Prahari, Guwahati), March 29.

2219. **Sareen, H.K.** : 1980 ; *Insurgency in North East India : A Study of the Sino-American Role.* New Delhi, Sterling Publishers.

2220. **Sarin, VIK** : 1968 : Challenge in the hills. *Indian Express,* May 10 : 6(7).

2221. ——— : 1968 : Refugee influx bars Tripura's progress. *Commerce,* Sept. 7 *(Supplement)* : 22-4.

2222. ——— : 1968 : The gathering storm. *The Assam Tribune,* July 7.

2223. ——— : 1980 : *India's North East in Flames.* New Delhi, Vikas Publishing House.

2224. **Sarkar, Anil** : 1986 : Wreath out of wild flowers *(In) Tribes of Tripura (Ed.)* by Sudhanshu Bikash Saha. Agartala. Agartala, Rupali Book Store : 77-80.

2225. **Sarkar, Dinesh Chandra**: 1948 : Monograph the Sakta Pithur : Description of Pithadevi Tripura Sundari of Udaipur, Tripura. *Jour. of Asiatic Society of Bengal,* 14(1).

2226. ——— : 1951 : Copper plates inscription of the time of the King Vijoy Manikyo of Tripura. *Jour. of Asiatic Society of Bengal,* 17(2) : 73-82.

2227. ——— : 1975 : Bangla Bhasha Bhashidiger Itihas samparke duti katha *(In) Tripura Prasanga (Ed)* by Swapan Sengupta. Agartala, Director of Public Relations & Tourism : 1-10 *(in Bengali).*

2228. ——— : 1979 : *Some Epigraphic records of the medieval period from Eastern India.* Delhi : 107-08.

2229. ——— : 1982 : *Silalekha : Tamrasasanadhir prasanga.* Calcutta. 65p. *(in Bengali).*

2230. **Sarkar, Jadunath** : 1940 : Ain-I-Akbari, *(Tr.) by H.S. Jarretti. Calcutta, Royal Asiatic Society of Bengal,* vol. II : 130 (This has Historical Reference of early Tripura).

2231. **Sarkar, Jadunath** *(Ed)* : 1948 : *History of Bengal, vol. II, Muslim Period.* Dacca, University Publication: 243, 301- 02, 425-26 (It has references of some old Rajas of Tripura).

2232. **Sarkar, M.** : 1982 : *Project Report for Tripura rehabilitation and plantation Corporation Ltd,* (for Official use). Agartala, Govt. of Tripura, Deptt. of Welfare for Sch. Caste and Sch. Tribes.

2233. ——— : 1986 : Forestry development in Tripura during the Five Year Plans *(In) Forestry Development of North East India (Eds.)* by Malabika Das Gupta *et al.* Guwahati, Omsons Pubs. : 192-203.

2234. **Sarkar, Narayan R.** : 1975 : *State Report on World Agricultural Census (1970-'71) in Tripura.* Agartala, Supdt. of Tripura Govt., 76p.

2235. **Sarkar, S.** : 1973 : Development of Tourism in Eastern States, *vis-a-vis* Tripura. *Journal of Lal Bahadur Shastri National Academy of Adminsitration,* 18(4), Winter : 551-53.

2236. **Sarkar, Shyamal** : 1988 : Cong-I ousts Tripura Front. *Statesman,* Feb. 5 : 1(1-5).

2237. **Sarkar, Shyamal** : 1988 : Inner-party weakness behind Tripura defeat? *Statesman,* Feb. 11 : 9(2-7).

2238. ——— : 1988 : Tripura's new guard raises fresh fears. *Statesman,* Feb. 13 : 9(2-6).

2239. **Sarkar, Shyamal** *and* **Chakraborty, Satyabrata** : 1988 : Major reverses for front in Tripura. *Statesman,* Feb. 4 : 1(2-4).

2240. **Sarmah, B.L.** : 1977 : *Socio-Demographic and Spatial relationship between large sized villages and urban centres in Assam, Manipur, Tripura and Arunachal Pradesh.* Delhi, M.Phil Dissertation, JNU, 118p.

2241. **Sarma, Girish Chandra** : 1989 : Against the wave in North Eastern States. *Assam Tribune,* Dec. 5 : 4(3-6), 7(3-5).

2242. **Sarma, R.M.** : 1980 : *Coinage of Tripura.* Varanasi, N.S.I. 18p.

2243. **Sarma, Ramani Mohan** : 1985 : Tripura in the Pre-Manikya period, *(In) Proceedings of North East India History Association, Sixth Session, Agartala (Ed)* by Jayanta Bhusan Bhattacharjee. Shillong, History Deptt., NEHU : 59-68.

2244. ——— : 1986 : *A Political History of Tripura*. Calcutta, Puthipatra.

2245. **Sarma, Kataki, Ratna Kandali** *and* **Das Bairagi, Arjuna** : 1938 : *Tripura Buranji or Tripura Desar Kathar Lekha*. Gauhati, D.H.A.S. (Original mss. is in the British Museum).

2246. **Secretariat Archives** : 1956 : *Letter of the Revenue Secretary, Govt. of Tripura, to the Deputy Secretary, Ministry of Home Affaris, Govt of India, No. 2934/Rev/69- 123/55, dated Agartala, 21 August, 1956*. Agartala, Secretariat Archives.

2247. **Secretary** : 1978 : *Tripura*. Agartala, Tribal Welfare Deptt., (21.11.1978) [Regarding the *Laskar* Community].

2248. **Sen, D.** : 1929 : Tripura : The most ancient of modern Indian States. Agartala, *Chunta Prakash (Extra-ordinary issue* dated 16-1-1929).

2249. **Sen, D.** *and* **N. Seehra** : 1977 : Fossil wood implements from Tripura. *Eastern Anthropologists*, 30(2) : 211-15.

2250. **Sen, Dinesh Chandra** : 1920 : *Folk-Literature of Bengal* (Tripura : The song of Samsher Gazi) : 136-50.

2251. ——— : 1926 : Trippera : The most ancient of the modern States. Agartala, *Chunta Prakash (Special Issue)*, 16 : 15.

2252. ——— : ? : *Brihat Banga* (2nd Part, XVIII Chapter) : 1013-50.

2253. ——— : ? : *Banga Sahitya Parichaya* : 1331-37, 1407- 39, 1850-60.

2254. **Sen, Dinesh Chandra** : ? : Banga Bhasha O Sahitya (5th edition) : 35, 74, 97, 151-52.

2255. **Sen, Kaliprasanna** *(Ed)* : 1336 TD : *Sree Rajmala*. Agartala, Pub. by the editor.

2256. **Sen, Kanti** : 1967 : Behind opposition defeat in Tripura. *Mainstream*, April 5 : 31(18-19).

2257. **Sen, Kshirode** : 1979 : Peace work in Tripura. *Himalaya : Man and Nature*, 2(10), March : 20-1.

2258. **Sen, Man Kumar** : 1971 : Massive influx of refugees in Tripura. *Sarvodya*, July 21 : 1(27-32).

2259. **Sen, Rabindra Nath; Nag, Pranab** *and* **Roy, G.C.** : 1977 : Some anthropometry of people of Eastern India. *Jour. of the Indian Anthropological Society* , 12(3) : 199-206.

2260. **Sen, Sipra** : 1985 : *The Tribes of Meghalaya*. Delhi, Mittal Publications, 170p.

2261. ——— : 1986 : *Arunachal Pradesh And the tribes : Select Bibliography*. Delhi, Gyan Publishing House, 232p.

2262. ———: 1987 ; *Tribes of Nagaland*. Delhi, Mittal Publications, 283p.

2263. ——— : 1992 : *Tribes and Castes of Manipur*. Delhi, Mittal Publications, 371p.

2264. ——— : 1992 : *Tribes of Mizoram*. Delhi, Gyan Publishing House, 448p.

2265. **Sen, Soumen** *(Ed.)* : 1985 : *Folklore in North East India*. Delhi, Omsons Publications.

2266. **Sen, Sumangal** : 1973 : Folk Arts. *Link*, March 11 : 59-61.

2267. ——— : 1975 : Terracotta silpa : Bange O Tripuraye *(In) Tripura Prasanga (Ed)* by Swapan Sengupta. Agartala, Directorrate of Public Relations and Tourism : 125-34.

2268. ——— : 1985 : Terracotta in Bengal and Tripura. *(In) Proceedings of North East India History Association, Sixth Session, Agartala (Ed)* by Jayanta Bhusan Bhattacharjee. Shillong, History Deptt., NEHU : 36-40.

2269. **Sen, Sumanta** : 1985 : 'Shanti Sena' to be revived. *Times of India*, Nov. 8 : 1.

2270. ——— : 1986 : Tripura CM caught in dilemma. *Times of India*, Dec. 28 : 1(2-5), 9(5).

2271. **Sen, Sumanta** : 1987 : Tripura needs more forces. *Times of India*, Jan. 2: 1(4-6).

2272. **Sen, S.N.** : 1929 : Rulers of Tripura. *Chunta Prakash* (Agartala, *Extra Ordinary Issue*), January 6.

2273. ——— : 1968 : Foreword *(In) Economic Problems of the Jhumias of Tripura* by J.B. Ganguly. Calcutta, Bookland Pvt. Ltd. iii.

2274. **Sen, Tripur Ch.** *(Ed.)* : 1924 : *Tripura Desher Katha*. Agartala, 42p. *(In) Bengali*, it is translated in 1964 *in Assamese* by Ratna Kandali *and* Arjun Das and entitled *"Tripura Desher Katha"*. It was originally written in Saka 1646).

2275. ——— : 1970 : *Tripura in Transition (1923 to 1957)*. Agartala, Published by author, 91p.

2276. **Senchoudhury, S.** : 1990 : The utilization of Biore sources in Agricultural production in Tripura. Paper submitted in symposium on *"Bioresorces of Tripura"* organised by Deptt. of life Science, Tripura University, March.

2277. **Sengupta, A.K.** : 1969 : Lushei-Kuki clans re- examined. *Eastern Anthropologist*, 22(3) : 349-59.

2278. **Sengupta, Gautam** : 1985 : Early medieval sculptures of Tripura : Some observations, *(In) Proceedings of North East India History Association, Sixth Session, Agartala (Ed)* by Jayanta Bhusan Bhattacharjee. Shillong, History Deptt., NEHU : 41-7.

2279. **Sengupta, K.P.** : 1932 : *The Rajmala*, vol. II (Agartala), 267 p. *and* vol. III (Agartala), 163p.

2280. **Sengupta, Kunal** : 1991 : HPC poses fresh threat to Mizoram's clan. *Statesman*, Feb. 28 : 7(3-4).

2281. ——— : 1991 : Concern over alcoholism in Mizoram : Round the States. *Statesman*, March 8 : 4(1-3).

2282. **Sen Gupta, P.** : 1970 : *Census of India 1961, vol. I, India, pt. IX : Census Atlas*. Delhi, Manager of Publications.

2283. **Sen Gupta, P.N.** *and* **Rao, R.K.** : 1957 : Studies on the living conditions, dietary habits and nutritional Status of the Tripuri, Rangkhal and Riang Tribes of Tripura State. *Bulletin Anth. Survey of India.* VI(1), January : 1-19.

2284. **Sen Gupta, R.D.** : 1973 : Prospect of industrial development. *Link,* March 11 : 63-4.

2285. **Sengupta, S.** : 1973 : Amader Tripura *(in Bengali). Ananda Bazar Patrika* (Calcutta), January 21.

2286. **Sengupta, Sankar** : 1990 : The Chakma : A Study of interaction between animism and popular Buddhism. *Folklore,* 31(9), Sept. : 187-203.

2287. **Sengupta, Sukhamoy** : 1973 : Tourism in Tripura : Possibilities in N.E. Region. *Link,* July 1 : 43.

2288. **Sengupta, Swapan** : 1975 : Tripuraye Sanskritik Jug, *(In) Tripura Prasanga (Ed)* by Swapan Sengupta. Agartala, Direc. of Pub. Rel. and Tourism : 113-24.

2289. **Serajuddin, A.M.** : 1984 : The Chakma tribe of the Chittagong Hill Tracts in the 18th Century. *Jour. Royal Asiatic Society.*

2290. **Shakespear, J.** : 1909 : The Kuki-Lushai clans (Manipur and Chittagong). *Jour. of the Royal Anth. Inst. of Great Britain & Ireland,* 39 : 371-85.

2291. ——— : 1912 : *The Lushai Kuki Clans.* London, Macmillan & Co., 250p (*Reprinted* by Tribal Research Institute, Aizawl in 1976).

2292. **Shanti Bahini** : 1983 : An open letter dated 25.11.'83 to Lt. General H.M. Ershad, Chief Martial Law Administrator of Bangladesh by the Shanti Bahini, drawing his attention to the manifold problems faced by the people of the Chittagong Hill Tracts by Central Executive, Jana Samhate Samity *(In) The Chakmas* by S.P. Talukdar. Delhi, Gian Pubg. House (1988) *: 159-62.*

2293. **Sharma, B.D.** : n.d. : Shifting cultivators and their development. *Jour. of Social Science and Humanities* (NEHU), 2(2) : 4-5.

2294. ——— : 1984 : Shifting cultivators and their development *(In) Socio Economic Aspects in Soil Conservation Activities with Special Reference to North Eastern Region* by

Soil Conservation Deptt., Shillong, Soil Conservation Deptt., Govt. of Meghalaya : 91-101 (Seminar held at Tura, 17-20 June, 1981).

2295. **Sharma, B.D.** : 1986 : Address by Dr. B.D. Sharma : Planning for Forestry in Tribal Areas *(In) Forestry Development in North East India (Eds)* by M. Das Gupta *et al.* Guwahati, Omsons Pubs : 241-80.

2296. **Sharmah, B.L.** : 1977 : *Socio-demographic and special relationship between large-sized villages and urban centres in Assam, Manipur, Tripura and Arunachal Pradesh.* Delhi, M.P.S. Dissertation, Jawaharlal Nehru Unviersity, 118p.

2297. **Sharma, S.** : 1980 : *Charmakar sampradayer samajik arthanaitik samiksha.* Agartala, Dir. of Research, Tribal welfare Deptt, 53p *(in Bengali).*

2298. **Sharma, Sudhir** : 1980 : *Socio-Economic Survey of the cobbler communities of Agartala Municipality and its adjacent areas.* Agartala, Directorate of research, 48p.

2299. **Sharma, T.C.** ; 1986 : Recent advances in prehistory and archaeology of northeast India. *Jour. of Assam Research Society,* XXVIII (1984-'85) [Stone Age Cultures of Tripura].

2300. ——— : 1990 : Archaeology and prehistory of North East India. *Proceedings of NEIHA, Eleventh Session,* Oct. 25-27, 1990, Manipur University , Imphal *(Ed)* by J.B. Bhattacharjee. Shillong, History Deptt., North Eastern Hill University.

2301. **Shillong Times** : 1982 : Editorial : Tripura District Council. *Shillong Times,* Jan. 23 : 2(1-2).

2302. ——— : 1982 : Editorial : Intra-region imbalances. *Shillong Times,* Feb. 20 : 2(1-2).

2303. ——— : 1982 : Tripura Newsletter : A New Face of Centre- State Discord. *Shi times,* Oct. 2 : 2.

2304. ——— : 1982 : Editorial : Forthcoming election. *Shi. Times,* Oct. 9 : 2(1-2).

2305. ——— : 1982 : Dispute over Jampui Hills : An avoidable misunderstanding. *Shi. Times,* Oct. 16 : 2.

2306. **Shillong Times** : 1982 : Editorial : Tripura C.M. plea. *Shi. Times*, Nov. 27 : 2(1-2).

2307. ——— : 1982 : Tripura Elections : Will Left Front return back to Power ? *Shi. Times*, Dec. 25 : 2(3-5).

2308. ——— : 1983 : Editorial ; Tripura verdict. *Shi. Times*, Jan. 15 : 2(1-2).

2309. ——— : 1983 : Editorial : Autonomy under VII Schedule. *Shi. Times*, June 18 : 2(1-2).

2310. ——— : 1983 : Editorial : District Council for Tripura. *Shi. Times*, Aug. 27 : 2(1-2).

2311. ——— : 1984 : Editorial : Chandrapur stalemate. *Shi. Times*, March 3: 2(1-2).

2312. ——— : 1984 : North Eastern Affairs : Chakmas get hell in Mizoram border. *Shi. Times*, July 14 : 2.

2313. ——— : 1985 : Editorial : A city by its own right. *Shi. Times*, April 6 : 2(1-2).

2314. ——— : 1985 : Editorial : Tripura Council Election. *Shi. Times*, July 20 : 2.

2315. ——— : 1985 : Editorial : Sixth Schedule in Tripura. *Shi. Times*, Oct. 19 : 2(1-2).

2316. ——— : 1986 : Editorial ; Tripura move for World Bank Loan. *Shi. Times*, Oct. 18 : 2(3-5).

2317. ——— : 1987 : 6 Tribals nabbed in Tripura. *Shi. Times*, Jan. 3 : 1(3), 6(5).

2318. ——— : 1987 : Editorial : Reassessment in Tripura. *Shi. Times*, Jan. 3 : 2(1-2).

2319. ——— : 1987 : Editorial : The Chakma Problem. *Shi. Times*, Jan. 17 : 2(1-2).

2320. ——— : 1987 : Editorial : The Chakma issue. *Shi. Times*, Jan. 31 : 2(1-2).

2321. ——— : 1987 : TUJS favours talks with TNV. *Shi. Times*, Feb. 7 : 3(3-5).

2322. ——— : 1987 : 3 TNV activists held in Tripura. *Shi. Times*, Feb. 19 : 1(2).

2323. ——— : 1987 : Appeal to save Chakmas. *Shi. Times*, March 12 : 4(4-5).

2324. **Shillong Times** : 1987 : Ominus Lull in Tripura. *Shi. Times*, April 25 : 3(1-3).

2325. ——— : 1987 : Chakmas set condition for return. *Shi. Times*, May 2 : 1(4).

2326. ——— : 1987 : An interview with CEM Tripura District Council. *Shi. Times*, July 6 : 2(3-6).

2327. ——— : 1987 : B'desh Dilly dallying on Chakma return. *Shi. Times*, July 30 : 3(1-3).

2328. ——— : 1987 : Editorial : Chakmas have a case. *Shi. Times*, Aug. 10 ; 2(1-2).

2329. ——— : 1987 : Editorial : Tripura in limelight! *Shi. Times*, Aug 13 : 2(1-2).

2330. ——— : 1987 : Chakma refugees set condition for return. *Shi. Times*, Sept. 2 : 3(1-3).

2331. ——— : 1987 : Rich reserve of gas in Tripura. *Shi. Times*, Sept. 3 : 3(1-2).

2332. ——— : 1987 : Tripura project for modern tea factory. *Shi. Times*, Sept. 19 : 3(4).

2333. ——— : 1987 : Chakma will be repatriated with gurantee of security . *Shi. Times*, Sept. 19 : 3(1-3).

2334. ——— : 1987 : Editorial : Buta Singh's visit. *Shi. Times*, Sept. 22 : 2(1-2).

2335. ——— : 1987 : Arunachal tells Delhi to expel Chakmas, Hajongs. *Shi. Times*, Sept. 28 : 1(4-6).

2336. ——— : 1987 : TNV in a flux. *Shi. Times*, Oct. 16 : 3(1-2).

2337. ——— : 1987 : Editorial : TNV affairs. *Shi. Times*, Oct. 30 : 2(1-2).

2338. ——— : 1987 : TNV killing operations in Autonomous areas. *Shi. Times*, Oct. 31 : 3(2-4).

2339. ——— : 1987 : Resurgence of TNV violence before polls. *Shi. Times*, Nov. 11 : 3(1-3).

2340. ——— : 1987 : Editorial : Welcome break through. *Shi. Times*, Dec. 3 : 2(1-2).

2341. ——— : 1987 : Editorial : Solution of the Chakma problem. *Shi. Times*, Dec. 4 : 2(1-2).

2342. ——— : 1987 : Editorial : TNV controversy lingers. *Shi. Times*, Dec. 18 : 2(1-2).

2343. **Shillong Times** : 1987 : TNV Guerillas kill 6 non-tribals. *Shi. Times*, Dec. 19 : 1(2-4).

2344. ——— : 1988 : Editorial : Massacre in Tripura. *Shi. Times*, Jan. 1 : 2(1-2).

2345. ——— : 1988 : Legacy of palace intrigue in Tripura. *Shi. Times*, Jan. 20 : 3(1-3).

2346. ——— : 1988 ; Chidambaram reviews counter insurgency steps in Tripura. *Shi. Times*, Jan. 24 : 1(2-3).

2347. ——— : 1988 : TNV men kill 31 more in Tripura. *Shi. Times*, Feb. 1 : 1(4-6).

2348. ——— : 1988 : 2 non-Tribals killed in Tripura. *Shi. Times*, Feb. 5 : 1(5-6).

2349. ——— : 1988 : Cong-I wrests power in Tripura. *Shi. Times*, Feb. 5 : 1(5-6).

2350. ——— : 1988 : In Tripura : Cong-I Ministry Assumes Office. *Shi. Times*, Feb. 6 : 1(6).

2351. ——— : 1988 : Disturbed Area Announcement with State Govt's consent. *Shi. Times*, \Feb. 6 : 4(3-4).

2352. ——— : 1988 : Editorial : Disturbed Tripura. *Shi. Times*, Feb. 11 : 2(1-2).

2353. ——— : 1988 : Tripura Governor reviews insurgency situation. *Shi. Times* Peb. 12 : 1(5-6).

2354. ——— : 1988 : Plea for popular pressure on TNV. *Shi. Times*, Feb. 17 : 3(1-2).

2355. ——— : 1988 : Railway expansion projects in North East. *Shi. Times*, Feb. 23 : 3(5).

2356. ——— : 1988 : Faleiro opens Loan Mela in Tripura. *Shi. Times*, March 28 : 1(3-6).

2357. ——— : 1988 : Editorial : Codification of customary laws. *Shi. Times*, April 5 : 2(1-2).

2358. ——— : 1988 : Editorial : Congress(I) TUJS alliance. *Shi. Times*, April 7 : 2(1-2).

2359. ——— : 1988 : Delhi against talks with TNV now. *Shi. Times*, April 18 : 1(5-6).

2360. ——— : 1988 : Cong-I wrests power in Tripura. *Shi. Times*, May 5 : 1(5-6).

2361. **Shillong Times** : 1988 : "Govt. determined to crush TNV"——— Majumder. *Shi. Times*, May 8 : 1(2-4).

2362. ——— : 1988 : Estimate says 3 Billion tonnes oil deposit in North-East. *Shi. Times*, May 11 : 3(2-3).

2363. ——— : 1988 : Editorial : Negotiation with insurgents. *Shi. Times*, May 23 : 2(1-2).

2364. ——— : 1988 : "Centre for autonomy of Jampui Hills" *Shi. Times*, June 7 : 3(1-2).

2365. ——— : 1988 : "Tripura Rly. Track to be ready by '89 end". *Shi. Times*. June 16 : 4(2).

2366. ——— : 1988 : TUJS resents authority. *Shi. Times*, June 17 : 1(2-4).

2367. ——— : 1988 : Rehabilitation, benefits to tribal insurgents offered. *Shi. Times*, June 23 : 3(1-2).

2368. ——— : 1988 : ITDC plan for development on Tourism in Tripura. *Shi. Times*, June 27 : 3(3).

2369. ——— : 1988 : Editorial : Forest Destruction in Tripura. *Shi. Times*, July 15 : 2(1-2).

2370. ——— : 1988 : Editorial : Fulminations at Dhaka. *Shi. Times*, July 18 : 2(1-2) (about *Chakma*).

2371. ——— : 1988 : Bangla H.C. Alleges : Extremists Preventing Chakma Return. *Shi. Times*, July 19 : 1(2-4).

2372. ——— : 1988 : Editorial : A choked highway. *Shi. Times*, July 26 : 2(1-2).

2373. ——— : 1988 : Fresh initiative for talks with TNV. *Shi. Times*, July 28 : 1(5-6).

2374. ——— : 1988 : Alleged apathy towards Tripura tribals. *Shi. Times*, Aug. 1 : 3(4).

2375. ——— : 1988 : Tripura's potential as major tea grower. *Shi. Times*, Aug. 2 : 3(1).

2376. ——— : 1988 : Editorial : Rumblings in TUJS. *Shi. Times*, Aug. 3 : 2(1-2).

2377. ——— : 1988 : Editorial : Talks with insurgents. *Shi. Times*, Aug. 12 : 2(1-2).

2378. ——— : 1988 : "Accord sanctioned by TNV Rank and File" : Hrangkhawl. *Shi. Times*, Aug. 14 ; 1(2-3).

2379. **Shillong Times** : 1988 : Editorial : TNV Accord. *Shi. Times*, Aug. 18 : 2(1-2).

2380. ——— : 1988 : Tripura can take off in Rubber Plantation. *Shi. Times*, Aug. 22 : 3(3).

2381. ——— : 1988 : Editorial : After the Accord. *Shi. Times*, Aug. 23 : 2(1-2).

2382. ——— : 1988 : TNV surrender next week likely. *Shi. Times*, Aug. 25 : 1(2-3).

2383. ——— : 1988 : Editorial : Wanted a positive initiative. *Shi. Times*, Aug. 27 : 2(1-2)

2384. ——— : 1988 : TNV surrender from Sept. 6. *Shi. Times*, Aug. 28 : 1(2-3).

2385. ——— : 1988 : 6th Schedule Amendment Bill only for Mizoram, Tripura. *Shi. Times*, Sept. 5 : 1(4-6).

2386. ——— : 1988 : TNV Guerillas surrender with arms. *Shi. Times*, Sept. 11 : 1(2-5), 4(2).

2387. ——— : 1988 : Hrangkhawl promises to make better Tripura. *Shi. Times*, Sept. 14 : 1(5-6).

2388. ——— : 1988 : Editoral : TNV rehabilitation. *Shi. Times*, Sept. 20 : 2(1-2).

2389. ——— : 1988 : Science Centre project for Tripura. *Shi. Times*, Sept. 26 : 3(6).

2390. ——— : 1988 : Editorial : TNV activists for Assam Rifles. *Shi. Times*, Sept. 27 : 2(1-2).

2391. ——— : 1988 : Editorial : The crucial Hill Section. *Shi. Times*, Oct. 11 : 2(1-2).

2392. ——— : 1988 : 'Hrangkhawl betrayed tribals cause'—— Dasarath. *Shi. Times*, Oct. 29 : 3(3).

2393. ——— : 1988 : Editorial : In fighting in Tripura. *Shi. Times*, Nov. 1 : 2(1-2).

2394. ——— : 1988 : Editorial : Change of guard *Shi. Times*, Nov. 18 : 2(1-2).

2395. ——— : 1988 : Tripura Tribal bodies plea with Governor. *Shi. Times*, Dec. 7 : 3(1-2).

2396. ——— : 1988 : Cong(I)-TUJS differ on Mizo Council demand. *Shi. Times*, Dec. 12 : 1(2-3) (Tripura).

2397. **Shillong Times** : 1988 : Editorial : Schedule Amendment-I. *Shi. Times,* Dec. 12 : 2(1-2).

2398. ——— : 1988 : Editorial ; Schedule Amendment-II. *Shi. Times,* Dec. 13 : 2(1-2).

2399. ——— : 1988 : TUJS criticises Sixth Schedule Amendment. *Shi. Times,* Dec. 14 : 1(2-3) (Tripura).

2400. ——— : 1988 : 35 die of enteric diseases in Tripura. *Shi. Times,* Dec. 21 : 4(3).

2401. ——— : 1988 : NEC to fund Tripura Highway construction. *Shi. Times,* Dec. 22 : 3(1).

2402. ——— : 1988 : Editorial : Tribal Demands in Tripura. *Shi. Times,* Dec. 22 : 2(1-2).

2403. ——— : 1988 : New Analysis : Bijay Hrangkhawl's next move. *Shi. Times,* Dec. 31 : 1(3-6), 3(5-6).

2404. ——— : 1989 : Editorial : Chakma talks fail. *Shi. Times,* Jan. 5 : 2(1-2).

2405. ——— : 1989 : Tripura to draw up industrial policy. *Shi. Times,* Jan. 5 : 3(1-2).

2406. ——— : 1989 : TNV-TUJS merger soon. *Shi. Times,* Jan. 7 : 1(6).

2407. ——— : 1989 : Rehabilitation of surrendered TNV activists. *Shi. Times,* Jan. 7 : 3(4).

2408. ——— : 1989 : Chakma orphans not sold : Agency. *Shi. Times,* Jan. 16 : 3(4).

2409. ——— : 1989 : Rebels reject Ershad's Dist. Council proposal. *Shi. Times,* Jan. 16 : 3(4-5).

2410. ——— : 1989 : No more for merger of TNV-TUJS. *Shi. Times,* Jan. 16 : 1(4-5).

2411. ——— : 1989 : Editorial : Laskars loss of privilege. *Shi. Times,* Jan. 25 : 2(1-2).

2412. ——— : 1989 : French collaboration for Tripura power plant signed. *Shi. Times,* Feb. 23 : 4(4).

2413. ——— : 1989 : Editorial ; An unpalatable controversy. *Shi. Times,* Feb. 23 : 2(1-2). (Tripura Chakma 72 orphans taken by *French Children Welfare Agency*).

2414. **Shillong Times** : 1989 : Editorial : Bill on Chakma Autonomy. *Shi. Times*, Feb. 23 : 2(1-2). (District Council of Mizoram under 6th Schedule).

2415. ——— : 1989 : Editorial : Tripuras Industrialisation. *Shi. Times*, March 8 : 2(1-2).

2416. ——— : 1989 : Tripura to launch attack on poverty. *Shi. Times*, March 18 : 5(5-6).

2417. ——— : 1989 : Bangla team to woo Chakmas home. *Shi. Times*, May 30 : 3(2-3).

2418. ——— : 1989 : Editorial : Jhuming reconsidered. *Shi. Times*, June 2 : 2(1-2).

2419. ——— : 1989 : Chakma influx unabated. *Shi. Times*, June 2 : 4(2).

2420. ——— : 1989 : Editorial ; An untimely initiative. *Shi. Times*, June 3 : 2(1-2).

2421. ——— : 1989 : Chakma refugees undecided about returning home. *Shi. Times*, June 3 : 3(1-2).

2422. ——— : 1989 : Editorial : The Faree Lingers. *Shi. Times*, June 13 : 2(1-2) (*Chakma*).

2423. ——— : 1989 : Tripura pineapple juice for Ṣoviets. *Shi. Times*, June 14 : 3(4).

2424. ——— : 1989 : Buta invites Majumdar to discuss Chakma. *Shi. Times*, June 17 : 4(1).

2425. ——— : 1989 : Tripura to import wood from Malaysia. *Shi. Times*, July 7 : 3(1).

2426. ——— : 1989 : Editorial : New menace. *Shi. Times*, July 15 : 2(1-2).

2427. ——— : 1989 : Editorial : Tripura's ordeal, *Shi. Times*, July 19 : 2(1-2) *(Chakma)*.

2428. ——— : 1989 : Insecurity among Chakma in Arunachal. *Shi. Times*, July 27 : 3(2-3).

2429. ——— : 1989 : District Council, Govt. hold debate in Tripura. *Shi. Times*, Aug. 3 : 3(1-3).

2430. ——— : 1989 : Tripura C.M. agrees to readjust port folios. *Shi. Times*, Sept. 15 : 3(4).

2431. ——— : 1989 : Editorial : Chakma problem intensifies. *Shi. Times*, Sept. 25 : 2(1-2).

2432. **Shillong Times** : 1989 : To the Editor : Aruanachal's harassment of Chakmas by an affected Chakma. *Shi. Times,* Sept. 26 : 2(5-6).

2433. ——— : 1989 : Politicians patronising Chakma influx in Tripura. *Shi. Times,* Oct. 3 : 1(1).

2434. ——— : 1989 : Chakma refugee students face urcertainity. *Shi. Times,* Oct. 4 : 3(2-3).

2435. ——— : 1989 : N.E. States need special economic norms. *Shi. Times,* Oct. 5 : 3(4).

2436. ——— : 1989 : Legal provisions await enforcement to present alienation of tribal land. *Shi. Times,* Oct 6 : 3(4-6).

2437. ——— : 1989 : Jampui Mizo plan their ownself government. *Shi. Times,* Dec. 29 : 3(1-2).

2438. ——— : 1990 : Siberian bird Sanctuary in Tripura. *Shi. Times,* Feb. 17 : 4(2).

2439. ——— : 1990 : TNV dissatisfied with Tripura Govt. *Shi. Times,* March 1 : 3(1-3).

2440. ——— : 1990 : Editorial ; Trans-border infiltration. *Shi. Times,* March 2 : 2(1-2).

2441. ——— : 1990 : Interview with Bijay Kumar Hrangkhawl : Infiltration is a great threat to tribals. *Shi. Times,* March 4 : 3(3-6).

2442. ——— : 1990 : Entire TNSA gang nabbed. *Shi. Times,* March 5 : 4(3-4).

2443. ——— : 1990 : CPI(M) demands Inner Line for Tripura Autonomous Area. *Shi. Times,* March 7 : 1(2-5).

2444. ——— : 1990 : TUJS demands corruption free Govt. *Shi. Times,* March 13 : 3(1-2).

2445. ——— : 1990 : Work on to seal Tichna Gas leak. *Shi. Times,* March 13 : 3(3-4).

2446. ——— : 1990 : Editorial : Sealing the border. *Shi. Times,* March 16 : 2(1-2).

2447. ——— : 1990 : New terrorist group in Tripura. *Shi. Times,* March 24 : 4(4) (TNSA).

2448. ——— : 1990 : TUJS demands district council elections. *Shi. Times,* April 6 : 3(2-3).

2449. **Shillong Times** : 1990 : Press Council's Dig at Tripura Government. *Shi. Times*, April 19 : 3(1-2).

2450. ——— : 1990 : Jampui Mizos up in arms. *Shi. Times*, April 25 : 3(1-3).

2451. ——— : 1990 : TNV to join ADC election fray. *Shi. Times*. April 21 : 3(2).

2452. ——— : 1990 : CPI(M)'s concern over influx in Tripura. *Shi. Times*, April 27 : 3(2-3).

2453. ——— : 1990 : Fish, sarees top smugglers list. *Shi. Times*, April 29 : 1(1).

2454. ——— : 1990 : Editorial : A Preposterous idea. *Shi. Times*, April 30 : 2(1-2).

2455. ——— : 1990 : Editorial : Chakma refugees unrelenting. *Shi. Times*, May 18 : 2(1-2).

2456. ——— : 1990 : ADC election last opportunity for Hrangkhal. *Shi. Times*, May 22 : 3(1-2).

2457. ——— : 1990 : TNV joins Cong(I) TUJS alliance. *Shi. Times*, May 31 : 4(5-6).

2458. ——— : 1990 : Editorial : Forest cover on decline. *Shi. Times*, June 16 : 2(1-2).

2459. ——— : 1990 : Security man killed, 4 rifles looted in Tripura. *Shi. Times*, June 25 : 1(1).

2460. ——— : 1990 : N E States to formulate Joint tourism development plan. *Shi. Times*, June 26 : 3(1-2).

2461. ——— : 1990 : N E States demand inner line permit withdrawal. *Shi. Times*, July 4 : 1(3-4).

2462. ——— : 1990 : 7 killed in Tripura District Council polls. *Shi. Times*, July 9 : 1(2-4).

2463. ——— : 1990 : Tripura poll violence toll now 11. *Shi. Times*, July 10 : 1(5-6). [Autonomous District Council Poll].

2464. ——— : 1990 : Congress(I) alliance dislodges left front in Tripura ADC. *Shi. Times*, July 11 : 1(2-4).

2465. ——— : 1990 : Editorial : Lawlessness in border areas. *Shi. Times*, July 12 : 2(1-2).

2466. ——— : 1990 : Tripura CM's warning against communal flare up. *Shi. Times*, July 14 : 3(1-2).

2467. Shillong Times : 1990 : TUJS to elect district council leader. *Shi. Times*, July 17 : 3(1-2).

2468. ——— : 1990 : Tripura elections prove Cong(I) hold on tribals. *Shi. Times*, July 17 : 4(4-5).

2469. ——— : 1990 : Editorial: MDC election violence. *Shi. Times*, July 20 : 2(1-2).

2470. ——— : 1990 : Editorial : Restore normalcy. *Shi. Times*, July 21 : 2(1-2).

2471. ——— : 1990 : Tripura will turn into Vietnam. *Shi. Times*, July 23 : 1(3), 4(3).

2472. ——— : 1990 : Tripura left front welcomes Central fact finding team. *Shi. Times*, July 24 : 3(1-2).

2473. ——— : 1990 : Editorial : Claim unrealistic. *Shi. Times*, Aug. 8 : 2(1-2).

2474. ——— : 1990 : Tripura CM's warning to Centre. *Shi. Times*, Aug. 14 : 3(1-2).

2475. ——— : 1990 : Editorial : Spurt of ragging. *Shi. Times*, Aug. 28 : 2(1-2).

2476. ——— : 1990 : Terrorist groups to be nipped in bud. *Shi. Times*, Aug. 28 : 3(1-2).

2477. ——— : 1990 : Laudable use of non-conventional energy. *Shi. Times*, Dec. 3 : 2(1-2).

2478. ——— : 1990 : Fresh Influx from Bangladesh. *Shi. Times*, Dec. 6 : 3(4-6).

2479. ——— : 1990 : President urges people to shun violence. *Shi. Times*, Dec. 11 : 1(2-3).

2480. ——— : 1990 : President opens new road. *Shi. Times*, Dec. 13 : 3(1).

2481. ——— : 1990 : Tripura to raise forest protection force. *Shi. Times*, Dec. 14 : 3(4).

2482. ——— : 1991 : Heavy rains may damage crops in Tripura. *Shi. Times*, Jan. 5 : 3(3).

2483. ——— : 1991 : Cong workers resent Tripura Govt. functioning. *Shi. Times*, Jan. 5 : 3(5-6).

2484. ——— : 1991 : Tripura tribal body resents state action. *Shi. Times*, Jan. 9 : 3(12).

2485. **Shillong Times** : 1991 : Security forces for Tripura. *Shi. Times,* Jan 9 : 3(13).

2486. ——— : 1991 : Record paddy production in Tripura. *Shi. Times,* Jan. 11 : 3(1).

2487. ——— : 1991 : Chakma refugee's plea to Bangla President. *Shi. Times,* Jan. 11 : 2(1-2).

2488. ——— : 1991 : Rumblings of dissent in Tripura Cong.(I) *Shi. Times,* Jan. 18 : 3(4-5).

2489. ——— : 1991 : Uncertainty persists about Chakma future. *Shi. Times,* March 5 : 3(4-5).

2490. ——— : 1991 : Ration quota for Tripura tribals doubled. *Shi. Times,* March 12 : 3(4).

2491. ——— : 1991 : Another extremist outfit in Tripura. *Shi. Times,* March 27 : 3(5-6).

2492. ——— : 1991 : Tripura ruling and opp. parties fear poll violence. *Shi. Times,* March 28 : 4(2-3).

2493. ——— : 1991 : Militants surrender with Arms. *Shi. Times,* March 31 : 1(5-6).

2494. ——— : 1991 : Bungling over TNV rehabilitation alleged. *Shi. Times,* April 1 : 3(1).

2495. ——— : 1991 : TUJS' uncern over Militant activities. *Shi. Times,* April 25 : 3(3).

2496. ——— : 1991 : 1934 booths for the Tripura Lok Sabha Poll. *Shi. Times,* April 29 : 3(1).

2497. ——— : 1991 : Record 17 candidates in 2 Tripura seats. *Shi. Times,* April 30 : 1(4).

2498. ——— : 1991 : "Great potential for developing economy of Tripura". *Shi. Times,* May 6 : 4(2-3).

2499. ——— : 1991 : 1 killed in Tripura poll violence. *Shi. Times,* May 7 : 1(1).

2500. ——— : 1991 : Bibhu Devi's tribal status questions by CPI(M). *Shi. Times,* May 25 : 3(1-3).

2501. ——— : 1991 : Tripura Tribal militants gun down 2 persons. *Shi. Times,* May 30 : 1(1) [ATTF].

2502. ——— : 1991 : CPI-M demand poll postponement in Tripura. *Shi. Times,* May 30 : 1(4-6).

2503. **Shillong Times** : 1991 : Editorial : Industrialisation and environment in N.E. *Shi. Times*. Aug. 1 : 2(1-2).

2504. ——— : 1991 : Plea for early repatriation of Chakma refugees. *Shi. Times*, Aug. 28 : 3(5).

2505. ——— : 1991 : Tripura traders threaten to pull out. *Shi. Times*, Sept. 4 : 3(4-5).

2506. ——— : 1991 : "Cong(I)-TUJS alliance intact" says CM. *Shi. Times*, Sept. 8 : 1(6-8).

2507. ——— : 1991 : "No links between ULFA and Tripura Militants". *Shi. Times*, Sept. 23 : 1(6-7) & 4(7).

2508. ——— : 1991 : "Harvest suffers due to ATTF threat. *Shi. Times*, Sept. 23 : 3(2-3).

2509. ——— : 1991 : Editorial : Travails in Tripura. *Shi. Times*, Sep. 24 : 2(1-2).

2510. ——— : 1991 : Prominent TUJS leader killed. *Shi. Times*, Sept. 27 : 1(8).

2511. ——— : 1991 : Another TUJS worker shot dead. *Shi. Times*, Sept. 30 : 1(6-7).

2512. ——— : 1991 : Militants, take over Jampui Mizo convention. *Shi. Times*, Oct. 2 : 3(1-3).

2513. ——— : 1991 : "TUJS did not demand change of leadership". *Shi. Times*, Oct. 2 : 3(5-7), 4(3-4).

2514. ——— : 1991 : Chakmas cry for help. *Shi. Times*, Oct 4 : 3(6-7).

2515. ——— : 1991 : Tribal girl dies of starvation in Tripura. *Shi. Times*, Oct. 7 : 1(2-3).

2516. ——— : 1991 : TUJS sets deadline for withdrawal of support. *Shi Times* Oct. 8 : 1(6-8).

2517. ——— : 1991 : ATTF ultras nabbed. *Shi. Times*, Oct. 11 : 1(6).

2518. ——— : 1991 : Tripura crisis : CM calls meeting with TUJS. *Shi. Times*, Oct. 11 : 1(2-5).

2519. ——— : 1991 : ATTF ambushes police escort : Two killed *Shi. Times*, Oct. 12 : 1(6-8).

2520. ——— : 1991 : Tripura incentives for industries. *Shi. Times*, Oct. 23 : 3(1-3).

2521. Shillong Times : 1991 : Tripura Govt. accused of abating infiltration. *Shi. Times,* Nov. 4 : 3(5). [Cong(I)-TUJS].

2522. ——— : 1991 : 100 die in Tripura gastro. *Shi. Times,* Nov. 6 : 1(5-7).

2523. ——— : 1991 : Two reasons why cancer is spreading fast. *Shi. Times,* Nov. 10 : 4(6-8).

2524. ——— : 1991 : Tripura CPI(M) heading towards split. *Shi. Times,* Nov. 12 : 1(2-5).

2525. ——— : 1991 : Peaceful bandh cripples normal life in Tripura. *Shi. Times,* Nov. 16 : 1(5-7).

2526. ——— : 1991 : Editorial · Shock in Tripura. *Shi. Times,* Nov. 16 : 2(1-2).

2527. ——— : 1991 : Rice in illegal activities along Indo-Bangla border. *Shi. Times,* Dec. 6 : 3(2-4).

2528. ——— : 1991 : Jampui Hills Mizos demand autonomy. *Shi. Times,* Dec. 9 : 3(1-3).

2529. ——— : 1991 : Tripura industries face closure. *Shi. Times,* Dec. 9 : 3(2-3).

2530. ——— : 1991 : Tripura govt. to hold talks with Hrangkhawl. *Shi. Times,* Dec. 16 : 3(4).

2531. ——— : 1991 : Tripura areas to be declared 'Disturbed'. *Shi. Times,* Dec. 17 : 3(2-3).

2532. ——— : 1991 : Mizos active for regional council. *Shi. Times,* Dec. 23 : 1(7-8).

2533. ——— : 1991 : Tripura beset with foreigners influx. *Shi. Times,* Dec. 25 : 3(2-4).

2534. ——— : 1991 : BSF Jawans kill six ATTF ultras in Tripura. *Shi. Times,* Dec. 25 : 3(3).

2535. ——— : 1991 : Starvation death toll rises to 450 in Tripura. *Shi. Times,* Dec. 31 : 3(2-4).

2536. ——— : 1991 : Measures adopted to control ATTF menace. *Shi. Times,* January 6 : 3(1-4).

2537. ——— : 1992 : ATTF threatens road stir from Jan. 20. *Shi. Times,* Jan. 8 : 1(2-4).

2538. ——— : 1991 : TUJS men to meet P.M. *Shi. Times,* Jan. 9 : 1(7-8).

2539. **Shillong Times** : 1992 : Tripura insurgency : Jacob urges negotiated settlement. *Shi. Times*, Jan. 10 : 1(2-4).

2540. ——— : 1992 : Red alert sounded in Tripura. *Shi. Times*, Jan. 14 : 1(5).

2541. ——— : 1992 : 3 Police men hurt in ATTF Attack. *Shi. Times*, Jan. 19 : 1(4).

2542. **Shome, S.G.** : 1973 : Education in Tripura : A new chapter. *Economic Times*, Feb. 4 : 4(1).

2543. **Shukla, S.P.** *and* **Agarwal, A.K.** : 1983 : The magnitude of the problem of agricultural labour in the N-E Region. *Jour. NEICSSR*, 7(1), April : 34-8 [Tripura].

2544. ——— : 1986 : *Agriculture in North Eastern Region*. New Delhi, National Pub. House : 143-44, 151, [Tripura].

2545. **Shyamacharan** 1987 : Tripura. *Chinikak* (Agartala), *Special Issue*, June 10 : 9.

2546. **Shyam Choudhury, N.K.** *and* **Biswas, S.K.** : 1963 : A trait of making earthen wares in the Mizo district and its cultural evaluation in Assam. *Bull. Anth. Survey of India*, 12(1-2).

2547. **Singal, D.S.** : 1980 : *Fertility differentials in Tripura, 1971 : A census analysis*. Bombay, International Institute for population Studies, 1979-'80.

2548. **Singh, Baldeo** : 1985 (?) : Tribal farmers and agriculture development of North East Region. : 179-92.

2549. **Singh, Birchandra Y.** : 1973 : Handloom handicrafts. *Times of India*, Jan. 21 : 12(6).

2550. **Singh, B.P.** : 1967 : High yielding and food resistant paddy varieties for Tripura. *Indian Farming*, July 22 : 17(4).

2551. ——— : 1987 : *The Problem of change : A Study of North East India*. Delhi, Oxford Uni. Press, 222p.

2552. **Singh, G.P.** : 1977 : Tripperah : The ancient Hill Kingdom. *North Eastern Spectrum*, 1(11-12), 1976-77 : 24-33.

2553. ——— : 1981 : The History and Culture of ancient Tripura : A re-appraisement, *(In) Proceedings of the North East India History Association (Ed)* by Jayanta Bhusan Bhattacharjee (1980). Shillong, Deptt. of History, North Eastern Hill University : 27-39.

2554. **Singh, G.P.** : 1990 : *The Kiratas in ancient India : Spotlight on North East*. New Delhi, Gyan Pub. House (Hill Tipperah).

2555. **Singh, Indera P.** *and* **Bhasin, M.K.** : 1979 : Ethnic and geographic frequency distribution of dermatoglyphic traits in India : A review. *Birth Defects : Original article series* (Delhi), XV(6) : 347-87 [Sikkim, Meghalaya, Tripura, Nagaland, Manipur, Assam].

2556. **Singh, J.D.** : 1980 : Tripura : Fear of tribal insurgency borns large. *Times of India*, June 26.

2557. **Singh, Jai Prakash** : 1985 : Tribal elements in the coinage of Tripura. *(In) Proceedings of North East India History Association, vol. 6 (Ed)* by Jayanta Bhusan Bhattacharjee. Shillong, Deptt. of History, North Eastern Hill University : 51-5.

2558. **Singh, Jogendra P.** : 1980 : Levels of Human Resources in North East India. *Jour. NEICSSR, IV(II), Oct. : 1-6 : [Tripura].*

2559. **Singh, J.P.** : 1982 : *Human Resources of North Eastern India*. New Delhi, Inter India Publications : 140-49.

2560. **Singh, J.P.** *and* **Ahmad, N.** : 1980 : Coinage and Economy of North Eastern States of India. *N.S.I.* (Varanasi), No. 10 : 115.

2561. **Singh, K.S.** : 1982 : The Postscript. *(In) Tribal Movements in India, vol. I (Ed)* by K.S. Singh. New Delhi, Manohar Pubs : 361.

2562. ——— : 1989 : Research Note : Ethnicity and Polity formation in tribal India. *Human Science*, 38(1), March : 77-82.

2563. ——— *(Ed)* : 1990 : *People of India, National Series : The Scheduled Tribes, Descriptive Data.* New Delhi, Anthropological Survey of India, 791p.

2564. Singh, K.S. *and* Mukherjee, B. : 1982 : Tribal movement in Tripura, *(In) Tribal Movements in India, Vol. I (Ed)* by K.S. Singh. New Delhi, Manohar Publications : 317-38.

2565. Singh, Ram Gopal : 1978 : *The Kukis of Tripura : A Socio Economic Survey.* Agartala, Tripura Govt. Press, 52p. (*Reprinted* in 1985 by Directorate of Research, 58p.)

2566. Singh, R.L. *(Ed)* : 1971 : *India : A Regional Geography.* Varanasi, National Geographical Society of India : 493-513.

2567. Singh, Tarlok : 1967 : Development of Tribal Economies in the hill areas, *(In) A Common Perspective for North East India (Eds.)* by Rathin Mitra *and* B. Das Gupta. Calcutta, Pub. by Pannalal Das Gupta : 200-08.

2568. Singha, Kailas Chandra : 1896 : *Rajmala.* Agartala, 62p. (*Reprinted* in 1984).

2569. ——— : ? : *History of Tripura, vol. III, chapter I.* Agartala.

2570. Singha, R.G. *(Tr)* : 1983 : *Loka Britter Aloke Koloi Sampradaya* by Pradip Nath Bhattacharjee. Agartala, Directorate of Research (1980), 121 p.

2571. Sinha, A. : n.p. : *Land alienation in Tripura : Preliminary hypothesis* (*Unpublished* paper.)

2572. Sinha, A.C. : 1984 : Managing social consequences of smallness : The developmental strategy for the small Indian Frontier State, *(In) Northeast Region : Problems and Prospects of Development (Ed)* by B.L. Abbi. Chandigarh, Centre for Research in Rural and Industrial Development : 11-23.

2573. Sinha, A.C. : 1986 : Conflicting images of the Indian core and periphery. *Jour. of Social Research* (Ranchi), 28-29, Sept. '85-March '86 : 85-97.

2574. Sinha, Kamaleshwar : 1970 : *Meghalaya.* Delhi, Publication Division : 73, 74, 76, 163, 170 [Tripura].

2575. Sinha, M. : 1990 : Fishing in the fallow N-E. *Amrita Bazar Patrika,* July 31 : 7(3-6).

2576. **Sinha, Rabindra** : 1985 : Bishnupriya Manipuris in Tripura : Past and Present, *(In) Proceedings of North East India History Association, vol. 6(Ed)* by Jayanta Bhusan Bhattacharjee. Shillong, Deptt. of History, North Eastern Hill University : 478-81.

2577. **Sinha, Raghuvir** : 1977 : *Religion and culture of North Eastern India.* New Delhi, Pub. by Abhinav, 120p.

2578. **Sinha, S.B.** : 1978 : *Socio-Economic Survey of the Noatia tribes.* Agartala, Deptt. of Tribal Welfare and Welfare of Scheduled Castes.

2579. **Sinha, Sachindra Lal** : 1968 : Freedom Movement in Tripura. *Amrita Bazar Patrika (Centenary Supplement)*, March 27.

2580. **Sircar, B.** *and* **Debnath, C.** : 1983 : Preliminary study to evaluate the nutritional status of Tripuri tribes near Agartala. Paper presented in *"International Symposium on Applied Physiology and Agroeconomics"*, Calcutta.

2581. **Sircar, D.C.** : 1951 : Copper plate inscription of the time of King Vijayamanikya of Tripura. *Jour. of Asiatic Society of Bengal*, XVII(2) : 76-77.

2582. ——— : 1983 : Foreword *(In) Tripura Through The Ages* by Nalini Ranjan Roychoudhury. New Delhi, Sterling Publishers : VII-IX.

2583. ——— : 1979 : *Some Epigraphical Records of the Medieval Period from Eastern India.* New Delhi, Abhinav Publications : 84, 89.

2584. **Smart, Robert B.** : 1866 : *Geographical and Statistical Report on the District of Tipperah.* Calcutta, Bengal Secretariat Office, 19p.

2585. **Smith, Vincent** : 1906 : *Catalogue of the coins in the Indian Museum (Calcutta).* London, Oxford Unviersity [Chapter III, A Description of the Tipperah coins].

2586. **Soil Conservation** : 1973 : *Scheme for permanent settlement of Jhumia cultivators through development of plantation crops by Fifth Five Year Plan, 1974-'75 - 1978-'79.* Gauhati, Soil Conservation Deptt., Assam, September.

2587. Som, T.K. : ? : *Participation of Tribal People (Riang) in rubber plantation industry in North Tripura district and its impact on their Socio-Economic status. Unpublished* Ph.D. Dissertation, Calcutta University.

2588. Som, Tapan Kumar : 1987 : Land utilisation and changing economy in the context of rubber plantation Industry : A micro-sociological study in North Tripura District. Proceedings of a Seminar on *"Impact of Land Reforms on North East India"*, organised by NEICSSR, Shillong on 24-25 April, 1987 : 1-14.

2589. ——— : 1987 : Changing Riang family composition : A micro- sociological study in Tripura. *Jour. NEICSSR, XI (2), Oct. : 44-50.*

2590. ——— : 1987 : Changing traditional authority structure : A case of Tripura Riangs. *Asian Studies* (Calcutta), 6(2), April-June.

2591. ——— : 1988 : *Book Reviews* : Changing Tripura [Tripura Administration : The Era of Modernisation by Banikanta Bhattacharyya, Mittal Publications, Delhi, Rs. 180/-] *Amrita Bazar Patrika, Sunday Supplement*, Feb. 5 : 26-7.

2592. ——— : 1988 : Shifting cultivation among the Riang : A micro study in Tripura. *Jour. Indian Anthropological Society*, 23(1), March : 45.

2593. ——— : 1988 : The Riang of Tripura : A Brief note on their religious beliefs and practices associated with child birth. *Vanyajati*, XXXVI (2), April : 3-7.

2594. ——— : 1988 : Transformation of Riang economy in the context of rubber plantation industry : A micro study in Tripura *Man in India*, 68(2-3), June-Sept : 145-66.

2595. ——— : 1989 : The Riangs of Tripura : A micro study on their religious beliefs and practices associated with witchcraft and diseases. *Jour. NEICSSR, 13(1), April : 18-25.*

2596. ——— : 1989 : *Book Review* : Homeless since partition "The Chakmas : Life and Struggle" by S.P. Talukdar, Gyan Publishing House, 29/6, Shakti Nagar,

Delhi-110 007, Rs. 150/-. *Amrita Bazar Patrika,* April 16 *(Sunday Magazine)* : 2(5-7).

2597. **Soppitt, C.A.** : 1884 : *Short Account of the Kuki and Lushai Tribes on North East Frontier.* Shillong.

2598. ——— : 1887 : *A Short Account of the Kuki Lushai tribes on the Northeast Frontier Districts —— Cachar, Sylhet, Naga Hills, etc. with an outline grammar of the Rangkhol- Lushai Language, and a comparison of Lushai with other dialects.* Shillong, Assam Secretariat Press.

2599. **Srinivas, M.N.** *and* **Sanwal, R.D.** : 1970 : Some aspects of Political Development in the North Eastern Hill Areas of India. *North Eastern Research Bulletin,* (Sociologu Deptt.), Dibrugarh University , I, Summer : 1-10.

2600. ——— : 1972 : Some aspects of Political Development in the North Eastern Hill areas of India, *(In) Tribal Situation in India : Proceedings of a Seminar (Ed)* by K. Suresh Singh. Simla, Indian Institute of Advanced Study: 117-24.

2601. **Sri Sankarnarayanan** : 1971 : Land revenue system and land reform measures in Tripura. *Proceedings of a Seminar of Census of India, 1971.*

2602. **Srivastava, M.P.** : 1968 : Industrial development possibilities of Agartala. *Economic Times,* Feb. 26 : 4(1).

2603. **Srivastava, L.R.N.** : 1968 : Habitation, Origin and Migration of a North Eastern Tribe. *Vanyajati,* 4 : 123-32.

2604. ——— : 1969 : The problem of modernization of the tribes of North-East India. *Bull. Cultural Research Institute.* (Calcutta), 7(2) : 21-5.

2605. **Srivastava, R.** : 1977 : Shifting cultivation in India. *Man in India, 57(4) : 331-44.*

2606. **Srivastava, S.C.** : 1987 : *Demographic profile of North East India.* Delhi, Mittal Publications, 343p.

2607. **Statesman** : 1970 : Editorial : Two more States. *Statesman* (Calcutta), Sept. 4:8(2-3).

2608. **Statesman** : 1975 : Editorial : Warning in Tripura. *Statesman*, Sept. 3.

2609. ——— : 1977 : Tripura tribals hold up land reform. *Statesman*, Jan. 23.

2610. ——— : 1979 : Violence in Tripura. *Statesman*, June 13 : 6(2-3).

2611. ——— : 1979 : Editorial : Tripura Scene. *Statesman*, Jan 14 : 6(2-3).

2612. ——— : 1980 : Tripura keen on tribal scheme. *Statesman*, March 20.

2613. ——— : 1980 : Tribal deserting border villages in Tripura. *Statesman*, April 12.

2614. ——— : 1980 : Tripura tribals plan agitation. *Statesman*, May 22.

2615. ——— : 1980 : Editorial : Tripura's morning after ...*Statesman*, June 18.

2616. ——— : 1980 : Tripura tribal extremist leaders held. *Statesman*, Aug. 4.

2617. ——— : 1980 : Two tribal youth found dead. *Statesman*, Sept. 5.

2618. ——— : 1980 : Tribals kill 5 traders in North Tripura. *Statesman*, Nov. 29.

2619. ——— : 1981 : Tribal influx continues. *Statesman*, June 29.

2620. ——— : 1981 : 3000 Bangladesh tribals cross border. *Statesman*, June 30.

2621. ——— : 1981 : Tribal Influx : Bangladesh charges against India. *Statesman*, Oct. 17.

2622. ——— : 1981 : 100,000 tribals face starvation. *Statesman*, Nov. 8.

2623. ——— : 1981 : Tribals raid police post in Tripura. *Statesman*, Nov. 22.

2624. ——— : 1982 : Tribals in Tripura intensify activity. *Statesman*, Jan. 14.

2625. ——— : 1982 : Tripura tribal leader held. *Statesman*, Jan 30.

2626. ——— : 1982 : Tripura tribals active. *Statesman*, May 28.

2627. **Statesman** : 1983 : Tripura Front's move on tribal council *Statesman,* Feb. 15.

2628. ——— : 1983 : Chakma Influx, a political issue in Mizoram. *Statesman,* July 1.

2629. ——— : 1987 : General alert in Tripura. *Statesman,* Jan. 19 : 1(5).

2630. ——— : 1987 : Fresh Chakma influx. *Statesman,* , Jan. 20 : 1(3).

2631. ——— : 1987 : The rebels arrested. *Statesman,* Jan. 21 : 16(5).

2632. ——— : 1987 : Tripura to list 'disturbed' areas. *Statesman,* Jan. 7 : 1(2-4).

2633. ——— : 1987 : Repatriation sure death for Chakmas. *Statesman,* Jan. 8 : 7(1-2).

2634. ——— : 1987 : Editorial : School for rebels. *Statesman,* Jan. 8 : 8(3-4).

2635. ——— : 1987 : Tripura border areas to be sealed. *Statesman,* Jan. 8 : 1(7-8).

2636. ——— : 1987 : TNV urges agitation for ethnic division of Tripura. *Statesman,* Jan. 14 : 16(3-4).

2637. ——— : 1987 : TNV may be outlawed soon. *Statesman,* Jan. 15 : 9(2-5).

2638. ——— : 1987 : General alert in Tripura. *Statesman,* Jan. 19 : 1(5).

2639. ——— : 1987 : TNV hideouts smashed. *Statesman,* Jan. 22 : 1(5).

2640. ——— : 1987 : TNV banned by Centre. *Statesman,* Jan. 23 : 1(2-3), 9(2).

2641. ——— : 1987 : Red alert in Tripura. *Statesman,* Jan. 26 : 9(2-3).

2642. ——— : 1987 : More refugees try to enter Tripura. *Statesman,* Feb. 2 : 9(5).

2643. ——— : 1987 : Chakmas prevented from returning, says Dhaka. *Statesman,* March 23 : 13(3-5).

2644. ——— : 1987 : Bangladesh agrees to take back Chakma. *Statesman,* April 27 : 1(2-3).

2645. Statesman : 1987 : Margis' ultimatum to Tripura. *Statesman*, June 29 : 7(2-4).

2646. ——— : 1987 : Tripura's natural gas resource largely unused. *Statesman*, July 9 : 3(4-5).

2647. ——— : 1987 : Editorial : warning up in Tripura. *Statesman*, Sept. 14 : 8(2-3).

2648. ——— : 1987 : Chakmas want deployment of peace keeping force. *Statesman*, Oct. 15 : 11(1-3).

2649. ——— : 1987 : Editorial : Violence in Tripura. *Statesman*, Oct. 17 : 8(2-3).

2650. ——— : 1988 : Security plan for Tripura. *Statesman*, Jan. 16 : 1(4).

2651. ——— : 1988 : Battle lines drawn for Tripura election. *Statesman*, Jan. 16 : 4(3-5).

2652. ——— : 1988 : Political luminaries descend on Tripura. *Statesman*, Jan. 24 : 7(2-4).

2653. ——— : 1988 : Cong(I) plea for more forces in Tripura. *Statesman*, Jan. 24 : 12(4-5).

2654. ——— : 1988 : 'Belated steps to curb TNV insurgency'. *Statesman*, Jan. 25 : 9(2-4).

2655. ——— : 1988 : More violence by TNV guerrillas feared. *Statesman*, Jan. 26 : 9(2-4).

2656. ——— : 1988 : More areas around Tripura border declared disturbed, *Statesman*, Jan. 28 : 1(4-5).

2657. ——— : 1988 : EMS confident of win in Tripura. *Statesman*, Jan. 29. 7(1-2).

2658. ——— : 1988 : Editorial : Protecting Tripura. *Statesman*, Jan. 31 : 8(2-3).

2659. ——— : 1988 : Central decision condemned. *Statesman*, Jan. 31 : 14(4-5).

2660. ——— : 1988 : Tripura people's confidence restored. *Statesman*, Feb. 3 : 9(5-6).

2661. ——— : 1988 : TNV not involved in all killings. *Statesman*, Feb. 4 : 9(6-7).

2662. ——— : 1988 : Dishonest victory, says CPI(M). *Statesman*, Feb. 5 : 1(4-5).

2663. **Statesman** : 1988 : 'Moral win for front' : Deb. *Statesman*, Feb. 5 : 9(3-5).

2664. ——— : 1988 : Army induction pre-planned. *Statesman*, Feb. 5 : 9(5).

2665. ——— : 1988 : 'Polls reduced to a farce' : Nirpen. *Statesman*, Feb. 6 : 9(4-7).

2666. ——— : 1988 : Vote bank of Cong(I), TUJS enlarged. *Statesman*, Feb. 6 : 9(5-7).

2667. ——— : 1988 : 'Tripura Day' in W.B. on Feb. 10. *Statesman*, Feb. 6 : 9(5-7).

2668. ——— : 1988 : TNV helped in Cong(I) victory. *Statesman*, Feb. 11 : 9(5-7).

2669. ——— : 1988 : People must resist TNV insurgents. *Statesman*, Feb. 17 : 13(3-4).

2670. ——— : 1988 : NSA enforced in Tripura. *Statesman*, Feb. 19 : 1(6-7).

2671. ——— : 1988 : Tripura C.M. denies army excesses. *Statesman*, March 20 : 3(4-5).

2672. ——— : 1988 : Editorial : Next step in Tripura. *Statesman*, March 26 : 8(2-3).

2673. ——— : 1988 : P.M. stresses stronger TUJS-Cong(I) bonds. *Statesman*, April 13 : 7(5-7).

2674. ——— : 1988 : Campaign for Tripura seat gathers momentum. *Statesman*, April 22 : 7(6-8).

2675. ——— : 1988 : Chakmas to be told to return. *Statesman*, May 6 : 3(4-6).

2676. ——— : 1988 : TNV men 'surrendering' to army. *Statesman*, May 7 : 7(3-4).

2677. ——— : 1988 : India's first pineapple juice concentration plant at Nalkata, Tripura. *Statesman*, June 10 : 7(1- 7).

2678. ——— : 1988 : Accord to end insurgency in Tripura. *Statesman*, Aug. 13 : 1(2-3).

2679. ——— : 1988 : CPI(M) alleges Congress(I)-TNV conspriracy. *Statesman*, Aug. 14 : 1(3-4).

2680. ——— : 1988 : Tripura. *Statesman*, Aug. 14.

2681. **Statesman** : 1988 : TNV to lay down arms by Sept. 12. *Statesman,* Aug. 15 : 1(5), 9(5).

2682. ——— : 1988 : Editorial : Farewell to arms. *Statesman,* Sept. 10 : 8(2-3).

2683. ——— : 1988 : Tripura's land problem needs to be solved. *Statesman,* Sept. 13 : 9(6-8).

2684. ——— : 1988 : Tripura C.M. Fears ethnic trouble. *Statesman,* Sept. 25 : 7(3-4).

2685. ——— : 1988 : Editorial : Tripura's Third Force'. *Statesman,* Sept. 26 : 8(2-3).

2686. ——— : 1988 : Tripura CPI(M) morale shaken. *Statesman,* Oct. 21 : 7(6-7).

2687. ——— : 1988 : Chakmas eager to return home but feel insecure. *Statesman,* Nov. 10 : 4(5-6).

2688. ——— : 1988 : More powers for Tripura, Mizoram councils. *Statesman,* Dec. 6 : 1(2-4).

2689. ——— : 1988 : TNV comes out as political party. *Statesman,* Dec. 11 : 1(8).

2690. ——— : 1988 : Editorial : TNV in the field. *Statesman,* Dec. 18 : 6(2-3).

2691. ——— : 1988 : Tripura-Assam highway. *Statesman,* Dec. 22 : 4(3).

2692. ——— : 1989 : Walkout in Tripura Assembly. *Statesman,* Jan. 3 : 9(2-4).

2693. ——— : 1989 : Tripura revokes policemen's right to form union. *Statesman,* Jan. 13 : 7(2-4).

2694. ——— : 1989 : TNLF renews 'sovereign Tripura' demand. *Statesman,* Feb. 1 : 12(3-5).

2695. ——— : 1989 : Students torture widens Tripura Cong-I rift. *Statesman,* Feb. 3 : 9(2-6).

2696. ——— : 1989 : Concern over rise in Tripura violence. *Statesman,* Feb. 9 : 4(4-5).

2697. ——— : 1989 : Round the State : Tension mounting in Tripura over land occupation. *Statesman,* March 8 : 11(4-5).

2698. ——— : 1989 : Drug racketeers active in Tripura. *Statesman,* March 16 : 4(1-2).

2699. **Statesman** : 1989 : Round the State : 'Tripura peaceful', says Gen. Krishna Rao. *Statesman*, May 8 : 10(4-5).

2700. ——— : 1989 : Round the States : Tripura law and order problems exaggerated. *Statesman*, May 15 : 13(3-4).

2701. ——— : 1989 : Chakma refugees. Dhaka keen on early repatriation. *Statesman*, May 18 : 1(2-4).

2702. ——— : 1989 : Rise in Trans-border crimes in Tripura. *Statesman*, May 19 : 13(1-2).

2703. ——— : 1989 : Chakma influx continues. *Statesman*, May 29 : 1(4).

2704. ——— : 1989 : Dhaka getting the better of Chakma militants. *Statesman*, May 29 : 9(2-7).

2705. ——— : 1989 : Influx continue. *Statesman*, June 2 : 1(6).

2706. ——— : 1989 : Biggest Chakma influx likely. *Statesman*, June 4 : 7(7-8).

2707. ——— : 1989 : Chakma appeal to help tribal refugees. *Statesman*, June 6 : 7(7-8).

2708. ——— : 1989 : 'Dhaka's hand behind killings in Chittagong Hill Tracts'. *Statesman*, June 8 : 9(2-4).

2709. ——— : 1989 : Editorial : Victims of Partition. *Statesman*, June 12 : 8(2-3).

2710. ——— : 1989 : Tripura to 'crush' TNLF. *Statesman*, June 29 : 4(3-4).

2711. ——— : 1989 : TNLF trying to build up base in Chittagong hills. *Statesman*, June 30 : 13(3-4).

2712. ——— : 1989 : Centre's silence worries Chakma leaders. *Statesman*, July 4 : 12(3-4).

2713. ——— : 1989 : Centre urged to take up Chakma issue with Dhaka. *Statesman*, July 10 : 9(3-5).

2714. ——— : 1989 : TNV dis-satisfied with accord implementation. *Statesman*, July 13 : 4(2-5).

2715. ——— : 1989 : ILO criticizes Tripura. *Statesman*, July 16 : 7(2).

2716. ——— : 1989 : Move to weaken TUJS. *Statesman*, July 25 : 4(2-4).

2717. **Statesman** : 1989 : Mass rigging hallmark of Tripura polls. *Statesman*, Dec. 19 : 4(1-2).

2718. ——— : 1989 : TUJS flays Cong(I) for rigging polls. *Statesman*, Dec. 22 : 7(3-4).

2719. ——— : 1989 : Unrest among Tripura hills tribes. *Statesman*, Dec. 28 : 7(2-4).

2720. ——— : 1990 : Tripura CPI(M) facing stiff criticism within party *Statesman*, January 9 : 4(1-3).

2721. ——— : 1990 : Tussle over funds in Tripura. *Statesman*, Jan. 15 : 7(3-4).

2722. ——— : 1990 : TNV's concern over influx. *Statesman*, Jan. 15 : 9(4-5).

2723. ——— : 1990 : The iron horse travels to the north-east. *Statesman*, Jan. 15 : 11(2-4).

2724. ——— : 1990 : CPI(M) had accepted the Inner Line system, TUJS demand. *Statesman*, March 6.

2725. ——— : 1990 : Tribals pawns in Tripura politics. *Statesman*, March 6 : 1(2-5).

2726. ——— : 1990 : TUJS flays Cong-I *Statesman*, March 15 : 4(5-6).

2727. ——— : 1990 : Tripura C.M. blasts about worsening law and order. *Statesman*, March 28 : 16(3-5).

2728. ——— : 1990 : Tripura to rationalize sales tax. *Statesman*, March 30 : 11(2-4).

2729. ——— : 1990 : Unruly scenes in Tripura house, *Statesman*, April 4 : 7(2-4).

2730. ——— : 1990 : TUJS imposes condition on Congress(I). *Statesman*, April 11 : 12(4-5).

2731. ——— : 1990 : Manipuris plan peaceful stir. *Statesman*, April 12 : 4(2-4). [Tripura-Manipuris].

2732. ——— : 1990 : Call for election boycott in Tripura. *Statesman*, April 14 : 16(6).

2733. ——— : 1990 : Plea for identity cards in Tripura. *Statesman*, April 16 : 7(6).

2734. ——— : 1990 : Tripura tribal students plan 'rasta roko' *Statesman*, May 3 : 4(6).

2735. Statesman : 1990 : Repatriation of Chakmas more uncertain. *Statesman,* May 17 : 4(1).

2736. ——— : 1990 : TNV Joins Congress(I), TUJS allience for Tripura polls. *Statesman,* June 5 : 4(2-4).

2737. ——- : 1990 : Chakma unwilling, to return. *Statesman,* June 5 : 9(6-8).

2738. ——— : 1990 : TNV to contest. *Statesman,* June 7 : 7(1).

2739. ——— : 1990 : Vendetta in Tripura. *Statesman,* June 7: 7(2-4).

2740. ——— : 1990 : CPI(M) fails to reach accord with Tripura dal. *Statesman,* June 8 : 16(4-5).

2741. ——— : 1990 : Battle lines drawn for ADC elections in Tripura. *Statesman,* June 11 : 7(3-5).

2742. ——— : 1990 : Violence before Tripura polls. *Statesman,* July 2 : 7(4-5).

2743. ——— : 1990 : TUJS in a dilemma over inner-line permit rules. *Statesman,* July 3 : 12(3-5).

2744. ——— : 1990 : 10 die in Tripura poll violence. *Statesman,* July 9 : 1(2-4).

2745. ——— : 1990 : Wild life in danger in Tripura. *Statesman,* July 10 : 5(1-4).

2746. ——— : 1990 : Tripura Council Poll : Absolute majority for Cong(I)—— TUJS alliance. *Statesman,* July 11 : 1(3- 4).

2747. ——— : 1990 : Editorial : Outcome in Tripura. *Statesman,* July 16 : 6(2-3).

2748. ——— : 1990 : Congress-I, CPI(M) blamed for Tripura violence. *Statesman,* July 17 : 4(5-6).

2749. ——— : 1990 : Tripura Poll violence worries Centre. *Statesman,* July 17 : 5(2-3).

2750. ——— : 1990 : Mufti's 'warning unnerves' Tripura coalition. *Statesman,* July 19 : 12(4-5).

2751. ——— : 1990 : Tripura Janata Dal wants ADC poll scrapped. *Statesman,* July 20 : 16(3-5).

2752. ——— : 1990 : CPI(M) trying to topple Tripura coalition. *Statesman,* July 21 : 12(2-4).

2753. Statesman : 1990 : Tripura Governor to convene all party meeting. *Statesman,* July 26 : 9(2-3).

2754. ——— : 1990 : Tripura tribals getting alienated. *Statesman,* Aug. 19 : 5(8).

2755. ——— : 1990 : Tension mounting afresh in Tripura subdivision *Statesman,* Aug. 28 : 6(1-3).

2756. ——— : 1990 : Region of terror in Tripura. *Statesman,* Sept. 11 : 3(6).

2757. ——— : 1990 : TUJS, CPI(M) oppose delimitation of constituencies. *Statesman,* Oct. 3 : 12(2-5).

2758. ——— : 1990 : Tripura killings on the rise. *Statesman,* Oct. 21 : 9(1-3).

2759. ——— : 1990 : Plea to develop North-East. *Statesman,* Oct. 21 : 9(2-3) [Agartala].

2760. ——— : 1990 : Buddhist statue found in Tripura. *Statesman,* Oct. 25 : 4(2-3).

2761. ——— : 1990 : Rehabilitation of Chakma refugees planned. *Statesman,* Oct. 30 : 4(1).

2762. ——— : 1990 : Chakma camps invite international. *Statesman,* Nov. 24 : 7(2-6).

2763. ——— : 1990 : New Tripura insurgent unit terrorising people. *Statesman,* Nov. 26 : 7(2-4).

2764. ——— : 1990 : Chakma leaders fear tribal influx. *Statesman,* Nov. 30 : 7(2-6).

2765. ——— : 1990 : Tripura C.M. warns of 'backlash' in Bangladesh. *Statesman,* Dec. 2 : 7(6-8).

2766. ——— : 1990 : Chakma support for Bangla agitators. *Statesman,* Dec. 4 : 7(3-4).

2767. ——— : 1990 : President's assurance to Tripura C.M. *Statesman,* Dec. 13 : 12(4-5).

2768. ——— : 1990 : Tripura day observed. *Statesman,* Dec. 19 : 3(4-5).

2769. ——— : 1990 : Agitation against Tripura Ministers. *Statesman,* Dec. 21 : 12(3-4).

2770. ——— : 1990 : Chakmas demand fair polls in hill tracts. *Statesman,* Dec. 21 : 12(3-4).

2771. **Statesman** : 1990 : TUJS, CPI(M) agree on refugees. *Statesman,* Dec. 24 : 9(2-5).

2772. ——— : 1990 : Denudation of Tripura forests. *Statesman,* Dec. 25 : 4(4).

2773. ——— : 1990 : Tripura C.M. criticizes CPI(M) hypocrisy. *Statesman,* Dec. 27 : 7(8).

2774. ——— : 1990 : Tripura to flush out extremists. *Statesman.* Dec. 27 : 7(8).

2775. ——— : 1990 : Infant killed by new tribal outfit in Tripura. *Statesman,* Dec. 28 : 12(4).

2776. ——— : 1990 : Fresh violence in Tripura. *Statesman,* Dec. 29 : 7(2-4).

2777. ——— : 1991 : Tripura Cong-I in shambles. *Statesman,* Jan. 5 : 7(2-4).

2778. ——— : 1991 : 'Law and order in Tripura better'. *Statesman,* Jan. 8 : 4(1).

2779. ——— : 1991 : Editorial : Vanishing forests. *Statesman,* Jan. 12: 6(2-3).

2780. ——— : 1991 : Tribal shot dead by Tripura rebel gang. *Statesman,* Jan. 23 : 7(5-6).

2781. ——— : 1991 : Chakma leaders reject Dhaka's proposal. *Statesman,* Feb. 12 : 9(1).

2782. ——— : 1991 : Tripura CM's charge against CPI(M). *Statesman,* Feb. 20 : 7(7).

2783. ——— : 1991 : U.N. steps on Chakma evacuees in Tripura. *Statesman,* March 12 : 4(2-4).

2784. ——— : 1991 : In fighting a challenge to Tripura coalition. *Statesman,* March 16 : 12(3-4).

2785. ——— : 1991 : Chakmas refuse to return. *Statesman,* March 26 : 4(2-4).

2786. ——— : 1991 : 'Tripura is aids-free'. *Statesman,* March 28 : 4(5).

2787. ——— . 1991 : Poll violence in Tripura feared. *Statesman,* March 28 : 4(6-7).

2788. ——— : 1991 : Arsonists target schools in Tripura. *Statesman,* April 2 : 4(2-3).

2789. Statesman : 1991 : TUJS-Cong(I) fall-out. *Statesman*, April 2 : 1(8).

2790. ——— : 1991 : Cong-I infighting worsens over Tripura candidates. *Statesman*, April 2 : 4(2-4).

2791. ——— : 1991 : Cong-I, CPI-M main rivals in Tripura. *Statesman*, April 9 : 12(4-5).

2792. ——— : 1991 : Tripura IAS officers' protest: 'Fair elections unlikely'. *Statesman*, April 12 : 11(1-3).

2793. ——— : 1991 : Call for election boycott in Tripura. *Statesman*, April 14 : 16(6).

2794. ——— : 1991 : Regional parties in North-East threat to Cong-I. *Statesman*, April 23 : 4(2-3).

2795. ——— : 1991 : Tripura, Mizoram and Cachar still cut off. *Statesman*, May 10 : 7(4-5).

2796. ——— : 1991 : Tripura rejects proposal for disturbed areas. *Statesman*, June 1 : 7(2-4).

2797. ——— : 1991 : Realignment of tribal forces in Tripura likely. *Statesman*, July 5 : 4(2-5).

2798. ——— : 1991 : Panel's proposal on CHT issue prompts 'limited autonomy' offer by Dhaka. *Statesman*, July 11 : 4(5-8).

2799. ——— : 1991 : Tripura Government in shambles. *Statesman*, Aug. 3 : 9(2-4).

2800. ——— : 1991 : Growing indiscipline in Tripura police. *Statesman*, Aug. 9 : 9(1-2).

2801. ——— : 1991 : Spurt in crime in Tripura. *Statesman*, Sept. 1 : 16(4-5).

2802. ——— : 1991 : Tripura projects to be cleared. *Statesman*, Sept. 3 : 4(1).

2803. ——— : 1991 : Seven killed in Tripura. *Statesman*, Sept. 3 : 4(2-3).

2804. ——— : 1991 : Concern over vandalism in Tripura Colleges. *Statesman*, Sept. 4 : 9(3-4).

2805. ——— : 1991 : Tripura C.M. beleaguered by dissidents. *Statesman*, Sept. 12 : 4(4-6).

2806. ——— : 1991 : Tripura C.M. trying to hide facts. *Statesman*, Sept. 26 : 4(2-4).

2807. **Statesman** : 1991 : Grain bins empty in Tripura. *Statesman*, Sept. 17 : 9(4-5).

2808. ——— : 1991 : Demand for 'national forum' on Chittagong Hill Tracts. *Statesman*, Oct. 3 : 9(6-8).

2809. ——— : 1991 : ATTF ambush escort vehicle, two killed. *Statesman*, Oct. 12 : 12(3-4).

2810. ——— : 1991 : Tripura Government denies starvation deaths. *Statesman*, Nov. 5 : 4(2-4).

2811. ——— : 1991 : Revolt in Tripura CPI(M) more pronounced, 100 leave party. *Statesman*, Nov. 8 : 12(2-5).

2812. ——— : 1991 : Gogoi urged to supply foodgrains to Tripura. *Statesman*, Nov. 8 : 8(1).

2813. ——— : 1991 : Dhaka unwilling to open border roads for India. *Statesman*, Nov. 24 : 12(3-4).

2814. ——— : 1991 : 'Struggle' to continue, feel CPI(M) rebels in Tripura. *Statesman*, Dec. 12 : 4(2-4).

2815. ——— : 1992 : Hunt for Tripura rebels stepped up. *Statesman*, Jan. 5 : 7(6-8).

2816. ——— : 1992 : Editorial : Hunger in Tripura. *Statesman*, Jan. 6 : 6(2-3).

2817. ——— : 1992 : BSF committing excesses : Tripura C.M. *Statesman*, Jan. 6 : 7(2-5).

2818. ——— : 1992 : Tripura tribals fighting among themselves. *Statesman*, Jan. 7 : 4(5).

2819. ——— : 1992 : Centre worried about Tripura situation. *Statesman*, Jan. 12 : 7(2-5).

2820. ——— : 1992 : ONGC to step up activities in Tripura. *Statesman*, Jan. 14 : 4(1).

2821. ——— : 1992 : Hydel project threatens historical battle field. *Statesman*, Jan. 15 : 16(4-6).

2822. ——— : 1992 : TUJS worried over tribal's migration to Bangladesh. *Statesman*, Jan. 21 : 7(6-8).

2823. ——— : 1992 Spate of violence in Tripura. *Statesman*, Jan. 29 : 16(4-6).

2824. **Statistical Department** : 1971 : *Statistical outline of Tripura, 1971*. Agartala, Statistical Deptt., Govt. of Tripura.

2825. ——— : 1976 : *Some Basic Statistics of Tripura, 1976*. Agartala, Statistical Deptt., Govt. of Tripura.

2826. ——— : 1981 : *Statistical Abstract : Tripura*. Agartala, Directorate of Statistics, Govt. of Tripura, 98p.

2827. ——— : 1983 : *Statistical Outline of Tripura*. Agartala, Statistical Deptt., Govt. of Tripura, 67p.

2828. ——— : ? : *National Sample Survey (Twenty Second Round): Land Utilisation Survey, vol. 7*. Agartala, Statistical Deptt., Govt. of Tripura.

2829. ——— : 1985 : *Some Basic Statistics of Tripura*. Agartala, Directorate of Statistics, Govt. of Tripura.

2830. **Subba, Tanka B.** : 1988 : Inter-ethnic relationship in northeast India and the "Negative Solidarity" thesis. *Human Science*, 37(4), Dec. : 369-77.

2831. **Sundar Rajan, K.R.** : 1988 : Spectre of instability. *Amrita Bazar Patrika*, Feb. 10 : 6(3-6).

2832. **Sur, H.K.** : 1986 : *British relations with the State of Tripura*. Agartala, Published by the author, 69p.

2833. **Surita, Pearson** : 1990 : A Passage to Burma. *Statesman, Sunday Miscellany*, March 18 : 1(1-5).

2834. **Survey of India** : 1981 : *Map of North Eastern Region of India*. Dehradun, Survey of India, 5p.

2835. **Sutherland, H.C.** : 1860 : Tipperah. *Calcutta Review*, 35(70).

2836. **Swell, G.G.** : 1967 : Problems of the Hill Areas. *Illustrated Weekly of India*, 88(16), May 21 : 52-3.

2837. ——— : 1967 : Tripura : demand for Scheduled Tribal Area. *Peoples' Democracy*, 3(30), July 23 : 5.

2838. ——— : 1974 : Tripura : Tribal unrest mounting. *Himalaya News Round-Up*, No. 1, Jan. 3 : 20.

T

2839. **Tagore, Rabindranath** : 1958 : *On the Edges of Time.* Bombay, Orient Longmans.

2840. **Talukdar, Sailen** : 1987 : Khadi and village industries in North East. *Assam Tribune,* April 24 : 4(1-2).

2841. **Talukdar, S.P.** : 1974 : The place of Chakma in Mizo society. *North Eastern Affairs,* 3(2-3), July-Dec. : 27-28 and 34.

2842. ——— : 1988 : *The Chakmas, Life and Struggle.* Delhi, Gyan Pubg. House, 250p.

2843. **Telegraph** : 1988 : Memorandum of understanding with TNV. *Telegraph* (Calcutta), Aug. 12.

2844. ——— : 1990 : Interview with Tripura Chief Minister Sudhir Ranjan Majumdar. *Telegraph,* July 9:1.

2845. **Tewari, C.P.** : 1978 : Need for a new model of development for hill areas. *Himalaya : Man and Nature,* 1(11), April : 25-7.

2846. **Thakkar, A.V.** : 1941 : Census of Assam Tribals. *Man in India,* XXI (4), Oct.-Dec. : 243-47.

2847. **Thakur, Pankaj** : 1982 : *India's North East.* Guwahati, Prakash Pubg. House, Assam.

2848. **Thakur, S.C.** : 1986 : Tribal turmoil in Bangladesh. *Assam Tribune,* July 22 : 4(3-6) [Chakma refugees].

2849. **Thanga, Lal Biak** : 1978 : *The Mizos.* Gauhati, United Pubs., 185p.

2850. **Thaosen, S.R.** : 1967 : Why the Hills and Plains do not unite ? *(In) A Common Perspective for North East India (Eds.)* by Rathin Mitra *and* B. Das Gupta. Calcutta, Pub. by Pannalal Das Gupta : 176-79.

2851. **Thompson, W.H.** : 1923 : Chakma. *(In) Census of India, 1921, vol. V : Bengal, pt. I, Report.* Calcutta, Govt. Press, 362p.

2852. **Thomton, E.** : 1857 : *Gazetteer of the Territories under the Government of East India Company and of Native State.* 997p.

2853. **Thusu, Kidar Nath** : 1962 : The Riang agricultural practices. *Bulletin of Anth. Surv. of India,* 11(3-4) : 157-74.

2854. **Times of India** : 1970 : Tripura. *Times of India,* Nov. 18.

2855. ——— : 1971 : Editorial : Tripura take-over. *Times of India,* Nov. 24 : 8(2).

2856. ——— : 1974 : Tribals on rampage. *Times of India,* Oct. 25.

2857. ——— : 1979 : Tripura tribals planning non-co-operation movement : *T.O.I.,* Jan. 5.

2858. ——— : 1979 : Tribal extremists are active. *T.O.I.,* Jan. 23.

2859. ——— : 1979 : Tripura's travails. *T.O.I.,* Jan. 29 : 6(2).

2860. ——— : 1979 : Tripura body revises stand on tribal bill. *T.O.I.,* Jan. 29.

2861. ——— : 1980 : Editorial : Tripura violence. *T.O.I.,* July 2.

2862. ——— : 1981 : TUJS calls for action on tribal-index. *T.O.I.,* Sept. 1.

2863. ——— : 1981 : Tripura, PLA, Manipur. *T.O.I.,* Nov. 26.

2864. ——— : 1982 : Tribal dialect in Tripura-Schools. *T.O.I.,* June 18.

2865. ——— : 1983 : Tripura rebel group returns to hide-out. *T.O.I.,* March 14.

2866. ——— : 1986 : Four Left Front supporters shot by TNV rebels. *T.O.I.,* March 12 : 1(1-3).

2867. ——— : 1986 : Five shot by TNV men. *T.O.I.,* April 6 : 1(5-7).

2868. ——— : 1986 : Changing Hill Tribals urge end to colonisation. *T.O.I.,* May 11 : 5(1-2).

2869. ——— : 1986 : TNV extremists kill 14. *T.O.I.,* Aug. 31 : 1(5-7).

2870. ——— : 1986 : Editorial : Carnage in Tripura. *T.O.I.,* Sept. 2 : 8(1-2).

2871. ——— : 1986 : TNV extremists ambush police jeep : Seven killed. *T.O.I.,* Sept. 14 : 1(1-3).

2872. **Times of India** : 1986 : Massive hunt on as TNV men slay 13. *T.O.I.*, Dec. 6 : 1(7-8).

2873. ——— : 1986 : Centre expresses concern over TNV killings. *T.O.I.*, Dec. 25 : 1(7-8).

2874. ——— : 1986 : TNV rebels kill four of family. *T.O.I.*, Dec. 26 : 1(7-8).

2875. ——— : 1986 : Total bandh in 3 towns. *T.O.I.*, Dec. 27 : 1(3).

2876. ——— : 1986 : TNV guerillas kill eight of family. *T.O.I.*, Dec. 27 : 1(1-3).

2877. ——— : 1986 : Editorial : Massacres in Tripura. *T.O.I.*, Dec. 27 : 6(1-2).

2878. ——— : 1986 : Chidambaram leaving for Agartala. *T.O.I.*, Dec. 28 : 1(1-2).

2879. ——— : 1986 : Tripura CM caught in a dilemma. *T.O.I.*, Dec. 28 : 1(2-5), 9(5).

2880. ——— : 1986 : BJP for 'drastic action' to halt Tripura killings. *T.O.I.*, Dec. 28 : 3(4).

2881. ——— : 1986 : Chidambaram has talks in Tripura. *T.O.I.*, Dec. 29 : 1(1-2).

2882. ——— : 1987 : Extremist tie ups in N East. *T.O.I.*, Jan. 8 : 1(2-5).

2883. ——— : 1987 : Steps urged to curb Chakmas' inflow. *T.O.I.*, Jan. 14 : 5(2-3).

2884. ——— : 1987 : General alert in Tripura. *T.O.I.*, Jan. 19 : 5(1-3).

2885. ——— : 1987 : Plea for UN force to 'save' Chakma. *T.O.I.* Jan. 22 : 7(1-2).

2886. ——— : 1987 : TNV banned. *T.O.I.*, Jan. 23 : 1(4).

2887. ——— : 1987 : Anti-extremist drive in Tripura. *T.O.I.*, Jan. 23 : 7(1-3).

2888. ——— : 1987 : TNV men kill 5 more non-tribals. *T.O.I.*, Jan. 26 : 1(1-2).

2889. ——— : 1987 : Chakmas raid village, kill tribesman. *T.O.I.*, Feb. 1 : 16(2-3).

2890. ——— : 1987 : TNV declared unlawful. *T.O.I.*, Feb. 5 : 1(7).

2891. **Times of India** : 1987 : Quit Tripura Notice by TNV to foreigners. *T.O.I.*, Feb. 7 : 1(7).

2892. ——— : 1987 : 'TNV enjoys Bangla govt's patronage'. *T.O.I.*, March 3 : 7(1-2).

2893. ——— : 1987 : Chakma influx continues. *T.O.I.*, March 21 : 3(2-4).

2894. ——— : 1987 : Editorial : The forgotten Chakmas. *T.O.I.*, March 25 : 6(1-2).

2895. **Tippera State Gazetteer** : 1905 : *Hill Tippera State Gazetteer (Statistics, 1901-'02).* Calcutta, Bengal Secretariat Book Depot, 21p.

2896. **Tiwari, S.P.** *and* **Chauhan, D.K.** : 1989 : Vanishing floral wealth and necessity of a green museum in North East India. *Jour. of Indian Museum* (New Delhi), XLV : 32- 40.

2897. **Tribal Research** : 1974 : Indebtedness and land alienation Survey of Tribal family under Mohanpur Block. *Bulletin of the Dir. of Tribal Research*, (Agartala), vol. 1, part I, II, III.

2898. **Tribal Research Institute** : 1978 : *The Lushais 1878-1889.* Aizawl, T.R.I. *(Reprinted)* [Hill Tippera Posts] : 6-9.

2899. ——— : 1986 : *A Brief Account of Reangs in Mizoram.* Aizawl, T.R.I., 104p.

2900. ——— : 1980 : *Foreign and Political Department Report, 1874 on Eastern Boundary of Hill Tippera.* Aizawl, T.R.I. (*Reprint* of 1874).

2901. ——— : 1983 : *Upajati unnayane grihita bivinna karmasuchi (in Bengali).* Agartala, T.R.I., 22p.

2902. ——— : 1992 : *The Lushais of Jampui Hills in Tripura.* Agartala, T.R.I. *(in Press).*

2903. —— : 1992 : *The Garos of Tripura.* Agartala, T.R.I. *(in Press).*

2904. **Tripathi, Satya Narayan** : 1987 : *Letters to the Editor* : North East and Geo politics. *Assam Tribune,* July 2 : 4(3-5).

2905. **Tripura Administration** : ? : *Rajmala : An Account of the Kings of Tripura (in Bengali)*. Agartala, Tripura Administration.

2906. ——— : 1958 : *Rehabilitation in Tripura*. Agartala, Deptt. of Refugee Rehabilitation, Tripura Admins., 41p.

2907. ——— : 1960 : *Annual Administration Report 1959-'60*. Agartala, Tripura Admn., 120p.

2908. ——— : 1961 : *Annual Administration Report of the Union Territory of Tripura for the year 1960-'61*. Agartala, Tripura Admn., 123p.

2909. ——— : 1962 : *Tripura Code, vol.II*. Agartala, Tripura Admn., 185p.

2910. ——— : 1962 : *Annual Administration Report of Union Territory of Tripura for 1961-62*. Agartala, Tripura Admn., 138p.

2911. ——— : 1963 : *Annual Administrative Report (1962-'63)*. Agartala, Tripura Admn., 57p.

2912. ——— : 1964 : *Annual Administrative Report of Tripura*. Agartala, Tripura Admn., 56p.

2913. **Tripura Agriculture** : 1962 : *Kahrif campaign in Tripura*. Agartala, Directorate of Agriculture, 11p.

2914. **Tripura Agriculture** : 1964 : *Conserve soil for more production*. Agartala, Directorate of Agriculture, 7p.

2915. ——— ; 1973 : *Fifteenth Report of Fisher scheme*. Agartala, Dir. of Agriculture, 8p.

2916. **Tripura Chief Commissioners** : 1972 : *Annual Administration Report, 1969-'70*. Agartala, Office of the Chief Commissioners, 87p.

2917. ——— : 1976 : *Annual Administration Report, 1972-'73*. Agartala, Tripura Chief Commissioner, 117p.

2918. **Tripura Chronicle** : 1973 : Tripura. *Tripura Chronicle* (Agartala), Nov. 1.

2919. **Tripura Community Development** : 1973 : *Community Development, 10th Report*. Agartala, Legislative Assembly Secretariat, 10p.

2920. **Tripura Cultural Affairs** : 1980 : Proceedings of a Seminar on *"National Integration"*, held on Nov. 2-3,

Agartala by Deptt. of Inf. and Cul. Affairs and Tourism, Govt. of Tripura.

2921. **Tripura Darpan** : 1984 : An interview with Binanda Jamatia. *Tripura Darpan, Special Puja Issue*, 20p.

2922. **Tripura Development** : 1965 : *Report of Evaluation Committee 1965*. Agartala, Deptt. of Development, 18p.

2923. **Tripura Education** : 1958 : *Side light on Education in Tripura* Agartala, Tripura Education Directorate, (part-I, 68p. part-II, 32p).

2924. ——— : 1958 : *College students problems in Tripura*. Agartala, Tripura Educational and Vocational Guidance Bureau, 17p.

2925. ——— : 1964 : *Who's who : Persons in Tripura who participated in the struggle for India's freedom 1818-1947*. Agartala, Education Directorate, 44p.

2926. ——— : 1967 : *Rajmala*. Agartala, Tripura Education Directorate.

2927. ——— : 1967 : *Facilities for medical education in India for students of Tripura*. Agartala, Tripura Educational and Vocational Guidance Bureau, 11p.

2928. ——— : 1967 : *Facilities for Technical Education in India for Students of Tripura*. Agartala, Tripura Educational and Vocational Guidance Bureau, 25p.

2929. ——— : 1970 : *An evaluation report on the facilities available to the students and the teachers for study and work in the Higher Secondary Schools in Tripura*. Agartala, Tripura Education Deptt. (Evaluation Organisation), 70p.

2930. ——— : 1970 : *Evaluation Report on Rural Manpower Programme : Kailashahar C.D. Block*. Agartala, Tripura Education (Evaluation) Deptt., 19p.

2931. ——— : 1970 : *Evaluation Report on Rural Manpower Programme : Kamalpur Block*. Agartala, Tripura Education Deptt. (Evaluation), 17p.

2932. ——— : 1970 : *Evaluation Report on the Industrial Estate: Arundhuti Nagar*. Agartala, Tripura Education Deptt. (Evaluation). 37 p.

2933. **Tripura Education** : 1970 : *Evaluation Report on Elementary Education during Plan Periods 1961-'66 in Tripura.* Agartala, Tripura Education Deptt., Evaluation Organisation, 49p.

2934. ——— : 1975 : *Secondary School Students Problem (in Tripura, class VIII-XI).* Agartala, Tripura Educational & Vocational Guidance Bureau, 97p.

2935. ——— : 1975 : *Education in Tripura at a glance.* Agartala, Education Directorate, 21p.

2936. ——— : 1975 : *Progress of education in Tripura, 4th Five Year Plan Period.* Agartala, Tripura Education Directorate, 24p.

2937. ——— : 1975 : *Tripura District Gazetteers.* Agartala, Tripura Education Deptt., 504p.

2938. **Tripura Excise Deptt.** : 1973 : *Tripura Excise 9th Report.* Agartala, Tripura Excise Deptt., 8p.

2939. **Tripura Govt.** : 1319 TE : *Report on the General Administration of the Tippera State for the year 1316 TE (1908-'09).* Agartala, Tripura Govt.

2940. ——— : 1919 : *Act 4 of 1329 TE Tripura Area, 1919 Sections 1618.* Agartala, Review Deptt., Tripura Govt.

2941. ——— : 1923 : *Tripura State and its Ruler.* Agartala, State Press, 8p.

2942. ——— : 1927 : *Investiture ceremony of his highness the Maharaja Manikya Bahadur.* Agartala, Govt. Press, 11p.

2943. ——— : 1937-1940 : *Tripura State, Consolidated Administration Report for 1937-1940.* Agartala, Tripura Govt.

2944. ——— : 1940-'43 : *Tripura State, Consolidated Administration Report for 1350-1352 TE (1940-'43).* Agartala, Tripura Govt.

2945. ——— : 1966 : Land carrying capacity under Jhum in Tripura. *Educational Miscellany,* vol. III, Nos. 1-2. Agartala, Directorate of Education, Govt. of Tripura, 23p.

2946. ——— : ? : *Draft Fourth Five Year Plan Tripura.* Agartala, Planning Deptt., Tripura Govt.

2947. **Tripura Govt.** : 1970 : *List of exhibit : Tripura Govt. Museum*. Agartala, Tripura Govt., Museum Deptt., 19p.

2948. **Tripur Kshatriya Samaj** : 1933-'34 : *Tripur Kshatriya Samaj Samkranta Bibaran Samgraha (in Bengali)*. Agartala, Tripura Kshatriya Samaj, 1343 TE (1933-'34).

2949. **Tripuri, Shyamacharan** *and* **Jamatia, Khagendra** : 1988 : "I was defeated by the TNV, TNV can not help tribals". (Report from tribal leaders). *Amrita Bazar Patrika*, Feb. 17 : 7(2-6).

2950. **Tripura Times** : 1970 : Stray thoughts on co-operative movement. *Tripura Times, Puja Number*, 1377BS : 14-6.

2951 ——— : 1981 : Positive change in rural Tripura. *Tripura Today*, July 15 : 2.

2952. **Tripura Upajati Juba Samity** : 1980 : *Memorandum to the Prime Minister of India submitted by the Tripura Upajati Juba Samity and Tribal Students' Federation*. Agartala, T.U.J.S., (September).

2953. **Tripura Welfare** : ? : *Strength of Achievement motivation and personality of two groups in Tripura*. Agartala, Deptt. of Welfare for Scheduled Caste and Schedule Tribes, Govt. of Tripura, 68p.

2954. **Tunga, Sudhansu S.** : 1975 : Aryanisation in North-East India : The Tipperas. *North Eastern Affairs* (Shillong), 3(4), Jan.-March : 27-8.

2955. **Tyagi, D.** : 1988 : *Book Review* : An Anthology of Tripura *ed* by J. Gan Chaudhuri (ed). New Delhi, Inter-India Publications (1985). *Eastern Anthropologist* (Lucknow), 41(2), April-June : 201-02.

U

2956. **United Bank** : ? : *Report of the fact finding survey on Tripura*. Calcutta, United Bank of India, 77p.

2957. ——— : ? : *District Credit Plan 1980-'82 : West Tripura*. Calcutta, United Bank of India.

2958. ——— : ? : *District Credit Plan 1980-'82 : South Tripura*. Calcutta, United Bank of India.

2959. ——— : ? : *District Credit Plan 1980-'82 : North Tripura*. Calcutta, United Bank of India.

V

2960. **Vadiveln, A.** : 1915 : *The rulling Chiefs, Nobles, Zamindars of India.* Madras, Longandham Bros.

2961. **Vaghaiwalla, R.B.** : 1953 : *Assam, Manipur and Tripura : Census of India 1951, vol. XII.* Delhi, Manager of Publications (2 Parts in 4 volumes).

2962. ——— : 1954 : *Census of India 1951, vol. XII, Assam, Manipur and Tripura, pt. I-A, Report.* Shillong, Printed at the Municipal Printing Press (Bombay).

2963. ——— : 1954 : *Tripura District Census Handbook : Census of India 1951, Tripura.*

2964. **Vanamali, N.** : 1975 : Tamil Parallels for Tripuri Proverbs. *Folklore,* 18(4) : 123-32.

2965. **Vanyajati** : 1980 : Editorial : Unrest in the North Eastern Region. *Vanyajati,* 28(3) : 1-2.

2966. **Venkataramayya Tiruvannamalai, S.** : 1962 : *Tripura rahasya on the mystery beyond the trinity.* Madras, Tiruvannamalai Ramanasraman, 258p.

2967. **Verma, B.** : 1988 : *Insurgency and counter insurgency.* New Delhi, Uppal Publishing House.

2968. **Vidyabinod, Chandrodaya** *(Comp.)* : 1968 : *Silalipi sangraha.* Agartala, Education Directorate, Govt. of Tripura (2nd ed).

2969. **Vidyarthi, L.P.** : 1975 : The future of traditional *primitive* societies : A case study of an Indian Shifting cultivation society. *Eastern Anthropologist,* 28(4), Oct.-Dec. : 313-26.

2970. ——— : 1986 : *Art and Culture of North East India.* Delhi, Publications Division : 62-3, 83-5.

2971. **Vidyarthi, L.P.** *and* **Rai, B.K.** : 1977 : *The Tribal Culture of India.* Delhi, Concept Pubg. Company.

2972. **Viswanath** *(Ed)* : 1967 : Demand of separate Regional Council by Chakmas of Mizo Hills. *Caravan,* June (ii). New Delhi, Delhi Press, 61p.

W

2973. **Wadia, F.K.** : 1975 : *Control of shifting cultivation in the North Eastern Region.* Shillong, Directorate (E & M), North Eastern Council Secretariat.

2974. ——— : 1980 : Control of Shifting Cultivation in the North Eastern Region *(In) Tribal Economy of the North Eastern Region (Ed.)* by T. Mathew. Gauhati, Spectrum Publication : 62-79.

2975. ——— : 1980 : Prospects for alternative sources of income and employment for tribal families *(In) Tribal Economy of North Eastern Region (Ed.)* by T. Mathew. Gauhati, Spectrum Publications : 196-205.

2976. **Webb, C.M.** : 1912 : Palaungs, Pales and Riang *(In) Census of India 1911, vol. IX, Burma, pt. I : Report.* Rangoon, Govt. Press : 278-79.

2977. **Webster, J.E.** : 1906 : *Letter from J.E. Webster, Esq I.C.S.* Officiating Secretary to the Govt. of Eastern Bengal and Assam. Judicial and General Department to the Commissioner of Chittagong Division, No. 3940-J dated Shillong, the 11th April, 1906.

2978. ——— : 1910 : *Eastern Bengal District Gazetteers : Tripura.* Allahabad, Pioneer Press, 119p.

2979. **Wolflang, C.** : 1984 : The North Eastern India, Socio-Economy aspects in soil conservation *(In) Socio Economic Aspects in soil conservation activities with special reference to North Eastern Region* by Soil conservation Deptt., Shillong, Soil Conservation Deptt., Govt. of Meghalaya : 115-21 (Seminar was held at Tura from 17-20 June, 1981).

2980. **Woodthorpe, R.G.** : 1873 : *The Lushai Expedition, 1871-1872.* London, Hurst and Blackett, 338p (*Reprinted* by Spectrum Publications, Gauhati) [It is on Lushai, Manipuri and Tripura].

2981. **Yapri** : 1981 : Tripura. *Yapri* (Kok-Borak-Bengali bilingual Weekly, Agartala), No. 1, July 16, 1981.

2982. **Yojana** : 1972 : Focus : The Reorganised North Eastern Region. *Yojana*, 16(2), Feb. 6.

ADDENDA I

2983. **Adhikari, O.S.** : n.p. : *Land alienation among tribals in Mohanpur Block, West Tripura District. Unpublished* microstudy.

2984. ——— : 1986 : A simple theoretic approach to the problem of land alienation *(In) Land Use Pattern in North East India (Ed)* by B.B. Dutta. Ludhiana, Gagan Publishers : 106-14.

2985. **Amrita Bazar Patrika** : 1984 : Animal and fisheries development in North East. *Am. Baz. Pat.,* Dec. 1 : 7(3-5).

2986. ——— : 1985 : North Eastern Affairs : Tripura's sick Tea Gardens. *Am. Baz. Pat.,* Feb. 23 : 3(4-5).

2987. ——— : 1985 : Tripura Scene : Defalcation and debauchery ended Jamatia. *Am. Baz. Pat.,* March 2 : 8(1-4).

2988. ——— : 1985 : North Eastern Affairs : Tales of Tribal Woe. *Am. Baz. Pat.,* April 13 : 5(4-5), 7(1).

2989. ——— : 1986 : Editorial : Security in North East. *Am. Baz. Pat.,* Jan. 29 : 6(1-2).

2990. ——— : 1986 : Editorial : Appeal to TNV. *Am. Baz. Pat.,* Feb. 28 : 6(1-2).

2991. ——— : 1986 : Attack on Chakma family protested. *Am. Baz. Pat.,* Nov. 12 : 6(5).

2992. **Assam Tribune** : 1986 : Tripura gets a new connection. *A.T.,* March 26 : 3(1-8).

2993. ——— : 1991 : Resuffle in Tripura cabinet soon. *A.T.,* Aug. 26 : 2(6).

2994. ——— : 1991 : Facing extinction in hills of north east. *A.T.,* Aug. 26 : 3(1-2).

2995. ——— : 1991 : Early repatriation of Chakmas urged *A.T.,* Aug 28: 5(6).

2996. ——— : 1991 : Problems of Tripura tea industry. *A.T.,* Sept. 2 : 6(5-6).

2997. **Assam Tribune** : 1991 : Intimidation on Tripura businessmen resented. *A.T.*, Sept. 4 : 5(1-2).

2998. ——— : 1991 : Jampui hill people want Regional Council. *A.T.*, Sept. 21 : 3(3).

2999. ——— : 1991 : Tripura to introduce Inner-Line Permit. *A.T.*, Sept. 21 : 21 : 5(4-5).

3000. ——— : 1991 : ATTF kill 2 in Tripura. *A.T.*, Sept. 27 : 3(4).

3001. ——— : 1991 : TUJS leader killed. *A.T.*, Sept. 28 : 5(3).

3002. ——— : 1991 : 'Rasta Roko' stir in Tripura. *A.T.*, Oct. 2 : 3(5).

3003. ——— : 1991 : TUJS never demanded change of leadership. *A.T.*, Oct. 2 : 3(5-8).

3004. ——— : 1991 : Tripura Govt. to impose TADA. *A.T.*, Oct. 12 : 1(6-7).

3005. ——— : 1991 : Meet on Chittagong Hill Tracts. *A.T.*, Oct. 22 : 3(5-8).

3006. ——— : 1991 : Cong(I) TUJS ties seem to come to an end. *A.T.*, Oct. 24 : 5(5-7).

3007. ——— : 1991 : Anti-Insurgency operation in Tripura begins. *A.T.*, Oct. 24 : 8(5).

3008. ——— : 1991 : More starvation deaths in Tripura. *A.T.*, Oct. 29 : 5(3-5).

3009. ——— : 1991 : Peace accord with TNV runs into rough weather. *A.T.*, Nov. 1 : 3(4).

3010. ——— : 1991 : Reports of starvation deaths 'totally baseless'. *A.T.*, Nov. 7 : 5(3-5).

3011. ——— : 1991 : Over 100 dead in gastro-enteritis in Tripura. *A.T.*, Nov. 7 : 6(3).

3012. ——— : 1991 : Starvation deaths in Tripura denied. *A.T.*, Nov. 7 : 6(1-3).

3013. ——— : 1991 : Probe panel on release of TRRB detenue. *A.T.*, Nov. 7 : 6(3-4). [Tripura Rajya Rakhi Bahini].

3014. ——— : 1991 : By-polls in four N.E. States assume significance. *A.T.*, Nov. 8 : 5(3-5).

3015. ——— : 1991 : Lack of hygiene-sense helps cancer-spread. *A.T.*, Nov. 11 : 3(6-8).

3016. **Assam Tribune** : 1991 : Prospect of BJP candidate bright : Tripura bypoll. *A.T.*, Nov. 13 : 3(1).

3017. ——— : 1991 : TPCC-I organisational polls from Nov. 17. *A.T.*, Nov. 13 : 3(4).

3018. ——— : 1991 : CPI-M in Tripura heading for formal split. *A.T.*, Nov. 13 : 3(5-8).

3019. ——— : 1991 : Agartala by poll 'acid-test' for Cong(I)-TUJS Govt. *A.T.*, Nov. 13 : 3(1-3).

3020. ——— : 1991 : 'No further split in Tripura CPI(M)'. *A.T.*, Nov. 15 : 5(3-5).

3021. ——— : 1991 : Common insurgent front formed in North East. *A.T.*, Nov. 30 : 3(5-6).

3022. ——— : 1991 : More Vayudoot service demanded. *A.T.*, Dec. 3 : 5(4). [Agartala *via* Kailasahar and Silchar].

3023. ——— : 1991 : Tripura seeks Rs. 1942'49 Crs for 8th Plan. *A.T.*, Dec. 3 : 5(3-5).

3024. ——— : 1991 : Lifting of RAP demanded. *A.T.*, Dec. 3 : 1(4). [Restricted Area Permit].

3025. ——— : 1991 : Tripura free from AIDS. *A.T.*, Dec. 6 : 4(6).

3026. ——— : 1991 : TUJS not to snap ties with Cong(I). *A.T.*, Dec. 6 : 4(5-6).

3027. ——— : 1991 : Financial help to Tripura's tea industry urged. *A.T.*, Dec. 7 : 5(5-6).

3028. ——— : 1991 : Jampui Mizos for Regional Council. *A.T.*, Dec. 9 : 1(5).

3029. ——— : 1991 : Editorial : Troubles in Tripura. *A.T.*, Dec. 9 : 4(1-2).

3030. ——— : 1991 : Mizos active for Regional Council. *A.T.*, Dec. 24 : 5(1-3) [Tripura-Mizos].

3031. ——— : 1991 : "TNV members will take to arms again" : Hrangkhawl. *A.T.*, Dec. 24 : 5(7-8).

3032. ——— : 1991 : TUJS condemns BSD atrocities A.T. Dec. 28 : 5(5-8).

3033. ——— : 1992 : Tripura CM escapes ATTF attack. *A.T.*, Jan. 4 : 1(1).

3034. **Assam Tribune** : 1992 : Pure Silver Coin of 16th Century Discovered. *A.T.*, Jan. 8 : 5(4-5).

3035. ——— : 1992 : ATTF's threat to strike all vehicles on NH from Jan. 20. *A.T.*, Jan. 10 : 5(3-5).

3036. ——— : 1992 : Hrangkhawl threatens stir in Tripura. *A.T.*, Jan. 10 : 5(2).

3037. ——— : 1992 : TUJS leaders to meet PM. *A.T.*, Jan. 10 : 5(1-2).

3038. ——— : 1992 : Centre firm to tackle insurgency in NE. *A.T.*, Jan. 10 : 1(2-4), 8(5-6).

3039. ——— : 1992 : Rs. 200 crs for oil exploration in Tripura. *A.T.*, Jan. 13 : 2(4-6).

3040. ——— : 1992 : Fate of Tipaimukh hydel project uncertain. *A.T.*, Jan. 18 : 3(6-8).

3041. ——— : 1992 : Tripura Govt. to complete four years in Feb. *A.T.*, Jan. 18 : 5(5-7). (Cong-I with TUJS coalition Govt).

3042. ——— : 1992 : New gallery in Tripura museum. *A.T.*, Jan. 20 : 5(6).

3043. ——— : 1992 : Govt. takes steps against ATTF threat. *A.T.*, Jan. 20 : 5(5-6).

3044. ——— : 1992 : Silver jubilee of AIR Agartala. *A.T.*, Jan. 26 : 3(6-8).

3045. ——— : 1992 : Tripura Govt. to introduce indentity cards. *A.T.*, Feb. 11 : 5(6-8).

3046. ——— : 1992 : Prospect of oil in Tripura bright. *A.T.*, Feb. 16 : 5(1-3).

3047. ——— : 1992 : Editorial : Change in Tripura. *A.T.*, Feb. 20 : 4(1-2).

3048. ——— : 1992 : Barman Ministry sworn in. *A.T.*, Feb. 20 : 1(2-4).

3049. ——— : 1992 : ATTF, TRRB demand homeland within Tripura. *A.T.* Feb. 24 : 5(2-4), [TNV, TNLF, TUJS, ATTF, TRRB].

3050. **Banerjee, Asis: Das Gupta, Malabika** *and* **Roy, Onkar Prasad**, 1992 : The Importance of Forests in the Economic Life of the Jhumias of Tripura *(In) Tribal Transformation in India, vol. I : Economy and*

Agrarian Issues (Ed) by Buddhadeb Chaudhuri. New Delhi, Inter India Publications *(in Press)*.

3051. **Banerjee, I.** : 1986 : Search of the lost tribe. *India Today*, Sept. 15 : 134-35 *(Mizo)*.

3052. **Bannerji, S.** : 1966 : Tipra and the Cognate Dialects : A study of Bodo Group of Dialects. *Educational Miscellany*, III(1-2), June-Sept.

3053. **Basu, Mahadeb Prasad** : 1990 : *An anthropological study of bodily height of Indian population*. Calcutta, Puthi Pustak : 60, 78, 200, 252, 253.

3054. **Berindranath, D.** : 1980 : Mythology of Zionist propaganda.....Mizos are the 14th lost tribe of Israel! *Blitz*, March 29 : 7.

3055. **Bhadra, R.K.** *and* **Mandal, S.R.** *(Eds.)* : 1991 : *Stratification hierachy and ethnicity in North-East India*. Delhi, Daya Publishing House, 310p.

3056. **Bhattacharya, Anil** : 1991 : Tripura : Gumti, Dam of Uprooted People. *The Hindu : Survey of the Environment (Annual*, Madras) : *65*.

3057 **Bhattacharyya, Gayatri** : 1988 : *Refugee Rehabilitation and its impact on Tripura's economy*. Agartala, 175p.

3058. **Biswas, Ashis K.** : 1991 : Surviving on roots, selling babies : The horror of starvation in Tripura. *Hindustan Times*. Nov. 30 : 1(1-5), 13(1-3).

3059. ——— : 1991 : Condemned to live. *Hindustan Times*, Dec. 15 *(Sunday Supplement)* : 1(1-8), 2(8).

3060. ——— : 1991 : Where does all the food go? *Hindustan Times, Sunday Supplement*, Dec. 15 : 2(1-8).

3061. **Census** : 1990 : *Census of India 1981, series 21 Tripura, Part 12, Census Atlas*. Delhi, Controller of Publications.

3062. ——— : 1991 : *Census of India 1991, series 24, Tripura*. Delhi, Controller of Publications.

3063. **Chakma, Subimal Bikash** : 1991 : Letters to the Editor : Chakma's plight. *Hindustan Times*, Nov. 30 : 11(6) [Chakma, Arunachal Pradesh].

3064. **Chakravarti, Mahadev** : 1990 : The New Zealand Baptist Mission and the beginning of Christian Missionary activities in Tripura *(In) Proceedings of North East India History Association, Xth Session, Shillong (1989) (Ed)* by Jayanta Bhusan Bhattacharjee. Shillong, Deptt. of History, North Eastern Hill University : 229-40.

3065. **Chakraborti, Satyabrata** : 1992 : CPI(M) bid to heal Tripura rift. *Statesman*, Feb. 11 : 4(1-4).

3066. **Chakraborty, Sujit** : 1991 : Near famine situation in Tripura's hill areas. *Assam Tribune*, Oct. 3: 2(3-6).

3067. ——— : 1991 : Tripura hill areas facing famine condition. *A.T.*, Nov. 6 : 5(1-3).

3068. ——— : 1991 : Plight of tribals in Tripura's hills. *A.T.*, Nov. 27 : 6(1-5).

3069. **Chakraborty, S.R.** : 1988 : *Special tables for Scheduled Castes and Scheduled Tribes : Census of India 1981 series 21, Tripura, part IX*. Delhi, Controller of Publications.

3070. **Chatterjee, Subhamoy** : 1991 : Cong-TUJs rift to favour CPM. *Hindustan Times*, Oct. 30 : 9(1-4).

3071. **Chaudhuri, S.** : 1978 : *Rajmala or an analysis of the chronicles of the Kings of Tripura : 1814-1887* by James Long. Calcutta Firma K.L. Mukhopadhyay (*Revised* edition).

3072. **Cuville, R.R.** : 1977 : The Tripuris of Tripura *(In) Church Growth in the Third World (Ed.)* by E. Roger *et al.* Bombay, 256p.

3073. **Danal, E.J. MacNamara** : 1958 : *The Encyclopedia Americana*. Washington.

3074. **Das, Jogendra Chandra** : 1990 : Population Education in Tripura *(In) Proceedings of North East India History Association, Xth session, Shillong (1989) (Ed)* by Jayanta Bhusan Bhattacharjee. Shillong, History Deptt., NEHU : 389- 92.

3075. **Das Gupta, Malabika** : 1992 : A neglected aspect of the alienation of tribal lands in Tripura : A Case Study of the Gumti Hydro-electric Power Project *(In) Tribal Transformation in India, vol. II : Socio-Economic and Ecological Development (Ed)* by

Buddhadeb Chaudhuri. New Delhi, Inter India Pubs *(in press)*.

3076. **Das Gupta, Malabika** : 1992 : The impact of LAMPS on the Marketing of Oranges in Tripura *(In) Tribal Transformation in India, vol. II : Socio-Economic and Ecological Development (Ed)* by Buddhadeb Chaudhuri. New Delhi, Inter India Pubs *(in Press)*.

3077. **Das Gupta, Malabika** *and* **Banerjee, Asis** : 1992 Jhuming as the way of life of the Jhumia : An analysis of data from Tripura *(In) Tribal Transformation in India, vol. I : Economy and Agrarian Issues (Ed)* by Buddhadeb Chaudhuri. New Delhi, Inter India Pubs *(in Press)*.

3078. **Deb, D.B.** : 1992 : *The Flora of Tripura State (in 2 vols)*. New Delhi, Mittal Publications *(in Press)*.

3079. **Deb Burman, Bijoy Kumar** : 1976 : Tripurai Kharchi O Ker Puja *(in Bengali) Gomati, Special Issue,* August.

3080. **Dev Varman, S.B.K.** : 1974 : *Nakhapilini Hamjagma* (Folklore). Agartala, Tribal Research Institute.

3081. **Dev Barman, T.J.M.** : 1958 : Origin of Tripura and its people. *Vanyajati,* 6(3) : 108-16.

3082. **Deb Sarma, N.C.** : 1985 : *Compilation of Tripuri Folk songs.* Agartala, Tribal Research Institute, 80p.

3083. **Directorate of Welfare** : ? : *Tribes and Tribal Welfare in Tripura.* Agartala, Directorate of Welfare for Sch. Tribes & Sch. Castes, Govt. of Tripura.

3084. **Dutta, Dwijendra Ch.** : 1976 : Gomati Dumbar Puran. *Gomati,* 11(687), March-April : 34-5.

3085. **Dutta, Jyotirmay** : 1987 : Land and Land Relations in Tripura *(In) Land Relations in North East India (Eds)* by B.B. Dutta *and* M.N. Karna. New Delhi, Peoples Pubg. House : 213-20.

3086. **Dutta, J.C.** : 1990 : A study into the Abwabs as in practice in Hill Tipperah and the attached Zamindaris in Chakla Roshanabad (Tripura) *(In) Proceedings of North East India History Association, Xth session Shillong (1989) (Ed)* by Jayanta Bhusan Bhattacharjee. Shillong, History Deptt., NEHU : 293-99.

3087. **Dutta, P.S.** : 1991 : Insurgency and the North East. *Shillong Times*, Nov. 28 : 2(3-8).

3088. **Gan Choudhuri, Jagadish** : 1976 : Tripurar Kak-Barak Prabad Bachan *(in Bengali)*. *Gomati*, Jan.-Feb.

3089. **Ganguly, J.b.** : 1991 : Community education movement among the tribals of Tripura. Proceedings of *Sixth World Conference of International Community Education Association* at Port of Spain, Trinidad-Tobago (West Indies) on 29 July-2 August, 1991.

3090. ——— : 1992 : The Process of transition from communal to individual land tenure system in Tripura *(In) Tribal Transformation in India, vol. I : Economy and Agrarian Issues (Ed)* by Buddhadeb Chaudhuri. New Delhi, Inter India Pubs *(in Press)*.

3091. **Ghosh, A.K.** : 1987 : Agricultural finance corporation. *Project Report for Gumti Catchment Development, Tripura* (forestry consultant was A.K. Ghosh).

3092. ——— : 1991 : Desertification of tropical evergreen rain forests in Tripura-consequence of social-political upheavels, I and II. *Himalaya : Man and Nature, XV (5), Oct. and XV(6), Nov. : 17-21.*

3093. **Ghosh, Kamalini** : 1984 : *Tribal Insurrection in Tripura*. M. Phil Dissertation, Central University, Hyderbad. (Book Links Corporation, Hyderabad).

3094. **Ghosh, S.** : 1988 : Tribal Jews step up campaign for recognition. *The Telegraph* (Calcutta), March 10 : 7 *(Mizo)*.

3095. **Haokip, L.**(*Ed*) : 1990 : *Kut festival Souvenir*. Imphal, Manipur State Level Kut Committee *(Mizo)*.

3096. **Hazarika, M.P.** : 1991 : NEC and the tribal areas. *Shillong Times*, Nov. 26 : 2(3-6).

3097. **Hindustan Times** : 1991 : Starvation claims 3 in Tripura. *H.T.*, Oct. 28 : 3(1-3).

3098. ——— : 1991 : Security beefed up in N-E States. *H.T.*, Nov. 5 : 10(1-4).

3099. **Hindustan Times** : 1991 : 99 Tripura CPM panel members quit. *H.T.*, Nov. 8 : 9(1-2).

3100. ——— : 1991 : Tripura's drinking water 'polluted'. *H.T.*, Nov. 11 : 20(1-2).

3101. ——— : 1991 : Tripura Palace losing glamour. *H.T.*, Nov. 25 : 6(3-5).

3102. ——— : 1991 : Jampui Mizos to lanuch agitation. *H.T.*, Dec. 9 : 6(6-7).

3103. ——— : 1991 : Tripura for talks with Mizo leaders. *H.T.*, Dec. 23 : 7(1-2).

3104. ——— : 1992 : Year of violence, famine in Tripura. *H.T.*, Jan. 4 : 6(6-7).

3105. ——— : 1992 : ATTF threat to disrupt transport. *H.T.*, Jan. 8 : 7(3).

3106. ——— : 1992 : Tripura CM resigns as TUJS withdraws support. *H.T.*, Feb. 18 : 1(4-6).

3107. ——— : 1992 : Editorial : The Agartala case. *H.T.*, Feb. 20 : 13(1-2).

3108. **Insaf** : 1992 : Round the States. *Shillong Times*, Jan. 1 : 2(8, last).

3109. **Lahiri, Dilip K.** : 1991 : Mizo life and culture and their folk superstitions beliefs. *Folklore*, 32(9), Sept. : 154-61.

3110. **Mandal, D.B.** : 1991 : *Garia : Tripura Jamatia Adibasider Puja O Uttsav (in Bengali)*. Calcutta, Sarodiya Gandhabanik.

3111. **Mukherjee, Sochindra Nath** : 1988 : Weekday Post : Army in Tripura. *Amrita Bazar Patrika*, Feb. 8 : 6(3-5).

3112. **Onkareswar** : 1992 : Tripura *(in Hindi). Saptasetu* (Guwahati), Feb. 14.

3113. **Prasad, R.N.** *and* **Agarwal, A.K.** : 1991 : *Political and Economic Development of Mizoram*. New Delhi, Mittal Publications : 15, 37, 125, 196, 234 (Tripura).

3114. **Purbanchal Prahari** : 1992 : Editorial : Tripura ki visfoltak sthiti. *Pur. Pra.*, Jan. 2 : 4(1-2) *(in Hindi)*.

3115. **Purbanchal Prahari** : 1992 : Tripura men jatayat band kamila-jula asor raha. *Pur. Pra.*, Jan. 22 : 1(7-8).

3116. **Purbanchal Prahari** : 1992 : Editorial : Tripura men ugrabad. *Pur. Pra.*, Feb. 17 : 4(1-2).

3117. **Ramesh, N.R.** : 1992 : *A study on geomorphology, quatarnary geology and associated cultural remains of West Tripura District, Tripura. Unpublished* Ph.D. thesis, Gauhati University.

3118. **Roy, Ash Narain** : 1991 : Fresh violence in Tripura likely : Turbulence in N-E-I. *Hindustan Times*, Oct. 27 : 1(2- 5), 24(1-2).

3119. ——— : 1991 : Turbulence in N-E II : Migrants change Tripura policy. *Hindustan Times*, Oct. 28 : 10(1-4).

3120. **Roy Bhowmik, A.B.** : 1968 : Jhum cultivation of cotton in Tripura should yield way to improved techniques. *Indian Farming*, 12, March 17 : 16-8.

3121. **Roy Burman, B.K.** : 1986 : *Community land system of the tribals and problem of institutional finance in Manipur and Tripura.* New Delhi, Council for Social Development *(Mimeo)*.

3122. ——— : 1992 : Issues in land reforms in N-E tribal area *(In) Tribal Transformation in India, vol. I : Economy and Agrarian issues (Ed)* by Buddhadeb Chaudhuri. New Delhi, Inter India Pubs *(In Press)*.

3123. ——— : 1992 : Historical Process in Report of Communal Land System and Poverty Alleviation Among Tribals *(In) Tribal Transformation in India, vol. 1 : Economy and Agrarian Issues (Ed)* by Buddhadeb Chaudhuri. New Delhi, Inter India Pubs *(in Press)*.

3124. ——— : 1992 : Crisis of identity among the Mizos *(In) Tribal Transformation, vol. III : Ethnopolitics and Identity Crisis (Ed)* by Buddhadeb Chaudhuri. New Delhi, Inter India Pubs *(in Press)*.

3125. **Saha, Sudhangshu Bikash** : 1984 (?) : *The History and Culture of the Tribal Peoples of Tripura.* Ph.D. Thesis, Calcutta University (?)

3126. **Samra, Myer** : 1991 : The Tribe of Manasseh : 'Judaism' in the Hills of Manipur and Mizoram. *Man in India, Special issue,* 71(1), March : 183-202.

3127. **Schwantzberg, Joseph E.** : 1988 : Tripura *(In) The Encyclopaedia Americana, International Edition, vol. 27.* Danbury, Grolier Incorporated : 125.

3128. **S.P.C.** *(Ed)* : 1977 : Tripura *(In) The New Encyclopaedia Britanica (Macropedia), vol. 18* . Oxford, University of Chicago : 714-15.

3129. **Sengupta, Sarthak** *(Ed)* : 1993 : *Tribes of North East India* : Anthropological perspective. Delhi, Mittal Pubs. *(in Press).*

3130. **Shillong Times** : 1992 : Agartala to attain full literacy. *Shi. Times,* Jan. 30 : 1(8).

3131. ——— : 1992 : Tripura likely to enter into country's oil map. *Shi. Times,* Feb. 14 : 3(2-5).

3132. ——— : 1992 : ATTF problem on the rise : Tripura CM convenes all party meet. *Shi. Times,* Feb. 16 : 1(7-8).

3133. ——— : 1992 : Cong-TUJS honeymoon ends : Tripura CM resigns, *Shi. Times,* Feb. 18 : 1(2-3).

3134. ——— : 1992 : High drama in Tripura : Barman new CM designate, swearing in to-day. *Shi. Times,* Feb. 19 : 1(2-5).

3135. ——— : 1992 : Editorial : Exit Majumdar. *Shi. times,* Feb. 19 : 4(1-2).

3136. ——— : 1992 : Pandemonium breaks out in Tripura Assembly. *Shi. Times,* Feb. 22 : 1(6-8).

3137. **Statesman** : 1987 : Tripura move to check tribal belligerency. *Statesman,* Jan, 14 : 10(2-3).

3138. ——— : 1992 : Editorial : Change in Tripura. *Statesman,* Feb. 20 : 8(2-3).

3139. ——— : 1992 : Tripura Governor's stance resented. *Statesman,* Feb. 23 : 9(6-7).

3140. **Takle, Rev. J.** : 1914 : *Application of Rev. J. Takle, Brahmanbaria, addressed to the Chairman, Agartala Municipality, dated Brahmanbaria, 22 March, 1914.*

Agartala (It is kept in the Record Room, Secretariat Archives, Govt. of Tripura).

3141. **Tribal Research** : 1986 : *A Brief account of Riangs in Mizoram.* Aizawl, Tribal Research Institute, Deptt. of Education (Mizoram), 104p.

ADDENDA II

3142. **Abedin, Joynal** : 1990 : Chittagong Hill Tracts seeks autonomy. *Hind. T.*, Dec. 21 : 13(1-2).

3143. **Allen, B.C.** : 1905 : *Assam District Gazetteers, Vol. II : Sylhet.*, Calcutta, Clarendon Steam Printing Works.

3144. **Amrita Bazar Patrika** : 1988 : The MLA Maharani. *Am. Baz. Pat.*, Feb. 20 : 4(5-6).

3145. ——— : 1990 : LF perturbed over infiltration in Tripura. *Am. Baz. Pat.*, March 11 : 7(1).

3146. **Assam Tribune** : 1986 : 4000 Chakmas deported to Bangladesh. *A.T.*, March 11 : 8(1).

3147. ——— : 1991 : Indo-Bangla talks on Chakmas begin. *A.T.*, Feb. 12 : 1(7).

3148. ——— : 1992 : 2 lakhs jobless. *A.T.* Feb. 29 : 8(5).

3149. ——— : 1992 : Tripura's new CM makes major impact on administration. *A.T.*, March 5 : 5(4-7).

3150. ——— : 1992 : Forest protection force for Tripura soon. *A.T.*, April 6 : 5(3-4).

3151. ——— : 1992 : Concern over tribal migration from Tripura. *A.T.*, April 21 : 394-60.

3152. ——— : 1992 : ATTF force schools to close in tribal areas. *A.T.*, April 27 : 5(6-7).

3153. ——— : 1992 : Tripura jute mill closed. *A.T.*, April 28 : 597-8).

3154. ——— : 1992 : World Bank aided project in Tripura. *A.T.* May 11 : 4(8).

3155. ——— : 1992 : Tripura perturbed with fresh influx of tribals. *A.T.*, May 18 : 5(2-4).

3156. ——— : 1992 : Insurgency plaguing Tripura for last 2 years. *A.T.*, May 28 : 5(4-5).

3157. ——— : 1992 : TUJS to bring out 'white paper' on ATTF violence. *A.T.*, July 29 : 5(2-5).

3158. ——— : 1992 : No more mass hysteria in South Tripura. *A.T.*, Sept. 8 : 5(1-2).

3159. **Assam Tribune** : 1992 : In Tripura : ONGC invests Rs. 500 cr. for oil and gas exploration. *A.T.* Aug. 4 : 5(1-3).

3160. ——— : 1992 : big houses in invest Rs. 3000 crs. for industrialisation in Tripura. *A.T.*, Aug. 11 : 5(1-3).

3161. ——— : 1992 : Tripura Govt's plan to eliminate insurgency. *A.T.*, Aug. 12 : 5(1-3).

3162. ——— : 1992 : 50,000 hectares earmarked for rubber plantation in NE. *A.T.*, Aug. 14 : 6(6-8).

3163. ——— : 1992 : Agartala-Guwahati bus service. *A.T.*, Aug. 14 : 3(5).

3164. ——— : 1992 : Drought hits North East. *A.T.*, Aug. 18 : 1(2-4).

3165. ——— : 1992 : TUJS gradually losing its identity. *A.T.*, Sept. 1 : 5(7-8).

3166. ——— : 1992 : Bangladesh forms committee for Chakma refugees. *A.T.*, Sept. 10 : 5(3-5).

3167. ——— : 1992 : Border fencing : Tripura Govt. proposal under consideration. *A.T.*, Sept. 13 : 2(5-6).

3168. ——— : 1992 : TUJS bails to build up any political image. *A.T.*, Sept. 16 : 5(2-4).

3169. ——— : 1992 : No trust motion against Tripura govt. defeated. *A.T.*, Sept. 19 : 1(2-4).

3170. ——— : 1986 : Torture and killing of tribals in Chittagong. *A.T.*, Oct. 9 : 4(7-8), 1986.

3171. ——— : 1992 : Editorial : Trends in Tripura. *A.T.*, Sept. 20 : 4(1-2).

3172. ——— : 1992 : Editorial : Tripura's Tribulation. *A.T.*, Oct. 22 : 4(1-2).

3173. ——— : 1992 : Editorial : Signals in Tripura. *A.T.*, Dec. 29 : 4(1-2).

3174. **Bangiya Sahitya Parishad** : 1967 : *Rajamala* (Bangiya Sahitya Parishad). Agartala, Education Directorate.

3175. **Bhattacharjee, J.B.** *(Ed.)* : 1991 : Proceedings of NEIHA, 12th Session (Jagi Road, Assam). Shillong, History Deptt., NEHU.

3176. **Bhattacharjee, J.B.** *(Ed)* : 1993 : Proceedings of NEIHA, 13th Session (Itanagan, A.P.), Shillong, History Deptt., NEHU.

3177. **Bhattacharjee, P.R.** : 1992 : A critical appraisal of the NEC schemes implemented in Tripura. Proceedings of a Symposium on *"Problems and prospects of balanced Regional Development in NEI and the role of NEC"*, organised by NEICSSR (Shillong) in collaboration of NEC (Shillong) on 27-28 July, 1992.

3178. **Bordoloi, B.N.** *(Ed)* : 1992 : Seminar on *"Tribal Women and Development"*, held on 4-6 April, 1992, organised by TRI, Guwahati *(Mimeo)*.

3179. **Borthakur, D.N.** *et al* : 1979 : Agro forestry based farming systems as an alternative to jhuming. proceedings of *Agro Forestry* Seminar on May 16-17, Imphal : 1-32.

3180. **Campbell, George** : ? : Languages from Tipperah and Cachar *(In) Specimens of Languages* by George Campbell. Calcutta, Bengal Secretariat Press : 204-217, 188-201, 168-186.

3181. **Chakma, B.B.** : 1992 : To the Editor : Unabated atrocities on Chakmas in Mizoram. *Shillong Times*, Sept. 15 : 4(3-4).

3182. **Chakma, Chamudhan** 1989 : Sri Chakma jatir itibritta brittantas. (hand written *unpublished* mass. in Bengali).

3183. **Chakravarti, Mahadev** : 1990 : Controversy on the designations 'Maharaja' and 'Manikya' : Some rare documents of Tripura. *Proceedings of NEIHA (Imphal), vol. 11*. Shillong, History Deptt., NEHU : 180-88.

3184. ——— : 1991 : People's participation in rural development *(In) Rural Development in North East India : Perspective, Issues and Experiences (Ed)* by R.K. Samanta. New Delhi, Uppal Publishing House : 69-93.

3185. ——— : 1992 : The TUJS : From Petition to Power *(In) Regional Political Parties in North East India (Ed)* by L.S. Gassah. New Delhi, Omson Pubs. : 226-240.

3186. **Chakraborti, M., Das Gupta, M.** *and* **Sircar, B.** : 1987 : *A study on the Lushais of Jampui Hills in Tripura.* Agartal Directorate of Research, Govt. of Tripura.

3187. **Chakraborti, Puranjan Prasad** : 1985 : *Rabindra Smriti Dannya Tripura (in Bengali).* Calcutta, K.P. Bagchi, 124p.

3188. **Chakraborty, Sujit** : 1992 : Special financial aid to Tripura demanded. *Assam Tribune,* May 12 : 5(1-3).

3189. ——— : 1992 : Concern at prolonged stay of refugees in Tripura. *A.T.* May 20 : 5(4-6).

3190. **Chakraborty, Sujit** : 1992 : Land routes of NE States through Bangladesh stressed. *A.T.,* May 25 : 5(3-5).

3191. **Chakraborty, Sujit** : 1992 : New height in violence by extremists in Tripura. *A.T.,* July 29 : 5(3-5).

3192. ——— : 1992 : Counter-insurgency operation in Tripura soon. *A.T.,* Aug. 3 : 5(6-8).

3193. ——— : 1992 : Plea for third force in Tripura. *A.T.,* Aug. 12 : 5(1-4).

3194. ——— : 1992 : NE States facing insurgency problems. *A.T.,* Sept. 12 : 5(1-4) [ATTF].

3195. **Chakraborty, Trailokyanath** : 1981 : *Jele Trish Bachhar O Pak-Bharater Yuddha (in Bengali)* Calcutta : 14-6.

3196. **Choudhury, Pratap** : 1992 : Regional Political Parties in Tripura : A Genesis *(In) Regional Political Parties in North East India (Ed)* by L.S. Gassah. New Delhi Omson Pubs. : 211-17.

3197. **Choudhury, Zaglul A.** : 1986 : Repartriation of Chakma refugees underway. *Times of India,* Nov. 25 : 16(2-3).

3198. **Dainik Sangbad** : 1988 : An interview with Shri B. Dutta Bhowmik. *Dainik Sangbad* (Agartala), Nov. 12.

3199. **Danda, Ajit K.** : 1989 : On ethnicity and political mobility. *Jr. of the Indian Anthropolgoical Society,* 24(3), Nov. : 210-11.

3200. **Danda, Ajit K.** : 1986 : Development perspectives and the rural poor. *Human Science,* 35(3), Sept. : 168-69 [Chandpur, Tripura].

3201. **Das, Jogendra Chandra** : 1991 : Historical writings of the Princely State of Tripura *(In) Proceedings of North East India History Association,* Twelfth session, Jagiroad *(Ed)* by J.B. Bhattacharjee. Shillong, History Deptt., North Eastern Hill University : 83-84.

3202. **Das Gupta, Malabika** : 1988 . Forest dwellers and forest development : Economic gains vs. environmental loss? The case of Tripura (In) *Proceeding of a Seminar on Forest Dwellers and Forest Development, 12th International Conference of IUAES (Ed)* by B. Chau B. Chaudhuri.

3203. ——— : 1990 : The continuity and change in the economic sphere of the jhumia tribal society of Tripura. *Jr. Anth. Surv. of India* (Calcutta), 39(2-3), June-Sept. : 133-42.

3204. ——— : 1991 : Will the creation of small farms through land reforms solve Tripura's agrarian problem? The search for an alternative solution *(In) Impact of Land Reforms in North East India (Ed)* by Malabika Das Gupta. New Delhi, Omsons Pubs : 105-12.

3205. **Dasgupta, Tarit Mohan** : 1990 : Tripurary Swadhinata Sangramer Smriti *(in Bengali). Gomati,* Ashar (July), Agartala : 1-11.

3206. **Datta, Brajendra Chandra** : 1972 : *Tripura Rajye Trish Bachhar (in Bengali).* Agartala, Khowai Division, 12p.

3207. ——— : 1986 : *Tripura Rajye Trish Bachhar (in Bengali), (Ed)* by J.C. Datta. Agartala, Belonia Division.

3208. **Datta, J.C.** : 1987 : Kaziana : A communal tax upon the Muslim subjects of Tripura. *Proceedings of NEIHA, vol. 8 (Kohima).* Shillong, History Deptt., NEHU : 214-21.

3209. ——— : 1990 : Land Tenure for the Capital Town of Agartala during the Princely Regime (1862-1947),

Proceedings of NEIHA, vol. 11 (Imphal). Shillong, History Deptt., NEHU : 243-47.

3210. **De, Ranjit Kumar** : 1990 : Socio-Economic Tensions in Tripura during the First World War. *Proceedings of NEIHA, vol. 11 (Imphal).* Shillong, History Deptt., NEHU : 216-25.

3211. **Deb, D.B.** : 1960 : *Vegetation of Tripura.* Agartala, Pub. by the author.

3212. **Deb Barma, Aghore** : 1991 : Land reforms in Tripura *(In) Impact of Land Reforms in North East India (Ed)* by Malabika Das Gupta. New Delhi, Omsons Pubs. : 101-04.

3213. **Deb Barma, Debpriya** *and* **Sarkar, Nepal** : 1980 : *Charmakar Sampradayer Samajik O Arthanyoitik Samikha : Agartala Sahar O Sahartali Sanlangna Anchal (in Bengali).* Agartala, Directorate of Research, 53p.

3214. **Dev Burma, J.M.** : ? : Origin of Tripura and its people. *Vanyajati,* 6(4).

3215. **Deb Burman, Mahimchandra** : 1334 B.S. : *Deshiya Rajya (in Bengali).* Agartala, Pub. by the author, 121p.

3216. **Dev Barman, Sahadev Bikram Kishore** *and* **Das, A.R.** : 1992 : Austric Elements in Tripura : A study in Ethno- genesis. *Jr. NEICSSR,* 16(1), April : 38-9.

3217. **Deb Burman, Shashadhar Vikram** : 1974 : *Kak-Thum : A guide book for words and conversation.* Agartala, Directorate of Tribal research, Tripura, 55p.

3218. **Directorate of Publicity** : 1970 : *Tripura on the March.* Agartala, Direc. of Pub., Govt. of Tripura, 45 p.

3219. **Directorate of Public Relations** : ? : *This is Tripura.* Agartala, Direc. of Pub. Rel. and Tourism, Govt. of Tripura.

3220. **Directorate of Research** : 1980 : *The Kai Pengs.* Agartala, Direc. of Research.

3221. **Dutta, N.C.** : 1982 : Agricultural Development in Tripura. *Jour. North Eastern Council* (Shillong), 5(1) : 32-35.

3222. **Economic and Political Weekly** : 1989 : Report : bullets instead of rice. *EPW,* XXIV (37), Sept. 16 : 2055.

3223. **George, S.T.** : 1992 : *The Chakma refugees in Tripura.* Delhi Gyan Pub. House, 175p.

3224. **Ghosh, G.K.** : 1992 : *Tribals and their culture: Arunachal Pradesh and Tripura, vol. II.* New Delhi, Ashish Pubg. House : 130-39.

3225. **Ghosh, M.** : 1984 : *Tribal Insurrection in Tripura.* Hyderabad, Booklinks Corporation, 68p.

3226. **Govt. of Tripura** : 1976-'77 : *National Sample Survey (31st Round, July 1976-June 1977) Jhum Cultivation in Tripura.* Agartala, Govt of Tripura.

3227. ——— : 1982 : *Project Report of Tripura Rehabilitation Plantation Corporation Ltd.* Agartala, Govt. of Tripura, Deptt. of Welfare for Scheduled Tribe and Scheduled Caste, 10p.

3228. **Hindustan Times** : 1992 : ATTF urged to give up violence. *H.T.*, Feb. 28 : 7(1-2).

3229 ——— : 1992 : Tripura kids prey to gall stone. *H.T.*, April 20 : 6(6-7).

3230. ——— : 1992 : Tripura extremists' in fighting surfaces. *H.T.*, April 25 : 7(4-5).

3231. ——— : 1992 : Editorial : Once more in Tripura. *H.T.*, Sept. 15 : 11(1-2).

3232. ——— : 1992 : States asked to check influx from Bangladesh. *H.T.*, Sept. 29 : 1(1-3).

3233. **Hugh** *and* **Colleen Gantzer** : 1987 : The warmth of Agartala. *Statesman, Sunday Miscellany,* Sept. 6.

3234. **Jha, Ajay N.** : 1992 : NE border still not well guarded. *H.T.*, Aug. 25 : 3(1-2).

3235. **Kamath, M.V.** : 1980 : Land of Seven Sisters. *Illustrated Weekly of India,* June 1-7.

3236. **Khan, Nurul Islam** *(Ed)* : 1977 : *Bangladesh District Gazetters (Comilla). Dacca, Pub. by the Editor, 56p.*

3237. **Linguistic Deptt.** : 1989 : Kokborok language of Tripura, second largest language after Bengali. Proceedings of a Seminar on *"Language"* held on Dec. 16-17, 1989 by Mysore Linguistic Deptt. in Agartala, Tripura.

3238. **Mahato, P.P.** : 1992 : *Tripurar upajati Samaj O' Sanskrite (in Bengali).* Calcutta, B.B. Prokasan.

3239. **Mandal, Debabrata** : 1984 : Jamatia *(In) Tribal Education in India (Eds)* by Biman K. Das Gupta *and* Ajit K. Danda. Calcutta, Anth. surv. of India : 12-4.

3240. **Mathew, J.** *(Ed)* : 1981 : *North Eastern Hill Regions of India : Problems and progress of development.* New Delhi.

3241. **Meghalaya Guardian** : 1990 : Tripura to have 'probelm of plenty' in power sector. *Meg. Gur.,* Sept. 3 : 5(2-4).

3242. **Misra, Prafulla** : 1992 : Chakmas : A tribe forlorn. *Shillong Times,* June 5 : 3(1-6).

3243. ——— : 1992 : Why ethnic assersions are on rise. *Shg. T.,* June 25 : 4(3-6), 5(5-6).

3244. **Nandi (Basu), Arati** : 1991 : Shifting cultivation in Tripura *(In) Shifting cultivation in India (Ed)* by Saradindu Bose. Calcutta, Anth. Surv. of India : 83-99.

3245. **Nath, Umasankar** : 1992 : Riang uprising in Tripura. *Unpublished M. Phil Dissertation, NEHU,* History Deptt.

3246. **NEC** : 1982 : *North Eastern Council : A Decade of Service.* Shillong, DIPR (NEC).

3247. ——— : 1992 : *North Eastern Region : At a glance.* Shillong, NEC.

3248. **North East Times** : 1992 : ONGC meeting power needs in Tripura. *N.E.T.,* March 9 : 7(1-3).

3249. ——— : 1992 : Over 200 tribals shot in CHT. *N.E.T.,* April 14 : 1(5-6) (Chakma).

3250. **Pal, Ranjit** : 1984 : *Tripurar Shramik Andolan O Ganatantrik Sangramer Itihas (in Bengali), vol. I.* Agartala, 39p.

3251. **Paul, Manas** : 1992 : Militant bodies keep Tripura in a state of ferment. *Shg. T.,* Sept. 17 : 3(2-6).

3252. **Poddar, Satyadeo** : 1991 : Social Changes in the Harijan Community of Tripura Since independence *(In) Proceedings of North East India History Association,* Twelfth Session, Jagiroad

(Ed.) by J.B. Bhattacharjee. Shillong, History, Deptt., North Eastern Hill University : 432-436.

3253. **Purbanchal Prahari** : 1992 : Editorial : Tripura men bhuk mari *(in Hindi). Pur. Pra.*, May 12 : 4(1-2).

3254. ——— : 1992 : Tripura men gyes ka pata lagane ke liye 500 caror ka nirdesh. *Pur. Pra.*, Aug. 4 : 1(6-7).

3255. **Radio Bangladesh** : 1986 : Marma. Radio Bangladesh *(Uttoran)*, Sept. 3, 10 and 17 *(Radio Talk)*.

3256. ——— : 1986 : Chakma. Radio Bangladesh (Uttoran), April 2, 9.16.23.30; May 21, 28 and June 4 *(Radio Talk)*.

3257. **Reang, Dhananjay** : 1992 : Ex-TNV leader forms parallel govt. *Shg. T.*, May 26 : 3(5-6).

3258. **Roy, Jagat Jyoti** : 1991 : Impact of land reforms in Tripura *(in) Impact of land reforms in North East India (Ed)* by Malabika Das Gupta. New Delhi, Omsons Pubs : 95-100.

3259. ——— : 1992 : The TUJS : A Regional Political Party *(In) Regional Political Parties in North East India (Ed)* by L.S. Gassah. New Delhi, Omson Pubs. : 218-25.

3260. **Roy, Raja Devashish** : 1992 : Chittagong Hills Tracts : The Ground realities. *Shg.T.*, Aug. 6 : 5(1-8). [Chakma].

3261. **Saha, A.K.** *and* **Bhowmick, Pradip K.** : 1992 : Family Welfare Programme, failure or success : A study of Anandanagar village under Agartala in the State of Tripura. *Man and Life*, 18(1-2), Jan.-June : 75-88.

3262. **Sanajaoba, Naorem** *(Ed)* : 1994 : *Manipur : Past and Present, vol. IV.* Delhi, Mittal Publications *(in Press)*.

3263. **Saptasetu** : 1992 : Bangladeshi Sharanarthiyon se des ki antarik suraksha khatre men. *(in Hindi). Saptasetu*, Sept. 4.

3264. **Scott, J. George** : 1901 : *Gazetteer of Upper Burma and the Shan State.* Rangoon, Supdt. Govt. printing (Burma).

3265. **Sen, Nabinchandra** : 1959 : Works of Nabinchandra, vol. II. Calcutta : 507-08.

3266. **Sengupta, Gautam** : 1992 : Whispering monuments of Tripura. *Shg. T.*, July 11 : 5(1-6).

3267. **Sengupta, Swapan** *(Ed)* : 1975 : *Tripura Prasanga (in Bengali)*. Agartala, DPRT, 205p.

3268. **Shillong Times** : 1982 : Editorial : No High Court for Tripura. *Shg.T.*, Nov. 6 : 2(1-2).

3269. ——— : 1986 : Worst of insurgency is over in North East. *Shg.T.*, Jan. 26 : 3(2-5).

3270. ——— : 1986 : The perennial problem of Chakma evacuees. *Shg. T.*, May 17 : 2(3-5).

3271. ——— : 1989 : Editorial : Chakma problem intensifies. *Shg.T.*, Sept. 25 : 2(1-2).

3272. ——— : 1992 : ATTF faces ethnic differences? *Shg.T.*, Feb. 1 : 3(7-8).

3273. ——— : 1992 : Tripura cabinet : expansion according to TUJS dictates. *Shg.T.*, March 5 : 1(6-8).

3274. ——— : 1992 : Repartiation of Chakma refugees seems bleak. *Shg. T.*, April 6 : 3(3-5).

3275. ——— : 1992 : Three-member panel formed to implement TNV Accord. *Shg. T.*, April 10 : 3(3-5).

3276. ——— : 1992 : Unokoti fair inaugurated : Barman given 'clean chit'. *Shg.T.*, April 11 : 1(6-8).

3277. ——— : 1992 : BDR massacre 200 Chakmas : Fresh refugee influx in Tripura feared. *Shg.T.*, April 15 : 3(4-6).

3278. ——— : 1992 : Tripura Panchayat Poll prospects bleak. *Shg.T.*, April 19 : 2(7-8).

3279. ——— : 1992 : Incidence of gall stone highest in Tripura. *Shg.T.*, April 20 : 3(4-5).

3280. ——— : 1992 : ATTF violence on rise. *Shg.T.*, April 23 : 5(7-8).

3281. ——— : 1992 : Tripura gastro toll rises to 156. *Shg.T.*, April 28 : 3(2-5).

3282. ——— : 1992 : Editorial : Troubled Tripura. *Shg. T.*, May 4 : 4 (1-2). (TUJS).

3283. **Shillong Times** : 1992 : Fresh massacre in Chttagong. *Shg.T.*, May 14 : 3(1-5), 6(4-6).

3284. ——— : 1992 : Insurgency plagues Tripura. *Shg. T.*, May 27 : 3(6-8).

3285. ——— : 1992 : Underground HPC demands separate State. *Shg.T.*, May 7 : 1(2-5). [Areas of North, Mizoram, Lakhimpur of Assam, Charachandpur of Manipur and Jampui Hills of Tripura].

3286. ——— : 1992 : Tripura, Assam Rifles companies beefed up. *Shg.T.*, may 28 : 4(1-2).

3287. ——— : 1992 : 125 Ultras surrender in Agartala. *Shg.T.*, June 5 : 3(7-8).

3288. ——— : 1992 : 'Repatriation of Chakma refugees on'. *Shg.T.*, July 5 : 1(2-5).

3289. ——— : 1992 : W. Tripura power project to help agriculture. *Shg.T.*, July 5 : 1(2-4).

3290. ——— : 1992 : Editorial : Tripura bulge. *Shg.T.*, July 7 : 4(1-2).

3291. ——— : 1992 : New industry incentives for Tripura announced. *Shg.T.*, July 17 : 3(1-3).

3292. ——— : 1992 : Elders demand 'Famine Code' in Tripura. *Shg.T.*, July 18 : 7(1-5).

3293. ——— : 1992 : Tripura on threshold of industrial boom. *Shg.T.*, Aug. 3 : 3(3-6).

3294. ——— : 1992 : Tripura's potential for rubber production. *Shg.T.*, Aug. 5 : 6(4-6) [W.Tripura].

3295. ——— : 1992 : Tripura Govt. draws up plan to eliminate extremism. *Shg.T.*, Aug. 13 : 8(3-6).

3296. ——— : 1992 : Editorial : Uninvited guests of Tripura. *Shg.T.*, Aug. 14 : 4(1-2) [Chakma].

3297. ——— : 1992 : Transit route through B'Desh likely to open. *Shg.T.*, Aug. 20 : 3(1-2).

3298. ——— : 1992 : Editorial : Unstable Tripura. *Shg.T.*, Aug. 31 : 4(1-2).

3299. ——— : 1992 : Look Back (*Shillong Times*, August 22, 1953) : Karimganj as a trade centre, capable of bearing entire supply to Tripura. *Shg.T.*, Sept. 2 : 4(1-2).

3300. **Shillong Times** : 1992 : 13 MLAs express no-confidence : Tripura ministry faces major crisis. *Shg.T.*, Sept. 14 : 1(2- 4).

3301. ——— : 1992 : TNV president issues ultimatum. *Shg.T.*, Sept. 15 : 3(4-8).

3302. ——— : 1992 : ONGC official killed in ATTF ambush. *Shg.T.*, Sept. 15 : 5(7-8).

3303. ——— : 1992 : Tripura CM suspects : Assam MP behind toppling bid. *Shg.T.*, Sept. 15 : 1(6-7).

3304. ——— : 1992 : Editorial : Chavan in North East. *Shg.T.*, Sept. 15 : 4(1-2).

3305. ——— : 1992 : BSF apprehends extremists near Indo-Bangladesh border. *Shg.T.*, Sept. 16 : 3(3-5).

3306. ——— : 1992 : Chakma Buddhist Association appeals to Central Government for intervention. *Shg.T.*, Sept. 16 : 3(5-8).

3307. ——— : 1992 : Khaleda's gesture softens Chakmas in C.H.T. *Shg.T.*, Sept. 17 : 3(4-5).

3308. ——— : 1992 : NEC funds micro-hydel schemes in North East. *Shg.T.*, Sept. 19 : 7(1-8).

3309. ——— : 1992 : Tripura coalition govt. wins no-trust move. *Shg.T.*, Sept. 19 : 1(2-4).

3310. ——— : 1992 : Editorial : Still in trouble. *Shg.T.*, Sept. 21 : 4(1-2) [TUJS, ATTF].

3311. ——— : 1992 : Two more AIR stations in Tripura. *Shg.T.*, Sept. 22 : 3(1-2).

3312. ——— : 1992 : Chavan convenes CM's meet : Centre concerned over infiltration in North East. *Shg.T.*, Sept. 23 : 1(2-7).

3313. ——— : 1992 : Anti-Insurgency operation stepped up in Tripura. *Shg.T.*, Oct. 9 : 3(6-8) [ATTF].

3314. ——— : 1992 : Editorial : Prospects in Tripura. *Shg.T.*, Oct. 16 : 2(1-2).

3315. ——— : 1992 : Urge to lift ban on foreigners in Tripura. *Shg.T.*, Oct. 30 : 3(2-4).

3316. **Singh, K.C.** : 1896 : *Rajamala*. Comilla, 566p.

3317. **Singha, Bhimsen** : 1992 : Letters to the Editor ; Manipuris in Tripura. *A.T.*, Feb. 28 : 4(3-5).

3318. **Sinha, Sunil** : 1992 : Tripura ki sajha sorkar vayvar men *(in Hindi). Saptasetu*, Sept. 18.

3319. **Sinha, Surajit** *(Ed)* : 1987 : *Tribal Politics and State systems in Pre-colonial Eastern and North Eastern India.* Calcutta, K.P. Bagchi, 336p.

3320. **Som, Tapan Kumar** : 1991 : Land utilisation and changing economy in the context of the rubber plantation industry : A micro sociological study in North Tripura District *(In) Impact of Land Reforms in North East India (Ed)* by Malabika Das Gupta. New Delhi, Omsons Pubs. : 113-36.

3321. **State Administration Report** : 1960 : *The Tripura Land Revenue and Land Reforms Act, 1960; Article No. 199(i) of the Act.* Agartala, Govt. of Tripura.

3322. **Statesman** : 1992 : Government urged to solve Tripura starvation problem. *Statesman*, Feb. 29 : 16(3-5).

3323. ——— : 1992 : More to bring together militant tribal outfits in Tripura. *Statesman*, March 3 : 12(3-5).

3324. ——— : 1992 : Jhumias yet to be rehabilitated. *Statesman*, March 7 : 16(3-5).

3325. ——— : 1992 : Editorial : Help for Tripura. *Statesman*, March 12 : 6(2-3).

3326. ——— : 1992 : TNV call for stir to Block National Highway. *Statesman*, March 14 : 7(5-7).

3327. ——— : 1992 : Hasina condemns Chakma massacre. *Statesman*, May 7 : 16(4-5).

3328. ——— : 1992 : Editorial : Anarchic Tripura. *Statesman*, May 11 : 6(2-3) [Chakma].

3329. ——— : 1992 : Saving Tripura's migratory birds. *Statesman*, May 27 : 12(5).

3330. ——— : 1992 : Autonomous District Council : Functioning leads to Congress (I)—TUJS rift. *Statesman*, July 18 : 16(4-5).

3331. ——— : 1992 : Tripura Cong(I) parochial. *Statesman*, Aug. 25 : 11(2-4).

3332. **Statesman** : 1992 : Tripura CPI(M) dissidents 'threatened' for speaking out. *Statesman*, Aug. 29 : 9(2-7).

3333. ——— : 1992 : Tribal Council Bills : TUJS leaders resent delay over assent. *Statesman*, Sept. 5 : 16(1-2).

3334. ——— : 1992 : Editorial : Tripura CPI(M) Malady. *Statesman*, Sept. 5 : 8(2-3).

3335. ——— : 1992 : Belligerence a way of life for Tripura Tribals. *Statesman*, Sept. 10 : 16(1-2).

3336. ——— : 1992 : Coordination bid by N-E rebels worries centre. *Statesman*, Sept. 11 : 16(4-5).

3337. ——— : 1992 : Editorial : Caution in Tripura. *Statesman*, Sept. 18 : 6(2-3).

3338. ——— : 1992 : Editorial : Outlook in Tripura. *Statesman*, Oct. 7 : 6(2-3).

3339. **Statesman** : 1992 : Editorial : Tripura charade. *Statesman*, Oct. 19 : 8(2-3).

3340. **Sukresware** *and* **Baneswar** : 1968 : *Rajmala*, Agartala, Govt of Tripura.

3341. **Tripura Agricultural** : 1981 : Provisional data on Number and Area of operational holding 1976-77 (Tripura). *Agricultural Situation in India*, XXXXI(5), August : 385.

3342. ——— : 1984 : Provisional data on Number and Area of operational holding 1980-'81 (Tripura). *Agricultural Situation in India*, XXXIV(1), May : 93-96.

3343. **Waheed, Padma** : 1992 : Letters to the Editor : Aids in NE region. *A.T.*, Aug. 8 : 4(3-4).

3344. **Yogi, A.K.** : 1991 : *Development of North East Region*. Guwahati, Spectrum Pubs., 84p.

PART III

APPENDIX A

Scheduled Castes and Scheduled Tribes of Tripura

(According to Order (Amendment) Act 1976 (No. 108 of 1976, dated the 18th September, 1979).

Scheduled Castes:-

Bagdi,
Bhuimali,
Bhunar
Chamar,
Muchi,
Dandasi
Dhenuar,
Dhoba,
Dum,
Ghasi,
Gour,
Gur,
Jalia Kaibarta,
Khar,
Kalindi,
Kan,
Kanda,
Kanugh,
Keot,
Khadit,
Kharia,
Koch,
Koir,
Kol,
Kora,
Kotal,
Mahisyadas,
Mali,
Mehtor,
Musahar,
Namasudra,
Patni,
Sabar.

Scheduled Tribes:-

Bhil,
Bhutia,
Chaimal
Chakma,
Garo,
Halem,
Jamatia,
Khasia,
Kuki including the following sub-tribes :-
(Baite, Belalhut, Chhalya, Fun, Hajango, Jangtei, Khareng, Khephong, Kuntei, Laifang, Lentei, Mizel, Namte, Paite, Paitu, Rangchan, Rangkhole, Thangluya).

Lepcha,
Lushai,
Mag,
Munda,
Kaur,
Noatia,
Orang,
Reang,
Santal,
Tripuri,
Tripura,
Tippera,
Uchai.

Source : Census of India 1981 : List of Scheduled Castes and Scheduled Tribes—P. Padmanabha (1981).

APPENDIX B

TRIBAL ADMINISTRATIONS

According to *1931 Census Report* and *Rajmala* the tribal administration had been formed with the Territorial Chief of Tripura who was later on called Tribal Chief. The following is the list of the officials:- *TRIPURI ADMINSTRATION*

Bachal:- Decorator in festival, ceremonies, marriages, etc.
Siuk:- Hunter and supplier of meat.
Koatia:- Distributor of betal leaf, garlands, incense, presadam.
Daitya Singh:- Holder of royal insignia.
Huguria and *Chiltia* : Attendants.
Apaia:- Supplier of fish and fuel-wood.
Chattra tuia:- Holder of umbrella.
Deoria and *Galim*:- Priest and his helper.
Sube Narayan:- Helper in feasts and festivals.
Sena:- Washer/Sweeper.
Joolai:- Attendant of queens.
Village Council of the Tripuri:-
Kami-fang:- *Chaudhuri* or Headman or Saredose.
Acai:-*Ojhai* or priest/sorcerer.
Kherpang:- *Karbari* or treasurer/secretary.
Khandal:- Peon/messenger.

REANG ADMINSITRATION

Kami Kachkao:- Chief/*Raja/Roy-Chaudhuri*.
Chapia Khan:- Prime Minister
Chapia:- Minister
Huklai Chaudhuri:- Zonal Chief
Chheng Krak:- Chief of army
Akcai:- Priest
Vaidya:-Physician
Yak Sunga:- Swordsman
Dalai:- Executor of corporal punishment
Dar-Kalim:- Assistant Priest
Bhandari:- Store-keeper

Khang Kalem:- Contribution collector
Hazari:- Attendant of Prime Minister
De-hazari:- Attendant of Minister
Karma:- Assistant swordsman
Dharia:- Helper to Chief Priest in annual ceremony
Daoa:- Messenger
Khandal:- Bodyguard to the Chief
Duguria:- Drum beater
Muria:- Elute player
Su-nai:- Flute player
Musa-nai:- Dance Master
Rica-nai:- Musician
Bau-nai:- Organiser of feasts
Som-nai:- Cook
Village Council of the Reang:-
Kach-kao:- Chief/*Chaudhuri* of a village
Yakcu:- Minister
Akcai:- Priest/magician
Khandal:- Peon
Kangreng:- Messenger

JAMATIA ADMINISTRATION

Hada Akhra:- *Mulluker Sardar*
Kherpang:- Manager
Daria:- Drum beater
Matai-balnai:- Carrier of images of deities
Village Council of the Jamatia:-
Kami-fang:- Village chief/*chaudhuri*
Acai:- Priest
Khandal:- Peon
Pushni:- Messenger
Kherpang:- Manager

CHAKMA ADMINISTRATION

Raja:- King
Dewan:- Minister
Talukdar:- District administrator
Khisha:- Administrator of a mouza
Karbari:- Village chief

Shola-ani Panchayat:- It consists of all the village chiefs.
Village Council of the Chakma:-
Karbari:- Village Chief
Bhandari:- Store keeper

UCHAI VILLAGE COUNCIL

Kami-fang:- Village Chief/*Choudhuri*
Kherpang:- Manager
Kaskas:- Store-keeper
Saksu:- Messenger
Tuisni:- Water-boy

Source : An Anthology of Tripura (1985) : 82-85.

APPENDIX C

GLOSSARY OF WORDS AND SHORT NOTES

Achai:- Priest

Aman:- Winter Paddy

Aush:- Autumn paddy

Bargadar:- Share-cropper

Bari:- House

Bhandari:- The Store Keeper

Bhatthi:- Traditional furnace

Chan:- A type of long sized grass

Chantai:- Non-Brahmin priest

Chem:- Sword (*Dao*)

Chhera:- Narrow stream

Chhonga Bhat:- Rice which is prepared by boiling in a bamboo tube with its opening closed with leaves etc.

Choudhury:- Village headman/Village Chief

Corridor system:- A plot of land is partitioned into long corridors to cultivate. Each corridor under cultivation is bordered with corridors under forests. When one corridor is exhausted the next with forests is to be brought under slash-and-burn cultivation while the abandoned corridor is planted with forest trees. By the time the last corridor is cultivated the first one where from the process started under corridor system comes under forest growth and the process restarts from the first corridor.

Dadan:- Credit taken from money lenders, crop advance

Dalui:- The counsellor

Daoa:- The musician

Darkalam:- The chief priest

Daya Hazara:- The drum beater

Dewan:- Administrator

Dugria:- Musician

Endogamy:- It is a marriage custom where a marriage is performed with a person who belongs to his own caste, clan and village.

Exogamy:- It is a marriage custom where a marriage is performed with a person who belongs outside his own caste group, clan and village.

Ghani:- An indigenous oil-crushing device.

· *Ghar Chukti Kar*:- Tax collected from each *jhumia* household family in the hills for their shifting cultivation's land revenue.

Hatam Bap:- Step father.

Hypergamy:- Marriage of a low caste woman with a high caste man.

Hypogamy:- Marriage of a high caste woman with a low caste man.

Huddas:- Titles.

Jamai khata:- Apprenticeship of the son-in-law in his father-in-law's house/Marriage by service.

Jhum Cultivation:- This is a kind of natural cultivation practised by the hill tribes in the hilly areas. The jungle in the hill is cleared by the people and burnt. The burnt ashes serve as the only manure. The seeds are sown broadcast by the people. In this field they cultivate for a year or two or so and thereafter they leave that field for a considerable period to gather fertility in the soil after a new growth of jungle on them. This is also known as 'Shifting Cultivation'.

Kami-fang:- He is known as *Choudhuri* or *Sardar*. He is the headman.

Kanda:- The attendant.

Kani:- A measure of area : 0.16 hectares.

Karbari:- Collector of rent and serve summons issued by the Dewan.

Katardafa:- Big caste.

Khanebadi:- Rent free homestead land.

Khas land:- Land under the state mangement.

Lekhiraj:- Rent free.

Lal:- Chief.

Lam Khojoy:- Ceremonial songs.

Lonkhai:- Bamboo basket.

Loonga:- Low marshy land lying in between hillocks, hills or elevation of earth.

Lunga:- Land soil.

Machan:- Raised platform.

Mahajan:- Professional money-lender.

Mroong:- A sect of the Tipras.

Muria:- The flutist.

Nicotiana tobacum:- Tobacco.

Nupa:- The village council of the *Darlongs*..

Ojha:- Magician priest.

Pachhra:- A cloth which is worn by women round their waists.

Palai:- The marriage broker.

Pan:- Piper betal.

Para:- Hamlet/small locality of a few households.

Pilak:- A village called Pilak. It is situated in Belonia sub-division in South Tripura. Here a good number of old stone images, gold coins, a number of teracotta temple plaques and sealings with depiction of stupa and Buddhist creed are found in and around *Pilak Pathar*.

Purani Rajbari:- Old palaces of *Maharaja*.

Puja:- Worshipping of God.

Rajkumars:- Princes of the Royal Family.

Rajmala:- A source-book of the 19th century in which has been written the chronicle history of the rulers of Tripura. According to Sri Kaliprasanna Sen, the original *Rajmala* written in Bengali, which had six parts and were compiled under six different rulers of Tripura. The first part of the *Rajmala* was compiled in the middle of the 15th century during the reign of Dharam Manikya.

Ria:- Brassiere.

Saikrak:- The distributor of meat after the *Pujas*.

Saluzai:- Songs for victory in war.

Supari:- Areca nut.

Taungya system:- In Burmese language *Taung* means hill and *ya* means cultivation. It is a method of growing trees along with crops. The shifting cultivators are granted to cultivate a selected patch of wild forests according to their traditional system. The cultivators sowing seeds of forest species supplied by the forest department along with their own.

Terrace cultivation:- It is practised on hill-slopes. Gradual low embankments of stones or earth are built to make the fields in different patches on the gradual slopes. The terraces thus formed are irrigated by artificially constructed channels. Soil can be conserved in the gentle hill-slopes if these are properly terraced. Erosion of hill-slopes is mainly caused by rain-water run off when the surface is free of any vegetation. Terracing hill-slopes causes a danger of erosion.

Thakur:- The people who are related to the Royal house are called *Thakurs*.

Thilkhang:- Engagement ceremony.

Tila:- Small hillock, elevation of earth, high land.

Tong-ghar:- Watch house on the jhum field. It is built on bamboo platform.

Tripurabda:- Tripura's own chronological era is called *Tripurabda*. It comes three years advance of the Bengali year. In 1980 AD, it is the year 1387 in Bengali era, while it is the year 1390 in Tripura era.

Tuisi:- A constable-cum-peon.

Village Mandalis:- Village Unions.

Zawlbuk:- Zawlbuk is a dormitory for the young Mizo unmarried boys. But this has now almost vanished.

APPENDIX D

LIST OF PERIODICALS AND NEWSPAPERS (USED AS SOURCE MATERIAL)

1. Adibasi (Orissa)
2. Ajanta (Agartala)]
3. American Anthropological Association (Washington)
4. Amrita Bazar Patrika (Am. Baz. Pat.) (Calcutta)
5. Ananda Bazar Patrika (Calcutta)
6. Anthropos (West Germany)
7. Art in Industry
8. Arun (Brahmanbaria, Tripura)
9. Asian Studies (Calcutta)
10. Asiatick Researches (Calcutta)
11. Asiatick Society of Pakistan (Dacca, East Pakistan now Bangladesh)
12. Asom Jagriti (Gauhati)
13. Assam Review (Gauhati)
14. Assam Tribune (A.T.) (Guwahati)
15. Bhaskar (Agartala)
16. Birth Defects : Original Article Series (Delhi)
17. Blitz (Bombay)
18. Bulletin of Botanical Survey of India (Calcutta)
19. Bulletin of Cultural Research Institute (Calcutta)
20. Bulletin of the Department of Anthropology (Anth. Survey of India (Calcutta)
21. Bulletin of the Deptt. of Anth. (Dibrugarh University)
22. Bulletin of the Deptt. of Anth. (Gauhati University)
23. Bulletin of the Institute of traditional cultures (Madras)
24. Calcutta Review (Calcutta)
25. Call
26. Capital
27. Caravan (New Delhi)
28. Chauraung (Agartala)
29. Chinha (Agartala)
30. Chinikak (Agartala)
31. Chunta Prakash (Agartala)

32. Citizen Weekend Review
33. Commerce
34. Dainik Sangbad (Agartala)
35. Desh (Calcutta)
36. Eastern Anthropologist (Lucknow)
37. Economic and Business Review (Amrita Bazar Patrika) (Calcutta)
38. Economic and Political Weekly (Bombay)
39. Economic Times
40. Educational Miscellany (Agartala)
41. Enlite (Baroda)
42. Epigraphia Indica
43. Evidence
44. Financial Express
45. Folklore (Calcutta)
46. Frontier (Madras)
47. Geographical Review of India of Geographical Society of India (Calcutta)
48. Geographical Society of India (Calcutta)
49. Gomati (Agartala)
50. Himalaya
51. Himalaya : Man and Nature (Delhi)
52. Himalaya News Round Up (Delhi)
53. Hindu (Madras)
54. Hindustan Standard (Calcutta)
55. Hindustan Times (H.T.) (Delhi)
56. Human Science (Calcutta)
57. Illustrated Weekly of India (Bombay)
58. Indian Antiquary (Bombay)
59. Indian Archives (Delhi)
60. Indian Educational Review
61. Indian Express (Ind. Ex.) (Bombay)
62. Indian Farming
63. Indian Folklore (Calcutta)
64. Indian Forest
65. Indian Forester (Dehra Dun)
66. Indian Geographical Studies : Research Bulletin (Patna)
67. Indian Journal of Adult Education
68. Indian Journal of Agricultural Economics
69. Indian Journal of Commerce

70. Indian Review of Public and Co-operative Economy
71. Indian Science Congress Bulletin (Calcutta)
72. India Today (Faridabad)
73. Japanese Journal of Ethnology
74. Journal of Anthropological Survey of India (Calcutta)
75. Journal of Asiatic Society (Calcutta)
76. Journal of Asiatic Society of Bengal (Calcutta)
77. Journal of Assam Research Society (Guwahati)
78. Journal of Bombay National Historical Society (Bombay)
79. Journal of Indian Anthropological Society (Calcutta)
80. Journal of Indian Education
81. Journal of Indo African Trade
82. Journal of Lal Bahadur Shastri National Academy of Administration
83. Journal of National Survey of Iconography (N.S.I.) (Varanasi)
84. Journal of North Eastern Council (Shillong)
85. Journal of North East Indian Council for Social Science Research (Shillong)
86. Journal of Royal Anth. Inst. of G.B. and Ireland (London)
87. Journal of Zoological Society of India
88. Jugantar (Calcutta)
89. Jwala (Agartala)
90. Karam (Agartala)
91. Khadi Gramodyog
92. Kurukshetra (Delhi)
93. Link (New Delhi)
94. Mainstream (Delhi)
95. Man in India (Ranchi)
96. Man and Life (Calcutta)
97. Mirror
98. Naba Bharat Times (N.B.T.) (New Delhi)
99. Nagarik (Agartala)
100. New Age
101. Newsletter : Zoological Survey of India
102. North Eastern Affairs (Shillong)
103. North Eastern Research Bulletin (Dibrugarh University)
104. North Eastern Review (Gauhati)
105. North Eastern Spectrum (Gauhati)
106. North East Times (Guwahati)

107. Panchayati Raj
108. People's Democracy (Agartala)
109. Peoples of Asia and Africa
110. Pines (Shillong)
111. Prabasi (Calcutta)
112. Prachi
113. Proceedings of North East India History Association (Proceedings of NEIHA) (History Deptt., North Eastern Hill University, Shillong)
114. Purbanchal Pehari (Guwahati) (*in Hindi*)
115. Quarterly Journal of Geographical Mining Meteoro. Soc. India (Agartala)
116. Quarterly Journal of the Mythic Society (Bangalore)
117. Quarterly Review of Historical Studies (Calcutta)
118. Rabi (Agartala)
119. Records of Geological Survey of India (Calcutta)
120. Records : Zoological Survey of India (Calcutta)
121. Royal Asiatic Society of Bengal, Letters (Calcutta)
122. Samaj
123. Saptahik Basumati (Calcutta)
124. Saptasetu (Guwahati) (*in Hindi*)
125. Science and Culture (Calcutta)
126. Seminar (Delhi)
127. Shillong Times (Shillong)
128. Social Mirror (Shillong)
129. Social Perspective
130. Social Research (Shillong)
131. Social Scientist
132. Social Welfare
133. South Asia Research (London)
134. Souvenir : North East India Geographical Society
135. Statesman (Calcutta)
136. Sunday (Calcutta)
137. Swarajya
138. Telegraph (Calcutta)
139. The Anthropologist (Delhi)
140. The Chinikok (Agartala)
141. The Englishman (Calcutta)
142. Times of India (Delhi)
143. Tirthamukh (Agartala)

144. Tribe (Udaipur, Rajasthan)
145. Tripura Darpan (Agartala)
146. Tripurar Katha (Agartala)
147. Tripura Review (Agartala)
148. Tripura Times (Agartala)
149. Uditi (Agartala)
150. Vanyajati (Delhi)
151. Vivekananda Kendra Patrika
152. Yapri (Agartala)
153. Yojana (Delhi)
154. Zoitschrift fur Morphologie und Anthropologie (Stuttgart).

AUTHOR INDEX

(References are according to the serial number of entries in the Bibliography)

Author Index

ADDENDA-I

ADDENDA-II

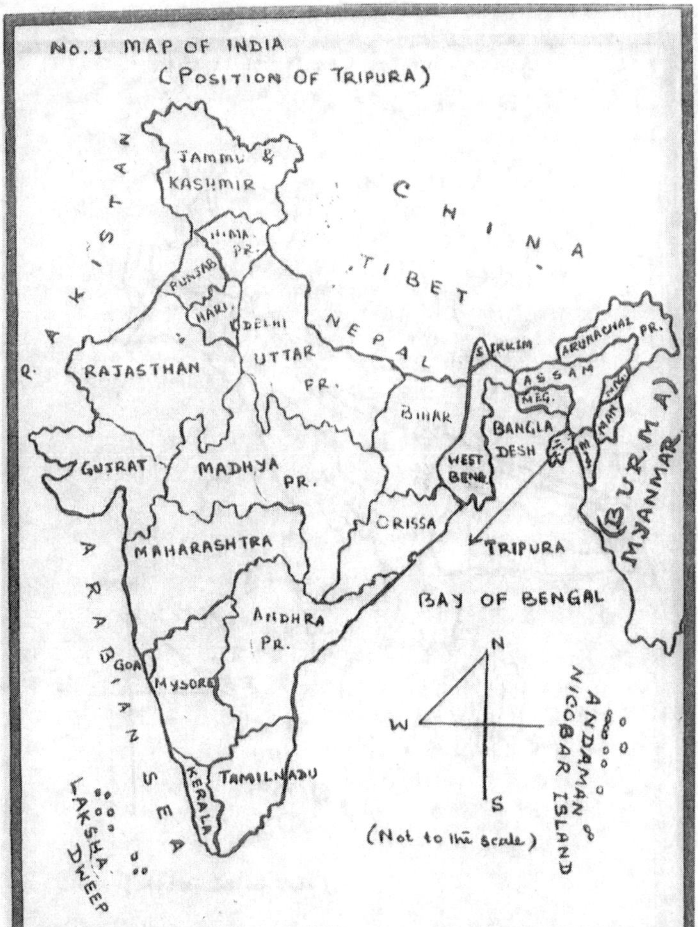

No.1 MAP OF INDIA (POSITION OF TRIPURA)

No. 2 MAP OF NORTH EASTERN INDIA
(Position Of Tripura)

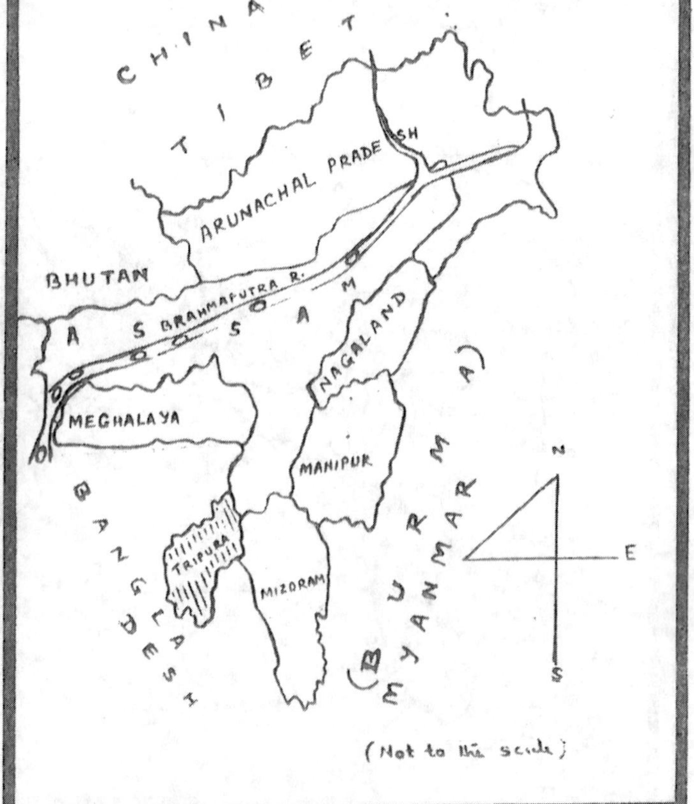

No. 3 MAP OF TRIPURA
(RIVERS & SUBDIVISIONS)

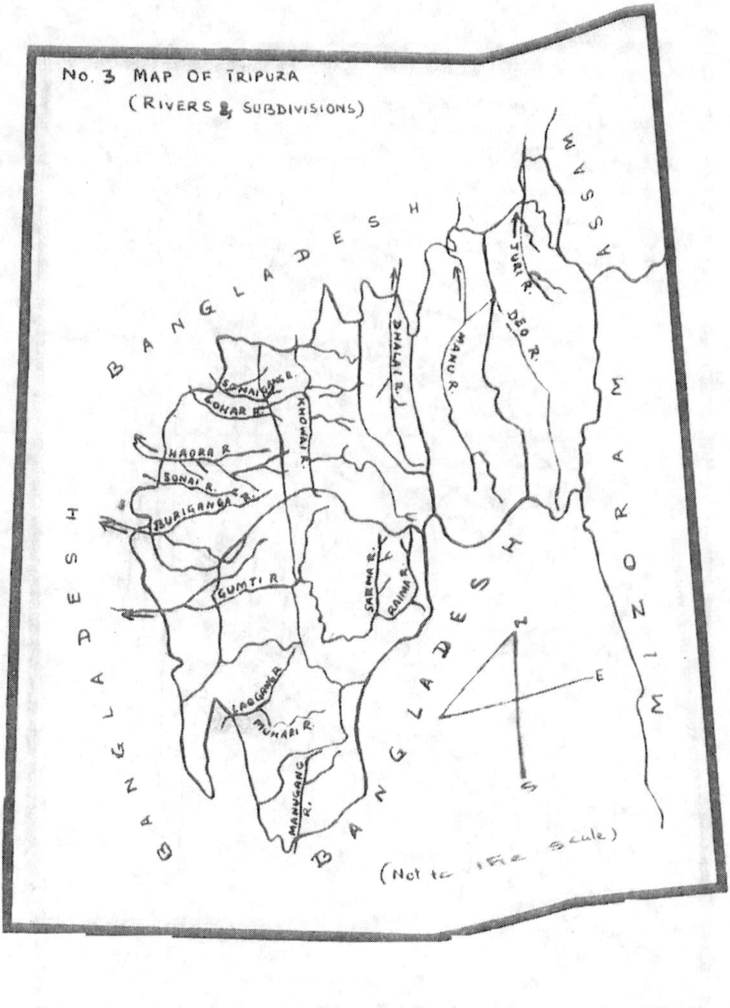

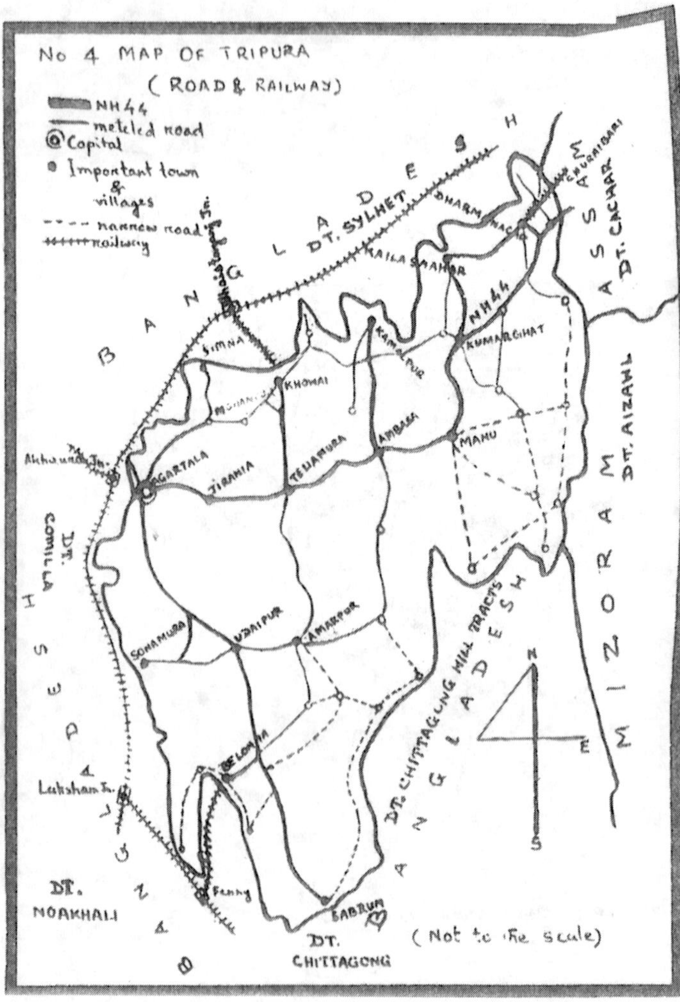
No 4 MAP OF TRIPURA
(ROAD & RAILWAY)
NH44
metled road
Capital
Important town & villages
narrow road
railway
BANGLADESH
DT. SYLHET
ASSAM
DT. CACHAR
MIZORAM
DT. AIZAWL
DT. COMILLA
DT. NOAKHALI
DT. CHITTAGONG
DT. CHITTAGONG HILL TRACTS
AGARTALA
TIRANIA
TELIAMURA
AMBASA
MANU
KUMARGHAT
KAILASAHAR
DHARMANAGAR
KHOWAI
SIMNA
MOHANPUR
KAMALPUR
SONAMURA
UDAIPUR
AMARPUR
BELONIA
SABRUM
Akhaura
Laksham Jn.
Fenny
N
E
S
(Not to the scale)

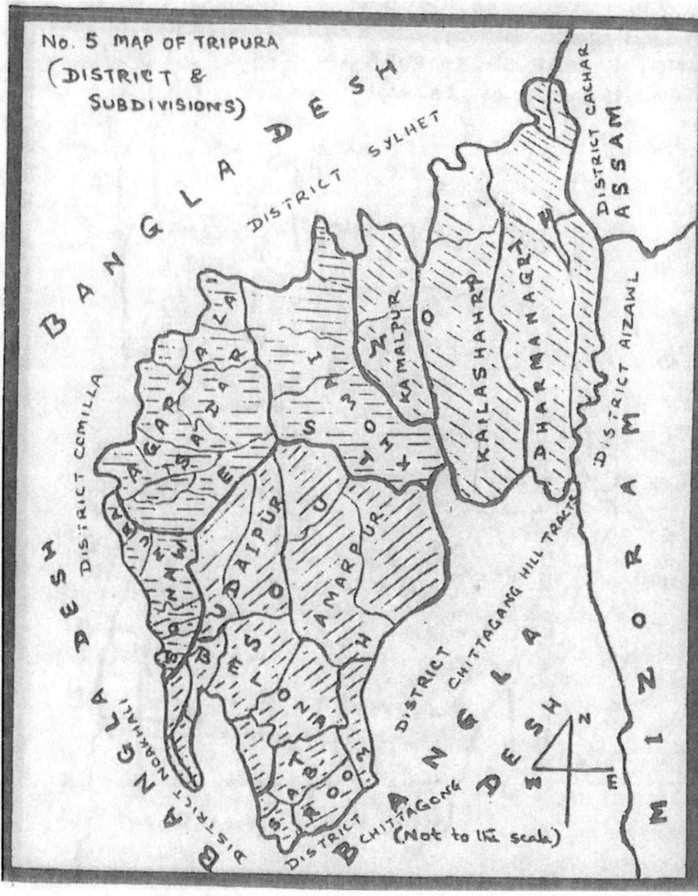
No. 5 MAP OF TRIPURA (DISTRICT & SUBDIVISIONS)

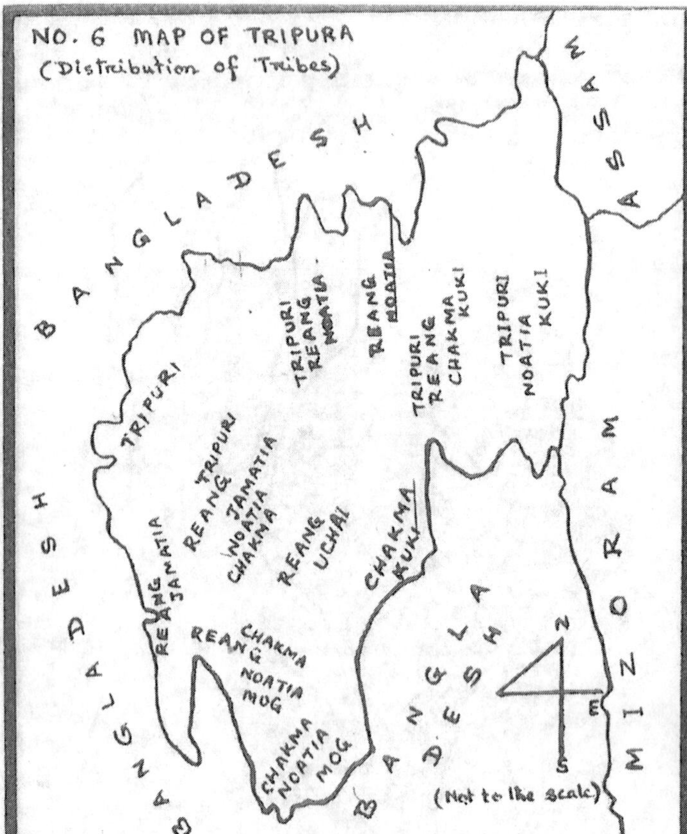

NO. 6 MAP OF TRIPURA
(Distribution of Tribes)

1. Process of Jhum cultivation

2. Noatia belle

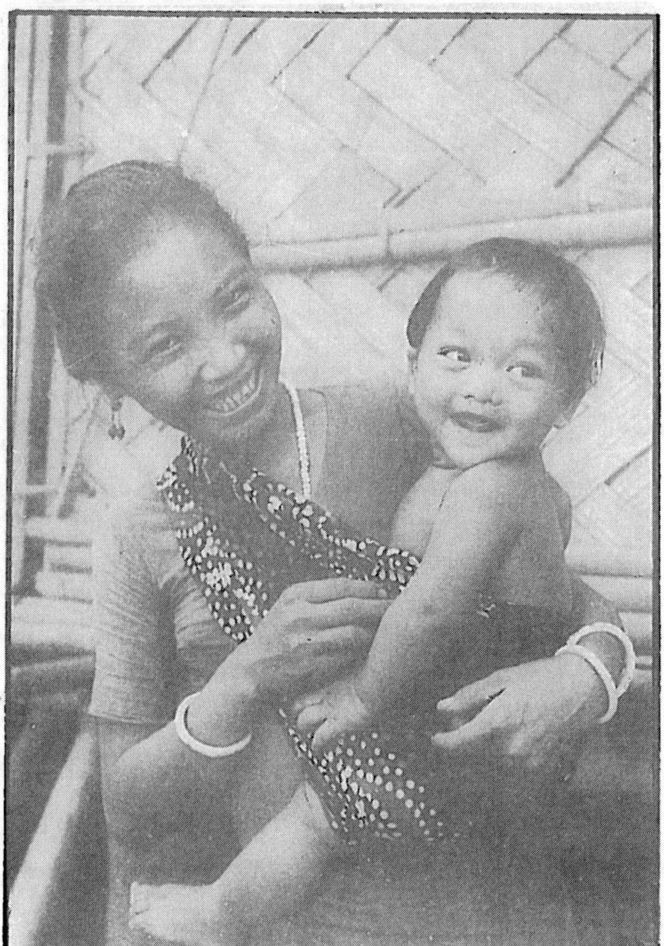

3. Tripurei mother and baby

4. Drinking water facilities in tribal area

5. Reang girls

6. Jamatia beli

7. Tribal hunting dance

8. MIZO KHOLAM DANCE

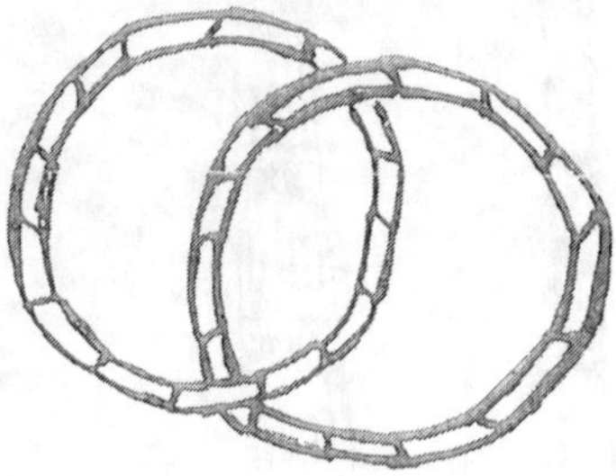

BALA

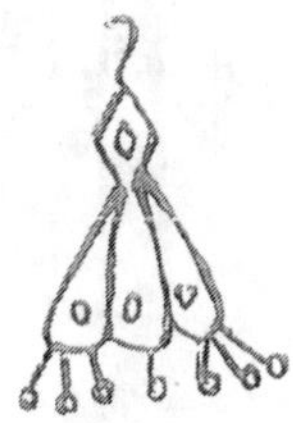

JUMḲHA

ṠUMRUI

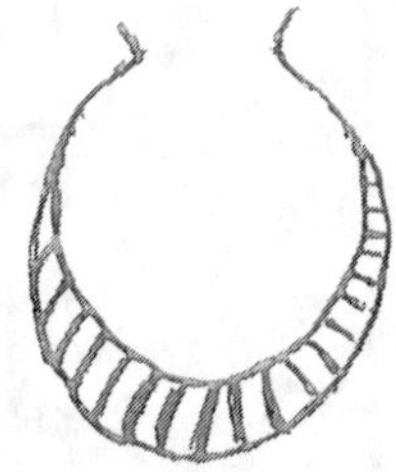

ANJULY

ANJULY

1. ORNAMENTS

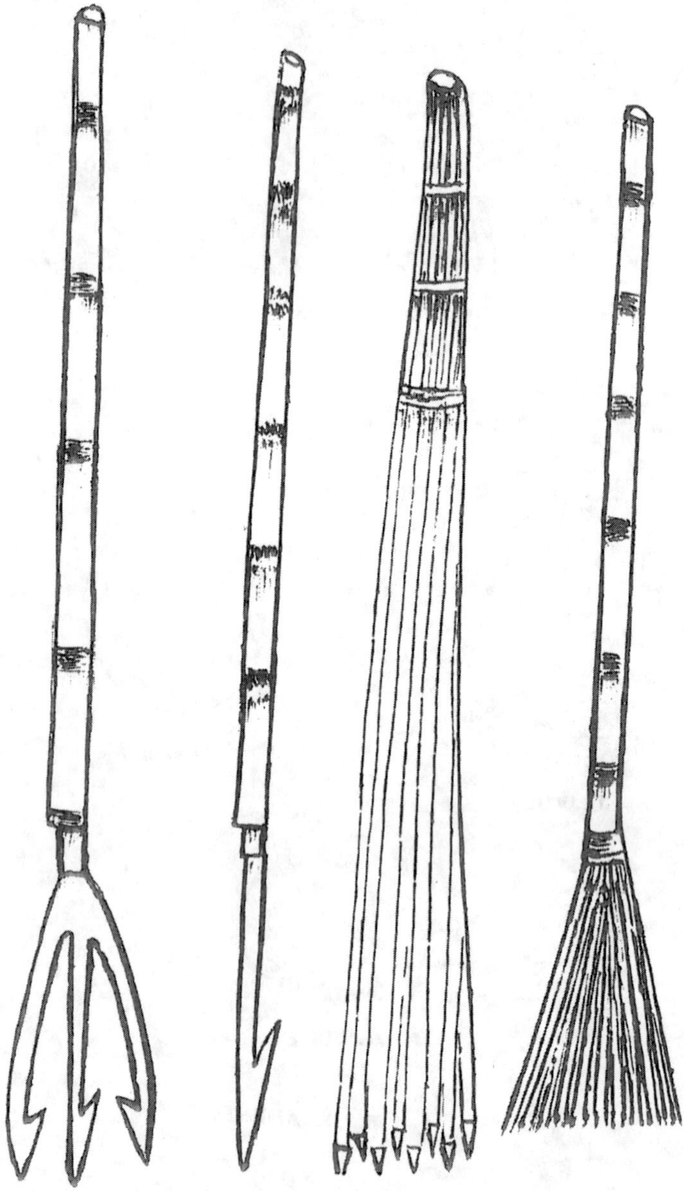

2. DIFFERENT TYPES OF SPEARS FOR FISHING

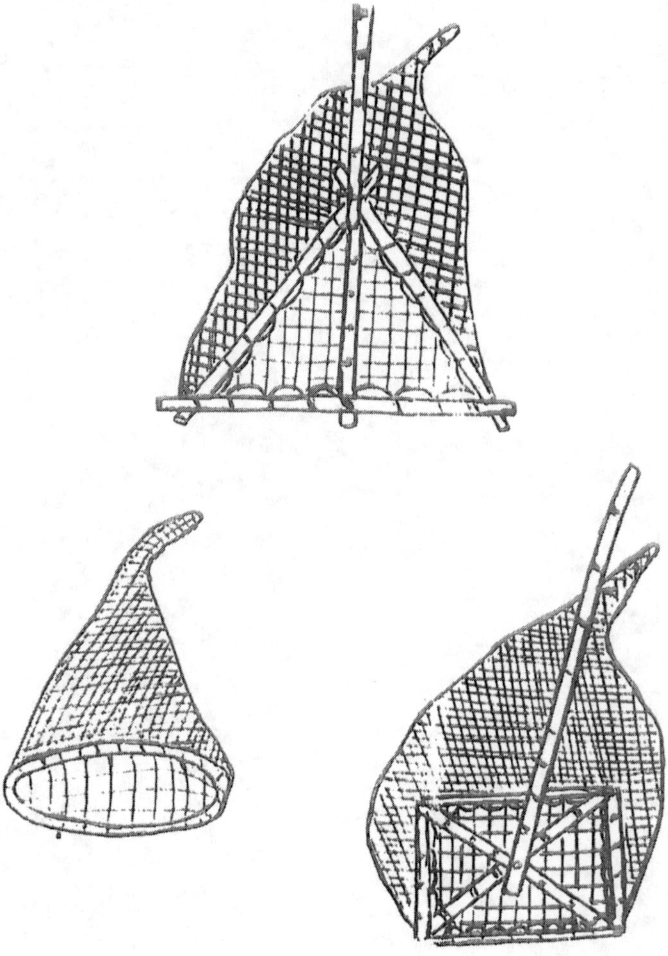

3. DIFFERENT TYPES OF FISHING NETS